D1324866

Storming Heaven

Storming Heaven

Class Composition and Struggle
in Italian Autonomist Marxism

SECOND EDITION

Steve Wright

Foreword by Harry Cleaver
Afterword by Riccardo Bellofiore and Massimiliano Tomba

PlutoPress
www.plutobooks.com

First published 2002; Second edition published 2017 by Pluto Press
345 Archway Road, London N6 5AA

www.plutobooks.com

Copyright © Steve Wright 2002, 2017

The afterword by Riccardo Bellofiore and Massimiliano Tomba first
appeared in the Italian edition of this book, published by Edizioni Alegre,
whom we thank for their permission to reprint it here. The text has been
translated by Steve Wright.

The right of Steve Wright to be identified as the author of this work has
been asserted by him in accordance with the Copyright, Designs and
Patents Act 1988.

British Library Cataloguing in Publication Data
A catalogue record for this book is available from the British Library

ISBN   978 0 7453 9991 1   Hardback
ISBN   978 0 7453 9990 4   Paperback
ISBN   978 1 7868 0116 6   PDF eBook
ISBN   978 1 7868 0118 0   Kindle eBook
ISBN   978 1 7868 0117 3   EPUB eBook

This book is printed on paper suitable for recycling and made from fully
managed and sustained forest sources. Logging, pulping and manufacturing
processes are expected to conform to the environmental standards of the
country of origin.

Typeset by Stanford DTP Services, Northampton, England

Simultaneously printed in the United Kingdom and United States of America

Contents

Foreword by Harry Cleaver   vi
Acknowledgements   xii

Introduction   1
 1. Weathering the 1950s   5
 2. *Quaderni Rossi* and the Workers' Enquiry   29
 3. *Classe Operaia*   58
 4. New Subjects   82
 5. The Creeping May   98
 6. Potere Operaio   120
 7. Toni Negri and the Operaio Sociale   140
 8. The Historiography of the Mass Worker   163
 9. The Collapse of Workerism   183
10. Conclusion   208

Postscript: Once More, With Feeling: A Bibliographic Essay   212
Afterword to the Italian Edition by Riccardo Bellofiore and
     Massimiliano Tomba   237
Bibliography   249
Index   278

Foreword

Amplified by a comprehensive new chapter updating research on and by Italian autonomist Marxists and a critical Afterword by Riccardo Bellofiore and Massimiliano Tomba, this second edition of Steve Wright's *Storming Heaven* is even more useful than the original, in two senses. First, while the earlier edition provided the most comprehensive analysis and understanding available in English of the innovations of Italian autonomist Marxists in the heyday of *operaismo*, the added chapter highlights newly available English translations of old texts, new Italian assessments of the past and carries the analysis forward, into the recent past and present, surveying the subsequent directions pursued by its main theoreticians in the years since. Comprehensive, but condensed into a single chapter, his survey has the feel of both a bibliographical essay and a sketch of what could be an entirely new book, were Steve to decide to delve as deeply into the recent literature that he summarises as he has done with the essential texts of *operaismo*. One can only hope.

The second way in which this new edition has a heightened usefulness is how it facilitates the intellectual and political mining of the autonomist tradition to inform contemporary decisions about confronting the present composition of class relations of struggle. Whether examining past variations and differences, or sketching present debates, by situating them all within their historical contexts and by showing how these autonomist theorists and militants harvested, yet winnowed, previous work, Steve has provided us with examples that show how demanding that theoretical innovations be based upon the analysis of the material conditions of class struggle can yield insights into 'What is to be done NEXT!' – which should be the purpose of all militant research, whether of past or present.

Riccardo and Massimiliano's Afterword adds their own critical perspective to Steve's analysis, highlighting what they see as the strongest aspects of *operaismo*, focusing particularly on the work of Tronti and Panzieri, and its legacies within '*post-operaismo*', i.e., among those who have retained central elements of the approach, abandoned others and innovated in new directions, of whom the best known is Antonio Negri. In this short text, their treatment is necessarily narrower than Steve's, and in the case of Negri, even more critical.

They are severe in their condemnation of what they view as Negri's building on the weakest aspects of *operaismo*. They write that in Negri's new formulations 'it is pointless to seek mediations, or to claim verifications of reality'. This erroneous path, they claim, has led Negri and like-minded *post-operaisti*, to formulate such concepts as the 'general intellect' and 'immaterial labour' in ways that 'lack all meaning' and led them beyond any recognisable form of workerism. While both concepts have been hotly debated, and I share aspects of their critique, their assertion that Negri et alia have come to embrace such concepts in a self-referential way, devoid of any analysis of 'reality', ignores the detailed researches on the kinds of labour characterised as 'immaterial' published in the journals *Futur Antérieur* (1991–92) and *Multitudes* (2000–) and elsewhere. Those researches provided material grounds for theorising the 'general intellect' and 'immaterial labour', regardless of how one judges the outcome. In the end, Riccardo and Massimiliano return to the central preoccupation of the *operaisti*, 'the reconstruction of the conditions that make possible antagonism within and against capital'. If we interpret 'reconstruction' to mean a close analysis of ongoing struggles that defy subsumption by capital, rupture its institutions and create alternatives, I can only agree.

Although Steve's new chapter and the Afterword both provide pointers to further desirable research and organisational efforts, I'd like to point even further, beyond the focus on developments among *Italian* autonomist Marxists, past and present, to related kindred spirits elsewhere in the world – whose interconnections formed, and still continue to form, a kind of international kinship network of more or less like-minded individuals and groups – a network whose mutually stimulating linkages have been largely unrecognised or forgotten.

In the beginning of his new chapter, Steve tells of the difficulties in gathering archival materials during a trip to England and Italy in early 1982 in the wake of the crackdown of April 1979 when the Italian state had used the terrorism of armed groups such as the Brigate Rosse to justify the arrest and jailing of thousands of its critics, a great many on trumped up charges.[1] Four years earlier, in the summer of 1978, I had made a similar journey of research and discovery, visiting many of the

---

1 We can observe just such a pattern of using the terrorism of the few to justify the repression of the many in Turkey, whose president, Tayyip Erdoğan, has been jailing thousands and rapidly removing all semblance of democracy and human rights in that country – a process that has resulted in his government's efforts to join the European Union being put on hold and its membership in NATO questioned. In the case of Italy, despite widespread condemnation, there was no such official EU response to the April 1979 crackdown and subsequent repression.

same people – in London, Paris, Milan and Padua. Like Steve, I was on the hunt for the origins of a set of new ideas. In my case, I had first encountered those ideas while participating in the political project that generated the journal *Zerowork* (1975–77), a project heavily influenced by both *operaismo* and the Wages for Housework Movement of the time – a movement born in Italy but which had spread rapidly in Europe and North America. Also like Steve, by talking to those more familiar with the history and reading the materials they dumped in my lap, I discovered many – though by no means all – of the Italian sources Steve has ferreted out and analysed so carefully in *Storming Heaven*.

But what struck me forcefully, and still fascinates me, was how in England, France and Italy I discovered even earlier roots, some in Europe but also, more surprisingly to me, some back home in the United States. Steve touches briefly on this international dimension in his first chapter 'Weathering the 1950s' where he mentions the way Danilo Montaldi, one of the earliest post-WWII Italian Marxists to begin rethinking class struggle from the point of view of workers, drew upon contemporary work by those in the American group Correspondence and the French group Socialisme ou Barbarie. For me to have had to voyage to Europe to discover such North American roots was nothing short of shocking.

It is true that Martin Glaberman – an important figure in Correspondence and its continuation, Facing Reality – had written a letter to those of us collaborating on *Zerowork* reproaching our failure to recognise or refer to their earlier efforts, which also put autonomous workers' struggles at the centre of both analysis and politics. But ignorant of that history, his scolding hadn't meant a great deal to me. It was not until I spent hours, first in John Merrington's study in London, then in archives in Paris and finally in Bruno Cartosio's office in Milan and poured over their collections of materials from the Johnson-Forest Tendency, Facing Reality, News & Letters and Socialism ou Barbarie – alongside all the Italian stuff – that the full impact of Martin's reproach struck home.

The phenomenon, or interrelated phenomena, that those of us working on *Zerowork* had failed to recognise had been a trans-Atlantic ferment in the late 1940s and 1950s in which an independent-minded array of individuals had ripped themselves away from earlier left preoccupations with the labour movement and political parties to return to Marx's own efforts to understand the materiality of workers' struggles, e.g., his close readings of the British factory inspectors' reports and his Workers' Enquiry, and through that return to rethink elements of his theory and the implications for their politics. This return, I discovered, had charac-terised the work of a wide variety of party dissidents, including C.L.R.

James, Raya Dunayevskaya, Martin Glaberman, and Grace Lee in the United States, Cornelius Castoriadis, Claude Lefort and Daniel Mothe in France, Danilo Montaldi, Raniero Panzieri and Mario Tronti in Italy. In much the same spirit, but with a professional focus on struggles in the past, were the so-called 'bottom up' Marxist historians of the period, such as Edward Thompson, Christopher Hill and Rodney Hilton. These individuals not only shared a common focus on the self-activity of workers but their writings and teaching would inspire a whole new generation of militants.

The elements for recognising the international character of this refocusing of research and organising on the self-activity of workers had all been available by the mid-1970s but scattered about in books and pamphlets, personal notes and memories of at least two generations of militants. A few individuals stood at what Alquati called 'nodal points' of this loose network. Grace Lee had personally established links between Correspondence and Socialisme ou Barbarie through contact with Castoriadis.[2] Bruno Cartosio, in a sense picking up where Mothe and Montaldi had left off, translated into Italian and published a collection of Martin Glaberman's writings.[3] In England, John Merrington had studied at Balliol, Oxford under Christopher Hill, had gone to Italy with Gramsci in mind and returned with a head (and suitcase) full of Tronti and Alquati. He and Ed Emery had provided to English militants, such as those involved in Big Flame, key translations of such Italian materials in various formats, including those published under the stamp of Red Notes. Peter Linebaugh, one of the editors of *Zerowork*, had studied with Edward Thompson and collaborated with comrades in London to study John and Ed's translations.

Ferruccio Gambino's voyages in the 1960s and 1970s repeatedly established or repaired communications across borders and across the North Atlantic. His study of workers' struggles at British Ford, translated and published by Red Notes, offered militants on the island a local example of the kind of analysis Alquati had done on Fiat and his critique of the French regulation theorists showed how they had inverted *operaismo*'s workerist perspective into a capitalist one.[4] Paolo Carpigano and Mario Montano had both studied elements of this history in Rome before joining the Zerowork collective. So too had Bruno Ramirez, who,

---

2 Grace Lee Boggs (1998) *Living for Change: An Autobiography* (Minneapolis: University of Minnesota Press), p. 65. For a brief account of their collaboration that includes Castoriadis' memories see www.zerowork.org/GenesisZ1.html.

3 Bruno Cartosio (1976) 'Introduzione' to M. Glaberman, *Classe Operaia, imperialism e rivoluzione negli USA* (Turin: Musolini).

4 The English translations of both works can be accessed at libcom.org.

having settled in Canada, had observed the influence of Correspondence and Facing Reality in that country and helped spread the ideas of the *operaisti*, influencing groups such as the New Tendency and the Toronto Struggle against Work Collective.[5] In Paris, Yann Moulier-Boutang had translated and circulated *operaisti* ideas in *Matériaux pour l'intervention* and *Comarades: revue militante dans l'autonomie*.[6] And, of course, major figures in the Wages for Housework Campaign, such as Mariarosa Dalla Costa, Silvia Federici and Selma James, were all familiar with developments in Italy. Selma's experience reached all the way back to Correspondence and her marriage to C.L.R. James, while Mariarosa's writings arose from participation in Potere Operaio, but dissatisfaction with its limited analysis of unwaged work.[7] While a few of the above individuals, who were best situated, provided partial verbal accounts, and a handful of brief notes, none had constructed a comprehensive narrative of the evolution of either these ideas or of the network of those sharing them through the decades of the 1950s–1970s. As has so often been the case with militants, down through the ages, they were more preoccupied with developing and spreading the ideas and organising around them than in reconstructing their history. Thus, my voyage in 1978 and Steve's in 1982.

The outgrowth of my discoveries was a distilled, brief summary of what I saw as the main innovations of this network, both theoretical and political, included in the introduction to my book *Reading* Capital *Politically* (1979). The outgrowth of Steve's efforts was his dissertation, recrafted into *Storming Heaven* (2002) that provided a much more thorough, and more focused analysis of the emergence and development of *operaismo* in Italy. Although I had learned to read Italian in order to access and understand the *operaisti* writings, I was delighted and excited to discover how Steve was turning his much better command of the language, both written and spoken, to the task of a more comprehensive analysis than I had been able to carry out. Many of us, preoccupied with

---

5   At long last, an analysis of the historical experience of these autonomist groups has been provided by John Huot, one of the participants. See, John Huot, 'Autonomist Marxism and Workplace Organizing in Canada in the 1970s' *Upping the Anti*, No. 18, August 2016. Accessed online at http://uppingtheanti. org/journal/article/18-autonomist-marxism.

6   One example: Matériaux pour l'intervention, *Les ouvriers contra l'etat et refus du travail*, 1973.

7   See Mariarosa's setting-the-record-straight statement on 'Women and the Subversion of the Community' and her cooperation with Selma James, written in response to assertions by James in *Sex Race and Class, The Perspective of Winning: A Selection of Writings 1952-2011* (Oakland: PM Press, 2012).

other projects but inspired by the past and unfolding, innovative work of Italian autonomist Marxists, are grateful for his ongoing work on this subject. That work has made him a key figure in the ongoing evolution of the international kinship network described above.

Harry Cleaver
Austin, Texas

Acknowledgements

2017 EDITION

First and foremost I would like to thank David Shulman at Pluto, who raised the possibility of a new edition of this book. In addition, I would like to thank: Harry Cleaver; all those who have helped with the translation and publication of this book in a number of other languages, especially Willer Montefusco, Riccardo Bellofiore and Massimiliano Tomba; two anonymous referees and Nik Papas for their comments on the additional chapter that has been written for this edition; and last (but far from least) Rosa, Ginevra and Sean.

2002 EDITION

This book began life as a doctoral thesis, inspired in large part by Ed Emery's work as translator and archivist. Over the course of its writing I became indebted to a number of people for their assistance: along with Ed himself, I would particularly like to mention my thesis supervisor Alastair Davidson, Vicky Franzinetti, Hilary Partridge and Larry Wright. I also benefited greatly from brief discussions with Ferruccio Gambino, John Merrington, Peppino Ortoleva and Marco Revelli. Jim Asker, Peter Beilharz, Carlo Carli, Pasquale Coppola D'Angelo, Richard Curlewis, Chris Healy, David Lockwood, Anna Marino, Sandro Portelli, Pierangelo Rosati (Hobo), Riccardo Schirrù and Jeff Soar all provided hard-to-find reference materials. My thesis examiners, Grant Amyot and Donald Sassoon, made constructive comments concerning its possible publication.

That a version of it has indeed finally appeared in print is largely due to the impetus provided by Patrick Cuninghame, John Hutnyk and Gioacchino Toni, combined with the enthusiasm of Anne Beech at Pluto Press. Along the way, I was sustained by the encouragement of the following: Franco Barchiesi, Jon Beasley-Murray, Volker Beyerle, Mike Brown, Verity Burgmann, Harry Cleaver, Steve Cowden, Massimo De Angelis, Nick Dyer-Witheford, Gra, Matt Holden, Sonya Jeffery, Pete Lentini, Bruce Lindsay, Angela Mitropoulos, Gavin Murray, Curtis Price, and Myk Zeitlin. A number of friends in Italy – Pino Caputo, Cosimo Scarinzi, Beatrice Stengel and Renato Strumia – have again been helpful with sources. Thanks too to John Holloway for help with a last minute citation.

Unless otherwise indicated, all translations are my own. Needless to say, all mistakes also remain my own.

I owe a special debt of gratitude to Rosa Lorenzon, who has long borne the intrusions of this project with a stoic tolerance and humour. I dedicate this book both to her and to our little rebels Ginevra and Sean.

Introduction

The cusp of the new century has seen something of an upsurge of the anti-statist left in Western countries and beyond, as part of a broader movement against global capital. If much of this resurgence can rightly be claimed by various anarchist tendencies, autonomist Marxism has also encountered renewed interest of late (Dyer-Witheford 1999). Given that the core premises of autonomist Marxism were first developed in Italy during the 1960s and 1970s, now is an opportune time to examine their origin and development within the stream of Italian Marxism known popularly as *operaismo* (literally, 'workerism').

By the late 1970s, *operaismo* had come to occupy a central place within the intellectual and political life of the Italian left. While its impact was most apparent in the field of labour historiography, discussions concerning the changing nature of the state and class structure, economic restructuring and appropriate responses to it – even philosophical debates on the problem of needs – were all stamped with workerism's character-istic imprint (Pescarolo 1979). Nor was its influence confined simply to circles outside the Italian Communist Party (PCI), as the attention then paid to its development by leading party intellectuals – some of them former adherents – made clear (D'Agostini 1978).

None the less, workerism's weight remained greatest within the tumultuous world of Italian revolutionary politics, above all amongst the groups of Autonomia Operaia (Workers' Autonomy). As the three major political formations to the left of the PCI plunged into crisis after their disappointing performance in the 1976 national elections, Autonomia began to win a growing audience within what was then the largest far left in the West. When a new movement emerged in and around Italian universities the following year, the autonomists were to be the only organised force accepted within it. With their ascent, workerist politics, marginalised nationally for half a decade, would return with a vengeance.

Curiously, these developments then engendered little interest within the English-speaking left. While the rise of Eurocommunism in the 1970s made Italian politics topical, encouraging the translation both of Communist texts and some of their local Marxist critiques, the efforts of the workerist left were passed over in silence. Little, indeed, of workerist material had at that point been translated at all, and what was available – pertaining for the most part to *operaismo*'s 'classical' phase during the

1960s – gave a somewhat outdated view of its development. It is not surprising, therefore, that on the few occasions when reference was made to workerism in the English language, it was often to a caricature of the Italian tendency. Despite this, workerist perspectives did succeed in touching some sections of the British and North American left. The advocates of 'Wages for Housework', whose controversial views were to spark a lively debate amongst feminists (Malos 1980), drew many of their arguments from the writings of the workerist-feminist Mariarosa Dalla Costa. In a similarly iconoclastic vein, the male editors of *Zerowork* set about reinterpreting contemporary working-class struggles in the US and abroad from a viewpoint strikingly different to those of other English-speaking Marxists (Midnight Notes 1990). Yet even these endeavours, while worthy of note in their own right, were to contain nuances quite different to those of their Italian counterparts, and could shed only limited light upon *operaismo* as it had developed in its place of origin.

Ironically, it would take the dramatic incarceration in 1979 of most of Autonomia's leading intellectuals for workerism to finally attract some attention in the English-speaking left. Once again, unfortunately, the image that emerged was a distorted one, focusing almost exclusively upon the ideas of one individual. Certainly, as the most intellectually distinguished of those arrested, and the leading ideologue of a major wing of Autonomia, Antonio Negri's views were of considerable importance. When *operaismo* was filtered via French theorists such as Deleuze and Guattari, however, as became the fashion in certain circles, the resulting *melange* – if not unfaithful to the development of Negri's own thought – served only to obscure the often fundamental disagreements that existed between different tendencies within both workerism and Autonomia. The paucity of translations has been remedied somewhat over the past two decades, with the appearance of anthologies such as *Radical Thought in Italy* (Virno and Hardt 1996), alongside some useful if brief introductory texts (Moulier 1989; Cleaver 2000). Still, the equation by English-language readers of workerist and autonomist theory with Negri and his closest associates remains a common one.

What then is workerism? Within the Marxist lexicon, it is a label which has invariably borne derogatory connotations, evoking those obsessed with industrial workers to the exclusion of all other social forces. Such a broad definition, however, could be applied with equal justification to many others of the political generation of 1968, and does nothing to pinpoint the specific properties of *operaismo*. The latter's origins lie, rather, at the beginning of the 1960s, when young dissidents in the PCI and Socialist Party first attempted to apply Marx's critique of political economy to an Italy in the midst of a rapid passage to industrial maturity. In this they were motivated not by a philological concern to execute a more correct reading of Marx, but the political desire to unravel the fundamental power relationships of modern class society. In the process, they sought to confront *Capital* with 'the *real* study of a *real* factory',* in pursuit of a clearer understanding of the new instances of independent working-class action which the 'Northern Question' of postwar economic development had brought in its wake (De Martinis and Piazzi 1980: v). In the words of Harry Cleaver, such a political reading

> self-consciously and unilaterally structures its approach to determine the meaning and relevance of every concept to the immediate development of working-class struggle … eschew[ing] all detached interpretation and abstract theorising in favour of grasping concepts only within that concrete totality of struggle whose determinations they designate. (Cleaver 2000: 30)

The most peculiar aspect of Italian workerism in its evolution across the following two decades was to be the importance that it placed upon the relationship between the material structure of the working class, and its behaviour as a subject autonomous from the dictates of both the labour movement and capital. This relationship workerism would call the nexus between the technical and political composition of the class. 'Slowly, with difficulty', Mario Tronti had proclaimed in 1966,

> and in truth without much success, the Marxist camp has acquired the idea of an internal history of capital, entailing the specific analysis of the various determinations which capital assumes in the course of its development. This has led justly to the end of historical materialism, with its hackneyed *Weltgeschichte*, but is still a long way from assuming, as both a programme of work and a methodological principle in research, the idea of an internal history *of the working class*. (Tronti 1971: 149)

This book traces the development of the central trunk of *operaismo*, which passed through the experience of the revolutionary group Potere Operaio (Workers' Power). In doing so, it seeks to gauge the analytical efficacy of that tendency's most distinctive category – class composition

---

* While the Italian original of this text reads 'the real stage [stadio] of a real factory', I believe this to be a typographical error.

– by measuring it against the emergence of new forms of political mobilisation during and after Italy's postwar economic 'miracle'. Rightly or wrongly, workerism saw itself engaged in an assault upon the heavens of class rule. To its mind, the only valid starting point for any theory that sought to be revolutionary lay in the analysis of working-class behaviour in the most advanced sectors of the economy. More than anything else, it was to be this quest to discover the 'political laws of motion' of the commodity labour-power which came to mark workerism out from the rest of the Italian left of the 1960s and 1970s.

At its best, the discourse on class composition would attempt to explain class behaviour in terms long submerged within Marxism, beginning with that struggle against the twin tyrannies of economic rationality and the division of labour. At its worst, *operaismo* would substitute its own philosophy of history for that of Marx's epigones, abandoning the confrontation with working-class experience in all its contradictory reality to extol instead a mythical Class in its Autonomy. At first inextricably linked, by the 1970s these rational and irrational moments of its discourse had, under the pressure of practical necessities, separated into quite distinct tendencies. By that decade's end, workerism's project had fallen into disarray, much like those who dared to build the Tower of Babel. And while it did not end well, the grandeur and the misery of its collapse offer important insights to those who continue to seek a world without bosses.

Two decades after 1968, Paul Ginsborg (1990), Robert Lumley (1990) and others would offer fine accounts of the Italian social conflict of the 1960s and 1970s, as well as the movements and outlooks bound up with it. To date, however, there has only been one book-length account of workerism as a distinctive stream within postwar Italian radical culture (Berardi 1998). Like its author, I believe that, of all the elements specific to *operaismo*, those relating to its thematic of class composition remain the most novel and important. Noting that for workerism this concept had come to assume the role played within Italian Communist thought by *hegemony*, Sergio Bologna (1977d: 61) would none the less caution that it is 'ambiguous. It is a picklock that opens all doors.' To discover how this tool was forged, and to assess the extent to which it might yet be of service, is the purpose of this book.

I

Weathering the 1950s

'So-called *operaismo*', noted Antonio Negri a year or so before his arrest in April 1979, had emerged above all 'as an attempt to reply politically to the crisis of the labour movement during the 1950s' (Negri 1979a: 31). A worldwide phenomenon, this crisis proved especially serious in Italy, where the crushing of revolutionary Hungary and the collapse of the Stalin myth dovetailed with a domestically induced malaise already hanging over much of the left. Together these dislocations were to become the primary concerns of a new approach to Marxism which would both anticipate the Italian new left of the 1960s and provide the soil from which workerism itself would directly spring.

THE PRICE OF POSTWAR RECONSTRUCTION

The 1950s were a period of profound transformation for Italian society. The aftermath of the Second World War left much of the economy, particularly in the North, in a state of chaos. Industrial production stood at only one-quarter the output of 1938, the transport sector lay in tatters and agriculture languished. A combination of inadequate diet and low income (real wages had fallen to one-fifth the 1913 level) meant that for large sectors of the population, physical survival overrode all other considerations. Yet by the end of the following decade the nation's economic situation was startlingly different, with dramatic rises in output, productivity and consumption: Italy's 'miracle' had arrived with a flourish (Clough 1964: 315; Gobbi 1973: 3).

Even as those working the land declined in number, the rate of growth in the agricultural sector actually increased slightly between 1950 and 1960. From the middle of the decade, as secondary industry began to develop extensively, excess labour-power was encouraged to embark upon an internal migration from countryside to city, and above all from South to North. While important new investments in plant were made in Italy's North-East (petrochemicals) and South (ferrous metals), the tendency remained that of concentrating large-scale industry in the traditional Northern triangle formed by Genoa, Turin and Milan. The most dynamic sectors located here were those bound up with the production of a new infrastructure: housing, electricity, petrochemicals, ferrous metals and autos. Industrial production had already matched prewar levels by the end of the 1940s; by 1953 it had jumped another 64 per cent, and had almost doubled again by 1961 (Lieberman 1977: 95–119). All of which moved one writer in the March 1966 issue of the *Banco Nazionale del Lavoro Quarterly Review* to note that

> the prodigious progress made by the Italian economic system in recent years, a progress the like of which has never been seen in the economic history of Italy or any other country. (De Meo 1966: 70)

Not that such growth sprang from a void, or that its progression had been linear, smooth. The fundamental premises of the 'miracle', instead, were established in the late 1940s only after a massive shift in the relations of force between the major classes. Italy's industrial base may have been profoundly disorganised in 1945, but as De Cecco (1972: 158) has pointed out, 'the situation was not at all desperate, especially in comparison with other [European] countries'. While neither the social dislocation caused by the war nor Italy's continuing dependence upon the importation of raw materials could be dismissed lightly, it was also true that much of the country's prewar fixed capital remained intact, or had even been enlarged due to wartime demands. If any major obstacle to accumulation existed, therefore, it was the working class itself. For many workers, and particularly those Northerners who had seized their workplaces during the struggle against Mussolini and the Wehrmacht, the future promised, if not the imminent advent of socialism – although this too was heralded in many factories – then certainly major improvements in work conditions and pay, along with a greater say over production in general. While it was hardly a return to the heady days of 1920, this new-found power within the labour process also allowed workers to flex their muscles beyond the factory walls, leading to freezes upon both layoffs and the price of bread. Yet no matter how restrained in reality, such assertiveness was still more than the functionaries of Italian capital were prepared to concede; for them, the path to postwar reconstruction could only pass through the restoration of labour docility. (Salvati 1972; Foa 1980: 137–62)

After their prominent role in the Resistance, the military defeat of fascism and Nazism in Central and Southern Italy ushered in a period of impressive growth for the parties of the left, from which the Communists – the current most firmly rooted in the factories – would benefit most of all. But the line which party leader Palmiro Togliatti proclaimed upon his return from exile in 1944 was to surprise and disappoint many members who, however ingenuously, associated the PCI with the goal of socialist revolution. Togliatti was too shrewd a politician not to recognise the lessons that the Greek experience held out to anyone contemplating insurrection in post-Yalta Western Europe, but it would be wrong to think that international considerations restrained an otherwise aggressive impulse to revolutionary solutions. Building upon the tradition of party policy established with the defeat of the Communist left in the 1920s, the PCI leadership was to advance a course which sought to unite the great mass of Italians against that 'small group of capitalists' seen as objectively tied to fascism. Within such a strategy the open promotion of class antagonism could only be an obstacle. The aim instead was to build a 'new party', one capable of expanding its influence within both the 'broad masses' and the new government, immune to the 'sectarianism' of those militants who spoke bluntly of establishing working-class power (Montaldi 1976: 87–8). Nor did this course alter with the fall of Mussolini's puppet 'social republic' in the North. For Togliatti, the decisive arena for gains in post-fascist Italy was to be not the world of the workshop or field, but that of formal politics, where accommodation with other social groups was a prerequisite for participation. The conditions under which the PCI had entered government at war's end were not entirely to its suiting, yet there is no reason to doubt the sincerity of his admission that the leadership had gone ahead just the same

> because we are Italians, and above everything we pose the good of our country, the good of Italy, the freedom and independence of Italy that we want to see saved and reconquered ... (quoted in Montaldi 1976: 99)

And the party was to be as good as its word. As Franco Botta (1975: 51–2) has shown, in the immediate postwar period the PCI moved 'with extreme prudence on the economic terrain, subordinating the struggle for economic changes to the quest for large-scale political objectives, such as the Constituent Assembly and the Constitution'. Togliatti (1979: 40) put it thus upon his return from the Soviet Union: 'today the problem facing Italian workers is not that of doing what was done in Russia'; on the contrary, what was needed was a resumption of economic growth within the framework of private ownership so as to ensure the construction of a 'strong democracy'. Togliatti urged working-class participation in such a project of reconstruction, envisioning recovery 'on the basis of low costs of production, a high productivity of labour and high wages', in the belief that the effective demand of the 'popular masses', rather than the unfettered expansion of free market forces proposed by liberal thinkers, would serve as the chief spur to economic expansion. (Quoted in Botta 1975: 57)

Would such an alternative model of development have been feasible in the 1940s? There is no simple answer to such speculation, although similar notions continued to inform the thinking of the left unions well into the next decade (Lange et al. 1982: 112; Ginsborg 1990: 188–90). What remains interesting is that, whatever the polemical tone of Togliatti's attack upon liberals like Luigi Einaudi, his own views on development shared more assumptions with such opponents than he realised. The most important of these affinities was the emphasis placed upon a substantial increase in productivity as the path to Italy's salvation. In practical terms, however, any rise on this score – which at that point in time offered employees the simple alternative of working harder or being laid off – could only be won at the expense of that level of working-class shopfloor organisation achieved during the Resistance. True children of the Comintern, for whom the organisation and form of production were essentially neutral in class terms, the PCI leadership saw no great problem in conceding – in the name of a 'unitary' economic reconstruction – the restoration of managerial prerogative within the factories. After all, wasn't productivity ultimately a problem of technique? The factories must be 'normalised', argued the bulletin of the Milan party federation in July 1945. The fact that new organs had been created which offered 'an ever-more vast participation and control of workers over production' could not mean the removal of 'labour' and 'discipline' from their rightful place at the top of the immediate agenda. Another party document from September of that year stated things more bluntly: 'the democratic control of industry by workers means only control against speculation, but must not disturb the freedom of initiative of senior technical staff' (quoted in Montaldi 1976: 259, 267). As one FIAT worker later put it:

I remember straight after the war Togliatti came to speak in Piazza Crispi – and then De Gasperi came – and they both argued exactly the same thing; the need to save the economy ... We've got to work hard because Italy's on her knees, we've been bombarded by the Americans ... but don't worry because if we produce, if we work hard, in a year or two we'll all be fine ... So the PCI militants inside the factory set themselves the political task of producing to save the national economy, and the workers were left without a party. (Quoted in Partridge 1980: 419)

In 1947, having invested so much energy in tempering working-class resistance to 'reconstruction', the parties of the historic left found themselves unceremoniously expelled from the De Gasperi government. Christian democratic political hegemony brought with it massive American aid, and the triumph of a model of industrial development that combined efforts to impose the unbridled discipline of the law of value in some sectors with selective state encouragement of others. In practice this involved production for the international market underpinned by low wages, low costs and high productivity; a sharp deflationary policy to control credit and wages; the elimination of economically 'unviable' firms, and the maintenance of high unemployment. To make matters worse for the labour camp, the union movement found itself split – with American and Vatican connivance – along political lines, enabling employers to open an offensive in the workplace against militants of the left parties and their union confederation, the CGIL (Confederazione Generale Italiana del Lavoro – the Italian General Confederation of Labour). (Ginsborg 1990: 141–93)

Closed in upon itself ideologically, its hard core of skilled workers disorientated by victimisation, the CGIL's isolation from the daily reality of the shopfloor would be symbolised by the loss in 1955 of its majority amongst the union representatives elected to FIAT's Commissione Interna (Contini 1978). Nor were the union's subsequent efforts to face up to its malaise helped by the significant changes then occurring within both the production processes and workforce employed in industry. Stimulated in part by the prospect of new markets which Italy's entry into the Common Market offered, investment in new plant by the largest Northern employers increased significantly in the second half of the decade (Lichtner 1975: 175–82; King 1985: 69–77). At the same time, the biggest firms began to recruit amongst a new generation of workers, men and women with little experience of either factory work or unionism. In all, Italy's manufacturing workforce would grow by 1 million during the years of the economic 'miracle'. At first these new employees were predominantly of Northern origin; as the 1950s drew to a close, however, entrepreneurs turned increasingly to the thousands of Southerners lured Northwards by the lack of jobs at home and the promise of a large pay packet (Alasia and Montaldi 1960; Fofi 1962; Partridge 1996). And just as such industrialisation only exacerbated differences between what had long appeared to be two discrete nations within Italy – the advanced North and semi-feudal Mezzogiorno – so too its benefits failed to extend themselves uniformly to all classes in society. As a consequence, the Italian labouring population which saw the 1960s draw near appeared markedly weaker and more divided than that of a decade before, a depressing view to which the lag of wage increases far behind those of productivity paid further mute testimony. (King 1985: 87)

THE AMBIGUOUS LEGACY OF THE HISTORIC LEFT

That 'unforgettable' year of 1956, as Pietro Ingrao has called it, marked a genuine watershed in the history of the PCI. As the first cracks appeared in the Soviet Party's facade, Togliatti pronounced ominously upon certain 'dangers of bureaucratic degeneration' in the USSR, vigorously denouncing all the while the rebellious workers of Poznan and Budapest as tools of reaction (Bocca 1973: 618; Ajello 1979: 389–90; Togliatti 1979: 141). Formally committing the party to the 'Italian road to socialism' it had followed for years, Togliatti also used the occasion to stamp out those insurrectionalist tendencies that lingered on within the PCI (Montaldi 1971: 369). Firmly embedded in a Stalinist matrix, such elements constituted in their own distorted manner what little that remained of the PCI's original class politics. A whole layer of middle-ranking cadre, who viewed Khrushchev with suspicion – not for complicity in Stalin's tyranny, but for having dared criticise him at all – found themselves slowly eased from positions of responsibility. The 8th Party Congress ushered a new levy of future leaders into the Central Committee, as an even greater 'renovation' occurred in the PCI's important federal committees, with the overwhelming majority of *Komitetchiki* henceforth party members of less than a decade's standing (Ajello 1979: 427). Whilst the most prominent of the older 'hards' managed, in exchange for their silence on current policy, to remain within the PCI's leading bodies, the small number of militants and functionaries who objected to the new regime were simply driven out of the party (Peragalli 1980).

Thus, if PCI membership would decline overall by the end of the decade, with a noticeable loss of liberal intellectuals disenchanted more with international events than the party's domestic policies, there was to be no exodus by rank-and-file Communists like those which devastated Communist parties in the English-speaking world. Indeed, when the PCI did emerge from its uncertainties it was to do so as a much-invigorated force, the correctness of its postwar course as a national-popular 'new party' largely confirmed in the leadership's eyes (Asor Rosa 1975: 1622).

For the other major party of the left, by contrast, 1956 would be experienced as a fundamental break. Always a strange political creature, the Italian Socialist Party (PSI) had been born anew in the final days of fascism. At that time its axis appeared decisively to the left of other Western Socialist parties, although the diversity of groupings within it lent a certain erratic bent to its political direction. Led by Pietro Nenni, Giuseppe Saragat and Rodolfo Morandi, its actions in the immediate aftermath of the war involved a juggling act. Vowing a continuing commitment to its close relationship with the PCI through the 'unity of action' pact sealed in the Popular Front period, the PSI also attempted to establish an identity independent of the Communist Party. Encouraged by its showings in the first postwar elections, the emphasis at first was placed upon 'autonomy', a notion that bore various connotations within the party. For some it represented aspirations to the mantle of 'revolutionary' party let fall by the moderate Communists; for others, it meant the construction of a mass social democratic party along British or German lines. In early 1947, midst the growing climate of the Cold War, the Socialist Party's reformist wing split away on an explicitly anti-Communist platform, a section of the party's left in tow; months later, the left parties were expelled from government. Both events were to have an enormous impact upon the majority of Socialists, winning a growing audience for those who saw the supreme political division as that between a socialist East and revanchist West, and any attempt to evolve a 'third way' merely a capitulation to imperialism. Following a brief period of non-alignment under the rule of a centre faction, the party's traditional critical support for the Soviet Union blossomed into support *tout court*. Indeed, by the outbreak of the Korean War, Nenni could be heard proclaiming his close identification with the USSR in the 'struggle for peace', and Morandi publicly dedicating himself to the Herculean task of cleansing the party of all traces of social democracy's corrupting influence (Libertini 1957; Vallauri 1978; Benzoni 1980: 33–70; Foa 1980: 270–81).

More than any other individual, Rodolfo Morandi embodied both the grandeur and misery of the Socialist Party left in the immediate postwar period. Its dominant figure both intellectually and politically, Morandi had first come to prominence not only as the author of an important study of Italian large-scale industry, but also as a leading domestic opponent of fascism. A convert to Marxism from the dynamic liberal-socialist circles of the 1920s, Morandi, like many left socialists of the interwar period, had devoted considerable energy to finding an authentic revolutionary 'third way' between bolshevism and social democracy. In this he paid particular attention to the vicissitudes of the USSR, which he judged from a viewpoint much influenced by Rosa Luxemburg's own brief but sharp pronouncements of 1918. Dubious of the statist nature of 'socialism in one country', Morandi reserved his greatest criticisms for the practice of class–party relations developed by the Comintern. Like many others in the left wing of the PSI, Morandi considered the 1921 split with the Communists a grave mistake, and looked forward to an eventual reconciliation between the two major tendencies of the Italian left. At the same time, he also understood that class unity could never be reduced to the fusion of party apparatuses: only if the dangers of substitutionism were confronted and defeated, he argued, would PSI–PCI reunification be feasible. In his councillist vision, the party was only an instrument – necessary but not sufficient – in the service of working-class unity. The revolution could be expected to usher in not a party-state, but a system of popular rule based on the democratic organs of the masses themselves (Agosti 1971: 173–83, 278–90).

If such was the theory, Morandi's subsequent efforts to realise it were uniformly disappointing. During the Resistance he pinned considerable hope upon the Comitati di Liberazione Nazionale (Committees for National Liberation) organised in the Centre-North, but most of these bodies soon revealed themselves to be little more than miniature parliaments, susceptible to all the wheeling and dealing of party politics. Those committees formed in the factories seemed, by contrast, to hold greater promise, being often dominated by Communist and Socialist militants with a class perspective. After the important role that the factory organisations played in the struggle against the German occupation, the Communist leadership pushed successfully for the committees' dissolution. In the words of the party historian Manacorda, PCI leaders were frightened that such militants might go 'so far in the course of the insurrection as to expropriate the capitalists and establish cooperative management of the works' (quoted in Ellwood 1985: 231). Instead the committees were replaced with 'management councils' which Morandi, as Minister of Industry in the second De Gasperi cabinet, did everything in his power to encourage. All things to all people, these joint councils of workers and employers quickly proved themselves to be no more than mechanisms to encourage working-class participation in postwar reconstruction (Craveri 1977: 184–207). Unable to extricate his earlier councillist notions from the poverty of such experiences, expelled from office by the Christian Democrats' anti-Communist offensive, Morandi sought to keep faith by embracing the aggressively Stalinist view of the world advanced by the newly formed Cominform. It was a step which marked the advent of Italian socialism's 'ten winters'; not until 1953 brought with it the death of Stalin would an inkling of light appear at the end of the 'Cold War tunnel' (Fortini 1977: 18).

With the benefit of hindsight, it is clear that a great part of the PCI's ability to weather the storms of 1956 lay with the complexity of its postwar culture. Blending the great native tradition of historicism with a resolutely 'popular' approach to social reform, the party succeeded in winning many self-perceived 'organic intellectuals' to its banner after 1945. Such a recipe for success may well have been concocted from equal parts of Croce and Stalin, as Fortini once quipped (Ajello 1979: 113). But above all it was flexible, able under Togliatti's auspices to move from an enthusiastic but superficial embrace of Zhdanov in the late 1940s to the accommodation of certain aspects of the liberal critique of Stalinism by the middle of the following decade. Not so that of the Socialist Party: its official Marxism-Leninism of the early 1950s, the product of Morandi's attempts at 'Bolshevisation', was rote learnt, doctrinal and arid, manifesting itself in conformity to the Soviet line and a rigid internal regime which stifled dissent. As a consequence, the arrival of 1956 came as a genuine shock for the PSI. For the majority of the dominant left faction in particular, the debunking of some of the myths surrounding Stalin and 'realised socialism' served only to puncture their own revolutionary pretensions, leaving them without any mask to cover a politics which was as reformist – if nowhere as coherent – as that of their Communist rivals.

The early 1950s had already seen the PSI lose support within the working class, gradually but inexorably, to the Communists. With Morandi's death in 1955, his efficient 'Leninist' apparatus fragmented into a number of competing machines, each vying to determine the Socialist Party's course. While some functionaries continued to genuflect towards Moscow, the more pragmatic elements around Nenni began to look for new waters in which to fish (Foa 1980: 268–9). Such opportunities were not long in coming. In the time-honoured Italian tradition of *trasformismo*, Nenni adroitly exploited the repression of Polish workers in Poznan to open a dialogue with Saragat, leader of the breakaway Social Democrats. By October of 1956, Nenni had succeeded in changing the 22-year-old 'unity of action' pact with the PCI to one of 'consultation'. When the 32nd PSI Congress was held six months later, Nenni moved into a commanding position within the organisation's leadership. From here he began to explore a number of possible courses of action, culminating in the early 1960s with the Socialists' return to a coalition government with the Christian Democrats (Della Mea 1967: 90–2).

PANZIERI AND THE LIMITS OF LEFT RENOVATION

To commentators outside the PSI, the growing fissures within that party seemed to reduce its internal life during the late 1950s to little more than factional manoeuvring (Barnes 1967: 64–71). Yet if the collapse of the Soviet Union as a model and guide served ultimately to consolidate the Socialist Party's slide towards social democracy, it also opened up space for a brief time to more critical enquiry within the party's left. To a new levy of Italian Marxists seeking, a decade later, to escape the political hegemony of the PCI, the names of that period – Gianni Bosio, Vittorio Foa, Franco Fortini – would become important reference points (Bermani and Cuzzaniti 1977; Bonini 1978; Forgàcs 1984). The most exceptional of these militant Socialists of the 1950s, however, was Raniero Panzieri, whose response to the uncertainties of the period was to grapple with the fundamental relation between class and organisation. Panzieri, of course, was not alone in this endeavour: amongst his contemporaries on the left, Danilo Montaldi (1994) in particular had similar concerns – even, at times, a clearer vision. But Montaldi, the son of a Bordighist, operated both by circumstance and choice on the margins of the official labour movement: what made Panzieri's line of development so novel, and ultimately influential, was that it struck out from the heart of the historic left itself. An anonymous tribute in *Classe Operaia* would later express Panzieri's uniqueness well: 'among the countless "leaders" of the organised movement', it said, 'only one had consciously chosen the path of his own defeat, because this led towards the working class' (*Classe Operaia* 1964g: 23).

Born in Rome in 1921, Panzieri's early intellectual formation was unusual for his generation in that it encompassed neither idealism nor historicism (Merli 1979: 91, 77). His writings of the 1940s, committed to the advancement of an authentically Marxist culture in Italy, were sometimes marred by a certain intolerance towards thinkers deemed renegades by Stalinism. But they were also concerned less with orthodoxy than the critique elaborated by Marx himself, characterised by the young Panzieri – in a pointed reference to the Crocean sensibilities of many Communists – as a rupture first and foremost with bourgeois thought (Rieser 1982: 47). After a period of involvement in party cultural affairs, Panzieri moved to Sicily in the late 1940s. There he became active in struggles over land redistribution, and worked with Ernesto De Martino and Galvano Della Volpe, amongst other prominent left intellectuals. 1953 saw Panzieri enter the PSI Central Committee; the following year, aged 33, he assumed the post of Cultural Secretary (Lanzardo 1975: 8–9). In time Panzieri established himself as one of the Morandians most open to critical self-reflection, turning that 'other', libertarian Morandi against the intellectual conformism which had come to grip the PSI left. His initial sallies, not surprisingly, were in the field of culture, where he argued that the poverty of postwar Italian Marxism was largely a consequence of the widely held equation between truth, party and class.

The fundamental task, he stated in early 1957, was 'to restore Marxism to its natural terrain, which is that of permanent critique', something which could only be accomplished by freeing it 'from the control of party leaderships and party directions':

> Only in this way – that is, only through the refusal of party-specificity [*partitarietà*], and the affirmation of its unity above and beyond political alignments – can Marxist culture rediscover its true function. (Panzieri 1973: 47, 50)

Although he did not state it in such terms, Panzieri already glimpsed that the much vaunted 'organic intellectuals' of Gramscian memory were now in practice organic only to the party machine. This did not mean, however, that he understood the 'cultural autonomy' of left intellectuals as either the abandonment of revolutionary commitment or a theoreticist return to 'origins or texts'. What was needed, instead, was an examination of 'the reality of the political and organisational movement of the popular classes': an undertaking, he predicted, which would prove richer culturally than either intellectuals or party leaders could imagine (quoted in Rieser 1982: 49).

In Panzieri's view, the theoretical reinvigoration of Marxism went hand-in-hand with the political renovation of the labour movement, and it was only natural that here he should take as his initial reference point Morandi's themes of direct democracy and the goal of Communist–Socialist unity. His earliest discussions of left renewal were quite moderate in tone, arguing that the 'natural terrain' of proletarian struggle lay within the framework of the postwar Constitution (Panzieri 1973: 36). Like most PSI members, Panzieri then still accepted the legitimacy of an 'Italian road'; what concerned him was to indicate within it 'the exceptional historic experience of unitary politics', which he characterised as its

> vision of mass action based on the presupposition of the necessary and concrete coincidence of mass struggles and the objectives of a critical, constructive, democratic vision of national problems. (ibid.)

This was a formulation to which few in the historic left would then have objected. In Panzieri's hands, however, the notion of 'mass action' quickly came to assume connotations quite different to those shared by the majority of Communists and Socialists. Appointed co-director of the PSI theoretical review *Mondo Operaio* in early 1957 after leaving the party's Central Committee, Panzieri soon found the journal to be the perfect vehicle for critical self-reflection. Working alongside him was Lucio Libertini, late of a small organisation of dissident Communists and Socialists opposed to the pro-Soviet stance of the major left parties (Benzoni 1980: 64–5). Over the following 18 months, *Mondo Operaio* established itself as a lively forum for debate, examining both current events and the work of Marxists – Lukács, Luxemburg, Trotsky – long passed over by the Socialist left (Della Mea 1967: 98). The most noteworthy aspect of *Mondo Operaio*'s new regime, however, was to be Panzieri's insistence that the final arbiter of the forms and goals of the struggle against capitalism must be the working class itself. Once again his starting point – that the Italian road to socialism ('*democratic* and *peaceful*') could not be confined to parliament – seemed modest enough; indeed, it was not dissimilar to the publicly stated position of Nenni himself (Vallauri 1978: 95–7). But Panzieri's argument went much further than that of the Socialist leader. While it was important, he held, for the left parties to make use of the constitutional arena, the struggle for socialism required that the labour movement be renovated '*from below* and in forms of *total democracy*' (Panzieri 1973: 102). For this to occur new institutions were needed, ones which must find their roots in the economic sphere, 'the real source of power'. Then the 'democratic road' would not become 'either a belated adherence to reformism, or simply a cover for a dogmatic conception of socialism' (ibid.: 110, 142).

Examining the experience of the historic left, Panzieri was particularly scathing in his criticism of the 'absurd identity between working class and party' consolidated by the experience of Stalinism. Against this, he argued, the collapse of Communist dogma made possible the reaffirmation – 'in all its vigour' – of 'the principle of class action as the autonomy of the exploited and oppressed classes in struggle for their liberation' (Panzieri 1973: 61, 62). In this vein he reprinted an article from the *Ordine Nuovo* period, in which Gramsci insisted that new proletarian bodies were needed to replace not only the capitalist state, but also the traditional organisations of the labour movement, since these had proved themselves 'incapable of containing such a flowering of revolutionary activity' (Hoare 1977: 77). At the same time, the Panzieri of the late 1950s was far from being an opponent of the party-form as such. Whilst he acknowledged that the PSI's surrender to social democracy was a genuine risk, he did not believe that the party should simply be left to fall into revisionist hands. Together with Libertini, Panzieri sought to show instead that, 'Of the party one can affirm with Marx: it is an educator which must be educated' (Panzieri 1973: 202). The recent experience of the historic left had seen the collapse of that 'necessary dialectical relation' between class and political vanguard and its replacement by 'the conception of the leading party, of the party which is the unique depository of revolutionary truth, of the party-state' (ibid.: 194). Still, both Panzieri and Libertini were confident that the questioning provoked by the events of 1956 would return the historic left to the correct path. This they identified with Morandi's original, anti-Stalinist vision of the relation between party and class, wherein

> the revolutionary autonomy of the proletariat becomes realised in the creation from below, before and after the conquest of power, of institutions of socialist democracy, and in the party's return to its function as the *instrument* of the class movement's political formation. (ibid.: 113)

Thus, without ever registering an explicit break in his thinking, Panzieri's pursuit of workers' control led him further and further away from the historic left's prevalent themes of class alliance and the constitutional road to socialism. As such, Panzieri's work of the period represents one of the first clear, if unspoken, ruptures with Togliatti's perspectives from within the labour movement itself. Not surprisingly, these views met increasingly mixed reactions from those within the mainstream of the Italian historic left (Negri 1979a: 41–2). To the Communist historian Paolo Spriano, such opinions smacked of 'left revisionism'; for the Socialist Lelio Basso, any talk about workers' control was of no practical relevance, since only the attainment of bourgeois democracy was currently on the agenda in Italy (Panzieri 1973: 118, 153).

If such glib judgements were unworthy of either critic, they none the less drew attention to the risk of excessive schematism that threatened all talk of autonomy in the abstract. Panzieri himself was acutely conscious of this. The demand for workers' control, he stated in 1958, could not be 'a literary motivation for historical re-exhumations, much less a miracle cure', but 'must emerge and make itself concrete within the reality of the working class, expressing its revolutionary autonomy' (quoted in Della Mea 1967: 100). As that year passed, Panzieri became more and more convinced that such an encounter could not long be avoided. Yet, as Sandro Mancini has rightly argued, such an aspiration was unattainable so long as the institutions of the labour movement remained Panzieri's only concrete point of reference – some sort of rupture was required (Lanzardo and Pirelli 1973: 14; Mancini 1975: 205).

As it turned out, Panzieri was soon to have just such a break thrust upon him. With the 33rd Congress of the PSI in 1959, the ascendance of Nenni's 'autonomist' faction became complete, and the goal of a joint Socialist–Christian Democrat government was brought one step nearer. One of the minor casualties of the new line was Panzieri, who was removed from *Mondo Operaio*'s helm. Summing up the workers' control debate in March of that year, he and Libertini held that it had run its course: what mattered now were practical measures, and in that sense the ball lay firmly in the court of the left parties and the CGIL. Notwithstanding the current course of the PSI, they concluded, 'We are increasingly convinced that the central theme of the Italian labour movement remains that of renovation' (Panzieri 1973: 239). There was little in Panzieri's personal experience, however, to justify such optimism. Despite re-election to the Central Committee, his isolation within the PSI continued to grow. In particular, his calls for greater rank-and-file involvement in policy and the reassertion of the left's 'revolutionary autonomy' sounded increasingly out of place in a party leadership maddened by the scent of a centre–left coalition (ibid.: 247–9). No prominent Socialist, he was forced to admit to Montaldi in October, had proved immune from its allure; all of the PSI's various factions were now united in a 'common vocation to government at any cost ... Even Libertini has been completely assimilated' (ibid.: 250, 251).

Towards the end of the year, an embittered Panzieri left Rome to work for the publishing house Einaudi in Turin. Here, in a strange city dominated by 'cold, smog and monopoly' (Panzieri 1973: 252), excluded once and for all from the inner councils of the Socialist left, his political career seemed finished. Having finally removed himself from the world of party intrigue, however, Panzieri was to discover the existence of small pockets of kindred spirits. Most were members of a younger political generation: in Milan, a group of left Socialists around Luciano Della Mea; in Rome, a circle led by Mario Tronti, many of them members of the PCI's long-troublesome cell at the university (Ajello 1979: 371, 395, 403–6). In Turin itself, he was to find a more eclectic group of political activists. Some, like Vittorio Rieser, had been members of Libertini's Unione Socialisti Independenti and associates of Danilo Dolci before passing to the PSI; others – like Romano Alquati, soon to arrive from Cremona and a period of political work with Montaldi – could lay claim to even less conventional backgrounds. More than a few also came from dissenting religious families, part of the local Valdese or Baptist communities (Panzieri 1973: 261; Merli 1977: 48; Piccone Stella 1993: 186–96). Whatever their origins, however, Panzieri's new associates all agreed that the growing moderation of the left parties and unions sprang first and foremost from their indifference to the changes wrought upon the Italian working class by postwar economic development. Deeply critical of the labour movement's present course, their disquiet was not in any way eased by the failure of its leadership to respond positively to the moderate revival of industrial unrest seen in 1959. In a letter written a fortnight before the close of that year, Panzieri indicated both the problem as he saw it, and the means to its resolution:

> If the crisis of the organisations – parties and union – lies in the growing difference between them and the real movement of the class, between the objective conditions of struggle and the ideology and policy of the parties, then the problem can be confronted only by starting from the conditions, structures and movement of the rank-and-file. Here analysis becomes complete only through participation in struggles. (Panzieri 1973: 254)

It was here, Panzieri believed, in 'full and direct political action', that a new, revolutionary role for intellectuals could finally be realised. 'Naturally', he added, 'none of this is new' (ibid.). On that point, at least, he was to be quite mistaken: with the aid of his new collaborators and their journal *Quaderni Rossi*, Panzieri now stood poised before an experiment which was to have enormous repercussions for the development of the Italian new left.

SOCIOLOGY: A SUITABLE WEAPON?

> The weapons for proletarian revolts have always been taken from the bosses' arsenals. (Tronti 1971: 18)

If the first great theme which *Quaderni Rossi* appropriated from the dissident Marxism of the 1950s was that of autonomy, the second concerned the possible utility of 'bourgeois' sociology as a means to understand the reality of the modern working class. Indeed, what Diane Pinto (1980: 243) has called *Quaderni Rossi*'s '"parallel" sociology' was to be formed precisely at the intersection between the group's rediscovery of *Capital* and its examination of certain recent developments in radical social science.

While it is true that Panzieri's openness to a critical use of sociology, like his critique of technological rationality, reveals a debt to Adorno, its direct inspiration lay much closer to home (Apergi 1978: 113–17; Meriggi 1978a: 91–116). What might loosely be termed an Italian radical sociology had already emerged after the war. This was largely confined to studies of the 'Southern question' which, apart from the accounts of peasant life by Ernesto De Martino, tended to present themselves primarily as works of 'literature' (Bermani and Bologna 1977: 10–20; Ajello 1979: 333–40). Industrial sociology, on the other hand, was relatively new in Italy. Having been imported from the US only recently in the form of 'human relations', the discipline was viewed with justifiable suspicion by many in the Italian labour movement (Lichtner 1975: 185; Massironi 1975: 46–57; Ajello 1979: 321–5). Exposure to the work of French writers such as Alain Touraine and Georges Friedmann helped to break down such hostility. By 1956, then, it was not uncommon for more critically minded left intellectuals to express commitment to the development of a left sociology capable of moving from literature to 'science' (Merli 1977: 48). Whilst the young Alessandro Pizzorno argued that too much had changed since the time of Marx and Lenin to privilege their thought within this project, for others, particularly within the PSI, the search for a meeting point between Marxism and sociology would become a serious pursuit. In its most extreme form, expressed by the Socialist Roberto Guiducci, the dissident Marxism of the 1950s went so far as to portray sociological enquiry as the means to establish a new 'organic' relation between intellectuals and working people, based upon the joint production of social knowledge 'from below' (Merli 1977: 17–19, 48–9; Apergi 1978: 111–12).

Interestingly, one of the earliest Italian instances of what would soon become known as 'co-research' had come from outside the labour movement altogether, in the work of the social reformer Danilo Dolci. A young professional who had abandoned his career to work amongst the Southern poor, by the mid-1950s Dolci had begun to make use of questionnaires and life stories as a means for the poverty-stricken to catalogue the wretchedness of their plight. Once a devout Catholic, Dolci's deep religious sense left him wary of any doctrine of class struggle, even as his propensity for non-violent direct action as a weapon of popular self-emancipation brought him into continual conflict with the powers that be. Long after they themselves had rejected his populism, Dolci's advocacy of the self-expression of the dispossessed was to remain with the group of Northern youths initially drawn to him, and later help propel a number of them towards *Quaderni Rossi* (Dolci 1960: 19; McNeish 1965; Negri 1983: 15, 17).

Individual life stories and interviews were also to play a central role in the work of Danilo Montaldi, who argued in 1958 that

the sociological method of interpretation is fundamentally foreign, even opposed, to the culture of reformism and Stalinism, which is based upon a fatalistic conception of progress and on the premise of a revolution from above ... (Montaldi 1994: 281)

Against a Marxism-Leninism 'of citations', Montaldi believed that certain sociological techniques could help in the development of revolutionary theory, which 'must be constructed from below in praxis and social analysis' (ibid.: 284). Such a view owed much in turn to two groups which had departed the Trotskyist camp at the end of the previous decade: in France, the organisation Socialisme ou Barbarie of Cornelius Castoriadis and Claude Lefort; in the US that of Correspondence led by Raya Dunayevskaya and C.L.R. James. Critical of the shibboleths which distinguished the Fourth International, these tiny groups devoted much of their energy in the 1950s to uncovering the authentic 'proletarian experience' hitherto passed over by party dogma (Lefort 1978; Binstock 1971: 140–71; Cartosio 1976). Of their many studies of working-class behaviour, the most sustained – the diary of the Renault militant Daniel Mothe, and a pamphlet on the condition of workers in the US – would find their way to an Italian audience chiefly through Montaldi's efforts. As Maria Grazia Meriggi (1978a: 159) has pointed out, *The American Worker* (Romano 1972) in particular had touched upon only the outward manifestations of class behaviour. None the less, it authentically documented the deep-rooted antipathy between factory workers and even the most 'modern' methods of production. For Montaldi, this Correspondence publication held a special significance because it expressed,

> with great force and profundity, the idea – practically forgotten by the Marxist movement after the publication of *Capital* Volume I – that before being the adherent of a party, a militant of the revolution or the subject of a future socialist power, the worker is a being who lives above all in capitalist production and the factory; and that it is in production that the revolt against exploitation, the capacity to construct a superior type of society, along with class solidarity with other workers and hatred for exploitation and exploiters – both the classic bosses of yesterday and the impersonal bureaucrats of today and tomorrow – are formed. (Montaldi 1994: 501–2)

The 1960 translation of Mothe's diary would evoke mixed feelings amongst a number of Panzieri's group, who found its anti-Leninist bent too 'anarchoid' and 'individualistic' for their taste (Panzieri 1973: 273–4). Yet none of them could deny that the Frenchman's reflections, along with the Correspondence studies, provided corroborative evidence of what they took to be the most important of their own discoveries. The first of these was that working-class antagonism to the capitalist organisation of labour, if often contradictory in form, was both permanent and universal. The second was that a profound 'structural separateness' (Bermani and

Bologna 1977: 31) had come to divide the class from those bodies – parties and unions – that claimed to represent it.

That not all in the circle were enthusiastic about the marriage of sociological technique and Marxism would be evident from Panzieri's later grumblings about the 'diffidence' of those 'motivated by residues of a false consciousness, namely by residues of a dogmatic vision of Marxism' (Panzieri 1975: 315). One such sceptic was Alquati who, as one of the few within *Quaderni Rossi* with some professional training in the field, had come to see the use of sociology as at best a stopgap, 'a first approximation' to that 'self-research' which the autonomous organisation of the working class demanded. If anything, Alquati (1975: 54; 1994) would later charge, it was Panzieri who had transgressed, as evidenced by his predilection 'to confide more in traditional social "science"' than the project of developing a properly Marxian reconstruction of the critique of political economy'.

Sensitive to the differences that separated him from Panzieri, Alquati none the less conceded that the insights offered by certain sociological techniques could indeed play an important part in the reinvigoration of Marxism. And as Cesare Bermani and Sergio Bologna (1977: 31) have since pointed out, *Quaderni Rossi*'s use of interviews and questionnaires to record working-class subjectivity was, 'even if it passed for sociology, at bottom oral history'. Of course, the uncritical use of these tools has frequently produced a register of subjective perceptions which do no more than mirror the surface of capitalist social relations (see, for example, Form 1976). Still, members of the group were usually not so naive as to ignore the relationship between such opinions and the behaviour of those who advanced them. Nor, for that matter, did they all believe, with Lefort (1978: 142–3), that the recounting of a limited number of individual testimonies permitted a concreteness and political clarity no larger survey could hope to match. In their opinion, the registration of working-class behaviours and perceptions had a vital part to play in fostering self-activity. The descent into pure empiricism could be avoided by setting such observations within an overall framework similar to that of Marx's own 'Enquête Ouvrière' of 1880, with its emphasis upon building up a composite picture of the technical and political dynamics of the workplace. Finally, like Marx, most of the journal's editors believed that if such a project was to succeed, it must be based upon mutual trust between researchers and workers. After all, only the latter, 'and not any providential saviours, can energetically administer the remedies for the social ills from which they suffer' (quoted in Bottomore and Rubel 1965: 210). From this point of view, as Dario Lanzardo (1965: 1–2) would then argue, 'co-research' was not simply an effective means to achieve results, but the very affirmation 'of a method of political work implicit in the general formulation of the critique of political economy'.

THE PROBLEM OF A 'SCIENTIFICALLY CORRECT' METHOD

If many within the Turin circle of *Quaderni Rossi*, including Panzieri himself, were partial to Weber (Alquati 1975: 24; Panzieri 1987: 332–3), it was also the case that Panzieri (1975: 315) saw Marxism, being itself a theory of capitalist society, as the pre-eminent sociology. This view, which he shared with the journal's Roman editors, had been in large part derived from the work of the Communist philosopher Galvano Della Volpe. A convert to Marxism after the Second World War, Della Volpe's most original contribution to Italian left culture was to seek to reconstruct Marx's method of investigation through a reading of the original sources. It was an unusual undertaking within a party then little concerned with the founder of 'scientific socialism', and to it Della Volpe, long hostile to Italian idealism, brought a viewpoint quite different to that of the majority of Communist intellectuals. However much the techniques of enquiry used in social or natural research might vary, he argued, there was but '*one logic* – the materialist logic of modern science' which underlay them all (Della Volpe 1980: 198).

Della Volpe expressed general admiration for the progress under capital which positive science, through its application of Galileo's experimental method, had achieved in developing coherent explanations of natural phenomena. All the same, the bourgeoisie had had no such success in the realm of social intercourse, being unable to unlock the secret to that class relation which reproduced its domination over labour. The reasons for this, Della Volpe believed, lay not so much with experimentalism, or its alleged inapplicability to the 'moral disciplines', as with the inability of the dominant class to exclude from its enquiry the subjective assumption that capitalist production relations were both natural and eternal. Marx, by contrast, had discovered capital's profoundly historical – and so transitory – nature only because he had remained true to scientific logic's refusal of apriorism. To Della Volpe's mind, the abandoned 1857 'Introduction' to *A Contribution to the Critique of Political Economy* possessed a fundamental importance in this regard, for within it Marx could be found scrutinising the basic building blocks of that conceptual apparatus later applied 'with maximum rigour and success' in *Capital* (Della Volpe 1980: 200). Armed with that critique of a priori reasoning which he had first enunciated in 1843, Marx here made use of historical, 'determinate' abstractions, hypotheses worked up from observation of the concrete – in this case, as Della Volpe emphasised, 'a specific historical society' – and continually re-submitted to it for verification. By these means Marx's enquiry, the opposite of a speculative philosophy which confused concept and reality, formed a methodological circle of induction and deduction, 'a circle that is historical, and therefore dynamic, moving from the concrete to the concrete ... therefore afford[ing] genuine development'. This, for Della Volpe, was the greatest triumph of the founder of 'moral Galileanism': not the elaboration of a pseudo-metaphysical attempt to comprehend the inner workings of the universe, but the application of science to modern capitalist society as 'materialist sociological economics' (ibid.: 186, 194, 209).

Della Volpe had been a marginal figure within the PCI before 1956, and his subsequent prominence within the party owed more to the diaspora of other Communist intellectuals than to a greater receptivity towards his ideas amongst the leadership. True to his self-image as an 'intellectual of the old style' (Colletti 1978: 323), the philosopher always steered clear of party policy. Many of his views most critical of orthodoxy thus lie hidden behind formal obeisance to 'dialectical materialists' such as Engels or Zhdanov, and his discussions of contemporary political themes, if somewhat unusual in formulation, can hardly be interpreted as attacks upon party doctrine (Guastini and Levrero 1970: 311; Bedeschi 1983: 89). Yet if Della Volpe himself never developed his reflections upon the critique of political economy beyond the initial problem of defining a correct epistemology, a number of his students were bolder. Writing in 1958, Lucio Colletti (1974: 3, 23) insisted that Marx's mature work was concerned not with '"general" laws, nonsensical truisms valid for all epochs', but 'with *one* society only, modern *capitalist* society'. Whilst directed chiefly against Soviet proponents of dialectical materialism, this reading of Marx also pointed a dagger at the heart of the PCI's historicism, which Colletti provocatively deemed non-Marxist (Ajello 1979: 349). Even more disturbing, according to the growing number of Della Volpe's critics within the Communist Party, were the political implications of such a stance for the strategy of an 'Italian road'. To their mind,

> by making Marxism a materialist sociology, that is a science of the modern bourgeois social-economic formation, 'dellavolpism' insisted more on the features common to various advanced capitalist societies than on the 'particular' and 'national' features that distinguished one country from another. (Bedeschi 1983: 90)

Judging such views to be the first step towards extremism, the philosopher's opponents launched their attack in 1962 through the pages of the PCI's cultural weekly *Rinascita*. The tone of the discussion, unlike earlier party debates, was generally civilised, but the eventual 'victory' of the historicist side was never seriously in doubt. Defeated, their opponents either retreated temporarily, or – like Colletti – left the party altogether.

The debt owed Della Volpe by the Italian new left, and *Quaderni Rossi* in particular, remains a controversial question. It is not difficult to draw direct connections between the two: Panzieri, for example, had worked with Della Volpe at the University of Messina during his sojourn in Sicily, while Tronti was well-known in the late 1950s as one of the philosopher's most vocal supporters (Fugazza 1975). At the very least, it could be said that Della Volpe's efforts to return directly to Marx cleared the ground for a new appropriation of the latter's thought able to bypass the dominant traditions of the Communist Party altogether. And if Della Volpe was too timid to engage in such a break publicly, Tronti would have no such qualms attacking Gramsci's thought in 1958 as an idealist philosophy whose purpose – the execution of an Anti-Croce – had largely been exhausted:

> For us the good sense of the philosophy of a given epoch is not the common sense of that epoch, distorted and mystified. It is necessary to discover the truth of the latter, through the historically determinate expression that it assumes. If philosophy coincides with good sense, we must mistrust philosophy. If through science we are able to express the common sense of things, it suffices to confide in science. (Quoted in Bosio 1975: 50–1)

Conscious of the seductive power of Gramsci's methodology, yet contemptuous of his epigones' tendency to neglect the critique of material conditions in favour of matters ideological, Tronti's closest associates simply turned their backs upon the philosophy of praxis. In its place they chose the path indicated by Della Volpe, who had refused to postulate the '"economic" and "ideological" as two separate levels of enquiry', looking for inspiration instead to Marx's critique of political economy (Schenone 1980: 174). In a period when that critique was largely unknown within the local branches of Italy's historic left parties (Ajello 1979: 348; Negri 1979a: 36), Della Volpe's insistence upon the actuality of *Capital* would leave an indelible mark upon Panzieri and his young friends. This was particularly so for Tronti, who in the mid-1950s had submitted a thesis on the logic of *Capital* at the University of Rome (Rossini 1980: 65). Echoing Della Volpe, Tronti would argue:

If the *logic of 'Capital'* is again substantiated today, it is because for working-class thought, the objective necessity of an analysis of capitalism has returned to the fore. The *instruments* of analysis are revised when the *object* of this analysis is rediscovered. If the object is capitalist society in the concrete – the modern world moment of capitalism – then the instrument can only be Marx's method that has provided the first and only scientific description of this object. One returns to *Capital* each time one starts from *capitalism*, and vice versa: one cannot speak of the method of *Capital* without transferring and translating this method into the *analysis* of capitalism. (Quoted in Asor Rosa 1975: 1640)

Pursuing this line of argument during the early 1960s, Tronti would also make clear the Romans' dissatisfaction with Della Volpe's own failure to follow through the radical thrust of his thought. If the recovery of the critique of political economy's actuality demanded an 'internal critique' to expunge Marx's work of its ambiguities and flaws, no less important was a confrontation with the vulgar Marxist ideologies prevalent within the labour movement. '*An ideology is always bourgeois*', Tronti insisted; to it the revolutionary must counterpose Marx's proletarian science and its 'ruthless criticism of all that exists' (Tronti 1971: 35, 33). Above all, Della Volpe had failed to understand that such a critique could not remain an academic exercise performed by 'pure Marxists'. Rather, it must become a moment of class struggle that retraced Lenin's path from the analysis of Russian capitalism in 1899 to its overthrow in 1917. 'Workers' power', Tronti concluded, 'the *autonomous* organisation of the working class – [this] is the *real* process of demystification, because it is the *material* basis of revolution' (ibid.: 37).

Similar sentiments were to be expressed by Asor Rosa in the second issue of *Quaderni Rossi*. Referring to unnamed 'scholars' who in recent years had 'dedicated their whole activity to reaching a more exact reading of Marx's thought', Asor Rosa (1962: 122–3, 125) praised their efforts to achieve the 'general demystification' of Marx's work as a great service which furnished the labour movement with 'precious theoretical instruments'. Despite this, however, there existed profound limits within their work, the most damning being an inability to advance to a '*real* notion', a '*scientific analysis*' of modern society. To accomplish this task, as *Quaderni Rossi* now sought to do, theory must step down from its ivory tower and present itself within the class struggle, since '*the only way to understand the system is through conceiving of its destruction*'.

Having taken Della Volpe's commitment to the reinvigoration of the critique of political economy as their own, Panzieri and the

Roman members of his circle would firmly reject both the philosopher's traditional approach to the act of theoretical 'production', and his acceptance of the intellectual's subservience to party politicians. As Emilio Agazzi recalled in the 1970s,

> in conversations during the early 1960s, Panzieri often pronounced a very severe judgement of Della Volpe and his 'theoreticism', of the inadequacies of his analysis, of his singular incapacity actually to apply that method of 'determinate abstraction' which, nevertheless, was his undisputed merit to have indicated – against the Stalinist and historicist deformations of Marxism – as the authentically Marxian method. (Agazzi 1977: 14)

At the same time, *Quaderni Rossi*'s critique of Della Volpe can be seen as incomplete, with the absence of a practical engagement with Italian class politics far from being the only obstacle hindering the philosopher's own efforts to constitute determinate abstractions adequate to the age of the assembly line. Indeed, despite its apparent empirical good sense, Della Volpe's understanding of how such tools are constructed had been deeply flawed. Apart from its blatantly scientistic starting point (Della Volpe 1980: 200), the chief difficulty of his reconstruction of Marx's method of investigation lay with its dependence upon the 1857 text as the key to *Capital*. As a careful reading of the 'Introduction' makes plain, however, Marx's generation of categories there differed from Smith and Ricardo only in the greater consistency with which it utilised that 'Galilean' logic of which Della Volpe speaks. Nor should this be surprising. Marx's later, first volume of *Capital* was guided by a new method of investigation which insisted that mere observation was not enough to penetrate beneath 'the direct *form of manifestation* of relations' to 'their *inner connection*' (Marx and Engels 1965: 191). Against this, Marx's understanding of the process of abstraction in the 'Introduction' still possessed what Rafael Echeverria (1978: 337) has called 'a markedly empiricist content, to the extent that it involves a simple generalisation from observable characteristics in reality'. Oblivious to this shift, Della Volpe continued to portray the 1857 text as if it really was informed by the unambiguous anti-empiricism of *Capital*. This confusion which would have its revenge most spectacularly in his discussions of politics, prone to generate 'the most typical weapon of the speculative method, the generic abstraction' (Montano 1971: 35).

Their uncritical use of the 'Introduction' would cause Panzieri and many workerists continual difficulties in disentangling the logical and historical moments of the critique of political economy. None the less, they were able to retrieve the most productive aspects of Della Volpe's reading of Marx: above all, the insistence that categories be historically determinate. 'Aspiring to a more operative theory,' Alquati (1975: 15) would later write, 'one founded on the new determinations offered in the immediate by the movements of a renovated working class, we theorised many "determinate abstractions".' As to which of these were most effective in grasping the class relations of contemporary Italy, however, Panzieri's group was soon to find itself sharply and irrevocably divided.

2

Quaderni Rossi and
the Workers' Enquiry

The first issue of Panzieri's journal appeared in the second half of 1961, making a big splash within the Italian labour movement. Exhausting its initial print run within a matter of weeks, *Quaderni Rossi* excited interest amongst politicians of the left, union officials, workplace activists and rank-and-file party members – even, if Alquati (1975: 26) is to be believed, amongst younger members of the nation's managerial elite. From the beginning, however, it was to be plagued by a series of crises. First to defect were the group's most prominent union associates. A year or so later, they would be followed by the circle around Tronti. Then, in October 1964, just when some internal order seemed finally to have been restored, the journal suffered the unexpected blow of Panzieri's death, from which it never fully recovered. While the editorial board of *Quaderni Rossi* continued to exert an influence upon the fringes of the labour movement until its dissolution four years later, no one could claim any longer that it bore much resemblance to the journal founded at the beginning of the decade.

For some critics, it is enough to label all collaborators of the original journal as 'workerists' – after all, most were guilty, in the words of Lelio Basso, of 'positing the centre of gravity of struggle within the factory' (quoted in Magni 1970: 36). As the growing polarisation within the group soon made clear, however, the common commitment to a new political practice was much weaker than the very different interpretations of class behaviour that divided the journal's editors. In reality, however, the workerist stream of Italian Marxism was to emerge fully blown only with *Classe Operaia* (Cacciari 1978: 45–7). Instead, it would be more apt to liken the first three issues of *Quaderni Rossi* to incubators, within which many of the themes central to classical *operaismo* were to receive their initial nourishment.

While Panzieri's new journal represented a novel experiment within the Italian left, its name evoked an earlier experience in the annals of left socialism, that of the French *Cahiers Rouges* associated in the late 1930s with Maurice Pivert. It was an apt reference: like Pivert before him, Panzieri had first hoped to win his country's Socialist Party to what he saw as a proletarian, revolutionary perspective, only to encounter an immovable hierarchy mesmerised by the lure of parliamentary office (Joubert 1977). It was also an ominous one, and the prospect that he might replicate Pivert's fate – banishment into the political wilderness at the head of a splinter group – filled Panzieri with dread. In March 1960, even as he made his first plans for the new publication, Panzieri would confess in a private letter that 'I see all paths blocked, the "return to the private" leaves me cold, the possible fate of the small sect terrifies me' (Panzieri 1973: 271).

Isolated in Turin from the factional intrigue of the capital, Panzieri located his path back from despair in the local CGIL's willingness to experiment with new approaches to political work. Following the shock of the 1955 defeat at FIAT, the national leadership of the union had been forced to admit that it was out of step with much of the workforce. 'The reality', confessed its secretary,

> is that we have not adequately examined the changes to the various aspects of productive life and the technical organisation of the wages structure which have occurred in enterprises. (Quoted in Mangano 1979: 13)

Union work, he concluded, had been too schematic, promoting political campaigns 'with a capital P' whilst ignoring the reality of changing work conditions. As a remedy, a number of practical changes were adopted, the most important of which was the acceptance of limited forms of collective bargaining so as to reflect differences in conditions from firm to firm. That was as far as the change went in much of the country. In the Turin CGIL, however, a war came to be waged against what the Socialist Vittorio Foa (quoted in ibid.: 16) termed the 'fossils'. These were functionaries who failed to see that the declining weight within production of that 'old type of worker upon which party and union had generally rested in the factory' (Pugno, quoted in Magna 1978: 309) demanded a new approach to the fight against employers. Foa, Panzieri wrote to Tronti in December of 1960, was 'very committed' to the production of a new review that addressed the real problems facing the working class. This, he felt, was a sign that 'at least here in Turin', it was necessary to distinguish between party and union in their relations with the class: 'Here the union – perhaps because of the terrible defeats suffered in past years – is relatively open to new themes ...' (Panzieri 1973: 283). As the organisation most in contact with the daily experience of workers, the CGIL – and in particular its metal industry union, the

FIOM (Federazione Impiegati Operai Metallurgici – the Metalworkers' Federation) – soon assumed in Panzieri's mind a privileged role as the vehicle best suited to lead the renovation of the Italian labour movement. A further antidote to despair came from the wave of industrial and political struggles which, having stopped for breath at the end of 1959, resumed the following year with greater intensity. With their national contract up for renewal, workers in the metal-mechanical sector had struck throughout the North in 1959, for the first time making widespread use of overtime bans. In some of the bigger firms a push from below for greater unity amongst workers, whatever their union affiliation, could also be discerned; at one plant in Turin for example, workplace delegates from all three major unions jointly organised the picketing (Bolzani 1978: 55). Far from quenching their combativity, the desultory results of the contractual struggle seemed only to fuel the anger of many workers, who chose to reopen the conflict in 1960 at the plant level. Starting in September, metal-workers held a series of national one-day stoppages – again augmented by overtime bans – which by December succeeded in opening a major split in capital's ranks, in the form of a separate agreement with the state employers' association. Common to this, in Turin and elsewhere, was a questioning of the struggle's management: more and more workers believed that this responsibility lay directly with their own assemblies, rather than with union officials (Panzieri 1973: 245–7). The struggles of (predominantly female) workers in the textile industry, freshly emerged from a process of restructuring and 'modernisation' even more frantic than that of other sectors, were more aggressive still, disrupting the flow of production through lightning stoppages which alternated by hour or shift ('checkerboard strikes'). While neither textile nor metal-workers were to achieve satisfactory results from such exertions, their new-found resolution was unmistakable, and pointed to a fundamental change in the tone of Italy's industrial relations (Bolzani 1978: 60–70).

The most overtly 'political' moment of this cycle came with the wave of demonstrations and street-fighting which gripped Italy in the summer of 1960, sparked by a government decision to allow the neo-fascist Movimento Sociale Italiano to hold its congress in the traditional working-class citadel of Genoa. The immediate effect of these protests, which saw more than a dozen workers killed by police before Prime Minister Tambroni was eventually forced to resign, was to open the door finally to a new centre–left coalition. Fought under the cross-class banner of anti-fascism, the July days have been dismissed by some as merely a 'defence and affirmation' of the values of that capitalist state erected after the Second World War (Del Carria 1979: 13). What is particularly interesting about the clashes, however, is the determinate role within them of the most recent generation of workers (Lerner 1980: 38). Almost none of these were old enough to recall the Resistance, let alone fascist rule – why then did they take to the streets with such ferocity? A *Rinascita* survey conducted amongst young Roman participants in the street-fighting provided an elementary clue: for many such young people, it discovered, fascism evoked the spectre of class domination in its purest form. 'I have never known fascism,' admitted one, 'although my father speaks badly of it. We are like slaves, work is a burden and I don't even make enough to live on. That is fascism to me – the boss' (quoted in Garzia 1985: 14). Hailing the role of young workers in the clashes, Panzieri (1975: 122–3) was to make a similar connection: the roots of fascism, he argued in the paper of the Turin PSI, lay in the factory, the source of the *padronato*'s power over society, and there it must be defeated.

In this way, a nominally 'anti-fascist' discourse led back to the most important question thrown up by the current industrial disputes, that of the relation between class behaviour and the organisation of labour in modern production. New labour processes and new workers foreign to the traditions of the labour movement did not spell the end of working-class struggle. Rather, it was within the most technologically advanced firms that – with the glaring exception of FIAT – the industrial conflicts of 1959–60 had been at their most fierce. To make sense of these problems, and to develop a coherent political strategy adequate to the changing face of Italian capitalism: this was the unifying thread binding the disparate forces which Panzieri brought together in the first issue of *Quaderni Rossi*. The cooperation of the local CGIL offered a door into the factory for the young intellectuals of the group to study working-class behaviour first-hand. Together, in what one wit was to dub 'anarcho-sociologism' (Alquati 1975: 72), they might yet develop 'a class political line' (Lolli 1962: 35) to defeat capital.

THE MEANING OF CAPITALIST DEVELOPMENT

Despite the postwar cycle of accumulation, many within the Italian left continued to see the words 'capitalism' and 'development' as polar opposites. Their view, expressed in the impeccably orthodox terms of the contradiction between relations and forces of production, was of an Italy held back by the stagnant forces of local capital, yet vulnerable to the proclivities of a crisis-ridden international economy. If others in the PCI and PSI rejected such an interpretation, and conceded the reality of Italy's 'miracle', they did so from a starting point which denied the inextricable connections between economic growth and the logic of capital, embracing technological development instead as an autonomous and innately progressive force. One of the most important marks of *Quaderni Rossi*'s political realism, by contrast, was to be its rejection of this false dichotomy. 'One could say', Panzieri (1975: 170–1) told a meeting of editors in August 1961, 'that the two terms capitalism and development are the same thing.' Now, however, development meant neither a generic 'progress' nor 'modernisation', but merely the extended reproduction of both the capital relation and the class contradictions which followed in its train.

Only a year before, in the same article which had acclaimed the role of young workers in bringing down the Tambroni government, Panzieri had depicted the 'clerical-fascism' of that regime as symptomatic of 'the capitalist refusal of any perspective of development, as oppression, blackmail, imbalances, unemployment, poverty'. The most important element behind this dramatic about-face was Panzieri's encounter with the essay 'La fabbrica e la società', Tronti's first sustained contribution to *Quaderni Rossi*'s attempted '*Marxian* purification of Marxism' (Tronti 1971: 36). The central purpose of his piece was to delineate the enormous changes that the generalisation of relative surplus value in the form of social capital had wrought within capitalist society. The emblematic case was that of mid-nineteenth-century Britain, where individual capitals had found themselves forced, both by 'the collective capitalist, with the violent intervention of the state', and the struggle of the working class, to shorten the length of the working day. As Marx (1976: 340–416) had demonstrated in the first volume of *Capital*, the response of British industrial capital had been to intensify the extraction of surplus value through 'decomposing and recomposing' the ratio between living and dead labour. This revolution in production techniques had greatly encouraged the development and eventual predominance of large-scale machine-based industry (Tronti 1971: 48, 53). Apart from prompting parallels with Italy's own postwar burst of industrial expansion, Marx's account of the arrival of the 'specifically' capitalist mode of production raised important questions as to the relationship between class struggle, development and forms of exploitation. The lesson to be drawn from the British example, Tronti argued, was that

> the pressure of labour-power is capable of forcing capital to modify its own internal composition, intervening *within* capital as essential component of capitalist development. (ibid.: 47)

Such a dialectic had continued after the introduction of a 'normal' working day. If working-class pressure forced 'the incessant development of the productive forces' upon capital, this process simultaneously entailed 'the incessant development of the greatest productive force, the working class as revolutionary class' (ibid.: 57). Here, too, capital faced the necessity of reorganising production, since 'it is only within labour that [capital] can disintegrate the collective worker in order to then integrate the individual worker'. Even if successful, however, each attack upon labour ultimately displaced the class antagonism to a higher, more socialised level, so that 'production relations become increasingly identified with the *social relation of the factory*, and the latter acquires an increasingly direct *political* content' (ibid.: 54).

Tracing the dimensions of this process of capitalist socialisation was Tronti's second aim in 'La fabbrica e la società'. Already in *History and Class Consciousness*, Lukács (1971: 91, 90) had argued that 'the fate of the worker becomes the fate of society as a whole', since the factory contains 'in concentrated form the whole structure of capitalist society'. According to Tronti, however, the advent of large-scale industry had seen the factory not only stand over society, but absorb it completely:

> When capital has conquered all the territories external to capitalist production proper, it begins its process of internal colonisation; indeed, only when the circle of bourgeois *society* – production, distribution, exchange, consumption – finally closes can one begin to talk of capitalist development proper ... At the highest level of *capitalist development*, the social relation becomes a *moment* of the relation of production, the whole of society becomes an *articulation* of production; in other words, the whole of society exists as a function of the factory and the factory extends its exclusive domination over the whole of society. It is on this basis that the machine of the political state tends ever-increasingly to become one with the figure of the *collective capitalist*, becoming increasingly the property of the capitalist mode of production and thus *a function of the capitalist*. The process of capitalist society's unitary recomposition, a process imposed by the specific developments of its production, can no longer tolerate a political terrain that is even formally independent of the network of social relations. (Tronti 1971: 51–2, 56)

While the subsumption of all social relations to capital brought with it the generalisation of the wage relation, the advancing proletarianisation of new social layers assumed a mystified form. 'When all of society is reduced to a factory, the factory – as such – seems to disappear', and with it 'labour-power itself as commodity'. This was only one of the topsy-turvy effects bound up with what Tronti called the *social factory*. No less important was the manner in which the state's assumption of the role of collective capitalist took the semblance of 'the possible autonomy of the political terrain from economic relations' (ibid.: 52, 53). In Volume III of *Capital*, Marx (1981: 428) had explained such obfuscations as inherent to the capital relation, and indicated as one of the functions of science the reduction of 'the visible, and merely apparent movement to the actual inner movement'. For Tronti (1971: 55), this stripping away of phenomenal forms could only be achieved by examining 'the state from the point of view of society, society from the point of view of the factory, the factory from the point of view of the workers'. Here, as before, can be found an echo of Lukács (1971: 21) who in 1919 had written that 'the Marxist method, the dialectical materialist knowledge of reality, can arise only from the point of view of a class, from the point of view of the struggle of the proletariat'. On the other hand, there was no celebration in 'La fabbrica e la società' of the arrival of social reality's 'full consciousness' along with proletarian self-awareness. In its 'ferocious *unilaterality*' Tronti's class science was to be no less partial than that of capital; what it alone could offer, however, was the possibility of destroying the thraldom of labour once and for all (Tronti 1971: 53).

The path to capital's demise was the final element developed in Tronti's essay. 'The machinery of the bourgeois state', he stated in conclusion, 'must today be smashed within the capitalist factory' (Tronti 1971: 59). It was a pronouncement that rested firmly upon the line of argument built up by Panzieri after 1956, but the manner in which Tronti proposed its realisation was characteristically novel. In the essay's most difficult passage, Tronti dwelt at length upon the political implications which arose from the twofold nature of labour under capitalism, which Marx himself had considered to be 'the whole secret of the critical conception' (Marx and Engels 1965: 199). It was mistaken, Tronti held, to picture the working class as a force which defeated capital from the outside, when in fact the commodity labour-power constituted 'the truly active side of capital, the natural site of every capitalist dynamic' (Tronti 1971: 56). To bring class rule to an end,

> the working class must discover itself materially as *part* of capital, if it wants to counterpose *all* of capital to itself; it must recognise itself as a *particular* aspect of capital, if it wants to be the latter's *general* antagonist. The collective worker counterposes itself not only to the machine as constant capital, but to labour-power itself, as variable capital. It must reach the point of having total capital – and thus

also itself as part of capital – as its enemy. Labour must see labour-power, as *commodity*, as its own enemy ... [so as] ... to decompose capital's intimate nature into the potentially antagonistic parts which organically compose it. (ibid.)

The most interesting aspect of this argument was that, without ever saying so explicitly, its solution for surpassing capitalist social relations pointed in a completely different direction to that traditional quest for workers' self-management of production which then informed the politics of the other editors of *Quaderni Rossi*. If, like all of Tronti's discoveries, that of the struggle against labour was derived through a process of logical deduction, it none the less brought back into the open an alternative Marxist approach to the problems which the parcellised labour of large-scale industry posed for those forced to endure it. And whilst it never became an explicit point of contention with Panzieri, Tronti's advocacy of antagonism between labour and labour-power was an early warning sign of the vast cultural chasm which would soon divide *Quaderni Rossi* in two.

With the appearance of 'La fabbrica e la società' in the second issue of *Quaderni Rossi*, Tronti rightly established himself as one of the most penetrating minds of Italy's heterodox left. In emphasising that relations of production were first and foremost relations of power, he was able to recover the political spirit of Marx's critique of political economy, while his identification of the political contradiction within the commodity form gestured towards a genuinely new anti-capitalist strategy. At the same time, 'La fabbrica e la società' bore within it a number of ambiguities and misconceptions soon to be transmitted to workerism itself. The most striking of these concerned the essay's central theme of the socialisation of labour under 'specifically' capitalist production, and the implications of this for the delineation of the modern working class. In unravelling this process, Tronti (1971: 50) had placed great store upon that '*scientific conception* of the factory' presented in Lenin's youthful study of *The Development of Capitalism in Russia*. There the factory had been understood not in an empirical sense as any establishment employing a large number of workers, but rather as one based specifically upon 'the employment of a system of machines for production' (Lenin 1977: 458–60). That Tronti would himself assign a strategic weight within the social factory to both large-scale industry and the workforce engaged within it was far from surprising; like the rest of *Quaderni Rossi*, he then agreed with Panzieri's assessment that the subversive strength of the working class, its revolutionary capacity, appears (potentially) strongest precisely at capitalism's 'development points', where the crushing preponderance of constant capital over living labour, together with the rationality embodied in the former, immediately faces the working class with the question of its political enslavement. (Panzieri 1980: 61)

All the same, Tronti seemed unable to reconcile this unambiguous championing of the workers in large factories with the notion of the social factory. In his next essay, he described the former as 'a social *class* of producers and not a *group* of miserable oppressed' prone to the 'unforeseen acts of disorderly protest' typical of a proletariat (Tronti 1973: 120). How did this sit with his earlier argument that now 'the entire social production becomes industrial production' (Tronti 1971: 52)? While it seems reasonable to assume that such talk implies the broadening of the category *productive labour* beyond the direct labour process, nothing of the sort was to be forthcoming in Tronti's work of the 1960s. With Panzieri, the 'scientific conception of the factory' was stretched to encompass 'the development of *industry* at a determinate stage of the development of capitalism' (Panzieri 1975: 256, my emphasis; Mancini 1977: 81–2). In Tronti's hands, by contrast, the notion of working class continued to refer exclusively to the employees – and only those engaged in manual labour at that – of Italy's largest firms. Thus if in one sense such reductionism served to focus attention upon the factory in a manner rarely seen within the Italian left since Gramsci's notes on 'Americanism and Fordism' (Sechi 1974: 14, 37), it also drained of meaning the workerist image of an ever-broadening proletariat within the 'social factory'. Having argued that the factory, rather than simply 'a construction that houses men [sic] and machines', was 'precisely the highest degree of capitalist production' (Potere Operaio 1973b: 5), the majority of workerists would, for the rest of the decade, catch little more than a glimpse of the world outside the immediate process of production.

CAPITALIST TECHNOLOGY AND CAPITALIST PLANNING

According to Negri, whose Veneto-based circle of young PSI dissidents entered Panzieri's network in time for *Quaderni Rossi*'s second issue, the project of reading Marx's *Capital* within the group 'was essentially, at the beginning, reading Volume I, and above all the chapters on machinery and large-scale industry' (Negri 1979a: 50). Panzieri's most important contribution to the early numbers of the journal would be devoted to the first of these questions. Succinctly reconstructing Marx's view of capitalist production as a system whose most adequate expression was found in machine-based industry, he challenged the view – then dominant amongst Italian Marxists – that technological progress somehow stood apart from class relations. 'The capitalist use of machinery is not', he argued, 'a mere distortion of, or deviation from, some "objective" development that is in itself rational.' On the contrary, machinery was determined by capital, which utilised it to further the subordination of living labour; indeed, in the mind of the capitalists, their command and the domination of dead labour in the form of machinery and science were one and the same (Panzieri 1980: 47, 48). It was this failure to recognise the intertwining of technology and class domination, he believed, which had undermined the CGIL's self-critique of the mid-1950s. 'The attention that has been correctly paid to the modifications accompanying the present technolog-ical and economic phases', Panzieri noted, was

> distorted into a representation of those modifications in a 'pure', idealised form, stripped of all concrete connections with the general and determining (power) elements of capitalist organisation ... New characteristic features assumed by capitalist organisation are thus mistaken for stages of development of an 'objective' rationality. (Panzieri 1980: 49–50, 51)

It was for Silvio Leonardi, who had played a central role in the CGIL's rethinking, that Panzieri reserved his sharpest barbs. Time and motion studies, 'human relations', even the restructuring and parcellisation of the labour process: all possessed for Leonardi an intrinsic rationality and necessity which their current use by capital could never obliterate. From this viewpoint, Panzieri observed,

> [i]t is not even suspected that capitalism might use the new 'technical bases' offered by the passage from the preceding stages to that of high mechanisation (and to automation) in order to perpetuate and consolidate the *authoritarian* structure of factory organisation ... the entire process of industrialisation is represented as being dominated by the 'technological' which leads to the liberation of man [sic] from the 'limitations imposed on him by the environment and by his physical capabilities'. (Panzieri 1980: 52)

Leonardi was unable, in sum, to see that an undifferentiated and 'objective' notion of rationality could never be used to judge capitalist production, because 'it is precisely capitalist "despotism" which takes the form of technological rationality' (ibid.: 54). Ricardo had accepted the reigning production relations as eternal, and declared that the 'proper' study of political economy should be restricted to the sphere of distribution. Like him, Leonardi and other latterday 'objectivists' granted capital a free hand in organising the workplace, focusing their attention instead upon 'the external sphere of wages and consumption' (ibid.: 61). Yet without 'the achievement of a dominance of social forces over the sphere of production', Panzieri argued, demands for improved working-class consumption and greater free time were meaningless, for it was above all as producers that humans suffered alienation at the hands of capitalism (ibid.: 64). Nor, he added, was the simple monetary growth of wages a useful measure of working-class emancipation and power, since so long as productivity proceeded to grow alongside them, the workers' expanding wage packets would represent no more than 'golden' chains (ibid.: 60).

Leonardi, Panzieri continued, had overlooked one of the most important political aspects of modern, continuous flow production. This was that while in one sense it offered capital 'new possibilities for the consolidation of its power', it also strengthened the hand of the 'collective worker' (that is, 'the various "levels" of workers created by the present organisation of the large factory'). In particular, the greater rigidity which modern production methods entailed gave the threat of working-class uncooperativeness 'enormous disruptive potential' (Panzieri 1980: 49, 51, 53). In fact, he went on,

> the specific element of the process of 'unitary recomposition' cannot be grasped if the connection between the 'technological' and politico-organisational (power) elements in the capitalist productive process is either missed or else denied. The *class* level expresses itself not as progress, but as rupture; not as 'revelation' of the occult rationality inherent in the modern productive process, but as the construction of a radically new rationality counterposed to the rationality practised by capitalism. (ibid.: 54)

Writing much later, the former workerist Massimo Cacciari (1975: 190–1) would fault Panzieri's essay on a number of counts. One of the most damning, in his opinion, was its 'ingenuous' vision of machinery's perfect functionality to the organisation of labour, a notion which had led its author to confuse the 'pure Taylorist' ideal of domination with the much more difficult task of realising it. Another weakness of Panzieri's analysis lay in its talk of the capitalist 'use' of machinery – a thoroughly inadequate way of denoting the material indivisibility of labour process and valorisation process. Similarly, the essay's argument that '[t]he relationship of revolutionary action to technological "rationality" is to "comprehend" it, but not in order to acknowledge and exalt it, rather in order to subject it to a new use: the socialist use of machines' (Panzieri 1980: 57) was markedly tamer than its call elsewhere for a 'radically new rationality' to supplant that of capital. Nor, finally, did Panzieri spell out how the tendency towards the rupture of the capital relation could be squared with his endorsement of socialism as workers' self-management of production, a notion which has too often been oblivious to the class nature of technological rationality. But to dwell upon these weaknesses can run the risk of forgetting the truly pioneering nature of Panzieri's essay. As Sandro Mancini (1977: 77) has emphasised, the piece 'undoubtedly represents the first demystifying analysis of technological rationality' produced by an Italian Marxist; with it, an understanding of the class relations immanent to existing forms of large-scale industry had taken an important step forward.

Following *Capital*, Panzieri had argued that with the growth of a capital's organic composition, the detailed regulation of production became evermore a necessity. 'Hence', he had concluded,

the development of capitalist planning is something closely related to that of the capitalist use of machines. To the development of cooperation, of the social labour process, there corresponds – under capitalist management – the development of the plan as *despotism*. (Panzieri 1980: 48)

In Panzieri's last major essay, entitled 'Surplus value and planning', the social implications of this line of argument were to be spelt out fully. Panzieri's starting point was a critical discussion of Lenin's views on the matter. Like the majority of socialists formed in the Second International, the Bolshevik leader had been of the opinion that economic planning in a capitalist society would violate the most fundamental laws of the latter, beginning with that private appropriation of wealth which constituted its very reason for existence. Limited state planning of a sort could exist – Germany during the First World War was a case in point – as could the 'planning' implied by oligopolistic practices, but with both of these activities came elements of instability which signalled the decadence of the monopoly form of capitalism (Lenin 1978a). In rejecting the idea that planning was inimical to the laws of capital, Panzieri was well aware that its proponents could turn for support to no less an authority than the first volume of *Capital* itself (Marx 1976: 470–80). All this proved, argued Panzieri (1976: 18–21, 22), was that Marx had not always been able to separate features peculiar to the phase of capitalism prevalent in his own lifetime from the general tendency of capital's development. In the modern world of the social factory, such a relationship no longer existed: there, on the contrary, planning had become 'the fundamental expression of the law of surplus value', stretching out from the workplace to assert its command over society as a whole.

With Marx (1976: 450), at least, the recognition of planning within the labour process as a necessary form of capital's 'despotism' could still serve as the basis upon which to construct an appreciation of contemporary planned capitalism. But this perception had been lost on Lenin, who,

[s]ince he [did] not see that capitalist planning with its concomitant socialization of labour is a fundamental form of direct production, [could] only understand capitalist technology and capitalist planning as totally external to the social relationship that dominates and moulds them. (Panzieri 1976: 6)

Believing planning to be intrinsically anti-capitalist, and forced moreover to act in a Russia isolated by the failed revolutions of Central Europe, Lenin had been unable to entertain 'the possibility that capitalist social relations may be present in socialist planning' which treated science and technique as socially neutral forces (ibid.: 21). As a consequence, 'the repetition of capitalist forms in the relations of production both at the factory level and at the level of overall social production' had proceeded apace in the USSR, with the doctrine of socialism in one country as an 'ideological screen'. Stripped, in this manner, of its critical faculties, Marxism in the Soviet Union had ultimately been reduced to a mere 'apologetic form of thought' (ibid.: 22).

As a critique of state economic planning, 'Surplus value and planning' held immediate relevance for the Italian historic left's political aspirations. The call for planning had been central to left ideology following the Resistance, being particularly dear to Morandi's heart. Panzieri's exploration of the power relationships immanent to the capitalist labour process had permitted him to shake off his earlier glib equation between socialist politics and planning. None the less, a commitment to some form of state direction of economic development continued to inform the outlook of the various factions of the PSI leadership after the turn of 1956, and now promised to be their specific contribution to any centre–left government (Spini 1982). Yet, in predicting the functionality of such a policy for the state's new role as representative of social capital, Panzieri (1976: 11–12) came to see its implementation as almost a naturalistic process stemming from the logic of capital itself. In his view, the class enemy was quite capable of solving all its internal contradictions, as 'the sole limit to the development of capital is not capital itself, but the resistance of the working class'.

Having correctly chided those who saw capitalist development in Italy as doomed to stagnation, Panzieri thus mistook a tendency within capital for its concrete manifestation, falling into the opposite error of overvaluing the prospects for smooth growth under a planned capitalism (Mancini 1977: 95). Further, by posing the only threat to capital as something allegedly external to it, Panzieri let fall the insights offered by Tronti's reading of capital as a class relation based on the forced unity of non-identical, and potentially antagonistic, elements. 'Surplus value and planning' was to display other weaknesses as well. These ranged from its confusion of the logical development of *Capital* with the actual historical course taken by the social relation, to its failure to elaborate upon the bonds linking the various forms assumed by capital's instrumental rationality in factory, society and state (Cacciari 1975: 194; Marramao 1975). None the less, like his essay on machinery, Panzieri's work on planning clarified *Quaderni Rossi*'s conviction as to the profoundly political nature of apparently neutral, thing-like processes, even as it laid bare the pretences of his former comrades in the PSI (Meriggi 1978a: 115).

A NEW WORKING CLASS

The existence of a new working class with needs and behaviours no longer commensurate with either those of the labour movement or capital was a theme that ran through nearly all of the major essays published in *Quaderni Rossi*. The most sustained discussion of the problem, however, was that carried out by Romano Alquati and his associates in their studies of two of Italy's major firms, FIAT and Olivetti. The 'Report on the New Forces', which Alquati was to present to a conference of the PSI's Turin federation in early 1961, drew primarily upon interviews with FIAT workers hired since the late 1950s, along with some of the firm's longtime CGIL activists. As an example of a 'workers' enquiry', the report was somewhat impressionistic and rudimentary. Even so, it registered problems undetected by the leadership of the traditional left. The latter, as Alquati had already noted in 1959, was now so often out of touch with working-class reality that 'sometimes it is enough to describe it ... at the level of common sense and in everyday language to produce a work of political and cultural interest' (quoted in Merli 1977: 48).

Like Olivetti, the FIAT of the early 1960s could hardly be considered a typical Italian company. On the other hand, the modern nature of its production process and value system, along with its size, marked it out both as a major pole of capitalist power and an industrial pace setter for the future. Additionally, as a former stronghold of class militancy now seemingly impervious to leftist influence, it stood as a symbol of the labour movement's current disarray. In fact, Alquati argued, the ground had begun to be dug up from beneath the CGIL's feet from as early as 1949. In that year the exploitation of the workforce had been intensified with the parcellisation of labour, followed after 1953 by the introduction of radically new forms of machinery which required little or no training to operate. By these means, management had been able to change the composition of its employees radically, first deskilling or marginalising its old core of professional workers, then introducing a mass of inexperienced youths to staff the expanded production lines (Lichtner 1975: 194–212). Indeed, such were the firm's new margins of manoeuvrability that, for a time at least, it was able to offer wage rates and social services for 'semi-skilled' labour which were amongst the best in the North. In these years, FIAT met with a certain success in projecting a new identity of high wages, valuable skills and dynamic career structures to overshadow its traditional reputation as a ruthless employer. If for some it embodied all that was benign about the Italian 'miracle', for many on the left, by contrast, FIAT evoked images of poor working conditions, company unionism, and a docile workforce besotted with consumerism. Both, however, could agree upon one thing, namely the success of FIAT management in constructing a *cordon sanitaire* around the firm, sealing it off from disturbances in the rest of the manufacturing sector (Partridge 1980: 429–30).

By contrast, the central thesis of the circle with whom Alquati worked was simple, if daring: in their opinion a whole series of objective and subjective processes were unfolding at FIAT such as to lay the basis for a resurgence of class struggle within the firm. The first task of 'co-research' was to strip bare the public myths attached to FIAT, and this the group accomplished with consummate skill. The much-vaunted 'FIAT wage' was shown to now lag behind that of many other Italian firms. It was also revealed that, far from acquiring new skills, most of the workers taken on since 1958 had remained in the bottom category of the gradings ladder, many of them working as 'common' labour on the assembly line. Finally, it was established that the prospects of a 'career' promised to a new generation of firm-trained technical workers simply did not exist (Alquati 1975: 31, 35–8). This, Alquati argued, was proof that the system of gradings which separated the great unwashed of the common labourers from the skilled workers and technicians did not have any basis at all in the 'objective' technical division of labour; instead, its function was fundamentally political, operating to make employees accept the existence of hierarchies within and without the factory as a natural fact, in order to combat the ever-clearer need of self-management which technological progress itself engenders in the executants. (ibid.: 42)

Unfortunately for FIAT management, the effectiveness of this attempt at mystification was increasingly desultory, inspiring a disappointment with conditions that frequently bred only cynicism as to the firm's structure and mode of operation. 'Absurd' is the adjective which most frequently recurred, Alquati (1975: 33, 36) noted, when newer workers described the nature of work at FIAT, and while such disillusionment might take three or four years to set in, once attained it was irrevocable. Many technicians sought to make up for their frustration at work through the purchase of such consumer goods as their higher wages permitted, but even this did little to appease them; its most common result, he argued, was only to add to the sense of ridiculousness surrounding their lives. Nor did such alienation automatically degenerate into nihilistic behaviour, as more orthodox Marxists might suppose. Indeed, the discovery of a political link between exploitation in the factory and the determination of social life beyond its walls by mass production – emblematic in a factory-city like Turin – led many of the 'new forces' most fixated with the acquisition of consumer goods to participate in nascent forms of collective resistance to management (ibid.: 39–40). The roots of the workforce's potential antagonism lay, therefore, in 'that very production which is the keystone of the system'. Particularly decisive had been the part played by the massive socialisation and deskilling of labour, which had served to empty work of its intrinsic content as concrete labour, rendering things 'the same for all'. But the progression from here to a political class consciousness was not for Alquati automatic. While most workers eventually dismissed the organisation of labour at FIAT as a 'bluff', only a minority had taken the further step of seeing collective organisation against capital as the logical answer (Alquati 1975: 40, 41–2). Nor did the latter perspective usually translate itself into sympathy for the CGIL or left parties, considered to be tired and ineffectual in their factory activity. Instead, for the most militant of the 'new forces',

the traditional organisational form of the union flows necessarily into the attitude and mentality of the old workers of the factory; between this process and integration they feel a reciprocal correspondence. (ibid.: 43–4)

Such attitudes led in turn to an 'inevitable vicious circle', with many young workers rejecting the union's demands as abstract, formulated by bureaucrats 'in Rome' themselves subservient to politicians. Meanwhile, those unionists who were genuinely interested in communicating with the new levy of employees felt increasingly daunted by the enormous gulf in age and values that separated them (ibid.: 44–7).

In this manner, and despite the absence of the term itself, Alquati's Report began that discourse on class composition – understood as the various forms of behaviour which arise when particular forms of labour-power are inserted in specific processes of production – which would soon come to be synonymous with workerism itself. While such a stress upon the relationship between material conditions and subjectivity, being and consciousness, had been a commonplace with Marx, too often his followers had approached the reality of working-class existence with rigid preconceptions deemed immutable through time and space. What was important about the Report, by contrast, was its refusal of that measuring stick of a 'completely mythologised class' which had inevitably led many left intellectuals to berate the real thing for its spontaneism and lack of socialist ideology (Alquati 1975: 64–5). This was not to say that Alquati rejected outright Lenin's discourse on organisation, simply that his was a peculiarly 'libertarian' brand of Leninism derived from Montaldi and some of the latter's international contacts. In particular, the argument in *What Is To Be Done?* that spontaneity is only con-sciousness 'in an embryonic form' (Lenin 1978b: 31) was read not as a dismissal of spontaneous actions, but as the recognition that the latter already possessed an innate political significance. Used in this manner, the term spontaneity drew attention to the already existing forms of 'invisible' organisation produced by workers in the absence of a formal class organisation under their control. Similarly, Alquati reasoned, if Lenin was right to insist that class consciousness be brought to workers from the outside, it was wrong to think that this could occur beyond the sphere of production itself. Finally, unlike the Bolshevik leader, who had been quite content to see the factory provide the necessary discipline for working-class struggle against capital, Alquati did not conceive of proletarian organisation as the mere reflection of the capitalist division of labour. Rather, it was a response to the latter's very irrationalism, one that prevented capital from moulding workers completely to its liking:

[T]he fundamental contradictions seem to me to be precisely those internal to technical-productive 'rationalisation', which creates mere executants and then in order to proceed must give them responsibility, which systematically separates and counterposes levels and then has to join them all together in a rigid system that annuls individuals and groups, posing shops etc. as minimum technological units ... which promotes a professional career and annuls professions .... (Alquati 1975: 68–9)

What this demanded, according to Alquati, was the exploration of the political nature of workers' daily problems on the shopfloor. In conversation, FIAT workers tended to move from criticising their individual job role to questioning the rationality of the firm's division of labour as a whole. Their critique – despite its often confused and naive form – revealed a preoccupation with 'the problem of workers' management, even if these young workers have never heard the expression':

The new workers do not talk abstractly of social revolution, but neither are they disposed towards neo-reformist adventures which leave untouched the fundamental questions of class exploitation as they verify them in the workplace. (Alquati 1975: 51)

If the collective possibilities which their individual belligerence to modern capitalist production offered could be conveyed to the 'new forces', then some hope for a consciously socialist development of that 'alternative line' already implicit in their actions was not misplaced (ibid.: 33, 48).

In this manner Alquati began to touch upon what, towards the end of the piece which served to introduce the Report to *Quaderni Rossi*'s readers, he would call 'the fundamental theme of Marxism-Leninism, of the transformation of objective forces into subjective forces': in other words, that of political organisation. He did not question the need for a separate party-institution; rather, the existing parties were condemned for failing to remain 'organic' to the class and the world of the factory that underpinned all social power. 'An organisation that responds to the actual reality of class exploitation': this was the goal to which Alquati aspired (1975: 71, 74, 72). It would also remain the least developed theme in his early work. Indeed, whilst always implicit, the notion of organisation as a function of class composition would lead a difficult existence within workerism so long as Lenin remained the principal reference point of its political discourse.

At the same time, Alquati's early work on FIAT was strongly imbued with that self-management ideology held in common by both Panzieri and the ultra-left which had so influenced Montaldi. In the Report, for example, Alquati counterposed a 'parasitic' management to workers 'united as producers'. Here his reading of class struggle followed Socialisme ou Barbarie in seeing the fundamental social division of labour as that between 'a stratum directing both work and social life, and a majority who merely execute' (Cardan 1969: 10; Alquati 1975: 71, 64). And if Alquati lacked Lenin's own heavy-handed determinism, he still at times presented the workers' thirst for self-management in plainly objectivist terms, speaking in his introduction to the Report of 'a structurally motivated demand to wield political and economic power in the firm and throughout society' (Alquati 1975: 69). In addition, this stress upon self-management and the polarity between 'order-givers' and 'order-takers' as the essential divide between the contending classes was to lead Alquati to some strange distortions when examining the relation between workers and technology. Like other *Quaderni Rossi* editors, he refused to accept that the process of rationalisation possessed any objective, class-neutral basis, seeing its 'classical' aim instead as being

the increase of capital's domination over labour through the increasingly forced technical decomposition of tasks in order to crush politically workers' class consciousness and so exclude them from the firm's policy decisions. (ibid.: 74)

Yet, in discussing this process, Alquati had nothing to say about the role played within it by machinery. Indeed, despite his use of Tronti's notion of 'the complex dialectic of "decomposition" and "recomposition"' in the later introduction, the Report itself assigned no great importance to the explanatory value which Marx's category of the organic composition of capital might possess for an assessment of class behaviour (ibid.: 68). As a consequence, his understanding of the deskilling engendered by mass production was at best equivocal. After having insisted on the political nature of the division of tasks and pay scales, he was led to consider deskilling to be 'as forced as it is false'. Even as old forms of professionality were destroyed, the incompetence of FIAT's managers, along with the 'increasingly parasitic' nature of its technical staff, returned more and more 'executive and technical' responsibility to the workers themselves. Later, in recalling the circumstances under which the piece had been written, Alquati would speak disparagingly of those who dwelt upon 'the presumed objective contradictions in the relation between man [sic] and machine', stressing instead the social aspect of the class antagonism within capitalist production (ibid.: 29, 74). Yet, while such an objection is an appropriate response to those who see technology as the fundamental problem of modern production, it also completely misses one of the major themes in Panzieri's reflections: namely that in determinate circumstances, class relations can themselves take the form of machinery. Without this element, Alquati's discussion in the Report of the 'collective worker' would still lack an understanding of the peculiarities of that *operaio massa* soon to be dear to workerism's heart.

In fairness, it must be pointed out that although both essays appeared in the first issue of *Quaderni Rossi*, 'The Capitalist Use of Machinery' had been written some time after the piece on FIAT. Moreover, in its wake Alquati's reflections upon Olivetti would advance quite a different position on the question. But there is another important point shrouded in ambiguity in the Report – its handling of the union question. On the one hand, Alquati was emphatic that the 'new forces' would have nothing to do with a body considered a spent force. Indeed, at times his own analysis hinted at a similar dismissiveness which drew unflattering comparisons between the top-down nature of the labour movement and that of the modern labour process. In the end, however, he was to shy back from such extremist conclusions, locating the main problem not in the union's function or organisational structure as such, but in the distortions introduced into these by the interests of the PCI and PSI leadership (Alquati 1975: 57–8). Unlike that regarding machinery, therefore, this ambiguity seems a fully conscious one, reflecting acutely the precariousness of *Quaderni Rossi*'s relations with the CGIL. According to Negri (1979a: 50), many in the group had already come to accept the characterisation of unions – advanced by Socialisme ou Barbarie, Correspondence and much of the traditional ultra-left – as 'completely bureaucratised' institutions functional only to capital. That the advocates of such a view had been swiftly dealt with in the past was a fact of which Alquati and others like him were only too aware. To avoid a similar fate, therefore, they found themselves forced to be, in the words of a Fortini essay, 'As Cunning as Doves' (Negri 1983: 101; Fortini 1965). Given this, perhaps one can see, along with an air of duplicity, even an element of momentary self-delusion in some of Alquati's more extravagant claims for the local FIOM. Amongst these was his question as to whether, given its new sensibilities towards young workers, it could still be considered a union at all. In any case, the Report was to achieve its aim, helping for a brief time to cement a close collaboration between leading Turin FIOM cadres and local *Quaderni Rossi* editors. For Alquati, in fact, this experience would be remembered as 'perhaps the only' example of the sort of practice Panzieri had originally envisaged with the journal's foundation (Alquati 1975: 46, 54).

Thus, while they served to deepen the group's understanding of recent changes within the Italian working class, Alquati's pieces on FIAT in the first issue of *Quaderni Rossi* were in many ways the product of a quite traditional, if dissident, political outlook. By contrast, his work dealing with Olivetti workers – the most complex and sustained of the journal's analyses of class composition – was to be enriched by Panzieri and Tronti's reflections upon the labour process. Written before the metalworkers' struggles of 1962 made plain the deep divisions amongst the journal's editors, it is important as a major transitional piece. Within it, a number of themes central to *operaismo* can be seen to emerge alongside, and in certain instances against, those conceptions which had informed Alquati's earlier work.

Olivetti, whose headquarters were situated some forty miles north-east from Turin in the town of Ivrea, was a company which at that time most fully embodied all the myths as to the coincidence between the interests of labour and capital. Owned by a family connected with liberal-socialist circles during the fascist period, the firm was noted for the presence both of its company union within the workplace, and of its owner Adriano Olivetti in the parliamentary arena (Negarville 1959). A maverick in a country where employers were traditionally happy to delegate such responsibilities to professional politicians, Olivetti was also one of the first of Italy's industrialists to sense the possibilities which industrial sociology could offer in securing domination over the labour process. He was also shrewd enough to recruit within progressive circles for the intellectuals ready 'to study' the Ivrea plant and its environs. Perhaps the best known of these would be the sociologist Franco Ferrarotti, whose effusive public enthusiasms for his employer's ideas prompted one Communist intellectual to declare that 'Olivetti is Allah and Ferrarotti his prophet' (Onofri, quoted in Ajello 1979: 325).

Alquati was fortunate in his work at Olivetti to receive the aid of ten or so workplace militants active in the local branch of the PSI. The initial response within the broader workforce, however, was more cautious: after the contributions made by previous left sociologists to the intensification of labour, few were prepared 'to lift a finger' to help research work which did nothing to benefit them. Alquati (1975: 83, 91) too was cautious: despite the industrial unrest of 1960–61, he was of the opinion that 'the reality of the proletariat today is one of political atomisation'. This fragmentation most commonly led to passivity; where resistance did occur, its isolation was such as to render it 'functional to the system'. Modern capitalism had shown itself to be a social formation which 'rationalises all aspects of social life, which plans exploitation on a world scale'. To defeat it, revolutionaries would have to break the 'blind empiricism' of localised conflicts, and discover a more global point of view from which to launch their attack.

In the past, Alquati argued, the relative quiescence of Olivetti had owed as much to Ivrea's isolation from Turin and its traditions of industrial militancy as to the paternalism of its owner. By 1961, however Adriano Olivetti was dead and his philosophy of class collaboration all but discredited; in its place, the firm's new management intended to utilise the command of fixed capital itself to guarantee its dominance over living labour. It was the struggle against this new organisation of labour – mass production regulated by the assembly line – which could, in Alquati's opinion, provide just the foil needed to overcome the present fragmentation of class organisation within the firm (Alquati 1975: 95, 117, 135, 141).

The most distinctive element of Alquati's Olivetti essay when compared with the earlier FIAT pieces, therefore, was the new emphasis that it placed upon the relation between workers and machines. Prompted in equal measure by Panzieri's reading of *Capital* and the more advanced form which mass production assumed at Olivetti, Alquati now judged the introduction of new machinery as a gauge of 'the general level and the quality of the relations of force between the classes in that moment'. With the growing application of Henry Ford's productive innovations to Northern industry during the 1950s, he noted, Frederick Winslow Taylor's goal of 'scientifically' disintegrating the proletariat as a political force had won an important victory: 'henceforth capital's command could develop through machines themselves' (Alquati 1975: 94–6, 105, 119). In this manner machinery became an integral part of socialised capital's edifice of domination, realised

> above all through its technology, its 'science', the diffusion of its structures of exploitation in social life, through constant capital which embraces all, from priests and police (both inside and outside the factory) to the Stalinists. (ibid.: 103)

This process, Alquati observed, had wrought fundamental modifications upon the traditional structure of command within the workplace. Although foremen at Olivetti remained responsible for the fundamental decisions affecting an individual worker's 'career' within the firm, their role – unlike that of their counterparts at FIAT – had become the supplementary one of minimising both the irrationalities of the line and the 'anomie' of their workers. In addition, the growing socialisation and concentration of capital had destroyed the autonomy once possessed by the smaller firms of the sector. Along with their independence there died a whole tradition of Communist politics. Reduced to managing moments within Olivetti's overall cycle, the owners of the *boîte* committed to providing components, maintenance or a retail outlet could no longer be seen as potential allies of the proletariat, but simply functionaries of capital (ibid.: 99–103, 156–7).

The possibility that management itself might forestall the full development of the fragmentation which came with assembly line production was also contemplated by Alquati. After Adriano Olivetti's experiments of the 1950s, his successors had shown themselves reticent to reduce workers immediately to simple appendages of constant capital, preferring to grant space for a token involvement in decision-making from the shopfloor. Such limited participation provided yet another buffer for the firm, one which reconstructed the atomised workforce in capital's image in a manner more advanced than one based upon naked despotism. In their own small way, these schemes provided the cornerstone for the insertion of the labour movement as a whole – or at least of the unions and PSI – into capital at the national level, a development for which the more farsighted entrepreneurs now clamoured (Alquati 1975: 139). The key to the successful integration of labour-power into the web of partic-ipation, Alquati argued, lay in management's ability to restore to work that meaning which the new organisation of labour had itself destroyed. Such an observation made clear the decisive shift that had taken place in Alquati's conception of the bonds linking workers to production. The message woven into the first writings on FIAT – that the proletariat was a class whose rightful place in command of the labour process had been usurped by a parasitic bourgeoisie – was now abandoned. Alquati still advocated the 'social regulation of the relations of production by the collective worker' as a 'necessary condition of socialism'. Now, however, his workers were producers only of surplus value for capital, and the self-management to which the most advanced of them aspired was that of the struggle against its domination (Alquati 1975: 140, 141). Since the simple dichotomy between order-givers and order-takers was no longer adequate to express the contradictions of the capital relation, the earlier discourse on workers as 'executors' also came to an end:

> Today the worker appears as executor only in the role of 'fulfilling' the plan, a role delineated in an abstract, global, generic, but political way. Therefore if workers today are 'executors', the sense of this word refers only to their political reification. (ibid.: 143)

Finally, while he continued to dwell at length upon the obstacles which the capitalist organisation of labour posed before the realisation of its own goals, Alquati no longer saw workers' opposition to such peccadilloes as the expression of a deeper process of rationality. To talk of capitalist development in terms of socially neutral productive forces which decadent relations of production had come to restrain was no longer adequate, and was replaced by an image of the open-ended opposition of class against class (ibid.: 142–3).

None the less, Alquati's emphasis upon the assembly line did not lead to any privileging of unskilled workers within the 'collective worker' such as could be found in some other contributions to *Quaderni Rossi* (Paci 1962: 165–6). As in his FIAT study, that of Olivetti assigned a key role to young technicians in the struggle to organise factory workers as a force against management. In Ivrea, he argued, the technicians' greater mobility within the firm granted them a global vision of sorts, making them the first to attain a class consciousness 'in new terms'. By dint of this mobility, they were also able to assume a vanguard role, communicating forms of organisation and struggle throughout the workplace (Alquati 1975: 142).

Beyond the specific situation of technicians, Alquati was also to uncover the exploitation by employees of the organisation's global structure as a means to pass on experiences of resistance and struggle (Alquati 1975: 143). Here was spontaneity in the true meaning of the term: workers' informal and often non-verbalised transmission of behaviours antagonistic to the logic of valorisation by means of the 'cooperative' structure they were forced to endure. It was, Negri explained years later, a discourse cloaked by Alquati in 'very abstract' terms, but one which his own group in the Veneto immediately recognised in the behaviour of workers at the petrochemical works of Porto Marghera:

> We began to follow a whole series of dynamics of sabotage: in fact no one had set out to commit sabotage, yet there existed a continuity of imperfect operations such that by the end the product was completely useless ... What is spontaneity? In reality it is my inability to establish an organisational, i.e. voluntary, precise, determinate relationship with another worker. In these conditions spontaneity acts through the very communication which the labour process as such, as a machine foreign to me, determines. (Negri 1979a: 64–5)

Alquati did not, however, believe that such behaviour would in itself lead to the recomposition of employees as a force against capital. Left to their own devices, individual forms of disruption were no match for management's own attempts at informal organisation, the most interesting at Olivetti being what workers there had come to call 'ruffianism'. This, Alquati (1975: 135–6, 153–4, 163) discovered, denoted the practice of those employees whose high output set the piecework norms for others. Ruffianism entailed contempt 'towards oneself, towards workmates [*compagni*], towards foremen, towards bureaucrats, towards the unions, towards the Commissione Interna, towards the parties'. It was the dialectical unification of 'the historical opposition of political atomisation and the socialisation of labour', and as such constituted 'the current guise of the "disposability" of the working class to the role of variable capital'. The existence of this behaviour demanded, not moral condemnation, but that the existing forms of refusal take a conscious and organised form. Now openly sceptical that the unions could contribute in any positive way to this process, Alquati portrayed the most important function of their continual divisiveness as the unwitting promotion amongst workers of 'the necessity of surpassing them with a political organisation'.

Alquati's investigation of Olivetti also underscored the identical form of the class relations in which the labour-power of both East and West had come to be ensnared. It was the modern USSR, he argued, which inspired private capitalism at all but the macroeconomic level, as it was young technicians in Poland and Hungary – 'authentic wage labourers' – who had shown that the 'spectre of proletarian revolution' was universal (Alquati 1975: 87, 104). From such sensibilities, common within the American and French ultra-left analyses that had touched *Quaderni Rossi*, Alquati would now draw out a sense of internationalism new to the Italian left (ibid.: 331). This was one based, in Bologna's words (1981: 11), not upon 'organisational vectors and ideological affinities', but rather upon the 'international homogeneity of the behaviours in struggle of productive workers'.

THE BIRTH OF WORKERISM

Piazza Statuto was our founding congress ...

(Potere Operaio 1973c: 208)

If the wage bargaining round of 1962 would at last see the FIAT workforce rouse itself to open strike action, their after-effects threw the various factions within *Quaderni Rossi* into violent collision. The immediate catalyst was provided by the Piazza Statuto riot of July, during which hundreds besieged the Turin offices of the smallest and most conservative of the three major union confederations, the UIL (Unione Italiana del Lavoro – the Italian Union of Labour), in what the broad consensus of the labour movement denounced as an assault by provocateurs and lumpenproletarians. Many of the demonstrators were themselves UIL members from FIAT, furious that their union had sabotaged their first big strike by signing a separate agreement with management. But this was lost at the time upon even the most militant union and party leaders, who preferred with Vittorio Foa to dismiss the whole affair as a 'manifestation of extremist pathology' and a 'diversion from mass action through the strike' (quoted in Lanzardo 1979: 58). A decade later, the event would be recognised by many union officials, including the new secretary of the UIL, as a positive turning point in the development of inter-union cooperation. In 1962, however, more simple answers were demanded: extremists, it was claimed, both of the right and left, were behind the troubles. While the likes of Paolo Spriano sought to play down the influence of a small group – 'students essentially' – whose outlook was 'tenaciously resistant to reality', others found in *Quaderni Rossi* a perfect scapegoat for their own inadequacies. Despite Panzieri's desperate efforts to disassociate his group from the riot, *Quaderni Rossi*'s already tenuous links with the CGIL and historic left now collapsed completely, and with them the very meaning of the journal's project as its founder had originally conceived it (ibid.: 54–5, 69–70, 207).

Even before Piazza Statuto, the Socialist Franco Momigliano had cast doubt upon the coherence of *Quaderni Rossi*'s approach to unions. Writing in the journal's second issue, Momigliano (1962: 108, 109) had centred his criticisms upon the group's denial that the unions' role was 'for the working class not only institutionally, but also objectively, of necessity, a contractual function'. For him, on the contrary, such a role was the whole basis of the unions' strength in society. It was naive, he believed, to project revolutionary connotations onto the most radical of the unions' measures to defend labour-power within capitalism. A more sensible course, he argued, was to work to broaden the scope of their power, so that conquests already won could form a springboard for further social reform.

To abandon its project and return to the fold, or to press on into the wilderness: this was the stark choice which seemed to face *Quaderni Rossi* after Piazza Statuto. While for Panzieri the subsequent break with the official labour movement proved traumatic, those closest to Alquati experienced it as the release from an increasingly impossible collaboration. Having correctly identified the estrangement between workers and unions, many of the Northerners now considered as completely mistaken the group's original premise that their reconciliation could be achieved in a form antagonistic to capital. For these *Zengakuren*, as they were then dubbed (Alquati 1975: 27), a new tack was required, one which drew sustenance directly from working-class struggle itself. The first effort along these lines was attempted by the Venetian circle, in the form of workplace rank-and-file committees organised in Porto

Marghera (Negri 1964a; Isnenghi 1980). With the revival of industrial activity amongst metalworkers in 1963, both the *Zengakuren* and the Roman members of *Quaderni Rossi* pushed for a concerted, autonomous intervention at the national level, starting with a more agitational form of publication than the existing theoretical review.

Starting directly from working-class behaviour also meant clarifying further the significance of those moments when its antagonism to capital refused to manifest itself openly. Already touched upon briefly and discretely by Alquati, the question of sabotage as a form of resistance would be explored at great length by Romolo Gobbi in a publication distributed at FIAT. During the previous July, argued *Gatto Selvaggio*, when

> open struggle was blocked by the unions, the workers, *consciously and collectively* coordinated by the worker-technicians, immediately *intensified sabotage within decisive areas identified through collective discussion.* After the separate agreement they CONTINUED THIS STRUGGLE IN MORE HIDDEN BUT POLITICALLY RELEVANT FORMS. (*Gatto Selvaggio* 1963: 1)

Brought to trial in late 1963 for producing an unauthorised publication that preached subversion, Gobbi could justly complain that the prosecution had completely ignored *Gatto Selvaggio*'s central argument, which was to indicate sabotage's limited contribution, outside of a revolutionary phase, to the development of class autonomy. 'More advanced forms of organisation' were needed, ones which could break the confines of the individual workplace; in this regard, Gobbi believed, Italian workers could learn much from the unofficial mass actions or 'wildcat strikes' which had proved so popular in France and Britain (quoted in *Quaderni Piacentini* 1963: 81–2).

Such a perspective, however, evoked little sympathy from Panzieri. Angered by what he saw as the 'biological hatred' of some in the Turin group for the left parties and unions (Panzieri 1987: 359), he had none the less reconciled himself to the view that the existing unions and parties were no longer 'a valid instrument for the generalisation of struggle'. Still, he remained dubious that any mass alternative could be constructed in the short term. In his contribution to the first issue of the new interventionist paper *Cronache Operaie*, Panzieri did not deny the 'concrete possibility' of uniting the disputes then in progress. He did criticise, however, those who extolled isolated disruptions of production for believing that such actions possessed a strategic moment capable of anticipating capital's development. As the strike wave faded away inconclusively, Panzieri's pessimism deepened. While he agreed that a more accessible format than *Quaderni Rossi* was required, Panzieri saw its main purpose to be 'the formation of a cadre linked to workers struggles without the pretence of representing or leading them'. Given this, the mass agitation advocated by some was currently out of the question (Panzieri 1973: 297–8, 299). Beneath such tactical differences, he insisted at an August editorial meeting, lay fundamental theoretical ones. These were evident in a recent essay by Tronti, which he considered

> a fascinating resume of a whole series of errors which the workers' left can commit in this moment. It is fascinating because it is very hegelian, in the original sense, as a new way of reliving a philosophy of history ... a philosophy of history of the working class. (Quoted in Lumley 1980: 129)

'There is probably', he continued, 'not one point on which we agree' (Panzieri 1973: 303). Raising the question of sabotage as an example, Panzieri characterised it as nothing more than the 'permanent expression of [workers'] political defeat'. The existence within one journal of two such divergent approaches was no longer tenable, he concluded: only a parting of the ways could offer a workable solution to the problem (ibid.: 303, 304).

The key issue for Panzieri, then, was the different connotations that he and the advocates of immediate action placed upon class behaviour. Perhaps Tronti and his associates were correct in saying that one could not 'trace the analysis of the level of the working class from the analysis of the level of capital'. All the same, 'a series of fragmentary refusals' like those evidenced in the recent struggles were no substitute for a coherent strategy based upon the material circumstances of the working class (Panzieri 1973: 291, 321). The path to the unification of workers against capital was still a 'very hard and weary one', and could find its 'permanent political reference' only in continued enquiries into the proletarian condition (ibid.: 254, 321).

Looking back, the points of confluence between Panzieri and the nascent workerists have become as clear as the depth of their disagreement. Like the later split between Potere Operaio and Lotta Continua ('Continuous Struggle'), that of 1963 flowed from personal as well as political differences, with neither side able to claim to have only benefited from the separation. After Panzieri's death, the uncritical use of sociology by some members of *Quaderni Rossi* seemed to confirm the workerists' worst suspicions. Yet the latter could hardly afford to feel smug, as their 'political experiment of a new type' soon brought submersion within Tronti's theoretical framework and that 'enchantment of method' which burdened it (Panzieri and Tronti 1975: 6). Finally, the discovery that a revolutionary mass movement was not yet on the cards would reopen the whole debate concerning the possible renovation of the labour movement which Piazza Statuto had seemed to close, leading to a further division in every way as painful as that from *Quaderni Rossi*.

3

Classe Operaia

With Tronti's journal began the classical phase of workerism's development. For all the different nuances within it, certain core features developed by *Classe Operaia* (*Working Class*) served to unite all its exponents: the identification of the working class with the labour subsumed to the immediate process of production; an emphasis upon the wage struggle as a key terrain of political conflict; the insistence that the working class was the driving force within capitalist society.

The new group was strongest in Rome and the Veneto, where defection from *Quaderni Rossi* had been almost total; elsewhere the situation proved less fortunate, with splits in Milan, Turin and Genoa. From the outset, therefore, *Classe Operaia* experienced an imbalance between the political weight which it assigned to different working-class concentrations – particularly in the North – and its own ability to intervene within them. It was a predicament heavy with irony for a group committed to mass political intervention, above all for the Romans, whose fascination with what Marx (1976) had defined as the 'immediate process of production' was of little avail in a city dominated by service industries. Nor could it bode well that such workplace intervention as did occur in Rome was left to the younger members of the group. Or in the words of Rita Di Leo, '"the adults" constituted the Politiburo, and didn't go to the factories' (quoted in Piccone Stella 1993: 200). Of all the components of *Classe Operaia*, only the Venetians were able to combine a certain numerical weight with what was then considered strategic location. It would be simplistic to reduce the tendency's later split – between those who chose entrism into the PCI, and those who sought to organise on its left – to this dichotomy. All the same, there can be no doubt that the factor of geographical location played an important if unrecognised part in the evolution of those paths (Negri 1979a: 80).

The 'very hegelian' essay by Tronti, which Panzieri had criticised in mid-1963, appeared in January of the following year as the editorial of *Classe Operaia*'s first issue. In it the most scandalous novelty of the new workerist ideology – the reversal of primacy between capital and labour – was clearly set out for the first time. Seeking to uncover 'the laws of development of the working class' so as to advance the cause of proletarian dictatorship, Tronti admitted:

> We too have worked with a concept that puts capitalist development first, and workers second. This is a mistake. And now we have to turn the problem on its head ... and start again from the beginning: and the beginning is the class struggle of the working class. (Tronti 1964: 1)

The current international restructuring of capital, he argued, could only be understood as a response to the movement of the working class, which today had become 'a social mass', possessing 'the same collective attitudes, the same basic practices, and the same unified political growth'. This homogenisation coincided with 'a period of in-between in working-class history', with workers both estranged from the existing labour movement – 'through which class consciousness usually expresses itself' – and lacking an adequate instrument with which to replace it (ibid.: 2). While the revolutionary process was 'assured', its progress would be quicker and easier if a section of the old movement could again play a leading role. In the meantime, workers still made use of the traditional institutions of party and union, albeit with little enthusiasm, while keeping for themselves 'an autonomous strategic perspective free from restriction and compromises'. Thus the task facing revolutionaries was to construct a new political outlook able to grasp 'the total viewpoint of the working class', carrying Lenin's political project of the seizure of power into the maturity of capitalist development analysed by Marx (ibid.: 4, 5).

THE CONJUNCTURE

Shortly after the *Quaderni Rossi* split, the leadership of the PSI reaped the rewards of its post-1956 course and entered Italy's first centre–left government. The marriage, blessed by both the Kennedy administration and the Vatican, had been finally consummated after a courtship of a year and a half. 'As of today', proclaimed the party daily *Avanti*, 'everyone is freer' (quoted in Franchi 1977: 82). Only seven months later, however, the coalition would be in the grips of a crisis – the first of many – as Socialists and Christian Democrats squabbled over the meaning and extent of the reforms necessary for Italy's development.

For *Classe Operaia*, the arrival of the centre–left was welcome if for no other reason than that it clarified the political lines between the workers in the factory and the reformists in Parliament: 'the class struggle is much too serious to be left to MPs' (*Classe Operaia* 1964b: 1). In particular, it laid bare the path that the planning demanded by the new socialised capitalism would have to follow. Unlike some in *Quaderni Rossi*, however, Tronti's group believed this transition to be far from smooth or organic:

> [T]he capitalist system will never be able to attain a perfect objective rationality of its mechanism of development ... [rather] it tends towards this as its maximum program ... The decisive *leap* to capitalist society properly speaking, organised around the production of the average rate of profit, occurs by means of a thousand delays, post-ponements, adjournments. (Tronti 1973: 114, translation modified)

Classe Operaia's starting point in determining the success of such a project was the recent cycle of struggles, which had indicated that sections of the working class – particularly in the metal industry – were no longer prepared to accept either wage restraint or the tightened work discipline imposed through technological innovation. The problem, as defined by the more astute of capital's political and economic repre-sentatives, was how to introduce an element of flexibility into industrial relations whilst keeping the situation within bounds functional to the continued accumulation of capital. In practice, the journal argued, this could only be achieved by means of an incomes policy which institu-tionalised the relationship between wage increases and productivity. Amongst the chieftains of the state – the *Palazzo*, as Pasolini once called it – Guido Carli, then Governor of the Bank of Italy, assumed a particular importance in *Classe Operaia*'s mind. Unlike the prominent Socialist Riccardo Lombardi, who mythologised planning as a significant step towards a post-capitalist society, Carli accepted its necessity as a measure to stabilise the existing order. Calling for a 'global policy' centred upon the relation between wages and productivity, Carli was prepared to accept a wage push to the extent that it forced more backward firms to modernise their productive and financial structures (*Classe Operaia* 1964c: 15).

Views such as these were proof, Tronti believed, that

> [r]aising the price of labour-power was a working-class act of force which coincided for a moment with a necessity of capital, and then overthrew it, surpassing and upsetting it ... the imbalance between wages and productivity is a *political* fact, and must be understood as a political fact and utilised as such. (Tronti 1971: 99)

The classical Leninist distinction between political and economic struggles was thus no longer applicable, since today the fundamental power relations in society were embodied in the sphere of production itself:

> *From the working-class point of view, political struggle is that which tends consciously to place in crisis the economic mechanism of capitalist development.* (ibid.: 111)

For Tronti, capital's development was best understood as a series of political cycles that did not, in any immediate manner, coincide with its 'economic' rhythms:

> [C]apitalist development runs along a chain of conjuncture. We say that each link of this chain will offer the occasion for an open conflict, for a direct struggle, an act of force, and that the chain will break not where capital is weakest, but where the working class is strongest. (ibid.: 101)

In line with such logic, classical *operaismo* rejected the Third Worldism then widespread within the Western new left. According to the youth-oriented journal *Classe e Partito*, edited by Asor Rosa and Franco Piperno amongst others (Scalzone 1988: 24), the peasant struggle in Vietnam could serve working-class internationalism, so long as the two were not confused. Moreover, 'in effect in Vietnam it is capital that is on the attack' (*Classe e Partito* 1966: 7). A less extreme position would be put by Alquati, who conceded the importance of struggles conducted by workers – if no one else – in the 'periphery'; yet for him too, their ultimate salvation lay with their counterparts in the developed world (Alquati 1975: 101).

If workers' struggles fell away with the recession of 1964, *Classe Operaia* could take consolation in the fact that the ruling class itself was suffering a disjuncture between industrialists and their ostensible representatives in the state. Thirteen years later, Carli would blame both the politicians and the industrialists. The first had failed to promote the cohesiveness of Italian society, which meant that by decade's end 'the ferment of protest, rather than stimulate reforms, accentuated the process of social decomposition and disintegration'. The second, he held, had 'never considered the state a social organization to which they are directly responsible' (Carli 1977: 185, 190). According to *Classe Operaia*, while the centre–left government shied away from implementing a coherent plan based on an incomes policy, preferring instead to impose discipline through a credit squeeze, employers were resorting to quite traditional weapons such as layoffs and speedups to attack workers in the factories. This, in its opinion, revealed

> the capitalist illusion of recent years – the political error of our class adversary – that of wanting to achieve direct control over the working class only at the end of a spontaneous process of economic development and through a spontaneous integration of labour into capital. (*Classe Operaia* 1965a: 1)

As for the politicians, their original scheme had failed because its essential prerequisite – a social democratic party able to draw workers into the orbit of the state – was still missing. Crippled by the defection of its CGIL cadre to a new Socialist Party of 'Proletarian Unity' (PSIUP), the PSI could still supply competent economists and politicians to the Palazzo, but no significant slice of the working class itself. With this project of integration a failure, and Socialist talk of planning little more than window dressing, Tronti's fear of a social democratic involution took new form within the PCI. Here Giorgio Amendola had expressed sympathy for the notion of planning and called for the formation of a single party of the left. His version of democratic planning, which drew sustenance from the same logic as that of Togliatti 20 years before, rejected the notion of an incomes policy. Instead it looked to increases in both direct and indirect wages as a means to stimulate effective demand and thus allow for full employment 'at the maximum level of productivity' (Amendola 1966: 399). In this way, he argued, the 'class dynamic' could play a stimulating role in economic development. Coupled with the workers' struggle within the framework of the Constitution as the 'national ruling class', 'defender of the interests of the whole Italian people', and 'bearer of the country's general needs', this would start to alleviate the problems 'exasperated' by those monopolies which since the 1940s had orientated Italy's economy towards production for foreign markets (ibid.: 587).

Unlike the rest of Western Europe, *Classe Operaia* insisted, in Italy the transition to the social factory had begun in the absence of a social democratic party. As a consequence, the possibility existed, for the first time, '*of reaching capital's maturity in the presence of a politically strong working class*' (*Classe Operaia* 1964e: 1), creating a situation of '*maturity without stabilisation*' (Tronti 1971: 117). This project Amendola and others like him, with their talk of a single party embracing the existing formations of the historic left, had come to threaten; everything turned upon preventing the success of their endeavour. For many of *Classe Operaia*'s editors, the exploration of class composition now paled alongside the pressing need to reclaim the Communist Party for revolutionary politics. Within the space of a year, Tronti's 'political experiment of a new type' had reverted to a tactic of a very old kind indeed (Sbardella 1980).

A NEW USE FOR OLD INSTITUTIONS

During the latter days of his involvement in *Quaderni Rossi*, Tronti had believed that 'the true organic integration of the labor unions within the programmed development of capitalist society' represented the most important threat to the struggle against capital (Tronti 1973: 109). With the decline of industrial struggle during 1964, however, he had been forced to reconsider such a view. *Classe Operaia* would subsequently insist that there were two sides to the union struggle,

> the *working-class* one, namely the incessant conflict around the division between necessary labour and surplus value; and the *union* one, namely the constant rationalisation of capital, stimulated by labour. (*Classe Operaia* 1964a: 22)

Gramsci, the group claimed, had offered 'perhaps the best definition of the permanent contractual and legislative character of the union' in the period before the Second World War. With the emergence of social capital, however, the union's function necessarily changed, becoming the 'occasional opponent and permanent collaborator of the democratic structure of society'. As a consequence, any strategy of union 'autonomy' from the party, such as sections of the CGIL had recently proposed, could only hasten the process by which the union became 'an increasingly organic function of capital's plan' (*Classe Operaia* 1964d: 26). If workers had consciously chosen to use the unions in their struggles of the past decade, this owed more to the PCI's absence from the factory than any intrinsic merits possessed by the CGIL itself. Indeed, the contempt of workers for union officials was now almost as great as their 'class hatred' for foremen, guards and technical staff – 'and so it will become, increasingly, in the future. But how to organise this, today, against the social boss?' (Tronti 1971: 100). Thus, while any 'union road to the working class' had to be ruled out, there did exist 'an undeniable union life to the working class' which made its continued use a tactical necessity (*Classe Operaia* 1964a: 22). In such circumstances, Tronti would argue, the best approach to unions was that taken by Lenin:

[I]n certain instances, some of which are very much present, tying the union to the party via a transmission belt still seems the most practicable path for the class struggle. (Tronti 1971: 115)

The key problem was to restore political organisation to the workers. 'There are moments', Tronti would soon proclaim, 'when all problems can and must be reduced to this one problem: organising the party' (Tronti 1971: 20). At first, however, the question of the party remained an open one. Indeed, until December 1964 the need for a 'political organisation' was spoken of in only the vaguest of terms within the pages of *Classe Operaia*. According to the editorial of the June 1964 issue, both the traditional parties as well as new forms – even, in contradiction with its other pronouncements on the matter, the unions themselves – were possible organs of struggle. The primary objective of organisation, it was argued, was '*to maintain the continuity of the open struggle*' (*Classe Operaia* 1964e: 1). Spontaneity, then, continued to be seen as a positive indication of the irreducible nature of the antagonism of labour to capital, of the 'inexhaustible combativity of the working class' (*Classe Operaia* 1964a: 5). All the same, there was general agreement within *Classe Operaia* that unless such struggles attained an explicitly political form, they would fall back to the union level and become coherent with capital's development.

In pondering whether their goal could be achieved outside the historic left, the group was also acutely conscious of the historic failure of earlier revolutionary Marxists to make any significant impact upon the Italian working class after the Second World War. The followers of Amadeo Bordiga had had the most success, but after a brief upsurge in the late 1940s their small party had dissolved into a number of warring factions that either returned to the political wilderness or else buried themselves away in the unions. The plight of Trotskyism had been even more bleak, reduced to eking out a semi-clandestine existence within the PCI. Neither of these fates particularly appealed to the editors of *Classe Operaia*; nor, for that matter, did they show any great interest in the first murmurings of Italian Maoism. Their reasons for such diffidence, beyond the vagaries of sectarian politics, were rational enough, being based on the realisation that a new organisation unable to command the support of a large slice of the working class was doomed to failure. This lesson, moreover, had been reinforced for the Venetians by their unsuccessful attempts to build workplace committees outside the official labour movement, a failure that led them temporarily to advance a more cautious approach to autonomous organisation.

Both the Northerners and Romans, then, were initially united in rejecting what they called 'Trotskyist tactics' and 'Chinese dances' (Tronti

1966: 32), even if their motives for doing so were rather different. For Tronti in particular, whose opinions had led to suspension from his local PCI section (Rossini 1980: 65), the search for a solution to the problem of political organisation had become a pressing need. Already in 'Lenin in England' it had been clear that, for him at least, the distance between the class and the official labour movement was no cause for celebration: the argument that the working class determined capitalist development, as radical as it seemed, only went so far. For Tronti (1971: 236), working-class struggle was like a great wave that tossed capitalist society and the class party on to the shore of a new conjuncture, spending itself in the process. From there, the initiative shifted to capital and/or the party, 'two opposing forms with the same content' – labour.

While such a conviction was understandable given the changed climate of the mid-1960s, it also revealed that Tronti could not conceive of the unification of the working class as a force against capital – what the workerists now began to call political recomposition – outside of a party-form. A number of other utterances appeared to belie this – for example, his argument later in 'Marx, labour-power, working class' that working-class power, unlike that of the capitalists, was by nature non-institutionalised, since it could exist separately from the official form of its representation (Tronti 1971: 240). At bottom, however, the thrust of his thinking presupposed a vanguard party. In the essay 'Classe e partito', published in *Classe Operaia*'s issue of December 1964, Tronti's starting point was the distance between the Communist Party and a working class which risked defeat if it confined its actions to the bounds set by capitalist accumulation. The crucial missing element, he believed, was 'the intervention of revolutionary will', inseparable from the 'irreplaceable function' of the party:

> Only through a subjective, conscious intervention from above, through a material force which allows the possession and command of the system's functioning mechanism to be destroyed; only through the social use of this force is it possible *not only* to foresee and anticipate the turning points in capital's cycle of development, *but also* to measure, control, manage and therefore to organise the political growth of the working class, forcing it to pass via a chain of conflicts at various levels and on various occasions ... [so as ultimately] to overturn the relation between the classes, to smash the state machine. (ibid.: 112)

Perhaps Trotsky had put it more eloquently with his analogy of the party as piston and the class as steam, but the sentiment expressed here was no different. Tronti's was a bluntly instrumentalist notion of organisation:

that the PCI had tended so far to adapt itself to capitalist development did not, in his opinion, mean that it could not be used against capital in the future. With this he combined another sensibility common to orthodox Trotskyism, locating the crucial site for such a transformation within the party's leadership. This 'collective brain' could re-establish a correct relationship with the class through its control of the scientific tools, the tactics and strategies necessary to manoeuvre capital into a vulnerable situation. The slogan to be worked around, he declared, was 'Give us the party in Italy and we will take Europe' (ibid.: 25).

Since the revolutionary party could not reasonably expect to encompass all the experiences of the class, it would have to maintain a certain autonomy, a tension, towards the workers as towards capital. This tension, Tronti held, was embodied in the figure of the revolutionary leader, no doubt as Napoleon had embodied the world-historical idea in Hegel's time. In 'Marx, labour-power, working class', Tronti was to indicate just how crucial he believed this figure to be:

> Lenin practised materially that overthrow of the relation between working class and capital which in Marx was only a methodological discovery, the partisan scientific foundation of a working-class point of view on capital. After Lenin, the working class can impose practically everything on capital. With one formidable condition: if it is armed from the outside with the intervention of tactics, with the direct leadership of the party ... by itself the working class can never arrive at this, and the party arrives there only when it contains a Lenin. (Tronti 1971: 254)

Thus, despite his fierce criticisms of traditional Communist intellectuals and their disdain for the reality of the factory, Tronti's main contribution to the struggle to overthrow the division between manual and intellectual labour was to propose instead that the intellectually trained become professional revolutionaries (Tronti 1971: 246). Not surprisingly, such an analysis attracted considerable criticism from others within the Italian new left. For Gianmario Cazzaniga, writing in the journal *Giovane Critica*, Tronti's arguments recalled in their idealism 'the positions of the young Hegelians'. Further, by locating the central contradiction in the head of the revolutionary leader, they showed themselves to be completely foreign to current debates 'in the international Communist movement' (Cazzaniga 1967: 33). Even Asor Rosa, one of Tronti's closest associates in the Roman group, was to baulk at this aspect of his analysis. Instead, he told a public meeting on *Operai e capitale* that Tronti needed to clarify this 'rather inexplicable or insufficient' point which seemed to present the tactical moment as *'the rule of the empirical, of the empiricism of the leader, whereas, vice versa, science would seem to be the total preserve of strategy'* (Asor Rosa 1967: 46). In this manner Asor Rosa touched upon another fundamental aspect of Tronti's discourse on politics: the relation between strategy – already embryonic within the class – and tactics, the property of the party. Such a notion remained dear to later workerists as well, with Negri citing it years later as 'one of the most precious legacies' of *Classe Operaia*. Through such a relation could be grasped not only the richness of daily struggles, but also the party's task of drawing out, like a modern day Socrates, their revolutionary significance. According to Negri, one of the main problems with *Classe Operaia* had been the presence within the group of many who overvalued the tactical moment whilst simultaneously undervaluing 'the institutional role of the Communist Party' (Negri 1979a: 84). In Tronti's work, however, the problem is different: there the party came to dominate both strategy and tactics as the privileged bearer of working-class science:

> [A] correct relation between class and party presupposes ... this *practical capacity* of anticipation and of direction of the class' movements in determinate historical situations: not only knowledge of the laws of action, but the concrete possibility of *acting*, in total possession of what could be called the theory and practice of the *laws of tactics*. In this sense the party is not only the scientific bearer of strategy, but also the practical organisation of its tactical application. The working class possesses a spontaneous strategy of its own motions and development: the party must observe it, express it and organise it. (Tronti 1971: 113)

Tronti was pessimistic as to the possibilities both of an autonomous working-class activity that could break the rhythm set by contractual struggles, and the political space available to construct a new organisation, as the continuing stagnation of the PSIUP demonstrated. It was not surprising, therefore, that Tronti's focus shifted to the PCI's redemption from a reformist leadership. The party function, he argued, could be performed 'only by an already existing political organisation, and only by a party cemented to the class as such' (Tronti 1978a: 24). The Communist Party thus had to be rebuilt as a party in the factory, so as to organise a blockage of production and therefore of profit, since 'Whoever controls and dominates [production] controls and dominates everything' (Tronti 1971: 235).

In light of this orientation, one of the most striking aspects of the whole Roman position within *Classe Operaia* would be its failure to provide any coherent structural analysis of Communist reformism. True, many pages of the journal after late 1964 were taken up with examinations of the PCI's evolution since the 1940s. But this material was largely descriptive in its account of party policy and ideology, focusing above all upon the gradual but apparently irreversible decline of the Communist Party's presence in the factory, and the corresponding drop in working-class membership. On occasion such dissatisfaction even filtered into PCI forums: for example, the 5th National Conference of Communist Workers of 1964, where one functionary relayed the common query of young workers: 'What does the party do? ... The unions organise struggles and strikes – what does the party organise? Only elections?' (quoted in *Classe Operaia* 1965b: 30). For *Classe Operaia*, the major blame for this state of affairs lay squarely with the choices made by the party leadership during the forties. At that time, when many Northern workers were still armed and in control of their factories, Togliatti had refused to work to consolidate the working class as an autonomous political force, tying it instead to the fate of a generic 'people'. From the 'new party' of the early 1940s, *Classe Operaia* argued – indeed, right back to Dimitrov's unveiling of the Popular Front at the Comintern 7th World Congress – a continuous thread could be traced to Amendola's proposal for a 'single party' of the left. But as to the reasons which had led the leadership of the major working-class party to choose this course over a revolutionary one, *Classe Operaia* had nothing to say (*Classe Operaia* 1964f; 1964h).

Tronti and his closest associates were quite adamant that the entrism they now proposed would be profoundly different to that of previous dissident Communist groups. These, they argued, had failed because they were lacking in 'a general perspective truly alternative to the official one' (Tronti 1971: 25). Nor did the Romans have any sympathy for Togliatti's successor Longo, who had publicly criticised many of Amendola's proposals. Longo too, in his time, had called for a 'single party' of the left, had sanctioned the right to a 'fair' profit, and had toyed with dropping the PCI's Communist label. Nor, finally, did they have much time for the party's 'official' left wing around Pietro Ingrao, which they condemned for its lack of a 'scientific vision' of the working class and its privileging of civil society as the crucial site of struggle (*Classe Operaia* 1965c: 9). Indeed, the Romans were not at first even prepared to concede that the Communist Party's reformist line might be tied either to its internal structure or to the Stalinist traditions of its past:

> It is clear that we are not interested in the theme of the relations between Togliatti and Stalin, of the leading role of the USSR, of the originality or otherwise of the PCI's line. We gladly leave it to the

Trotskyists: this is not the heart of the problem. The heart of the problem lies in the relation between the PCI and the working class. (*Classe Operaia* 1964h: 13)

Later Tronti's faction would be more reasonable, admitting that the question of the party's line could not be separated from that of its structure (Artioli 1967: 4). Still, from now on the fate of the class was inseparable from that of the party, in a struggle that moved both against capital and towards the party. If Amendola's efforts to recast the PCI as an all-embracing social democratic party proved successful, capital would finally be able to gain control of the class. While the ruling class was still not sophisticated enough to bring the PCI into the state, a 'single party' would be a different matter. If, on the contrary, the left of the labour movement could be regrouped so as to leave the social democrats in a minority – something never seen before in the transition to social capital – then the balance of forces would shift towards the workers (Tronti 1966: 32).

Beyond any political objections that might be raised to such a position, its most distinctive attribute was to be its patent impracticability. By 1966 the Romans were prepared to gamble everything on halting the 'social democratisation' of the PCI, including the existence of the journal and national group. 'We think that in great part we have exhausted the reasons for our direct political presence', they were to write in May of that year (Tronti 1966: 32). Yet within a party where the major left current commanded the support of perhaps 20 per cent of active members (Amyot 1981: 157), *Classe Operaia*'s own forces could only be considered minuscule. In addition, they were to find themselves the object of an aggressive public campaign by sections of the party leadership, which did not shy away from slander plain and simple. 'Who pays them?', the Turin page of the party daily *L'Unità* had asked rhetorically in early 1964, while leaving its readers in no doubt that *Classe Operaia*'s voluminous output of publications depended upon the purse strings of big business (Minucci 1964). In the face of such vehemence, the group had been able to do little more than seek consolation in the unrest which the incident provoked within the local party (*Quaderni Piacentini* 1964). By 1966 *Classe Operaia* would be reduced to celebrating the reunification of the Socialist Party with Saragat's PSDI (Partito Social Democratico Italiano – the Italian Social Democratic Party) as a signal both of social democracy's marginalisation, and the temporary reprieve of the PCI and PSIUP (*Classe Operaia* 1966). Of all of Tronti's closest associates, only Asor Rosa maintained – for the moment – a ruthlessly pragmatic approach to the historic parties, which he characterised as 'now nothing more than transitory meeting places for revolutionary militants' (Asor Rosa 1966: 23).

CLASS COMPOSITION

Nobody has discovered anything more about the working class after Marx; it still remains an unknown continent. One knows for certain that it exists, because everyone has heard it speak, and anyone can hear fables about it. But no one can say: I have seen and understood. (Tronti 1971: 18)

Within *Classe Operaia*, as in Panzieri's group, research on working-class behaviour continued to revolve around the studies of Alquati. Later he would deem his work of that time as the product of 'Five Years of Solitude': as projects which, artisanal and exploratory in nature, could only offer hypotheses to be taken up practically at some future date (Alquati 1975: 11). None the less, having established his conceptual framework in *Quaderni Rossi*, Alquati's central concerns turned to following the complex bonds between the class and its ostensible representatives, and to mapping out the former's patterns of 'invisible' organisation. In his first contribution to the new journal, Alquati focused upon the FIAT wildcat strikes of 1963, which he saw as indicative not of backward, 'anarchoid' behaviour, but of a new, compact, mass vanguard in motion. The most important property of these wildcats lay in their refusal to play by the established rules of industrial relations; instead, they were unpredictable, they excluded the union from the direction of the struggle, and '*they demanded nothing*' (ibid.: 187, 192). At the same time, Alquati believed, it was wrong to see such strikes as anything but transitional phenomena, a temporary measure until a more adequate form of organisation could be found. 'Carrying the permanent struggle beyond the "wildcat"', he went on,

> demands above all a 'beyond' of anticipation, of theory, of organisation, of strategy and *therefore* a 'beyond' of the international organisation of revolutionary political struggle ... At FIAT, as in the entire Italian working class, the workers already look to the final battle. (ibid.: 197)

Leaving aside this triumphalist note, the most interesting aspects of 'Lotta alla FIAT' are bound up with its explicit rejection of self-management ideology, and its attempt to identify the connecting thread which ran from open forms of struggle like the wildcat to more subterranean forms of resistance. Polemicising at length with the union left grouped around the Turin CGIL, Alquati dismissed their plans for workers' control as unwitting attempts to bind labour to accumulation. Instead he pointed to recent stoppages in which 'the revolutionary consciousness and will of the workers expressed itself above all in the refusal to address positive demands to the boss'. Such independent action, he concluded, demonstrated that workers had begun to grope their way towards a goal entirely different to that envisaged by Bruno Trentin and his ilk: the organisation of a '"political" self-management outside of capitalist production against the "general political power" of capital' (Alquati 1975: 189, 193).

Developing its thematic of class composition in this manner, Tronti's group came to reject a notion of class consciousness as the mere aggregate of each worker's *Weltanschauung*. Struggle, rather, was seen as the greatest educator of the working class, binding the various layers of the workforce together, turning the ensemble of individual labour-powers into a social mass, a mass worker. It was through struggle that class autonomy most clearly differentiated itself not only from the movements of capital, but also from 'the objective articulation of labour-power' (Alquati 1975: 225). As Negri put it in his essay 'Workers without allies':

> [T]he working class is increasingly closed and compact internally, and searches within itself to articulate its ever greater unity in organisation ... today the *whole* working class in struggle is the vanguard. (Negri 1964b: 18)

Identifying the subterranean paths by which class recomposition moved was, however, to prove a far more difficult task; at times, indeed, the workerists' talk of the compactness of the class merely stood as an admission that its inner workings remained opaque to them. The limits of *Classe Operaia*'s approach were particularly evident in its argument that passivity should be understood as an instance of class antagonism, a form of 'organisation without organisation' (Tronti 1971: 262). According to Alquati (1975: 191), the reticence of workers to join in union-sponsored token strikes could be read not only in a traditional manner as a lack of class identity, but also as a refusal to sanction empty gestures which did nothing to challenge capital's command over their labour-power. Against this, Sandro Studer has suggested that the path to understanding such behaviour lies in examining

> the daily relationship between workers and productive forces, which is always an ambiguous relationship, where both the acceptance and refusal of capitalist labour coexist, where workers' passive objectification

and subjective (collective) resistance coexist within the subsumption of labour-power to the productive process. (Studer 1977: 59)

For his part, Alquati was not to pursue the matter beyond the limits already set by his work in *Quaderni Rossi*. All the same, his work would be amongst the first to address, however implicitly, an apparent contradiction within classical workerism. This lay in its insistence upon the permanent nature of labour-power's antagonism to capitalist relations of production, while at the same time talking of a 'technological path to repression' (Negri 1967: 11), by which capital could successfully destroy the political quality of given concentrations of working-class power.

Unlike many Marxists, the editors of *Classe Operaia* never believed that the 'making' of the working class within a particular social formation was an event confined to a single period. Rather, it was the result of an ongoing interplay between the articulations of labour-power produced by capitalist development, and labour's struggles to overcome them. But which element was the more potent: the continuity of struggle, or capital's ability to decompose its antagonist? Was the proletarian subject really destroyed by the reorganisation of production which periodically followed industrial conflict, or was it like some single-celled creature, which could be infinitely divided whilst still retaining its genetic code intact? Was it enough to say, with Negri and Tronti, that capital's restructuring simply displaced class conflict to a higher and more socialised level? Finally, what role if any did the problem of memory play in the reproduction of class antagonism?

These questions would become paramount at the end of the following decade. In the mid-1960s, however, most workerists seemed happy to posit a determinate relation between the workforce's material articulation within the organic composition of capital – the 'technical composition' of the class – and its struggle to overturn such subordination in pursuit of a new political unity. Whilst still associated with *Quaderni Rossi*, Alquati had already stepped beyond such reductionism, intertwining his assertion of labour's inherent hostility to capital with a sense of the peculiar problems thrown up by the vast cultural gulf which separated the million new workers of the 'miracle' from their older workmates. By the time of *Classe Operaia*, Alquati had deepened his understanding of shopfloor culture further, placing an increasing emphasis upon the coherence that the transmission and filtering of memory between successive generations of workers lent to the immediate experience of production. In this regard, his best work of the period was to be a study of those ex-party 'factory Communists' who provided an internal vanguard for the industrial working class of Turin. It was these factory activists, he argued, formed in the struggles of the miracle and now politically homeless, who would ultimately decide the fate of Tronti's project of the working-class 'use' of the PCI (Alquati 1975: 274–302). By stressing the dialectic between such militants and the workplace culture which nurtured them, Alquati thus began to move away both from conventional Leninist notions of vanguard organisation, and *Classe Operaia*'s own simplistic characterisation of the working class as a single, homogeneous mass. In this manner, his thematic of 'invisible' forms of class organisation came to acquire a certain substance, gesturing towards those elementary units of working-class resistance which, based upon both the organisation of labour and social networks, have been explored at length by certain radical American writers (Weir 1981). In other respects too, Alquati would continue to supply *Classe Operaia*'s most sober assessments of working-class behaviour. Emphasising the need to locate Italian developments within an understanding of accumulation and proletarianisation as worldwide phenomena – '"socialist" countries included' – he was of the opinion that if the unification of the class was now 'decisive' it was also 'partial'. In Italy, he continued,

a stumbling block to approaching the structure of labour-power at the social level is the extreme differentiation between the levels of capitalist exploitation in the various zones, sectors, firms. (Alquati 1975: 222, 223)

An appreciation of the Italian working class, therefore, could not be exhausted by its description as a 'compact social mass': rather, such homogeneity stood as a goal for which to fight. And more than any other editor of *Classe Operaia*, Alquati was sensitive to the existence of a working-class experience outside the workplace. Forty years before, Otto Rühle had insisted:

Only in the factory is the worker of today a real proletarian ... Outside the factory he [sic] is a petty-bourgeois, involved in a petty bourgeois milieu and middle class habits of life, dominated by petty bourgeois ideology. (Rühle 1974: 41–2)

Alquati's view was diametrically opposed to that of the old Council Communist. Taking his cue from the category of *social factory*, he argued that no moment of a worker's life could escape the reach of direct capitalist domination:

Turin is considered the 'factory-city'. And it's even true that there isn't one aspect of the 'social life' of the city that is not a moment of the 'factory', understood in the Leninist sense as 'social relation of production'. But it is also the 'factory-city' because according to the census more than 60 per cent of its 'labourers' are industrial workers, because the mass of *factory workers* is concentrated in the city, working in factories and living around them. There is no simple, clearcut distinction, then, between the plants where surplus value is created, the residential zones where labour-power reproduces itself, and the centres of administration of the movements of variable capital, of commodities, products and semi-worked primary and auxiliary materials. (Alquati 1975: 230)

At the same time, *Classe Operaia*'s insistence upon the centrality of productive labour in the direct production process would severely restrict Alquati's understanding of class relations outside the world of immediate production. Thus, despite its promising beginning, the rest of his article on Turin as a 'factory-city' explored only the connections between different plants in the cycle of the metal industry. Similar limitations emerged within his piece on the 'green factory' of agriculture, which ended rather than began with the realisation that '*one of the most urgent analyses to be made is that of the social fabric of class recomposition*' (ibid.: 272).

Introducing *Classe Operaia* to a new generation of readers in 1979, Negri (1979b) was to confess with some justice that 'our mass worker smelt badly of the Putilov works'. Curiously, in the course of an earlier polemic, he had come to the opposite conclusion about the journal. Then he had complained that the likes of Tronti and Cacciari, 'who today go on and on about working-class centrality', had at that time 'fully recognised the productive nature of socially mediated labour' (Negri 1979a: 11). A similar position has been advanced by Giovanni Bossi (1975: 260), for whom the classical workerist discourse encompassed not only the political leadership of workers in the large factories over the rest of the class, but also 'the socialisation-massification of the figure of the working class beyond immediate production'. Such an understanding of what Bossi has called 'the capitalist use of the articulation of the territory', however, is impossible without a fully developed notion of circulation and reproduction, both of which *Classe Operaia* lacked. At best, as exemplified by the work of Alquati, the 'social fabric' would be discussed only to the extent that it offered a means to communicate or block struggles. Furthermore, it is puzzling that a journal such as *Classe Operaia*, which is remembered as the birthplace of the 'mass worker thesis', should have had so little to say about the enormous impact which migration then wrought upon the whole of working-class culture in the North. If, as Bologna (1981: 17) later recalled, 'part of workerism was an analysis of the formation of the industrial proletariat of the 1960s, the passage from countryside to factory', then this was true only in terms of its impact upon the workplace. Next to nothing, for example, would be said about the problems – of housing, transport, social life – which their relocation brought for the new levy of industrial workers. Where the question of migration was taken up in *Classe Operaia*, it was simply in terms of its function as one of the objective bases of the 'liquidation' of the peasantry as a class separate from productive workers. Alternatively, it was understood as a moment of the mobility of labour-power; even in the latter case, discussion would be confined to migration within the Veneto region rather than from South to North (Di Leo 1964; Tolin 1965).

Reviewing some American studies a few years later, the workerist Ferruccio Gambino (1968) would insist that the gates of the factory stood firmly closed to the mainstream sociologists of that nation. A cynic might have added that if this was so, *operaismo* itself remained trapped inside. There is, in fact, more than a grain of truth in the contemporary critique of *Classe Operaia*'s outlook – advanced by one of its own associates in the pages of *Rinascita* – as 'factoryist'. According to Accornero (1965), Italy was reduced to the industrial triangle, and the working class to the productive workers of the large factories in the North. In the end, however, the journal's chief failure would lie not so much in its reductionism, although this would create problems enough, but rather in its habit of bringing to too-hasty a conclusion the necessarily complex matter of developing political strategies adequate to the autonomous class behaviour which it had been its privilege to identify.

A CLASS SCIENCE?

For working-class thought, the moment of discovery has returned. The days of systems-building, of repetition, and vulgarity elevated to the status of systematic discourse are definitively over. What is needed now is to start again, with a rigorously one-sided class logic – courage and determination for ourselves, and detached irony towards the rest. (Tronti 1964: 4)

When, in 1966, Tronti's contributions to *Quaderni Rossi* and *Classe Operaia* were reprinted in the book *Operai e capitale*, they were to be overshadowed there by a previously unpublished essay on 'Marx, labour-power, working class'. Written in the same year as *Lire le Capital*, the piece was also, in its own way, a symptomatic reading of the critique of political economy. As the title suggests, it took as its starting point two central categories in Marx's work in order to draw out the methodological premises for a class science. Unlike some of Althusser's epigones, however, Tronti did not believe that such a science could ever depend upon purely internal proofs for verification. If theory necessarily informs practice, allowing us to order 'facts' and to pierce the world of mere appearance, then it was equally true that certain theoretical advances were possible only by means of practical breakthroughs. In this vein Tronti set out to filter a reading of Marx through the struggles of the early 1960s, seeking to escape the 'petrified forest' of vulgar Marxism which presently dominated the thought of the Communist movement. For classical workerism, as Negri (1983: 94) has noted, theory was a weapon to be used 'both as a scientific lever and as a practical club'. The working class was crude and menacing: so too must be its science. All great discoveries – 'ideas of simple men which seem madness to the scientists', as Tronti put it – had been made by 'dangerous leaps', by breaking 'the thread of continuity'. Today too a new horizon was demanded: 'blind, minute analyses' were best left to pedants (Tronti 1971: 11, 12).

'Knowledge is tied to struggle. Who knows truly hates truly.' The working-class point of view was thus 'a non-objective social science which makes no pretence of objectivity', its motivation being fuelled instead by the class hatred 'of that part which wishes to overthrow society' (Tronti 1971: 14, 232, 245). In the introduction to his unpublished *Critique of Hegel's Philosophy of Law* of the early 1840s, Marx (1975a: 187) had first proclaimed that part to be the proletariat, whose secret was '*the dissolution of the hitherto existing world order*'. Thus the first section of Tronti's essay sought to find, within Marx's early works, the gestation of the category labour-power, that peculiar commodity sold by the worker to capital. According to Tronti, its origins could be traced back to the *Economic and Philosophical Manuscripts*, a piece he was anxious to recover from the hands of those humanists and existentialists who had so bedevilled Althusser. But the pre-1848 texts were marked by considerable confusions, from which Marx had been freed only after a push from the outside:

> Abstract labour already exists as labour-power in Marx before 1848. Labour-power already exists as commodity. But it is only the revolutionary passage of '48 which lays bare in Marx's head the theoretical process that will carry him to discover the *particular* content of

the commodity labour-power. The latter is no longer tied simply – through the alienation of labour – to the historical figure of the worker, but rather – through the production of surplus value – to the birth of capital itself. (Tronti 1971: 130)

It was this practical catalyst, he asserted, which had allowed Marx both to fuse and to surpass the thought of Hegel and Ricardo. Here Tronti echoed the approach of Raya Dunayevskaya, whose text *Marxism and Freedom* had emphasised the dialectic between theory and class activity:

All of history is the history of the struggle for freedom. If, as a theoretician, one's ears are attuned to the new impulses from the workers, new 'categories' will be created, a new way of thinking, a step forward in philosophic cognition. (Dunayevskaya 1958: 89)

Tronti's approach to theoretical discovery was very much the same, with the added qualification that an often fortuitous relationship existed between enquiry and its results. Indeed, in certain circumstances serendipity could even become a methodological principle:

[U]nknown worlds wait to be explored, and the vicissitudes of those who try to find a new route to the Indies, and *precisely because of this* discover other continents, are very close to our current mode of procedure. (Tronti 1971: 5)

Here, it would seem, there was no place for teleological rabbits pulled out of the hat at the last instance. Yet Tronti was himself to prove far from consistent in applying such an open-ended notion of theoretical enquiry; ultimately, his critique would remain trapped within its own conceptual terms, a metaphysic unable to realise that interaction with the real world for which it yearned.

This weakness would reveal itself most fully in the central section of 'Marx, labour-power, working class', wherein Tronti sought to deepen *Quaderni Rossi*'s earlier reading of capital as a power relation. So-called economic laws, he argued, had to be rediscovered as political forces, behind which lay the motor of working-class struggle. This was true above all for the cornerstone of the critique of political economy, the law of value. It was wrong, Tronti held, to interpret this law as proof that workers produced all wealth in society: such an argument was both moralistic and incorrect. The crucial point, rather, was that in assuming labour as the measure of its value, capital had acknowledged its dependence upon a unique commodity, one with the potential to destroy it completely (Tronti 1975: 225, 230). From this point of view,

> [t]he labour theory of value means *labour-power first, then capital*; it means capital conditioned by labour-power, set in motion by labour-power ... *Labour is the measure of value because the working class is the condition of capital.* (ibid.: 224–5)

To refuse such a function within the valorisation process, Tronti believed, would prove the most coherent means to dismantle the class relation. Now that labour, with the generalised use of mechanised production, had lost 'all individual character, and, consequently, all charm' (Marx and Engels 1972: 39), such a strategy of opposition to wage labour found its material reference point in the modern working class, which

> has only to look at itself in order to understand capital. It has only to combat itself in order to destroy capital. It must recognise itself as political power, and negate itself as productive force. (Tronti 1971: 261)

In posing the antagonism between capital and labour in these terms, Tronti could claim no less a precursor than Marx himself, for whom a communist society was one in which work – the tyranny of economic necessity – would no longer regulate people's lives. According to the German revolutionary, capital was not a thing to be taken over and managed in a new fashion, but a social relation based upon a process – the self-expansion of value – which must be abolished as a prerequisite of human freedom (Marx 1975b: 278–9). When, after him, most leftists had envisaged their goal instead as a society at whose centre stood the workers reunited with their products, only a handful were to raise their voice in opposition. One of these was James Boggs, a former member of Correspondence whose critique of American unionism would appear in the pages of *Classe Operaia*. In *The American Revolution*, Boggs pictured a looming 'workless society', in which it would be 'technologically possible for men [sic] simply to walk out on the streets and get their milk and honey'. To his mind, the strongest push for such a compact would come not from factory workers, busy defending their jobs, but from the 'outsiders' whom society had marginalised. 'The workless society', he concluded, 'can only be brought about by actions and forces outside the work process' (Boggs 1963: 53, 58). Tronti's line of thought led him to exactly the opposite conclusion: only those who actually produced surplus value could block its accumulation, and with it the reproduction of the capital relation. Yet if such an argument was rigorous in its logic, Tronti's efforts to give substance to the crucial passage from a mass of individual labour-powers to a class of workers would prove less successful.

'What the working class *is* cannot be separated from *how it struggles*' (Tronti 1971: 200). Having established the sphere of production as the privileged terrain within which, through struggle, the class composition of workers experienced a 'political leap', Tronti turned to what he saw as currently the most widespread form of working-class opposition to capital. This, he claimed, was exemplified by the passive, sullen denial of any but the most minimal collaboration within the labour process. If passivity was sometimes the product of a political defeat, as Panzieri had held, it could also arise in the wake of a new level of capitalist development. According to Tronti, these two manifestations had become entwined 'in the past few decades'; while passivity remained a barrier to revolutionary activity, it also represented 'an opting out of the game, a flouting of the social interest' (ibid.: 202, 261, 262). Having reached this point, however, the essay's argument simply ground to a halt, unwilling or unable to delve beneath the surface appearance of the phenomenon of passivity. Instead, Tronti's refusal to budge from the highly abstract realm inhabited by 'pure' labour-power would lead him to postulate a series of suggestive if ultimately vacuous notions, such as his description of passivity as a form of 'organisation without organisation'. Last but not least, it led him to take refuge in the triumphalist assertion that 'Many experiences have failed. *Ours will not fail*' (ibid.: 259, 262).

Polemicising with the latterday *Quaderni Rossi* and its efforts to construct a 'model' of socialist society with which to inspire workers, Asor Rosa would argue:

> If there are reasons why the working class must overthrow and smash the domination of the capitalist system, they certainly cannot be found outside the material, objective characteristics of the class itself – Marx has at least taught us this. (Asor Rosa 1965: 39)

From this vantage point, perhaps the most important bequest of 'Marx, labour-power, working class' lay in its instruction that the Italian new left discover 'what has happened in the working class since Marx' (Tronti 1971: 263). In the pursuit of such understanding the work of Tronti himself, with its hermetically sealed categories, could only be of limited utility. Ironically, the ability to push parts of Marx's conceptual apparatus towards their limits, in the process discerning certain aspects of workers' behaviour without leaving the realm of theory, had become both his gift and his doom. Like Moses before him, Tronti would glimpse, but not himself enter, the promised land.

THE END OF *CLASSE OPERAIA*

As early as 1965, Tronti (1978a: 29) had argued that the existence of groups such as *Classe Operaia* was symptomatic of the labour movement's current weakness, and could only be short-lived. Resuming this theme two years later, he was to deny that the recent round of contractual struggles posed any serious threat to capitalism. The social system based upon the accumulation of value for its own sake was young and vibrant, with most of the Third World's population yet to be conquered by the wage relation:

> The simple growth of this immense mass of industrial labour-power, and within it the internal passage from proletarians to workers, will be the true challenge of the final days of the second millennium, and not the technological futurism of those who see in the automated factory all labour being transferred to machines ... (Tronti 1967a: 28)

Not only did capital continue to rely upon workers, Tronti went on, but the latter themselves still needed capital for their own growth and development as a social force. The class was neither strong enough nor mature enough to overthrow the capital relation, although it was now possible to manage the latter through the party. From the earlier strategy of workers within and against capital, and of revolutionaries within and against the party, there now followed 'the party *inside* and *against* the state'. In fact, he believed, even a working-class use of social democracy had become possible:

> Power is everything in cases such as these. Only the relations of force are decisive ... There is no solution that can be tactically excluded *a priori*. Tactically, all solutions are good. (Tronti 1967b: 26, 27)

As Lenin had said: 'the revolution is a dirty affair ... one can't make it with clean hands' (ibid.: 27). By any means necessary, then – except outside the institutions of the official labour movement.

While the Northern workerists were more sanguine than Tronti about the prospects of their continued organisational autonomy, they too saw the revolutionary renovation of the historic left as an unavoidable task. As Negri would later remember in his autobiography:

> Throughout those years our conviction was that, given a determinate level of consistent crises and the construction of [new] moments of organisation, the official labour movement would line up within the revolutionary process. It would be forced to. What a frightening error! How ingenuous and myopic on our part ... (Negri 1983a: 98)

None the less, the main thrust of the Northerners' approach to political organisation continued to centre upon the need to maintain and generalise the fight within production. To their minds, the Romans' emphasis upon entrism – at a time when the level of industrial conflict was again on the rise – was ludicrous. A full twelve months before the last issue of *Classe Operaia* appeared in 1967, the division into two factions had already effectively taken place, with only a handful of editors, like Alquati, maintaining a certain distance from both camps. Whilst this separation did not lead to their immediate rejection of the existing labour movement, nor even end their theoretical collaboration with Tronti's inner circle, it did mark a fundamental prioritising by the more radical workerists of industrial agitation over inner-party politicking. If a working-class 'use' of the PCI existed, then it was one that stemmed from militant organisation in the workplace. As workerism entered a phase of 'practical enthusiasms and theoretical depressions' (*Metropolis* 1978: 7), the hypotheses of the *Classe Operaia* years stood ready to be tested in the heat of conflict.

4

New Subjects

By 1968, the unrest which characterised campus life in the US, West Germany and Japan had become an international phenomenon, reaching even into the Eastern bloc before exploding in France with the heady days of May and June (Ortoleva 1987, 1988). More so than in any other advanced capitalist society, however, the Italian 'Year of the Students' heralded a broad wave of social conflict that would peak in 1969 with the 'Hot Autumn' of the Northern factories. Italy's was a 'creeping May', and if its Movimento Studentesco (Student Movement) (MS) had then only recently emerged from beneath the shadow of the official student organisations, it lost no time in moving to overtake its foreign counterparts. In so doing, it placed on the agenda the possibility of an effective worker–student alliance the likes of which campus radicals elsewhere could only dream.

University occupations and demonstrations were not unheard of in the Italy of the mid-1960s. A number of brief but widespread mobilisations had taken place in response to the centre–left government's moves to rationalise higher learning, while in spring 1966 the Roman campus had been in turmoil after a student was killed by fascists. The cycle of struggles which opened in early 1967, however, was much more profound in scale than anything before, involving at its peak thousands of university and high school students throughout urban Italy, and quickly paralysing much of the education system. Lively and confrontationist, the new movement was notable not only for its size, but also for its efforts to redefine the very notion of politics, constructing forms of organisation – above all, the permanent 'assembly' – which simply and brutally swept the traditional student bodies aside.

Along with the new-found industrial muscle of technical workers, the rise of the MS was the most distinctive feature of social conflict in Italy during the first half of the *biennio rosso** of 1968–69. As the product of social strata whose behaviour could not be reduced to that of simple labour, the actions of students and technicians raised important questions for *operaismo*'s understanding of class composition. Yet in the immediate aftermath of the *Classe Operaia* split, many workerists seemed

---

* Literally, 'red biennium'; it evokes the Italian strike-wave of 1919–20.

incapable of grasping the significance of such forces. As Bologna would confess more than a decade later:

> I remember our embarrassment in interpreting the underlying social mechanism, in understanding the relationship between the movement in the universities and the formation of the working class. In my opinion, this also determined our great political marginalisation during the 'anti-authoritarian' period from Autumn 1967 to the beginning of 1968, when we were incapable of assessing the nature of the student movement. (Bologna 1981: 14)

Such isolation would be alleviated by the middle of 1968, as the movement itself became increasingly preoccupied with the industrial working class, and a number of prominent members of the Roman MS moved to embrace the workerist credo. But it would only really be broken with the migration of student cadres to FIAT Mirafiori in spring 1969, by which time many Northern factories were in turmoil, and the very nature of the 'student question' – now subsumed to that of the mass worker – had changed beyond recognition.

POTERE STUDENTESCO

The reasons for the rapid collapse of the 'official' Italian student bodies in 1967 are not difficult to discern. Student numbers had begun to expand with the partial liberalisation of access to tertiary education in 1961, although the structure of secondary schooling continued to handicap the chances of youth from blue-collar families. By the middle of the 1960s the Italian system of higher learning was suffering as much from overcrowding, poorly equipped facilities and antiquated courses as any other in Europe. With graduate employment becoming more and more of a problem, it was not surprising that the earliest of the new style of campus disturbances – at Trento in 1966 – was highly corporatist in nature. Still, it would be simplistic to deduce the origins of the new movement from nothing more than the disjuncture between Italian universities and the needs of capitalist development. Along with the rest of the industrialised world, the mid-1960s in Italy witnessed the fruition of a deep-rooted normative crisis amongst young people, signs of which *Quaderni Rossi* had already charted in Italian industry. It also registered the beginnings of a specific 'youth' subculture rejecting many of the dominant values of civil society (Piccone Stella 1993; Mangano 1999). Expressed through music and dress, through changing attitudes towards the family and work, such values found particularly fertile ground amongst members of the Communist and PSIUP youth federations. For many of the latter, the example – and mythology – of China and its 'Cultural Revolution', along with that of their nation's own Resistance, served to condemn as failures both the meagre showings of the 'Italian road', and the monstrosities of the Soviet experience (Viale 1978: 19; Moroni 1983). True, other far-left currents, including workerism, made some advances within these organisations. But it was the spectacular images of anti-imperialist struggle in Asia and Latin America which first fired youthful imaginations in the mid-1960s, leading many young militants to condemn the historic left's purely verbal solidarity with movements of national liberation (Bobbio 1978: 9–12). Nor was this break with traditional politics confined to those young people emerging from the mainstream left. A similar restlessness was also detectable within the Catholic world, with dissident Catholic students coming to play an important role in the MS, and after within left groups as diverse as Lotta Continua and PDUP (Partito di Unità Proletaria – the Party of Proletarian Unity) (Cerrato 1999). As Asor Rosa (1968: 198) would astutely note at the time, the new student movement had attained a significance unique in postwar Italian politics, because it represented nothing less than 'the first example of a mass struggle without party control'.

The rejection of its hegemony did not mean, however, the immediate severance of all ties to the historic left. Indeed, the first phase of struggles in 1967 saw student actions whose leaders – hotly asserting the movement's autonomy from the left parties – were often still nominal members of the latter or their youth federations. Various justifications were then offered for this peculiar relationship. For some student activists, the MS represented an important split within the 'middle class'; whilst the movement needed to organise autonomously, it was still obliged to look to the working class – and thus its party, however revisionist – to lead the popular 'historic bloc'. This position, common at Milan's State University, also struck a responsive chord in many of the more conservative sections of the local PCI (Camboni and Samsa 1975). For other young militants, the renovation of the historic left as a revolutionary force was still an open question. Like the workerists, they perceived the labour movement's major problem as one of a healthy base held back by a reformist leadership, and looked to pressure exerted both within and without the parties to rectify the situation. Others, finally, were of the opinion that for the moment, and whatever their policies, the left parties – and the PSIUP above all – afforded a useful channel of rank-and-file communication until something better came along (Hellman 1976: 250).

The very schizophrenic nature of the PSIUP, with a leadership dominated by older associates of Morandi quite out of touch with – and, more importantly, incapable of disciplining – the party's younger militants, made such a use seem feasible to many for a time. Similar attempts to utilise the Communist youth federation would meet with varying results. While youthful dissent and sympathy for 'extremist' politics were tolerated in places such as Reggio Emilia, in other localities – for example Pisa – exclusion came swiftly for those who strayed beyond the bounds of the party's dominant postwar traditions (Cazzullo 1998: 41–2). This general mood of intolerance did nothing to improve the increasingly strained relationship between the PCI and politicised youth; Amendola's portrayal of the student movement as an enemy to be defeated only added fuel to the fire. Despite the more conciliatory position advanced by others in the party leadership during 1968, the membership of its youth federation continued to decline. By 1969, relations between the PCI and MS in all major cities except Milan had effectively collapsed, and a number of factions within the student movement began to amalgamate into new national organisations seeking to challenge the PCI's dominance of working-class politics (Luperini 1969; Hellman 1976: 272).

While struggles circulated throughout the major university centres in Italy, the MS swelled to mass proportions in only a few localities during 1967, and it was the experiences in these cities – above all Turin and Trento – which gave the new movement its initial orientation in pursuit of 'Student Power'. Influenced in part by the German and American campus movements, this new ideology was turned by its young theoreticians into a peculiarly Italian concoction. To their minds the tyranny of the academic 'barons' and the discriminatory nature of university admission were only an expression of the more general power relations within society. 'Authoritarianism', wrote Carlo Donolo (1968: 78) at the time, 'is a new word for an old fact: exploitation.' Yet if such a generic notion of domination was perhaps the major weakness of Student Power as an ideology, its very breadth left it open to a number of quite different readings. In its first emanation, in Trento, the call for Student Power stressed the sectionalist interests of students; even in its most radical form, it rarely went beyond the demand for 'universities to the students, factories to the workers'. In Turin, by contrast, emphasis was from the beginning placed upon the social continuity of class rule. Echoing *Quaderni Rossi*'s thesis of the social factory, Luigi Bobbio and Guido Viale held that

[t]he social system of advanced capitalism increasingly takes the form of a network of totalitarian institutions aimed at the total control and domination of the persons subject to it ... Authoritarianism in a neo-capitalist world is not a hangover from feudalism; it is the fundamental form of class domination, to which all social institutions are subordinated. (Bobbio and Viale 1968: 222)

In their view, the role of the MS was to challenge schools' function as 'a direct instrument of subordination' which, through the organisation of consensus and passivity, 'manipulate the students, persuading them to accept the division of labor and hierarchic stratification of roles on which our society is based' (ibid.: 223). Europe's historic left and unions were considered little better, since they confronted social conflict only to keep it within the confines set by capital: 'The only thing these organisations still have to offer is a career' (ibid.: 222). If the immediate targets in Turin were again the class nature of admission and the power of professors, the continuous nature of domination throughout society ultimately raised the problem of joining with the working class to generalise the conflict gripping academe. Elsewhere however, sectionalist interests or Third Worldism reigned supreme. In Rome, talk of a worker–student alliance made little ground before 1968, with its proponents likely, in Scalzone's words, to be 'drowned out by whistles and cat-calls' and dismissed as 'one of the PCI, a "politico"' (Piperno and Scalzone 1978: 75).

'LABOUR-POWER IN FORMATION?'

Despite its relative isolation, workerism would leave its mark upon at least one of the Movimento Studentesco's most important debates. In February 1967, during an occupation of the University of Pisa, dissidents within the 'official' left student organisation drew up a document that set out to delineate both the class location of students within Italian capitalism and their relationship to working-class struggle. Rewritten and partially reformulated a few months later as the *Tesi di Pisa*, their analysis had considerable impact during the early days of the movement, being praised by Rossana Rossanda (1968: 65) of the PCI left as 'the most complex and persuasive of the MS's "theoretical" attempts'.

Gianmario Cazzaniga and the other authors of the *Tesi* played a central role in the local group Il Potere Operaio, which would later supply much of the leadership of Lotta Continua. They had first been formed politically within the organisations of the historic left, where they had come into contact with the networks around Panzieri and Tronti. Il

Potere Operaio was a hybrid group ideologically, containing workerists as well as radicals motivated by more conventional Marxist-Leninist and Third Worldist precepts. It was also one of the few far-left formations then able to command respect within the new student movement. If elsewhere, Cazzaniga (1967) had written critically of *Classe Operaia*, the influence of *Quaderni Rossi* – and, to the lesser extent, that of Tronti's journal – was clearly discernible within the *Tesi*. A qualitatively new model of capitalism, the document argued, was currently emerging. Capital's ever-increasing centralisation had 'profoundly' altered its laws of development, and the enormous growth of its organic composition was now leading to the 'disappearance' not only of the tendential fall of the rate of profit, but the law of value itself. As a consequence, class composition could no longer be conceived as a simple function of the valorisation process, but must of necessity also be examined in terms of the social division of labour (Cazzaniga et al. 1968: 174).

According to the *Tesi*, there had always existed intermediary strata in capitalist society, 'social figures of the waged, who as such are formally producers of surplus value, but who are not internal components of the working class'. Now, however, capital's socialisation had reached such a magnitude that the barrier separating them from blue-collar workers had begun to fall (Cazzaniga et al. 1968: 173). This was particularly the case for those engaged in intellectual labour, whose subsumption was of growing urgency for capital. Such a process was not, however, without attendant risks for the class relation. Even as the incorporation of science and intellectual labour within constant capital strengthened the latter's political power over the potentially insubordinate, deskilled 'masses', the parcellisation and generalisation of intellectual labour generated an 'intellectual proletariat' open to an anti-capitalist struggle in pursuit of both material and political demands (ibid.: 171, 172). For its part, the labour market was forced to undergo a 'radical evolution' so that it could be 'planned in time and space', alongside 'the 'growing average rate of qualified labour-power' demanded by capital. As a consequence, the state was increasingly compelled to intervene in order to guarantee tertiary training as a 'long term productive social cost' (ibid.: 167, 171). Since schooling was 'the place of production of qualified labour-power, counting as a social cost in the cycle of capital's enlarged reproduction', the student must be understood first and foremost as labour-power 'in its process of qualification' (ibid.: 176–7).

Although they were to prove no less flawed than other contemporary Italian attempts to grasp the nature of intellectual labour, the *Tesi* are distinctive for a number of reasons. Perhaps the most important of these was their location of students within capital's total circuit of reproduction, as an early attempt to make concrete *operaismo*'s allusion to a horizon beyond the immediate process of production. Caught none the less between the implications of the social factory thesis and the political significance of productive labour, the *Tesi* ultimately followed earlier workerist texts in privileging the latter. The student was already a proletarian by virtue of a subordinate location within the university division of labour. To the extent that existing stipends became a fully-fledged wage, she would be transformed from an 'impure social figure on the margins of the valorisation process' into a fully-fledged 'wage worker producing surplus value' (Cazzaniga et al. 1968: 177).

While this argument was to generate the greatest controversy upon the appearance of the *Tesi*, little serious effort was made by its authors to sustain or develop the point before more orthodox critics. For contemporaries concerned with its practical implications, the document was also marred by a discussion of students which perceived them only from the restricted viewpoint of what they would eventually become. By contrast, one of the proponents of Student Power could boast:

> If we do not offer a definition of the student, if we underrate politically both their social background and their 'probable' future class position, we do this in order to reflect something that has emerged from the struggle, which is, precisely, the *specific political negation* which the students have made of their 'past' and of their 'future', not evading the problems raised, but passing through and beyond them, affirming the 'present' as history to be constructed ... the definition of the student is given by the student struggle ... (Rostagno 1968: 203–4)

While plainly demagogic, such a position was infinitely closer than the *Tesi* to the spirit then prevailing within the early MS. Finally, the document's chance of having a lasting impact on the MS were severely hampered by its conception of student relations with the labour movement. On the one hand, it advocated the eventual formation of a new revolutionary party, and exalted the new movement's discourse on anti-imperialism, direct democracy and confrontation. On the other, the call for a student 'union' to defend the particular interests of nascent labour-power as one component within the labour movement as a whole, only grated with the dominant student thematic of autonomy from all existing social institutions. For this reason above all, the document was to be largely forgotten by the end of the decade: when cited, it was as an artefact left over from the old movement, not a weapon suited to the needs of the new.

WORKERS AND STUDENTS UNITE

With the dissolution of *Classe Operaia*, any organised presence of 'pure' workerists was confined to the North-East of Italy, where Potere Operaio veneto-emiliano (POv-e) dominated the region's far left. Although the group soon came to wield considerable influence over its own local MS, Pov-e's relations with student politics were quite different to those of its Pisan namesake, whose members were always at pains to distance themselves from the Venetians. Years later, Negri would attempt to explain the differences between the two Workers' Power groupings in terms of their respective social composition. According to him POv-e, unlike the Tuscan formation,

> was overwhelmingly working-class, so that student problems, which were fundamental for the Pisans, were always mediated via a rather difficult debate within Potere Operaio veneto-emiliano. (Negri 1979a: 93)

Whatever the truth of this, throughout 1967 and 1968 the workerists closest to POv-e clung unflinchingly to the world of *lavoro operaio* ('blue-collar work'). In their view, the only political problem of any consequence still left unsolved from the experience of *Classe Operaia* was the relation between the class and the labour movement. One senses that for them, as for Piperno at that time, many of the student movement's concerns smacked of the merely '"personal" or superstructural', and as such were simply dismissed as irrelevant (Piperno and Scalzone 1978: 74).

With such attitudes commonplace, it should come as no surprise that Pov-e's journal had paid no attention to the student movement before the middle of 1968. By that time, a fundamental shift could be discerned within the most important components of the MS, with the proponents of Student Power now finding themselves challenged by more traditional ideologies stressing the primacy of the working class in social conflict. The criticisms of Oreste Scalzone (1968: 2) – not yet a workerist, but already prominent within the faction-ridden Roman MS – were not untypical of such views. After conceding the potency of Student Power's anti-institutional critique, Scalzone argued that it had also engendered a widespread mistrust of 'the party as an institution', the 'revolutionary vanguard of the proletariat'. Without the latter, the MS would remain confined to the university, ultimately exhausting itself as nothing more than a privileged revolt by 'bourgeois children'. While lacking Scalzone's socialist moralism, many student activists were increasingly conscious of the limits of a struggle conducted wholly within the university. As the whole edifice of Italian society began to appear as an obstacle to the reform of higher learning, even the most sectionalist advocates of Student Power looked with interest to a working class that was again stirring itself into action. Thus one of the first of the movement's factory commissions was formed in Trento; by the middle of the year, the first steps towards a practical linkage with workers had been made in all the other major university cities (Boato 1978: 228–32).

It was this 'turn to the class' which led POv-e to display public interest in the development of the MS. The first discussion of students carried the significant title of 'Fiat Edison Marzotto University – one struggle against one boss', and was published in the early days of May 1968. Noting the growing preparedness of students to reply to state force in kind, as witnessed by the March clashes at Valle Giulia in Rome (Ginsborg 1990: 304), the article expressed a certain condescending pleasure that the MS had finally moved beyond 1967's generic themes of protest. In the process, it had discovered the need to join with workers in 'an *open and general struggle against the entire plan of capital*'. Whilst most students came from bourgeois families, the MS represented an attempt 'to negate their own class origin in order to be a revolutionary class'. To take things forward, the workerists demanded 'the generalised wage for all' (Pov-e 1968c: 1, 4). Unlike the notion of a 'political wage', however, which in a few years would play a central role in Potere's Operaio's discourse on political recomposition, the aim for Pov-e of the 'generalised wage' seems not to have been that of organising students as part of the proletariat. True, the 'generalised wage' was important for allowing access to university for working-class youngsters. POv-e's primary interest, however, lay elsewhere, in seeking the means by which an effective relation between students and workers could be realised outside academe. Worker–student unity, it was argued, could only be consummated in the environs of the factory, where capital's plan 'is most organised, and from whence it draws its strength'. Thus, whatever other ways such unity might have been conceived, for POv-e it would from the beginning entail the submission of student interests to the promotion of workers' struggles, an attitude which understandably outraged wide sections of the MS (Boato 1978: 198).

As many student activists were then discovering, their efforts to support industrial struggles, and in particular to promote a rank-and-file control over them, met not only with frequent interest on the part of workers, but also hostility from union officials jealously protective of their 'turf'. Even the FIOM, the component of the CGIL most open to 'new' political discourses, agreed to discussions with students only on condition that the latter accept its 'monopoly over the class' (Viale 1978:

50). In such circumstances, the widespread antipathy amongst student activists for POv-e could only have been deepened by the group's continued circumspect behaviour before the 'official' representatives of labour. Indeed, so cautious was POv-e at this time that it actively discouraged efforts to circumvent the CGIL:

> We have said before that the Movement reaches its maximum point of growth in the awareness of the necessity of contact and organisation with the working class, which in Italy is still identifiable with the union organisation of the Labour Movement. It is clear that if the Student Movement seeks direct and organisationally effective contact with the working class, it cannot dream of doing so outside the class union: direct contacts are always precarious, and often lack possibilities of generalisation ... (POv-e 1968c: 4)

If one reason for this outburst can be traced to the tendency's fear of isolation, another lay in the fact that the split with Tronti's closest supporters still remained unclear in the Veneto for much of 1968. Pov-e thus continued to maintain relations with left currents within the PCI, even organising a joint conference with them, 'Students and Workers', in June. As the workerists argued in *Potere Operaio*:

> [T]he organisational channels which permit contact with the working class [are not] confined to the union. Despite the reformist lines to which their leaderships are committed, the parties of the labour movement are still class parties by dint of the composition and characteristics of their base. (ibid.: 4)

Not surprisingly, many on the far left objected to such arguments. Harshest in its criticisms was the Marxist-Leninist tendency within the Pisan Potere Operaio, for whom this utterance was yet one more proof that

> *workerist and spontaneist praxis cannot escape its internal logic*, but rather converges into the reformist, and evermore clearly counter-revolutionary strategy of the official institutions of the labour movement. (Quoted in Boato 1978: 231)

The struggles of workers at Montedison's Petrolchimico plant in Porto Marghera that summer, in which POv-e was to play an important role, would set the group on a final collision course with the parties and unions of the left. While the ambiguities inherited from *Classe Operaia*'s discourse on the historic left did not long survive this conflict, the chemical workers' struggles only confirmed the group in its interpretation of worker–student relations. Worker–student unity was projected by POv-e as a *'new organisational form'* consummated in the often violent mass picketing of late July (POv-e 1968a: 35–6). In practice, this 'unity' meant the 'working-class use' of the MS as a channel of communication against the bosses and, where necessary, union leaders as well (POv-e 1968j: 4). One workerist leaflet summed up the question thus:

Only if the union between workers and students, under the leadership of the working class, becomes an organisational and continuous fact, will the student movement conserve its political weight and significance. (POv-e 1968a: 31)

A more sophisticated workerist attempt to grapple with the political role of students emerged in Sergio Bologna and Giairo Daghini's detailed, first-hand reconstruction of the French May. Here students were presented as detonators of class struggle, the 'acting minority' of which Daniel Cohn-Bendit had spoken in his famous interview with Sartre (Bologna and Daghini 1968: 20). French students were praised for having triggered 'the most formidable and concentrated mass refusal of the job [*posto di lavoro*] ever seen in an advanced capitalist country' (ibid.: 35), in the form of a general strike by at least 9 million workers. At the same time, it was conceded that this had not been sufficient to overcome the gulf separating students in the streets from workers in the occupied factories (ibid.: 49–51). It was in their conclusion, however, that Bologna and Daghini introduced a new twist to their tendency's reading of worker–student relations. First, they drew a parallel with the defeat suffered in 1920 by Turin's metalworkers, who had stood firm but alone in their factory strongholds. In future, argued Bologna and Daghini, workplace occupations must act as 'trampolines' to launch 'decisions of a practical-political type, which must then translate themselves into the organisation of the social circuit of struggle'. Such a schema offered students a privileged role as intellectual labourers, for in order to be successful, 'these mechanisms of working-class struggle must be entirely reconstructed at the theoretical level' (ibid.: 52–3).

While this attempt to grasp the peculiar contributions which the intellectually trained might offer to revolutionary politics was passed over by the rest of the tendency, it is no less true that POv-e's approach to students only prefigured the general practice of the extra-parliamentary organisations formed with the Hot Autumn. Within a few years, indeed, Potere Operaio (1972d) was to ascribe greater legitimacy to students' struggles within the education sector than did a number of its rivals. In 1968, however, the resurgence of industrial strife would see the specific problems of students overshadowed by those of the mass worker; only with the crisis of the far left during the mid-1970s would some workerists begin

> to rethink entirely the relation between intellectual strata and the working class, between detonators of a knowledge or of particular knowledges, and productive workers. (Bologna 1981: 15–16)

TECHNICIANS – THE MISSING LINK?

Occasionally present in the disputes of the early and mid-1960s, it was only really in the latter half of 1968 that Italian technical workers came into their own as an industrial force in Italy. The epicentre of their mobilisation over wages and the reorganisation of production lay between two poles. The first contained the highly qualified workers of Milan's electronics sector, then the most dynamic within the network of large and medium-sized manufacturing plants of that city. The second was based upon the employees of various industrial research facilities in the North and Centre (Lelli 1971; Dina 1972; Low-Beer 1978; Lumley 1990). With tertiary training increasingly common amongst them, such workers were unusually sensitive to events in the world of higher learning; many followed the vicissitudes of the MS with great interest. For those workerists such as Bologna wary of the theory and practice of 'external' vanguards, these technicians, with their strikes, demonstrations and workplace occupations, seemed momentarily to offer 'the ideal vector' – a 'bridge' between workers and students, to defeat the gulf between factory and university struggles (Bologna 1981: 15). In Italy at that time, as in much of the West, the terms of Marxist debate on technicians had largely been set by the French sociologist Serge Mallet. The central thesis of his 1963 book *The New Working Class* held that capitalist development, far from deskilling all layers of the workforce, had led to a substantial rise in the level of qualifications and skills. Along the way, it had created a stratum of specialised workers who occupied a strategic place in the planning and execution of production. According to Mallet, a deep-rooted sense of frustration with capitalist property relations was widespread amongst such technicians, many of whom yearned to exercise their own control over production (Low-Beer 1978: 14–22). In the expressive prose of Andre Gorz, whose *Strategy for Labor* advanced similar positions in the following year:

The impossibility of living which appeared to the proletarians of the last century as the impossibility of reproducing their labor power becomes for the workers of scientific or cultural industries the impossibility of putting their creative abilities to work. (Gorz 1967: 105)

For Mallet, the adherence of technical staff to a strategy for socialism – understood as a society whose norms found sustenance in the self-management of production – was a viable political hypothesis which he was to pursue actively as a member of the left socialist PSU (Partie Socialiste Unifié – the (French) Unified Socialist Party) (Howard 1974). While certain exponents of classical *operaismo* such as Tronti (1967a: 28) were dismissive of 'a couple of technicians boasting they produce surplus value by pushing buttons', others, following Alquati's work in *Quaderni Rossi*, would treat the problem more seriously. One such workerist was Bologna, who possessed first-hand experience in organising white-collar staff from his days as an Olivetti employee. In a brief account of 'The discourse on technicians', Bologna (1965: 15) set out to confute a notion popular in Italy amongst the leaders of the CGIL left. For the latter, technicians represented 'not only the expression, as labour-power, of the most advanced level of capital, but also the political expression of the most advanced movements of the class'. This interpretation, Bologna claimed, simply re-echoed all the Second International debates around the labour aristocracy, and risked using purely sociological criteria to make political distinctions within the working class. Further, the theory of the technician as a 'revolutionary' figure was, at least in the minds of its French proponents, tied to an empirically invalid assumption. This was that the deskilling and massification of modern production had reduced the majority of workers to depoliticised atoms lacking 'a general vision of the mechanism of production' (ibid.: 16). For Bologna, instead, '*no sociological distinction between the various levels of labour-power can lead us automatically to a specific discourse on technicians*' because politically 'advanced' sectors could not be deduced *a priori* from the structure of the labour process. Only a *post festum* analysis 'following the path traced by workers' struggles' could determine their relationship; until then, the role of technicians in the struggle against capital could only be an open question (ibid.: 17).

By early 1969, with many technicians actively engaged in industrial disputation, such tentative conclusions were no longer adequate. More concrete was the document produced by employees of the Comitato Nazionale Energia Nucleare (CNEN – the Nuclear Energy National Committee) laboratories near Rome. There the presence of former members of the local student movement amongst staff helped to ensure that many of the central industrial themes of 1969 – flat wage increases, the attack on grading scales, decision-making in the hands of assemblies rather than union officials – were prominent. Scientific research, it was argued, was not a neutral and benign force currently misused by the bourgeoisie. In the age of mass production, science had become indispensable to capital, as necessary to the task of class domination as to the process of valorisation (Piperno et al. 1969: 173–6). Furthermore, the latterday socialisation of labour had subordinated research and development to Taylorist norms of production. Both in the parcellised and repetitive nature of its labour process, and in the structure of its rates of pay, the modern research institute was now organised according to the same criteria as industry generally. Wage differentials, for example, were 'functional to the maintenance of a quite precise hierarchical-repressive structure and, ultimately, to the political control of the mass of workers'. While a small minority of specialists wielded considerable power within this pyramid of command, the great mass of technical staff, especially those without tertiary training, were simply forced to endure the organisation of labour (ibid.: 186).

Interesting as it was, the CNEN paper's desire to emphasise the deskilled and factory-like nature of labour for the majority of workers at CNEN led it to say very little about the peculiarities of technicians as specialised workers. This question was to be taken up instead in early 1969 by Bologna in 'Technicians as producers and product', an essay he co-authored with Francesco Ciafaloni, a Marxist from outside the workerist tendency. In these authors' opinion, the label technician could be applied to all those workers, whether manual or white collar, whose role in production was based upon the performance not of simple labour, but of skills acquired through specialised training. Such a broad definition, they acknowledged, embraced 'most workers in a complex and diversified society'; none the less, it retained a certain heuristic value due to its ability to link together workers 'in otherwise unrelated situations' (Bologna and Ciafaloni 1969: 152). In this sense, then, it applied most adequately to those employees who, even if massified, were separate from the mass worker: namely, those staff involved the conception as well as execution of production. The subsumption of such labour-power to capital, if an actuality, was only formal, since the peculiar 'tools' for which they are sought on the labour market – in particular, the social knowledge which they physically embodied – could not yet be easily separated and counterposed to them as fixed capital.

Bologna and Ciafaloni (1969: 151) began their discussion by noting the diametrically opposed connotations that the 'proletarianisation' of technicians had come to assume within the Italian left. For some, technicians constituted the central core of the modern working class in quest of self-management; for others they were personnel whose compromising location in producton made them fit only to intervene in others' struggles as external cadres. A different interpretation held that technicians were workers with no distinctive attributes at all, yet another that they were employees with their own specific struggles to fight within the general front against capital. Favouring the last of these conceptions, Bologna and Ciafaloni criticised Mallet's outlook for its potential corporatism. The very nature of many technicians' relation to their product – over whose contents they already exercised far greater control than workers on the line – offered limited but real possibilities of enjoyment, and thus identification with the existing division of labour. Given this, 'a struggle of technicians for self-management could easily transform itself into a struggle to become a *ruling technocracy*'. In any case, the initial assumption held by Mallet – that the mass of semi-skilled workers had been co-opted by capital – was, 'at least in Italy, empirically false'. While it would be mistaken to say that the mass worker's struggles were intrinsically revolutionary, it would be just as absurd to deny their current breadth and intensity (ibid.: 160). Bologna and Ciafaloni's harshest criticisms, however, were reserved for those who saw technicians as nothing but the raw material for the revolutionary party. To begin with, the great majority of the intellectually trained, who were currently inserted in the labour market as either technicians or executants of 'cognitive roles', were quite different from the vanguard of declasse bourgeois intellectuals bearing 'socialist' consciousness to the masses of Lenin's day. Such a formulation was, in any case, politically objectionable, since it restated 'the division of roles between leaders and led, which is what we want to combat' (ibid.: 159).

According to Bologna and Ciafaloni (1969: 153), the peculiar status of technicians as workers who embodied their 'capital' revealed the limitations of conceptions which posited the basis of class domination within production 'in subservience to a machine'. While such a forced dichotomy between social relations and machines risked undermining their own depiction of technology as 'a political response' to working-class struggle (ibid.: 154), Bologna and Ciafaloni's emphasis upon the division of labour went to the core of the problem of specialised labour. If the pyramid structure of the modern firm derived its sustenance solely from the logic of class domination, it was within the layer of intellectually trained staff that the effort to establish a neat bifurcation between functions of command and functions of production collapsed (ibid.: 155). Yet a motivation for these employees to challenge capital did exist, according to Bologna and Ciafaloni. Ironically, they offered here the same contradiction as that advanced by Mallet, counterposing the technicians' supposed autonomy in production to the reality of the 'passively repetitive' work which many of them had come to endure (ibid.: 158). If by dint of their social origin and function within the firm, neither clerical nor managerial staff were likely to engage in a collective questioning of the organisation of labour, it was 'precisely technicians who constitute a possible exception to this rule' (ibid.: 156). The essay's final note was one of caution. Given that 'the main victims of the present division of labour' remained the manual workers, it was impossible to determine in any objective manner how and why particular technicians would take their side. In part this was because 'the factory has not yet been analysed as a social reality', in part because 'the alignment of technicians is not a given, but a product of struggles'. Not just any struggles, however; technical staff also had to challenge that division of labour from which many of them benefited. Consistent with workerism's precepts, Bologna and Ciafaloni located the unifying thread of such an attack in the wage struggle: but this, they insisted, could not become a magic formula, since capital was always able to effect new divisions in pay. To be serious, the struggle by technicians against the division of labour within the firm would have to be joined to an attack upon the division between manual and intellectual labour within society as a whole, starting with 'a profound critique of the education system and its complete overthrow' (ibid.: 157).

In this manner 'Technicians as producers and product' pointed towards a strategy involving workers, both specialised and semi-skilled, in alliance with students as 'pre-workers'. Recognising that the potentially positive relationship between technical workers and their work demanded that their struggles be closely entwined with those of the mass worker, the essay none the less acknowledged a specific role for the former. Unfortunately, as with Bologna and Daghini's earlier discourse upon students, such an approach was to be quickly swept away with the enthusiasms of the Hot Autumn. If echoes of their position could still be detected at Potere Operaio's 1970 conference (Berardi 1998: 115), the situation had changed fundamentally by the following year. Infatuated with the theme of insurrection, the group would finally dissolve the specific attributes of technical workers into those of industrial labour as a whole. Now all labour was simple labour, and technicians faced with the choice of either bolstering capital's command, or else acting as 'an agent in the enemy camp' (Potere Operaio 1971h: 15). Once again, the problems of complex labour would have to await the uncertainties of the mid-1970s for a more balanced assessment by the workerist current.

5
The Creeping May

In December 1967 a number of prominent intellectuals associated with the radical wing of *operaismo* met to discuss the nature of international class struggle during the interwar period. The venue was the University of Padua, where Negri had recently assumed the Chair of State Doctrine and was now busy establishing a foothold for the tendency within the academic world. Attempting to situate historically many of the assertions advanced in Tronti's *Operai e capitale*, the contributions ranged across various subjects, from the German council movement to the British General Strike and John Maynard Keynes' work on the dynamic of effective demand (Bologna et al. 1972). The pivotal experience of the period, however, was seen as that of the US, where workers had clashed with a capital able to make the leap to its social form in the absence of a social democratic party. Above all, it was claimed, Roosevelt's New Deal had realised practically what Keynes' *General Theory* had grasped in only a mystified form. The wage was now an independent variable, and nothing short of an income policy underpinned by the legal organisation and regulation of the working class could hope to prevent a repetition of the disaster of 1929 (Ferrari Bravo 1972: 108–14).

THE MASS WORKER TAKES FORM

Within the workerism that followed *Classe Operaia*'s demise, mass worker and the wage became inseparable themes. If until the Padua conference this class figure remained somewhat indistinct, a 'social mass', now the mass worker began to assume flesh and blood. It possessed three decisive attributes: it was massified, it performed simple labour, and it was located at the heart of the immediate process of production. Individually interchangable but collectively indispensable, lacking the bonds which had tied skilled workers to production, the mass worker personified the subsumption of concrete to abstract labour characteristic of modern capitalist society (Bologna 1972: 13, 23). It was a 'crude, pagan race' (Tronti 1968: 46), bent on destroying not only that factory regime which, to Engels' (1959) mind would always be with us, but any force which subordinated the fulfilment of its needs to the dictates of dead labour.

With its organisational presence restricted to the North-East of Italy for most of 1967 and 1968, it was only natural that *operaismo*'s political work and discussion of class composition would at first focus upon Emilia-Romagna and the Veneto. The North was then in the grip of a widespread industrial restructuring, based for the most part upon the intensification of labour rather than any significant investment in new plant (Graziani 1979: 86–7). As elsewhere in the North, the recession in these two regions also offered employers a perfect opportunity not only to attack pockets of dead time in production, but also to pursue what Massimo Paci (1973: 89–92, 133) was to call the 'masculinisation of employment'. According to Franco Donaggio (1977: 20–1), only one factory in Porto Marghera continued to hire workers in the mid-1960s, recruiting predominantly amongst males in their twenties or thirties. Elsewhere in the North-East, owners achieved the same result simply by laying off women and the oldest and youngest of the men (POv-e 1967d: 2).

The growing homogenisation of labour by age and gender within many of Italy's large and medium-sized industrial concerns during the late 1960s acted to reinforce that compactness encouraged by the spread of mass production techniques (Paci 1973: 161–2). One crude indicator of this declining weight of skilled manual labour amongst workers as a whole was the changing fortune of apprentices. As fewer and fewer positions required prolonged periods of preparation in school or factory, the percentage of industrial employees holding apprenticeships dropped dramatically, from 12.8 per cent in 1961 to 4.6 per cent in 1970 (ibid.: 223). The traditional system of grading pay by skill also began to assume new connotations: having once served in part to defend the wages and conditions of skilled workers, its original rationale had been increasingly undermined from the 1950s onwards by the fragmentation of work tasks intrinsic to mechanisation. Under such circumstances, the grading system proved a flexible tool with which Italian managers could redefine job roles without resorting to more sophisticated methods such as 'job evaluation' (Regini and Reyneri 1971: 112). The same semi-skilled task frequently fell under quite different pay classifications from one firm to the next, rendering any material distinction between many 'qualified' and 'common' workers increasingly blurred (Paci 1973: 153). Promotions, too, reflected this transformation, coming to signify less the acquisition of new skills than an acknowledgement of seniority (Regini and Reyneri 1971: 105).

That gradings had become a problem was already a widely-held belief at the beginning of the 1960s, and the struggles of that time had registered a muted push against the existing division of the workforce into four categories (Paci 1973: 163). The solution agreed to by unions and employers in 1963, however, had simply been to divide the second-lowest category further into two levels of 'common workers'. This trend was continued by the metalworkers' contract of 1966, which also split the top category of 'specialised worker' in two (Regini and Reyneri 1971: 72, 107). That employers would seek the further stratification of their workforce is not difficult to comprehend, but the fact that support for the new categories was no less widespread amongst union officials perhaps requires explanation. For the CGIL in particular, with its faith in technical progress still formally intact, the increase in the number of gradings – and with it, a growing spread in pay – was of great importance, a mark of the further specialisation and skill demanded by economic development. If some of its functionaries were critical of the existing system, this was due not to any doubts as to the rationality of its division of labour, but only capital's ability to administer it fairly (ibid.: 108). The worth and dignity of skills was a faith held dear not only by the more conservative sections of the FIOM, but also by champions of workplace democracy like Bruno Trentin, who would confess at the height of the mass challenge to gradings:

> I believe that professional qualifications are still a goal and a patrimony of workers ... It is not a weapon of the boss, and I don't see, therefore, why the boss should not pay for it ... (ibid.: 76)

If such an attitude does much to explain the distance between many workers and the CGIL in 1968 and 1969, the irony of the restructuring of the mid-1960s was that ultimately it acted to strengthen the forces of labour whilst greatly restricting capital's manoeuvrability. By selecting young adult males as those supposedly best suited to the rigours of mass production, employers effectively ruled out the use of other components of the labour market as an industrial reserve army. When added to the growing absorption of young people by mass education, and the declining rate of migration Northwards, this handicap served to strengthen the rigidity of an industrial workforce already partly homogenised by the deskilling of mass production techniques. For the first time since the war, the relations of force within Italy's urban labour market were no longer stacked in capital's favour. When workers began to perceive this shift, they would set out to bring enormous pressure to bear upon the Italian industrial relations system precisely at its weakest point: the categories of 'skill' which until then had furnished its cornerstone (Paci 1973: 168).

WORKERS AND WORKERISM IN PORTO MARGHERA

Within the Italian petrochemical sector of the 1960s, technical and white-collar staff constituted a noticeably high proportion of employees (Cacciari 1968: 592). This did not mean, however, that most workers in the major petrochemical plants – whether classified as 'manual workers', 'technicians' or white-collar 'employees' – were any less massified or in possession of greater control over production than their counterparts in manufacturing (Zandegiacomi 1974: 26–7). The traditional craft workers of Porto Marghera had already been forced down the 'technological path to repression' during the 1950s; the relatively higher qualification of those who replaced them was in large part a distorted recognition of the greater technological sophistication of production within the chemical industry. Like their counterparts at FIAT, many of the new chemical workers had come from the countryside; indeed, in a region that epitomised the process of industrialisation in the absence of urbanisation (Patrono 1980: 96), many continued to live in a rural setting. What, if anything, made their workplaces different from Mirafiori was on the contrary the apparent perfection of the tyranny of fixed capital. Here, the very nature of the production process – a highly automated system demanding attention around the clock – guaranteed the subordination of employees even more fully than the car industry's assembly line. Thus in Porto Marghera, no less than in Turin, a mass worker would slowly take shape during the years of the economic miracle. By 1967, five or six years of workerist intervention at Porto Marghera had begun to bear fruit at Montedison's large Petrolchimico plant. There POv-e could claim as adherents both younger workers fresh from the outlying countryside, and a number of long-time CGIL militants elected to the firm's Commissione Interna (Pasetto and Pupillo 1970: 96; Perna 1980). Frustrated with the regional union's refusal to organise around health and safety – a perennial concern in an industry plagued by a high accident rate and silicosis – in August POv-e members called a stop-work meeting which voted for strike action. Fearful of being outflanked at a plant where its base was already weak, the local union ratified the decision. The brief stoppage which followed saw only 500 employees take part, yet the implications of the episode were disturbing, as one local newspaper reflected:

There remains the (preoccupying) fact that the 'Chinese' were able to impose their objectives on unionists of consumate experience. Of the 10 per cent who heeded the strike call, almost all were youths in their twenties, 32–33 years of age at the most. It is a warning which cannot be ignored; it means that there is a cog loose somewhere ... (quoted in POv-e 1968a: 13)

It was the group's first major independent action, one that left it cautiously optimistic about the future. For the following year, none the less, POv-e continued to promulgate *Classe Operaia*'s traditional discourse on the working-class 'use' of party and union. Whilst the revisionism of the PCI's leadership was measured for the first time against the performance of Communist parties in other continents (POv-e 1967c: 3), the workerist message remained the same. The labour movement might be integrated into the capitalist system elsewhere in the West, but in Italy the party's rank-and-file – 'its truly revolutionary base' – still blocked this tendency. It was mandatory, then, to join the struggle 'against the reformists in the party' to that 'against the boss in the factory' (POv-e 1967a: 1; 1967j: 1). In fact, claimed *Potere Operaio*, the goals of reclaiming the party in the workplace and defeating modern planned capitalism were inter-twined, since

[t]oday the political terrain on which the relation of force between workers and capitalist is measured is that of the factory, and the wage-productivity relation is the key to the whole functioning of capitalist society. What yesterday was economic, today is the only real political terrain; what yesterday was political, today has become appearance ... (POv-e 1968b: 4)

Thus, until events in 1968 shattered the group's belief in any possibility of the official labour movement's renovation, the question of the Communist Party's future remained an open one. True, some articles in the workerist journal called for a new, mass revolutionary party during 1967. Others the following year, though, continued to put the ball firmly in the court of the PCI, 'that great Communist Party' which workers 'have always seen as their own', and which now 'must choose' between social democracy and class struggle (POv-e 1968b: 4; 1968d: 4).

A similar ambivalence then informed POv-e's understanding of the CGIL. As with the Communist Party, the group's view of the union before that point had been deeply contradictory. In this it was marked both by hostility towards the top-down efforts at cooperation between the three major confederations – for whose sake the CGIL seemed prepared to capitulate its few remaining class principles and the belief that the 'class' union was still susceptible to working-class influence. Thus, while in one article the refusal of CGIL parliamentarians to vote against the Socialist Party's 'five year plan' was seen as confirmation that all unions were within capital's logic, other pieces called for 'true' union autonomy. 'Union bureaucrats are paid by the workers', stated an article of November 1967, 'we must impose the interests of the workers upon them' (POv-e 1967b: 1; 1967f: 1, 4; 1967i: 2). In one respect, such differences reflected ongoing differences of opinion amongst workerists as to the unions' long-term worth; as has been seen, the demarcation between 'extremists' and 'entrists' had still by no means clarified itself fully amongst the North-Eastern exponents of *operaismo* (Bianchini and Pergola 1980). On the other hand, such pronouncements were the product of POv-e's belief that regional specificities also had their part to play in defining the relation between workers and the labour movement. Thus, while the PCI of Emilia-Romagna – the central regulator of the local capitalist economy – was dismissed from the beginning as a lost cause (POv-e 1967h), the group's assessment of the Veneto party was for a time much more open-ended.

Above all, however, POv-e was acutely conscious that Italian workers, on the defensive after the disappointing contract struggles of 1966, were not yet prepared to venture far beyond the cover of either party or union. During 1967 there were to be no appeals in *Potere Operaio* for militants to form autonomous committees, even if one article noted the emergence in some workplaces of

> forms of autonomous working class organisation and initiative, for now still in an embryonic state, but susceptible to further development (POv-e 1967f: 1).

Instead, if any alternative in the factory to the revisionism of the PCI and CGIL was held up, it was to be the traditional delegate structure of the Commissione Interna, with numerous articles that year advising workers to pressure their workplace representatives into fighting the reorganisation of production. If, as the Petrolchimico dispute of August made clear, even these bodies were not immune to the corrupting influence of reformism (POv-e 1967g: 4), this was not cause for undue despair: what mattered most was not so much the organisational form assumed by workers' struggles as their content. Counselling workers to use 'the wage thematic' belatedly discovered by the unions, the issue of *Potere Operaio* for July 1967 looked forward to an imminent political struggle within the workplace, one which placed 'everything in discussion: staffing levels, hours, overtime, holidays' (POv-e 1967e: 4).

In Porto Marghera, the opportunity for this 'guerrilla warfare in the factory', as *Potere Operaio* was to call it in late 1967 (POv-e 1967i: 2), appeared the following summer when production bonuses came up for negotiation. The chemical contract made provision for marginal percentile adjustments, varying from category to category, but the local workerists struck upon the demand of a flat 5000 lire increase for all: an objective both egalitarian and, they felt, one which most workers would deem 'worth fighting for' (POv-e 1968a: 16). It proved to be a shrewd move, with the popularity of the idea forcing the CGIL once again to take up demands advanced by the group. Opening in late June, the dispute saw a dozen stoppages before its climax, in early August, with a demonstration in which thousands of chemical workers converged upon the neighbouring town of Mestre, effectively isolating it from the rest of the Veneto (ibid.: 39). From the beginning of the conflict the question of leadership was hotly disputed. After workers involved in discussions with MS militants were threatened with expulsion by the union bureaucracy, the site of decision-making shifted firmly to the mass meetings (ibid.: 26–9). The strikers' tactics throughout were aggressive, with stoppages on alternate days designed to disrupt production, and mass picketing to intimidate those still prepared to work. The biggest card, however, would be played on 29 July, when strikers threatened to reduce the size of the skeleton staff traditionally left to oversee the plant, prompting a lockout (ibid.: 37–8; Tarrow 1989: 169). This object lesson in the vulnerability of continuous flow processes, along with the effectiveness of rank-and-file organisation, did much for the prestige of POv-e at the plant. Yet the group still found itself pitifully weak outside the workplace, and powerless to prevent a final agreement between management and unions enshrining percentile increases by category. The dispute also shattered once and for all any ambiguity about 'using' the union. If it was 'stupid to talk of "betrayal"', as POv-e argued a few months later, that was because the CGIL, no less than the other union confederations, had become a tool of capital. Henceforth, workers would truly be thrown upon their own resources in fighting the employers and state (POv-e 1968a: 42, 46; 1968g: 1; 1968h: 3).

'FRANCE IS NEAR'

One event which contributed to the growing assertiveness amongst Italian workers was the French general strike of May and June 1968. The May days had a galvanising effect upon the Italian far left as well, with both Leninists and libertarians holding it up as a verification of their policies. The workerist assessment of May was also largely positive, and if *Potere Operaio* agreed with Marxist-Leninists that the key element missing in France had been a revolutionary political organisation, it was equally adamant that such a body must take a mass form internal to the class (POv-e 1968i: 2). One of the first to review some of the literature that had poured out of France in the aftermath of May was Massimo Cacciari, whose defection to Tronti's camp would not lessen his ongoing interest in the intricacies of class composition. Cacciari cuttingly dismissed those – like Andre Glucksmann – who continued to preach the lessons of *What Is To Be Done?*, when on the contrary it was increasingly evident that

> struggle manifests and massifies itself *completely within* the determinate production relations, and it is *from here*, finally, that it tends to 'socialise' itself ... There no longer exists, for the class, a 'politics-outside', external to its own *mass* location in the advanced capitalist cycle. (Cacciari 1969: 454, 455)

The French May also prompted *operaismo* to deepen its critique of self-management as a weapon against capital. Indeed, despite his dismissal of vulgar Leninists like Andre Glucksmann, Cacciari's greatest venom was reserved for those who saw workers' management of production as the gateway to some idyll of democracy practised to its ultimate degree. Self-management's fundamental flaw, he argued, was that it challenged not the capitalist mode of production as a whole, but simply the right of its current functionaries to hold sway:

> [I]n this manner self-management disarms the class: in place of the formidable instruments which it has discovered and strengthened *against* the capitalist production relation, it offers a model of 'liberation' which is objectively reactionary even in terms of the capitalist production relation itself. (Cacciari 1969: 459)

The ideology of self-management, he insisted, found its roots in the most backward sectors of the class, still jealously clinging to their traditional skills. It was these strata which comprised the base of the Western Communist parties, and from whence their reformism drew sustenance; in the meantime, liberation from labour, not the liberation of labour, had become the aim of modern revolutionary politics (ibid.: 460).

The identification of the self-management project with the base of the French Communist Party (PCF) would no doubt have surprised many in France, not least members of the PCF itself. The assessment offered by Bologna and Daghini (1968: 17–18) was more balanced, recognising that self-management had meant very different things during the general strike. True, for the majority of its advocates it held out nothing more than 'workers' management of their own exploitation', while the Communist wing of the French labour movement revealed its political dishonesty by conjuring up the spectre of 'left opportunism' each time the phrase was mentioned. For the most radical students, however, such as those of the Mouvement du 22 Mars, the term evoked something fundamentally different: a meeting place where they and workers could discuss the question of power (ibid.: 30). Self-management's real critique, however, had come from those young unskilled workers at Renault who had called for a minimum wage of 1000 francs a month. This exorbitant demand, claimed Bologna and Daghini, had threatened 'to blow up' the labour market, and was symptomatic of the collective egoism of workers keen 'to negate their own figure as producers':

> It was the refusal of labour which emerged at the end of discussions of self-management, and not the acceptance of a better and more human organisation of labour itself. (ibid.: 42, 46–7)

More than any other single event, the French May accelerated radical *operaismo*'s final abandonment of the tactic of a working-class 'use' of the PCI. If the general strike had further demonstrated that workers' spontaneity both refused the unions' policies whilst retaining those bodies as an elementary means of organisation and communication, the role of the French Communist Party in contrast had been one of containment and provocation (Bologna and Daghini 1968: 51–2). It was the PCF which had brought the Communist-led component of the union movement to heel during the June negotiations with the state, and it was the PCF which had most vehemently denounced the far left. Within Italy, the assessment of one former *Quaderni Rossi* editor – 'when it comes to the crunch, the PCI will not behave differently to the PCF' (Masi 1968: 56) – also came to be accepted by POv-e and its allies in Rome. Having claimed as late as its May issue that 'the working class has always seen in the PCI its party, a party that wants to be revolutionary' (POv-e 1968e: 4), any positive portrayal of the Communist Party disappeared from the pages of *Potere Operaio* after July. By March 1969, Luciano Ferrari Bravo (1969: 36) of POv-e was advancing the proposition that the French May held the same significance for the Communist movement as that of August 1914 for the Second International. According to Scalzone, the PCI leadership's march towards participation in a 'new majority' of government parties, coupled with its firm commitment to capitalist development, was confirmation that

> [t]he open clash between the real autonomy of the class movements and the control of the opportunist organisations of the labour movement is in the nature of things. It happened in France; it will happen in Italy ... (Scalzone 1969: 6)

Why so drastic a shift in *operaismo*'s critique of the PCI? One cause was the realignment of forces within the tendency itself, as increasing numbers of Tronti's immediate supporters chose the PCI after the June conference, 'Students and Workers' (Boato 1978: 295). Beyond this, both observation of the French May and their own difficulties at Porto Marghera helped to bring home to workerists the untenable nature of their traditional tactics. Indeed, despite what many on the far left deemed its too conciliatory tone, the tendency's attempt to intervene at factory gates had already provoked a number of clashes with PCI activists (Negri 1979a: 91–2; Bologna 1988). Yet if Piperno (1969: 37) was to come closest to capturing the essence of the Communist Party when he dubbed it 'the working-class articulation of capitalist social organisation', the PCI was far from identical with the French Communist Party. Perhaps, indeed, it was the very differences between the two that most concerned the workerists, and their hostility became explicit just as the PCI was making its greatest efforts at dialogue with the MS. It would be foolish to interpret the outstretched hand of certain party leaders as anything more than an attempt to utilise the new mass movement for their own ends. In the long run, though, such an accomodating flexibility seemed to pose even more of a threat to the independent existence of groups such as POv-e than the confrontationist approach taken by the French party. Such a risk was, in the end, academic; as it transpired, the PCI's openness would soon disappear along with much of its major left tendency, finally driven from the party in 1969 (Amyot 1981; Garzia 1985).

If more than a little pessimism underlay *operaismo*'s appraisal of political developments in Italy, the growing wealth of experiences in class militancy and autonomous organisation were a source of encouragement to the tendency's decision to finally strike out alone. In this respect too, the French general strike played an important part in altering expectations as to the timescale of social change. 'For the first time we are not afraid of confrontation', *Potere Operaio* announced in May (POv-e 1968d: 1). While speaking of the '*long and patient*', if '*unstoppable work of organisation*', the paper now extolled the new forms of struggle in evidence (POv-e 1968f: 4). Above all, the breadth of discontent under De Gaulle, combined with the French Communist Party's 'deaf but frontal' blockage of the strike wave, lent a sense of urgency to class antagonisms already heightened by the challenges to Western imperialism emanating from the Third World (POv-e 1968i: 2).

Nor was such optimism entirely unwarranted. If the French events projected to Italian workers some sense of the enormous energy and creativity latent within their class, their own student movement indicated that different and more effective forms of organisation existed than the traditional ones assumed by party and union. As discontent with the labour movement's performance within the workplace mounted, growing numbers of workers were to take matters into their own hands (Regalia et al. 1978; Reyneri 1978: 51–2, 74). The most famous of such early initiatives was taken that June by militants at the Milan offices of the tire firm Pirelli. Angry with their unions' poor handling of recent struggles over contracts and work conditions, they had formed a body – the Comitato Unitario di Base (CUB – United Rank-and-File Committee) – destined to mark a new phase in Italian industrial conflict (Mosca et al. 1988; Lumley 1990: 183–95).

The situation at Pirelli in 1968 was in many ways emblematic of Northern Italian industry as a whole. Although staff numbers had declined overall in recent times, there had been a considerable influx of young male workers into the firm, with management taking advantage of their inexperience to speed up production (CUB 1969: 18; Pietropaolo 1970: 68). Like POv-e's cell at Montedison, the CUB brought together not only younger workers relatively new to politics, but also those experienced party and union activists dubbed 'factory communists' by Alquati (Pasetto and Pupillo 1970: 96; D'Agostini 1974: 199–200; Basilico 1976: 281). The CUB also worked closely with members of both the MS and left groups – including Sergio Bologna (1988), who helped to write some of their documents. Less anti-union to begin with than extra-union, it sought to overcome the divisions imposed by competition between the CGIL, the CISL and the UIL. In its first document, the group stressed the need to build working-class power through struggles over working conditions in individual departments; these in turn, it held, would lay the basis for a general struggle 'to invest all of Pirelli'. Struggle over workplace matters, it argued, could not be dismissed as irrelevant to political struggle, since 'the significance of exploitation is political' (CUB et al. 1970: 100, 103). The CUB's primary purpose, the committee continued in another piece, was to contribute to the planning of working-class struggle, since only this could defeat 'the general plan of capital's exploitation' within which the unions, through the national contracts, were increasingly inserted (ibid.: 99–100, 104).

Beyond its insistence that the direction of industrial action remain in the hands of the workforce itself, the most striking aspect of the CUB experience at Pirelli was the practice, beginning in the middle of June, of the self-limitation of production. The 'go-slow' was a relatively novel occurrence in Italy. As one of the best accounts of the period has explained, it was immediately effective because it upset 'the balance between the cost of the strike to the firm and to the workers which practice had established and almost made legitimate' (Regalia et al. 1978: 112). Leaving no space for unions to intervene, hostile to the existing organisation of labour, the 'go-slow' proved a great success at Pirelli (CUB et al. 1970: 131–2). Soon the CUB phenomenon had spread to a number of major factories in Milan, lending encouragement to discrete minorities of workers in other parts of the country to go and do likewise. In Porto Marghera itself, POv-e's cell at Petrolchimico reformed as a Comitato Operaio (Workers' Committee), which presented itself as

a new organisation which does not intend accepting the ensnarement of struggles and mystification of perspectives which the party, unions and other organisations advance. Our immediate objective is to create a network of working-class links capable of leading struggles. (Quoted in Pasetto and Pupillo 1970: 105)

At the same time, with the student movement increasingly losing direction and impetus, the North-Eastern group drew closer to other workerist fragments around the country. Together with small groups in Milan and Turin and a sizeable section of the Roman MS, plans were laid for a new national journal, the first since *Classe Operaia*'s demise (Scalzone 1988: 130–7). When *La Classe* finally did appear in May 1969, it was to shift workerist attention back to its initial source of inspiration – FIAT's Mirafiori plant in Turin.

'WE WANT EVERYTHING'

By the late 1960s, FIAT's traditional image as an island of relative privilege for factory workers had begun to tarnish. In particular, the frantic pace of production had become increasingly unacceptable for growing numbers of Mirafiori's 50,000 workers, as the firm's annual staff turnover of 10 per cent attested (Castellina 1969: 13). By this time around 60 per cent of FIAT's employees were from the South, many of them living in difficult circumstances in a city whose social services and housing sector were ill-equipped to meet their needs (Partridge 1996: 86). In July 1968 the journal *Quaderni Piacentini* published excerpts from a union questionnaire aimed at gauging FIAT workers' commitment to industrial action over shorter hours and piecework rates. Conducted on a scale far beyond the means of *Quaderni Rossi* or similar groups, the survey drew a massive 20,000 replies. Out of this complex mosaic of perceptions, the widespread hatred for the FIAT environment emerged with great clarity. 'The work rhythm is exhausting', complained one employee. 'We work too much and enjoy too little', wrote another, adding 'they treat us like slaves, and if someone speaks up they are punished severely'. Some insisted that they were 'tired of strikes', but the majority's attitude towards management was belligerent, and the conviction that 'We must give FIAT no respite' was a common one (Ciafaloni 1968: 86, 84, 89, 90). Unions were criticised for their disunity and the ineffective, symbolic nature of their stoppages, which should instead attempt to bring maximum 'disorganisation' to the firm. This combative mood was matched by an openess towards the MS, with one worker even floating the possibility of striking three days a week 'if the unions are all united, and if the students intervene (without them nothing can be resolved)' (ibid.: 88, 90).

For the rest of the year and into early 1969, FIAT remained at simmering point, with strong turnouts for two national strikes: one over improved pensions, and one against the regional wages zones which had traditionally kept Southern pay levels below the national average. December 1968 registered a new high point, with a joint call by local unions for a half-hour stoppage in protest at the killing of two Sicilian labourers by the police. 'For the first time', Angelo Dina (1969: 136) noted soon after, 'an internal strike had been successful throughout FIAT.' The struggle came out into the open yet again in April, sparked once more by the death of Southern demonstrators at the hands of the police (Revelli 1989: 41). It was to follow the pattern already established elsewhere in the North, with the most qualified workers the first to stir themselves, and the lower categories moving in their wake. Associates of Panzieri now in the Turin PSIUP, who had worked long and hard amongst the specialised workers concentrated in FIAT's Auxiliary departments, gained broad support amongst these 8000 staff for a system of workplace delegates to negotiate piecework rates (Giachetti 1997: 46; Ferraris 1998). As the unrest slowly spread along the firm's cycle of production, however, its demands changed radically. Few of the semi-skilled workers in the assembly and paint shops showed interest in the auxiliary employees' programme; instead they called for substantial, flat wage increases and immediate passage up to the second category of pay (Revelli 1989: 42–3). Organising lightning stoppages which flared up and down the FIAT line, 'common' workers made their Italian debut as 'direct protagonists of struggle', pushing towards 'a profound modification of relations within the working class, and the refusal of the existing division of labour' (Reyneri 1978: 63–4). Such action was to signal a revolution in Italian industrial relations, the coming of age of *operaismo*'s mass worker as a social subject.

Before May, only a few small groups within Turin's MS – remnants of *Quaderni Rossi* and *Classe Operaia* – had carried out a modest political intervention at FIAT. The rest of the movement, still dominated by conceptions of Student Power, continued to lie under the malaise which had come to grip most campuses. The events at Mirafiori lent a new lease of life to the local MS, and by the end of the month its members began to make regular appearances at the factory gates. There they were to encounter more than one hundred cadre newly arrived from the Potere Operaio groupings of Tuscany and the North-East (Giachetti 1997: 38). Curiosity also brought many line workers to the activists' meetings. By June, hundreds of workers could be seen making their way after each shift to this new 'assemblea operai e studenti', there to discuss the state of play at FIAT and to organise the almost daily stoppages which now racked the firm (ibid.: 58; Fraser 1988: 224–7).

The influence of *La Classe* was at first prevalent within the assembly. In particular, the workerists' emphasis upon material needs as the fundamental cement of class solidarity evoked a strong response from workers previously indifferent to leftist rhetoric. As never before, large numbers of those who had at best defied factory discipline in purely individual ways began to show an interest in organised class struggle (Virno 1989). The reaction of Alfonso Natella to an invitation to meet with students – 'What the fuck, I've got nothing to lose, I'll go and see what these turds have to say' – was typical of many young Southern immigrants in 1969. Also typical was his surprise to discover that 'the things that I'd thought for years, as long as I'd worked, the things I'd believed only I felt, were thought by everyone' (Balestrini 1971: 93, 132–3). For such workers, talk of bigger pay packets and slower work rhythms bore a concreteness missing from much of leftist propaganda, while the struggle to achieve them held out the possibility of a new, collective identity. As Natella recalled in the book *We Want Everything*:

At times we had failed to understand each other or agree because each of us was used to speaking in a particular way – as a Christian, as a lumpen, as a bourgeois. Finally, however, in deeds, in the fact that we had made the struggle, we could all speak in the same way. We discovered that we all had the same needs, the same necessities, and that it was these that made us all equal in struggle. (ibid.: 133)

For *La Classe* and its successor *Potere Operaio*, the materiality of the demands advanced by production workers in the lowest categories cut a swathe through the pretensions of those on the left who talked of the 'new socialist man'. 'The working class has no ideology to realise', the workerists argued in October, since

> the starting point for its struggles are material needs that have to be satisfied. The new and irreducible fact in the workers' struggle is the demand that, wherever capital is found in either a private or collective form, it should be removed from control over living labour in order to break the vicious circle of labour-toil, of work as slavery. (Potere Operaio n.d.: 19)

Like *Classe Operaia* before it, the group around *La Classe* was to centre its understanding of working-class political composition upon the question of the wage. Just what exactly the wage thematic then meant for the tendency, however, was not always clear. In its most general form, it would entail the fight for 'more money, less work', a fight which both increased workers' control over the use of their labour-power, and disengaged their renumeration from productivity. Here talk of the wage suggested much more than a mere increase in income, being inseparable from opposition to the gradings and pace of production which weakened and divided workers as a force in society. It was, in other words, the refusal of the existing division of labour, the struggle to appropriate all social wealth outside the logic of commodity relations. This was the sense of Bologna and Daghini's criticism of those leftists who bemoaned workers' disinterest in 'qualitative' demands at a time when even employers 'now see the working class only as a "wage variable"':

> Must we therefore leave every discourse on the wage to the adversary? Must we continue to remain prisoners of bourgeois ideology and its divisions/oppositions between 'economic' and 'political', between 'qualitative' and 'quantitative', between 'party' concerns and 'union' concerns? (Bologna and Daghini 1968: 18)

Yet if emphasising the political nature of the wage struggle made good sense at a time when the prevalence of collective piecework linked pay directly to productivity, many within the tendency were also guilty of reading all aspects of the struggle at Mirafiori within the terms of the wage-form. Take Tronti (1969: 508) for instance, whose commitment to the PCI had not completely extinguished his influence upon *La Classe*: 'For today's worker – correctly – hours, tempos, piecework, bonuses are the wage, pensions are the wage, power itself in the factory is the wage'. In his later reconstruction of the period, Guido Viale (1978: 181–93) of Lotta Continua was to make much of this reductionism, portraying the influence of its proponents as no less destructive than that of certain self-proclaimed 'Marxist-Leninists'. More balanced was the critique he voiced during the creeping May itself. Then he argued that the workerists were 'endemically incapable of grasping all of the political implications of a struggle of these dimensions': in particular, the latter's demonstrated 'capacity of subjective initiative'. Formed completely outside the official labour movement, this had come to invest 'all aspects of the clash' (Viale 1973: 58). In the end, amongst prominent workerists only Bologna would at that time raise doubts about such a use of the wage, noting with Ciafaloni that the exclusive focus upon the struggle for flat wage increases,

> even if very correct in principle, can lead to an insufficiently clear confrontation with the problems of the aims of production and the distribution of power. (Bologna and Ciafaloni 1969: 157)

The lack of clarity in workerism's discourse on the wage was most evident in *La Classe*'s call for the generalisation of 'the wholly political content' of the objectives raised at FIAT and other industrial concentrations. The vehicle for this was the demand for a social wage 'equal for all', whether engaged in productive labour or not. In this schema, the relative wage became a measure of power, an indicator of the existing balance of force between the two classes. While such a view was underpinned by an innovative political reading of Keynes' own 'discovery' of labour as an independent variable in capitalist society (Negri 1967), *La Classe* invested little effort in explaining the links between the various articulations of labour-power. Nor, for that matter, did advocacy of a social wage open the tendency to a more balanced assessment of political problems outside the immediate process of production. Thus, despite its growing talk of the social sphere, *La Classe* would also rail against those

> who, instead of making a correct class analysis, identify the 'left of the people' in those most discontented, ultimately organising only poor devils, the sexually repressed, adolescents with Oedipal complexes, students in conflict with the family, lunatics, wretches, filmmakers

in crisis, anguished noblewomen, sex maniacs, bourgeois anxious for expiation, the phobia-ridden etc. ... (quoted in Viale 1978: 178)

The workerists' understanding of the slogan 'from the factory to society' assumed a more concrete form on 3 July. When the unions called a strike that day over high rents, the worker–student assembly upped the ante with an afternoon demonstration before FIAT's main gates, in Corso Traiano. Soon things spilled over into street fighting in the surrounding suburbs. The clashes were to continue into the early hours of the morning, as rocks and molotovs were pitted against the tear gas of the *carabinieri* (Ginsborg 1990: 316, Giachetti 1997). Dubbing the affair an 'insurrection', *La Classe* was exultant:

It's been 20 years since the workers of FIAT have been able to show themselves in the streets, fighting hand-to-hand with the police and coming off victorious. (*La Classe* 1969a: 193)

In its aftermath, the assembly called a national conference of autonomous workers' committees for late July. The venue was to be Turin, 'the most advanced moment of a process of struggle which runs throughout Italy, and the political reference point for the whole Italian working class' (Assemblea operaia di Torino 1969: 41). Yet the workerists' assessment of Corso Traiano would also contain a note of disappointment. In their opinion, the 'extraordinary level of class autonomy' displayed in Turin had still proved insufficient to provide direction to the clashes. A new revolutionary organisation was needed, one capable of 'discovering, generalising and transforming the political contents emerging from workers' struggles, and more generally from mass struggles, into preordained revolutionary violence'. If, on the other hand, such a vehicle dedicated to the defeat of social capital and its state remained absent, working-class autonomy risked 'being overturned into a dangerous occasion for the class enemy's counterattack'. In such circumstances, the reorganisation of capital's organic composition would take its toll upon the compactness of the mass worker (*La Classe* 1969b: 48, 49). Measured in these terms, the national conference of CUBs was to be a failure for *La Classe*. Writing in August, Piperno described the gathering in Turin as one that had projected 'a disquieting sensation ... of the disjuncture between intentions and results'. In particular, it had been unable to move beyond the theme of autonomy, of 'the strategic programme elaborated by the mass struggles that is now the patrimony of the movement'. This, however, was no longer enough: what the present occasion demanded was nothing less than the restoration of 'Leninism's primacy of tactics over strategy' (quoted in Bobbio 1978: 39).

THE EMERGENCE OF THE GROUPS

For the workerists, a prime example of how *not* to construct the new revolutionary organisation would be provided by the Unione dei Comunisti Italiani (Union of Italian Communists), for a brief period the largest group within the 'anti-revisionist' left. From its birth of Trotskyist and Stalinist parents, the Unione's elephantine structure, its cult of leader Aldo Brandirali ('our staunch and steady guide') and its puritanical defence of family life and 'normal' sexual behaviour were a source of both fascination and horror for other leftists (Ciafaloni and Donolo 1969; Violi 1977). Dubbed 'a religious phenomenon straight out of the Counter-Reformation' by Ciafaloni (1970: 69), the Unione was initially dismissed by the workerists as a bunch of 'buffoons' intent upon dredging up the worst moments of the Communist experience. The Maoist group's activities came to assume more sinister connotations, however, after some of its members clashed with striking Milan workers disinclined to accept its particular path to salvation. 'Organisations of this type', *Potere Operaio* insisted soon after,

> practitioners of *squadrismo* against working-class pickets [and] the exaltation of the work ethic ... are nuclei of bourgeois resistance, associations of the class enemy, and must be dealt with as such, in the Leninist manner. (Quoted in Vettori 1973: 92)

As the Unione's spectacular growth turned as quickly to decline in the latter part of 1969, the MS began to break up into a series of national and local organisations. The first to emerge was a new, countrywide Potere Operaio. In Milan, the two major tendencies within the movement at the State University parted ways, one gathering around the paper *Avanguardia Operaia*, the other retaining the title Movimento Studentesco for its peculiar brand of Maoist-Stalinist politics. In a similar fashion the group that published the journal *Il manifesto*, expelled from the PCI in late November, attempted to gather its widely scattered sympathisers into the semblance of an organisation. The last major current to form came together around those in the Turin worker–student assembly most critical of the workerists' discourse on wages; together with large numbers of student activists around the North, they prepared to launch the paper *Lotta Continua*. With its immediate purpose thrown into doubt by the liberalisation of access to university won in 1969, and its guts torn out by such splits, the Italian MS now effectively disintegrated, replaced by a new force: the 'extra-parliamentary left' (Bobbio 1978: 40–3).

Potere Operaio, Lotta Continua, Manifesto, Avanguardia Operaia: there were dozens of other, minor organisations, with the most varied politics, but only these four of the new groups had any significant national presence, albeit one dwarfed by the Communist Party. Committed to the formation of a new leadership within the working class, each had a share of workplace militants, above all in their respective strongholds: the Veneto, Turin, Rome and Milan. Still, to a greater or lesser degree, all drew their cadre from the same stuff as the student movement that had spawned them. Representative of widespread discontent amongst the new strata of intellectual labour-power, it would be vacuous to dismiss the majority of the groups' members as 'petty bourgeois', but also naive to accept at face value their self-image as vanguards of the industrial working class. That the ludicrous formulae of the Unione had offered safety, certainty and stability for militants close to exhaustion was widely recognised (Ciafaloni and Donolo 1969: 220). It had yet to be seen, however, whether the cadre of the new organisations, with the garb of 'professional revolutionary' obscuring the specificity of their own class needs, would be fundamentally different. At the time, however, few in the Italian new left seemed able to sense the dangers inherent in the formation of these 'micro' parties. Of such sceptics, perhaps the most perceptive were Ciafaloni and Donolo, who had argued back in July 1969 that the tendency to form new 'revolutionary' organisations was more symptomatic of the student movement's demobilisation than of a qualitative leap forward. The warning with which they concluded their reflections that summer was to prove as prophetic as it was unheeded:

> The revival of student struggles and their functionality to workers' struggles can only emerge from a revival of 'their own' struggles and an encounter with workers not as 'politicians', but as one group of workers to another ... If one struggles without clear objectives, the sole aim being to raise hell and 'form cadres', then in reality all that will be formed is a new sector of the political class. (ibid.: 226).

'WE ARE ALL DELEGATES!'

Even as POv-e and other workerist groups came together to form Potere Operaio, unrest again began to circulate in factories with the struggle to renew industry contracts. In Porto Marghera checker-board strikes broke out, organised for alternate days; in FIAT, where a fresh wave of young Southern workers had arrived over the summer to work at Mirafiori and FIAT's new Rivalta plant, similar stoppages occurred on alternate hours, throwing the productive cycle once more into chaos. In such circumstances, the workerists' pessimistic assessment of the limits of autonomous workplace organisation would be momentarily put aside. 'It is difficult to believe', enthused one writer in *Potere Operaio*, 'that the working-class struggles now taking place can be brought back within the established order of things' (Potere Operaio n.d: 18, 29). Their traditional emphasis upon the large factories was being confirmed, the workerists claimed, by the lead provided by these 'great epicentres of workers' autonomy' (ibid.: 16). Likewise the 'rejection of work', which was no longer merely the property of a 'small minority of "vanguard" left-wingers', but had become the expression of a mass movement (ibid.: 46). It would be enough to have the existing union contract demands immediately ratified, the group argued, for the struggle to consolidate itself and prepare to move forward with the 'process of political unification and organisation' (Potere Operaio 1969b). Rather than a merely Italian phenomenon, the workplace upheavals made the project of a 'Red Europe', capable of defeating capitalism East and West, a viable one.

When the struggles of autumn resumed in 1970, as workers sought to improve upon industry-wide contracts through plant-level agreements intended to further enshrine the new egalitarian demands, the workerists were forced to face the most disconcerting aspect of the creeping May: the resurgence of the union movement. That a temporary revival of the confederations was possible had not been ruled out by *Potere Operaio*, which had argued in October 1969 that

> the workers in struggle will not drop the trade union as an instrument of unification until political class-recomposition has fully achieved the leap to full autonomous organisation. (Potere Operaio n.d.: 17)

Far from abandoning such bodies, however, large numbers of militant workers moved closer to the most radical of the unions during 1970, particularly in factories bereft of unofficial committees. Apart from their accommodation of the new egalitarian demands, the chief reason for the changing fortune of Italy's metal and chemical unions lay in their adoption of the movement of workplace delegates then spreading through much of industry. A chaotic mixture of initiatives arising from both the shopfloor and without, the movement bore different connotations from one instance to the next. In some workshops, the delegates were seen as nothing more than watchdogs over the industrial contract. In others, where their primary source of loyalty lay with workmates rather than union, delegates took a much more aggressive role in challenging the factory hierarchy. Similarly, in some factories delegates were simply appointed from above, or else elected from a list recommended by officials; in others any worker, union member or not, was eligible to stand. Whatever the specific circumstances, however, the delegates' councils, with their roots planted in individual work groups, came to be embraced by workers in more and more factories after 1970, supplanting or subsuming the older and smaller Commissioni Interne drawn from plant-wide elections (D'Agostini 1974; Romagnoli 1975).

The strategy of co-opting the delegates – 'riding the tiger', as it was then popularly known – was abhorrent for many union officials, who saw in the new movement yet another challenge to their declining influence. As their more astute colleagues realised, however, accepting the delegates as the bottom rung of a reunited union movement promised to recapture much of the ground lost since the war. The endorsement of this new approach by the bureaucracy would not be long in coming: by December 1970 the CGIL, through a mixture of self-criticism, mass pressure and opportunism had formally adopted the delegates and their factory councils as 'the rank-and-file structure of the new unitary union'. When in the following year the CISL (Confederazione Italiana Sindacati Lavoratori – Italian Confederation of Workers' Unions) assumed a similar stance, talk of unification proceeded apace, although ultimately only the metal unions of each confederation would step beyond the new mood of cooperation to seek organisational fusion (Grisoni and Portelli 1977: 189).

From its beginnings in 1968, the majority of workerists were to spurn the delegates' movement outright. The original PSIUP call for the election of negotiators of piecework rates was dismissed as a form of self-exploitation. Many in Potere Operaio (n.d.: 30) also followed Lotta Continua in rejecting any approach that did not concentrate leadership functions within the mass of workers as a whole. The chief reason for Potere Operaio's refusal of the delegates' movement, however, stemmed from the workerists' fear that it might become a Trojan Horse through which the confederations could reconquer the factory (Grisoni and Portelli 1977: 187–8). Along with the tendency's conviction that the union-form was now incapable of challenging the capital relation, such intransigence drew sustenance from the links which Potere Operaio and similar groups had come to establish with a militant fringe of workers completely opposed to the confederations (Bobbio 1978: 59). As with Lotta Continua, Potere Operaio's tragedy would lie in its inability to combine support for such militants at FIAT or Petrolchimico with a battle to defeat union officialdom's designs upon the delegates' movement elsewhere. In other words, most of the group's leading members were unable to see that the processes of class composition and recomposition might be quite different outside the most 'advanced' poles of capitalist accumulation. That at least some workerists recognised what was at stake is clear from an issue of *Potere Operaio* of November 1969, where one anonymous writer posed the group's options in stark terms:

> If we do not absolutely maintain *a continuous relation between new forms of organisation and mass struggles*, we can safely say that the rank-and-file committees will end up as nothing more than one of the many articulations of the union in the factory … There is a precise battle to be conducted in the mid-term over what we have called the average level of autonomy, the terrain of the objective proliferation of rank-and-file committees in the individual moments of the post-contract struggles. If, through sectarianism or illusion, we continue to consider the work team or shop delegates as definitively destined to constitute the transmission belt of union control over struggles, then it will be much more probable that the rank-and-file committees will be reabsorbed into the articulation of the democratic union than vice versa. (Potere Operaio 1969c: 4)

Ignoring such warnings, the majority of workerists chose in effect to abandon to the confederations those militant workers still unconvinced by the tendency's critique of unionism. In doing so, they would help to make their fears of union recuperation a self-fulfilling prophecy (Bobbio 1978: 66). As a consequence, Potere Operaio would encounter great difficulties in building a factory presence outside established strongholds like Petrolchimico; there as elsewhere, a number of its activists would choose to participate in the new councils of delegates (Scalzone 1988: 121).

The newly legislated Statuto dei Lavoratori would institutionalise many of the gains made in larger workplaces, and lend certain legal rights to the unions. Coupled with their patronage of the delegates and the egalitarian demands of the mass worker, the unions would soon prove successful in overtaking most of the radical rank-and-file factory groups of the creeping May (Pasetto and Pupillo 1970: 108–18; Bologna 1980a: 29; Perna 1980; Giugni 1987: 240). While Lotta Continua remained influential at FIAT, and the CUBs sponsored by Avanguardia Operaia continued to spread through Lombardy, the unions' resurgence was to have direct consequences for workerism's political ambitions. In the crucial years of the early 1970s, the tendency's major organisational expression would turn away from the problem of class composition, towards the all-or-nothing gamble of 'militarising' the new revolutionary movement.

6

Potere Operaio

For the brief years of its existence, the revolutionary organisation Potere Operaio would represent a unique moment in the development of workerism. At a time when many young people in the West attempted to repeat the success of Bolshevism, the experience of the self-styled Leninists of Potere Operaio was to parallel in certain striking ways that of German ultra-leftism during the early Weimar Republic. Anti-parliamentarian, contemptuous of work within the unions, committed to an insurrectionalist perspective, the line of Potere Operaio was soon to be, as Scalzone (1980: 249) later reflected from prison, 'caught in the eye of the hurricane, like a kind of modern KAPD' [Kommunistiche Arbeiter Partei Deutschlands – the Communist Workers' Party of Germany]. And as with that far-distant organisation, the failure of Potere Operaio to realise its ambitions was to throw many of its members' central tenets into crisis. If Potere Operaio was in a very real sense the word of classical *operaismo* made flesh, its difficulties would also make plain the flaws in both the theory of the 1960s and the workerists' attempts to implement it.

CRISIS OF CLASS COMPOSITION

The energy and creativity of the mass worker of 1969 was to bubble over into the early 1970s as the years of 'permanent conflictuality'. It was a time when tens of thousands of working people engaged in a practical questioning of the existing organisation of labour, in the process radically transforming the form – if not vocation – of the Italian union movement. As for the generation of young workers politicised in those years – or at least the males amongst them – their mood was captured with humour and verve by the comic strip character Gasparazzo, whose adventures briefly graced the pages of Lotta Continua's daily newspaper in 1972. Gasparazzo was an immense success: a Southern migrant who loathed wage labour, militant in his outlook but wary of the official labour movement, his private world was full of uncertainties but also permanent rebellion. As such, he quickly became the emblem of the group which most faithfully embodied the best and the worst of the new politics thrown up in 1968. Like that of his organisation, Gasparazzo's outlook was a fundamentally optimistic one: despite continual setbacks, there was always an unspoken sense that ultimately his class would triumph over adversity (Del Carria 1979: 172–3).

Writing in October 1972, the leadership of Lotta Continua (1974: 2151) would reflect that, notwithstanding 'great differences in content, in style of work, in the conception of organisation', their group shared one important notion with Potere Operaio. This, they continued, was the idea that the construction of a revolutionary party was possible only on the basis of a rupture with the traditions of the Third International. If this was so in part, it was equally true that the two groups had long been divided in their respective assessments of the mass worker's prospects. For Potere Operaio, in contrast to Gasparazzo, these prospects had seemed far from bright in the immediate aftermath of the Hot Autumn. Disappointed that the combativity then expressed in the factory had not led to an explicit political challenge to capital's rule, Potere Operaio would begin not only to re-examine the relation between class composition and organisation, but to reconsider the very meaning of its central category. That sections of the Italian state were prepared to respond to class struggle with terrorist tactics, such as the December 1969 bombing of a Milan bank which left 16 people dead (Ginsborg 1990: 333–4), lent a further urgency to the project.

As with all theoretical shifts within *operaismo*, such a reassessment would be prompted primarily by developments in social conflict. The earliest, if faintest, of these was the political upsurge of 'Black Power' in the American ghettoes, which the journal of POv-e had interpreted in unambiguous class terms:

> American Blacks do not simply represent, but rather *are*, the proletariat of the Third World within the very heart of the capitalist system ... The Blacks have learned from the Vietnam War – to which they have been sent as cannon fodder – that the proletariat cannot wait indefinitely for a (white) working class like the American one, dominated as it is by reactionary (union) organisations ... *Black Power means therefore the autonomous revolutionary organisation of Blacks.* (POv-e 1967c: 3)

In the late 1960s, this goal was to be pursued most successfully by a Detroit-based circle of African-American activists influenced both by mavericks like James Boggs and more conventional Marxist-Leninists. During its short life their League of Revolutionary Black Workers, with which the Italian organisation established links, was to play a significant role within the local auto industry, organising 'revolutionary union movements' outside and against the traditional union structure (Gambino 1986; Georgakas and Surkin 1998). Because the Detroit experience affected Potere Operaio while the latter was still in its early factory-orientated stage, however, the problem of racism remained important for it only in so far as Black workers represented a specific stratum of the workforce. As a consequence, the workerists' defence of autonomous workplace organisations for African-Americans was to follow pragmatic lines quite alien to the nationalism that inspired many League members. Not surprisingly, Potere Operaio failed to draw any positive lessons from the work of Black militants beyond the shopfloor, arguing that the level of class struggle was superior in Europe, since on that continent migrant workers had brought the rage of the ghetto into the factory (Potere Operaio n.d.: 23). By the time that the Italian group had moved on from conceiving workplace struggles as necessarily more advanced than those in the streets, the radical wing of the Black movement in the US had largely been beaten into the ground. As a consequence, Potere Operaio was to seek the reference point for its theoretical revision in the new 'wind from the South'.

Another factor that contributed to the workerist reassessment of its class analysis was the emergence of women as collective subjects of social change. While the second wave of feminism would become a mass phenomenon rather later in Italy than in the English-speaking world, the 'germ of women's rebellion' (Ciuffreda and Frabotta 1975: 7) had already been present within the student movement of the late 1960s. At that time, however, neither the MS nor the extra-parliamentary left that succeeded it were to pay anything but lip service to the struggle against the oppression of women. For its part, Potere Operaio's initial approach to the problem of sexual domination emerges clearly in its February 1970 appraisal of women workers recently hired by FIAT:

> Ten thousand underpaid workers make it possible for the owner to realise an enormous profit and in this way to break up the struggle for the abolition of categories ... Women are being hired by FIAT Mirafiori somehow like Blacks were hired by the Detroit auto industry in the 1930s. It is about time to stop shedding tears about women's 'equality', [which] like every lecture about civil rights is fucked up. Capital has already 'equalised' women at Mirafiori, assigning them to the assembly lines. (Potere Operaio n.d.: 53)

Betraying a certain ill grace, the article's conclusion was to accept the arrival of this new levy as a *fait accompli*; the real problem was how women workers might be organised in an anti-capitalist manner.

Such attitudes within the far left were to prompt small groups of female militants to establish their own circles, organising a variety of activities from discussion groups to campaigns over abortion and childcare. The most ambitious of these early attempts at women-only organisation was Lotta Femminista, a group centred – like Potere Operaio, from which its central figures had departed by 1972 – upon the Veneto region. For Lotta Femminista, Potere Operaio's acceptance of the viewpoint of the male workforce evaded the deep-seated contradictions existing within the class in favour of the male workers' hegemony:

> In seeing women as the instruments of capitalist attack upon the wage, PO navigates in dangerous waters. The traditional motive for attacking the migrant worker, especially if he or she is Black (or an Italian Southerner), is that their presence threatens the conquest of the indigenous working class. It is exactly the same thing that is said of women in relation to men. The anti-racist (and thus anti-nationalist and anti-sexist) point of view, the point of view of struggle, is to discover the organisational weakness that permits the more powerful sections to be divided from those with less power. In other words, to discover the organisational weakness which, by permitting capital to plan this division, defeats us. Today this question is one of the fundamental questions that the class must confront. (Lotta Femminista 1972: 18–19)

Already on record as supporting the independent organisation of African-American workers in the US, it was a rebuke for which Potere Operaio had no answer. Lotta Femminista's most famous contribution to workerist debate, however, was Mariarosa Dalla Costa's small pamphlet *The Power of Women and the Subversion of the Community*, soon to become well-known in international feminist circles (Malos 1980). In it Dalla Costa set out to demonstrate that in performing domestic labour, women not only reduced the costs of necessary labour, but themselves produced surplus value. In doing so, she would be the first of the workerists to advance a coherent case for the claim that the extraction of surplus value could occur outside the sphere Marx had designated as the direct process of production. While glossing over the strategic implications of her argument, Potere Operaio showed itself happy to accept Lotta Femminista's demand of 'Wages For Housework' as further support for its own calls for a social wage. Even here, however, the condition of women was seen only as an addendum to the group's understanding of class composition, at best stimulating a greater interest in the problem of the reproduction of labour-power without addressing specific issues of either gender or sexuality (Potere Operaio 1971b).

Undoubtedly the greatest factor in broadening Potere Operaio's perceptions of working-class life would be the increasing restlessness of Italy's Southern population. Once again, however, the group's initial outlook was to be firmly cast in a 'factoryist' mould. The very first issue of the new *Potere Operaio* presented migrant workers as a vanguard force in the mass struggles,

> the starting point for political work at a European level, provided you don't make the mistake of approaching them in their condition as 'immigrants', but – as was the case in Turin – within the struggle of the factory, and within the content that the struggle there proposes. (Potere Operaio n.d.: 12)

In other words, the group dismissed outright the need to confront any of the peculiar social problems facing those who had come to the city for work. Similarly, Potere Operaio's early discussion of the Mezzogiorno set out to establish agricultural labour as productive in Marx's sense of the word. Attacking what it saw as the Communist myth of a separate Southern society, a 'pre-capitalist production formation' still awaiting the promise of the Risorgimento, Potere Operaio indicated that Italian agriculture had been tied to industry for close to a century. Today the social labour involved in agriculture was identical to that at FIAT, since the factory was not simply 'a construction housing men [sic] and machines'. More daringly, the group acknowledged that capitalist relations of production could partake of a wide variety of forms in time and space. In the Italian rural sector, it believed, they had assumed forms 'of political control which utilise feudal rights: the wage as price of labour-power is paid in an underhand manner through the concession of use and the juridicial ownership of small tracts of land'. In addition to the extraction of surplus value, the key factor binding agricultural labourers to factory workers was their mobility, which for Potere Operaio was 'the novelty with the most significance and duration in the "internal history" of Southern labour-power'. Tens of thousands from the Mezzogiorno, it pointed out, had refused the misery of village life over the past 15 years; if many had later returned home, they had brought back with them new experiences and demands. As a consequence, Southerners were now increasingly inclined to demand wages rather than land as the solution to their problems, while for their part Northern workers were learning to embrace the explosiveness of proletarian violence as their own (Potere Operaio 1969a: 4, 5). In a similar fashion, migrant workers were circulating struggles within Europe and beyond, as part of an inter-national cycle of struggle not seen since the years immediately following 1917 (Gambino 1969).

Potere Operaio's approach to the 'Southern question' demonstrated workerism's growing preparedness to make good its notion of social factory and stretch the capital relation beyond the wage. All the same, its framework was still one of a society polarised between *lavoro operaio* and the bourgeoisie. In their midst, there vacillated 'a congerie of social figures with indeterminate social connotations – students, white-collar workers, professionals'. Once again, the hegemony of industrial workers was not questioned. If the thread binding together the new political composition was presented as a 'minimum guaranteed wage for all labour-power', it was also held that the revolt and spontaneity of the countryside could only develop under the guidance of the class struggle and organisation of factory workers (Potere Operaio 1969a: 5).

When in the second half of 1970, part of the population of Reggio Calabria rose in revolt over proposed government changes to that city's regional status, the majority of the far left condemned the disturbances as the work of fascists. The PCI agreed with their judgement, adding its general disapproval of politically motivated violence (Bobbio 1979: 90–3). For Potere Operaio, which like Lotta Continua supported the uprising, the events possessed on the contrary 'the characteristics of a mass insurrection'. If it was true that the far right had succeeded in instrumentalising discontent there, this was because in the South 'the traditional left is defunct, the revolutionary left still absent'. Above all, the group insisted, the revolt had 'opened eyes to a mass push – widespread amongst proletarians – which presses violently against the institutions' (Potere Operaio 1972g: 2).

With the Reggio disturbances, Potere Operaio's belief that the struggles of workers engaged in the direct production of surplus value were necessarily more advanced than those of proletarians outside it collapsed completely. Much to the amusement of more orthodox leftists, Potere Operaio began to apply Lenin's distinction between political and economic struggles to its analysis of the industrial front. With the Hot Autumn, it argued, class struggle had broken free from the bounds of accumulation, snapping the link between class domination and development. By refusing to function as a mere economic factor, the mass worker had disrupted the functioning of the law of value, forcing capital to rely more and more upon the direct intervention of the state to hold the class relation together. Stopping short of the final confron-tation, however, workers had become isolated in the factories, their gains whittled away by inflation and layoffs. If the militants formed in

1968–69 continued on their current path they faced a massive defeat, for the crisis was 'inevitably the crisis of the factory struggle' (Potere Operaio 1971g: 38). In such circumstances, Lenin's categories again became relevant. Economic struggles, the group explained, were defensive, tied to labour-power's efforts to improve its lot within capital, while political struggles were those which attacked the relations of production. In the prevailing conditions of crisis, the factory had become a hostile terrain for workers, and there could be no direct continuity between the two levels. Only with the conscious intervention of a party constituted 'externally but not extraneously' to the class could this qualitative leap be effected (Potere Operaio 1971e: 35).

Returning in this manner to its arguments of mid-1969, Potere Operaio threw over its earlier exclusive identification of the category *mass worker* with the workers of the large factories. In dismissing as opportunist Manifesto's emphasis upon factory struggles, the workerist group rejected what it called 'the conception of the working class tied to the structure of production – by necessity therefore tied statistically to employment' (Potere Operaio 1971f: 38). The present crisis both proletarianised and 'de-workerised' labour-power, and whilst this process apparently confirmed the PCI's calls for a class alliance between workers and the so-called 'middle classes', in reality it pointed to an 'objective recomposition' of the class which extended far beyond the minority of productive workers:

> The new political composition of the class, the connotation of the majority of employed labour as proletariat, is not given in the objectivity of the production processes, nor can it be grasped and represented in an institution, in an ideology, in the formation of a homogeneous consensus or opinion. On this terrain the stratification, the differences multiply and exercise their weight ... No, the political figure of the reunified proletariat is given only as estrangement, as antagonism, as struggle against the capitalist system, as will of destruction and as communist programme. (Potere Operaio 1972e: 1)

Here, for the first time in *operaismo*'s history, any necessary relationship between the labour process and class behaviour was to be denied. Revolutionary subjectivity now posed itself outside and against capital, so that the central problem of recomposition became the relation between factory workers and the growing numbers of the unemployed. The biggest danger, according to Potere Operaio, was 'factoryism', the term by which it characterised productive workers' defence of their positions at the expense of the jobless. As long as its actions remained confined to the workplace, the Italian class risked repeating the American experience of the late 1940s, when the strongly organised workers in Northen industry had been unable to prevent capital's use of unemployed Southern labour-power against them (Potere Operaio 1971c). The solution, on the other hand, did not lie in the widespread leftist demand of jobs for the unemployed, since that would play into the hands of a class enemy only too ready to link income to employment (Potere Operaio 1972c). What was needed instead was a guaranteed or political wage for all. During the 1960s factory workers had struggled to separate wages from productivity: now the slogan of the guaranteed wage summed up a strategy to separate wages from labour, asserting the reproduction of proletarian needs over and against the requirements of capital (Potere Operaio 1971a).

The most theoretically sophisticated version of Potere Operaio's new championing of the broad proletariat over factory workers was that advanced by Negri in his *Crisi dello Stato-piano*, the main preparatory document of the group's 3rd Conference of September 1971. Its chief source of inspiration was Marx's original 'Rough Draft of the Critique of Political Economy', written in the late 1850s as its author sought frantically to commit 'at least the fundamentals of his economic theory to paper "before the deluge"' (Rosdolsky 1977: 7). Then only recently translated into Italian by the workerist Enzo Grillo, the *Grundrisse* (Marx 1973) already appears in Negri's reading as a pre-eminently modern text capable of anticipating the capital relation's development well beyond the era in which it was written. Not that Negri (1971: 127) believed that the 'Rough Draft' could be utilised uncritically; if Marx had displayed enormous percipience, he reasoned, it was also true that the subsequent course of capitalism demanded that certain of his categories be modified. Central to Negri's reading of the *Grundrisse* was his appropriation of the category *tendency*, by which he understood the historical unfolding of capital's immanent contradictions as social antagonisms. The tendency was 'in no sense a necessary and ineluctable law governing reality', but rather 'a general schema' that 'defines a method, an orientation, a direction for mass political action' (ibid.: 125). In the 'Rough Draft', Marx (1973: 693) saw this passage reach fruition with the real subsumption of labour to capital, as the latter pursued 'The increase of the productive forces of labour and the greatest possible negation of necessary labour', realised in 'The transformation of the means of labour into machinery'. For Negri, it was within this process that an understanding of the passage from a mass of individual labour-powers to a class subject in the form of a 'social individual' became possible (ibid.: 115–17). If capital's use of mass production had led it to empty labour of all its particularity, this measure, far from reducing workers to simple economic factors, had cut them free from all ties to their work, laying the basis for their broader, more potent unification. Hence Marx's category of abstract labour had itself become a revolutionary subject, for whom the constriction of commodity relations appeared both petty and irrational (ibid.: 118). Today, as a special supplement to *Potere Operaio* proclaimed in May 1971, the mass terrain of class conflict was nothing less than a 'proletarian assault upon social wealth' accumulated by capital (Potere Operaio 1971a).

Exactly what positive goals proletarians were pursuing in their struggle against capital had never been clear in *Classe Operaia*. Potere Operaio, by contrast, explicitly rejected the normative value that Marxists had traditionally assigned to the goal of labour freed from the domination of capital, replacing it with an ethic of consumption unfettered by the dictates of accumulation. Yet if such an approach stemmed from a refusal of that asceticism which many on the left hoped to impose upon working people, it also drastically simplified the problems involved in reappropriating the wealth produced under the logic of capital. At its worst, the conception of communism and revolutionary struggle which some workerists were to develop during the 1970s can be characterised as a sort of 'capitalism without labour' (Preve 1984: 71–3). In the process they were to forget, as Lotta Continua would point out in early 1971, that 'what this society produces is not social wealth but commodities, that is wealth for the bosses and poverty for the proletarians'. In order to build a new society, Potere Operaio's critics argued, rather more was required than the simple seizure of the existing pool of commodities (quoted in Bobbio 1979: 78).

Developing its own innovative approach to the world outside the factory in its campaign to 'Take Over the City', Lotta Continua was also critical of Potere Operaio's abandonment of the central category once shared by the two groups. Writing in early 1972, Adriano Sofri accused the members of Potere Operaio of substituting the Southern unemployed for the protagonists of the Hot Autumn, by dint of a logical rigour that 'bordered on madness':

> That the working class of the large factories is not only an occupational datum, but the most conscious and organised sector of the proletariat, and that it verifies this fact in struggle, no longer seems to count. That the Southern unemployed are something quite different to FIAT workers, both in terms of awareness of the social and political mechanisms of exploitation, and class unity and organisation, no longer counts either, given that both are identified with that dilated definition of the working class. Not only is the struggle of the unemployed bestowed with a positive class significance identical to

that of spontaneous struggle in the factory. More than this, the struggle of the Southern proletariat or unemployed is deprived both of that formidable and decisive support which is working class organisation, and the overall strategy against the division of labour which the latter incarnates. (Quoted in Della Mea 1972: 88–9)

In its reply, Potere Operaio insisted that Sofri had misunderstood the group's position: the polemic against 'factoryism' did not in any way deny 'the hegemonic function which the workers of the large factories must have – as guide, as point of reference and direction – over the entire movement' (Potere Operaio 1972b: 6). None the less, Sofri's criticisms fed upon the growing doubts which certain members of Potere Operaio – such as those, like Negri (1983: 124), sympathetic to the theme of 'Take Over the City' – were again expressing as to the relation between class composition and political project. With the resurgence in 1972 of factory-based conflict over industry contracts, which in Milan saw regular confrontations between mass pickets and *carabinieri*, Negri's wing of the group would return the workers of the large firms to their former privileged position within the workerist credo. In the process, such members of Potere Operaio began to question the very meaning of a revolutionary organisation that was not rooted first and foremost in the workplace.

Internal polemics were to cripple Potere Operaio as a political force in the year that preceded its dissolution in mid-1973. When the debate came to revisit the political significance of the mass worker, a handful within the group continued to push on towards abandoning all reference to the category. Writing a little before the controversy began, one such anonymous contributor to the February 1972 issue of *Potere Operaio* insisted that workerism had reached a theoretical dead end. In order to break free, the tendency would be forced to refuse 'blind voluntarism' and confront 'the sour taste of crisis'. Now that the traditional articulation posited by workerism between technical and political composition had assumed a 'much larger and more pregnant' form with the expansion of the capital relation beyond the factory, the old conceptual apparatus had become less and less useful (Potere Operaio 1972a: 22). In particular, they went on,

a series of simplifications once useful for us, like the 'mass worker', no longer serve. We need something that is both more and less than this. We need a figure of a proletariat which experiences the crisis, the repressive cyclical nature of production as much as prices and inflation, and on the other hand we need the figure of a proletariat which suffers exploitation throughout the entire day ... (ibid.: 23)

Just what such a figure would be was not explained. Instead, the problem would have to wait until the middle of the decade and Negri's theory of the *operaio sociale*, the arrival of which would finally call the whole meaning of workerism into question.

BUILDING THE ARMED PARTY?

The mass worker believes only in real parties, credible ones ... (Alquati 1980: 30)

Insurrection, militarisation of the movement and armed party – phrases inseparable from the ideology of Potere Operaio – would continue to haunt the workerists long after the group's demise. Having failed to link Autonomia with the Brigate Rosse (Red Brigades), some of the magistrates directing the '7 April 1979' case centred their investigation instead upon the common past of those detained in Potere Operaio. In doing so, their chief charge was to be that the organisation had planned an insurrection in 1971 (Ferrajoli 1981: 54). If on closer examination this grand design would prove to be nothing more than the preparation of petrol bombs for a Milan demonstration, the new tack of the prosecution, as two of the accused were to indicate, revealed a wilful ignorance of the workerist group's whole project:

In the first place, is working-class autonomy or has it ever been in fact, an insurrectional phenomenon? The very first thing we need to do here is to clear up a misunderstanding – the one pursued by the Roman judge – that is, the resurrection of an insurrectionalist thematic that was the historical property of the 1968 group *Potere Operaio*. Agitation for an insurrectional perspective (which never even began to become a theory, far less an insurrectionary practice) constituted a last resort to articulate leninist goals (vieux-leninist?) on a theoretical and 'workerist' corpus, and above all, on a transformation of its referent, of the *social* subject of the struggles which '68 had begun to reveal in all their breadth. *Potere Operaio* said insurrection for the same reasons Lotta Continua said 'Take over the city' and *Il Manifesto* (Yes, Magri himself) put forward guerrilla warfare in the factories. The judges obviously forget, or better still, they are obliged to conceal by whatever means possible, the small detail that P.O. was the very first group to take note historically of the impractibility and inadequacy of that attempt at articulation, and to dissolve. (Negri and Ferrari Bravo 1981: 24)

Yet in defending Potere Operaio so, Negri and Ferrari Bravo were themselves guilty of smudging over the profound disagreements which had separated it from the other major far left organisations in Italy. In a mundane sense, what they said was perfectly true: the workerists' actual practice of violence was little different to that of thousands of other leftists. As for the dabblings of some of Potere Operaio's leadership with their own clandestine structures, these too were modest by the standards of the time (Palombarini 1982: 81–6). Indeed, if members of Potere Operaio had not shown themselves backward in the manufacture of molotov cocktails for use against the *carabinieri*, neither did they possess the reputation of certain more doctrinally moderate groups for settling political differences with monkey wrenches. Ideologically too, the thematic of an unavoidable armed struggle against the state, as exemplified by the efforts of the Vietcong, was an important part of the extra-parliamentary groups' common patrimony, and one which marked them off from a PCI leadership deemed revisionist. Whilst differences within the far left as to the meaning of armed struggle then ran deep, 'on the "if"', as Scalzone (Tracce 1983: 26) would later point out, 'there were no doubts'. What did distinguish Potere Operaio, however, was its conception of insurrection as a pressing, imminent necessity. Crash or crash through was the message Potere Operaio broadcast to other revolutionaries after 1970; if 'the party of the insurrection' was not built, it argued, the only possible outcome would be 'the general defeat of the movement' (Potere Operaio 1971d: 5).

The roots of such a discourse lay in the group's pessimistic assessment of the Hot Autumn's outcome. Yet, to begin with at least, the answer to the insufficiency of 'continuous struggle' in the factory was seen to lie in the greater centralisation of existing radical working-class forces, rather than the constitution of an organisation separate from them. This task was to be entrusted to new factory-based 'political committees', through which Potere Operaio hoped to lay the basis for 'general *scadenze* of struggle and the class party' by channelling discontent into 'precise moments of struggle and obtainable objectives' (Finzi 1971: 37). Spurned by its half-sister Lotta Continua, Potere Operaio launched the committees in the early months of 1971 together with Manifesto, a group with which it had little in common, if not a mutual isolation from the rest of the far left (Bocca 1980: 54; Berardi 1998: 132–4). Not surprisingly, as the progeny of such mismatched parents, most of the political committees soon proved practical failures.

For the rest of the group's short existence, the majority within Potere Operaio was to reiterate again and again its diagnosis of an impotent far left, and a working class trapped in a dead end. From its beginnings with *Classe Operaia*, workerism's political point of reference had oscillated constantly – and not always with coherence – between the two poles of 'mass work' and the 'vanguard party'. In other words, between what it saw as the dictates of contemporary class composition, and the strictures imposed by the manoeuvring of the class enemy. By privileging the latter from the late 1960s onwards, Tronti and his associates had begun to abandon *operaismo*. Now, little more than a year after its formation, the group showed itself to be equally 'obsessed by the reality of the adversary' (Negri 1979a: 111), leaving those who found the solution inadequate – like Sergio Bologna (1980b: 180) and Franco Berardi (1998: 116) – little option but to depart.

The precise contours of the vanguard party visualised by Potere Operaio were to be spelt out by Negri in *Crisi dello Stato-piano*. Before a state 'casual and arbitrary' in its behaviour, its efforts to hold the capital relation sustained only by hatred and 'the desperate will of class survival', nothing less than a return to the Leninist problematic of insurrection could direct mass struggle towards a satisfactory conclusion. While the raw material of this process was the whole layer of militants formed within the last cycle of conflicts, the danger existed that, in the absence of a further leap forward, this vanguard would risk 'suffocation' at the hands of 'pre-constituted levels of autonomy and class spontaneity'. If the formal structure of the party would not necessarily follow the Bolshevik model, its function as the privileged subject of recomposition was not in doubt:

> The vanguard has to prove capable of interpreting the mass tendency to appropriation and channelling it against the enterprise, against the factory-command that is imposed on the class ... Action by the vanguard alone is empty; action by the mass organisms alone is blind. But it is equally dangerous to attempt to merge the two moments into unified mass vanguards. (Negri 1971: 132, 133)

Despite Negri's denials (1971: 132), Potere Operaio's conception of the revolutionary party would owe more to the 'theory of the offensive' which had flourished briefly within the Communist movement of the early 1920s than to any notion held by Lenin (Cacciari 1978: 58). Embraced by both left communists and the extremist wing of Bolshevism, condemned by Lenin himself as 'insane and harmful' (Harman 1982: 214), the strategy of forcing the pace of class struggle through the exemplary actions of the party found its most intelligent advocate in Georg Lukács. For the latter, it represented the means to shake off 'the Menshevistic lethargy of the proletariat' (quoted in Löwy 1979: 161). Admittedly, the most significant attempt to apply it in practice – an uprising in Central Germany during March 1921 – had proved disastrous. All the same, the only thing available to those determined to ground a militant approach to class unity within the theoretical baggage of the Communist movement, whilst avoiding some variant of a United Front between existing labour organisations, was precisely the theory of the offensive. Having spurned as futile any such alliance with the historic left, it is perhaps not surprising that Potere Operaio would turn instead to such a spectacular notion of vanguard organisation. In doing so, it also rejected a third path, that of seeking the meaning of its political project within the behaviours of the class, so turning its back upon what was precisely 'the theoretical novelty of Italian workerism' (Berardi 1998: 130).

Workerism's interest in the theory of the offensive had first been roused during Italy's creeping May, in an essay penned by Giario Daghini (1971) for the September 1968 issue of *Aut Aut*. While this initial discussion of the question failed to separate the elements specific to the theory from a more general discourse upon the necessity of revolutionary violence, this was no longer so in 1971, when Potere Operaio stated explicitly:

> If the crisis of autonomy before the bosses' attack prevents us from assuming the permanency of significant levels of attack on the part of the *autonomous* behaviours of the workers' struggle, then the problem of shifting the relations of force in favour of the working class can only be resolved, from the beginning, by the hypothesis and realisation of instruments adequate to an offensive strategy. (Potere Operaio 1971d: 4)

Yet, for all the group's talk of 'acting as a party' – a slogan then shared with Lotta Continua – it would be mistaken to think that Potere Operaio genuinely believed that it could undertake such a project alone. For one thing, the group, with perhaps three or four thousand militants to its name, continued to lag behind the other nationally based organisations in both size and influence. Most of its members, furthermore, were still concentrated in the traditional strongholds of Rome and the Veneto, outside which, as Scalzone was to report from Milan in December 1970, the climate was all too frequently 'hostile, inhospitable, icy, lukewarm? Certainly little enthusiasm (for us)' (quoted in Bocca 1980: 55). Conscious of such limitations, Negri's intervention at the 1971 conference was to demonstrate a realism singularly lacking in his preparatory document:

> When we say that we are not a party, we are saying that we are not a weapon adequate to the conquest of power, that we are not capable, today, of this ... Comrades, saying this raises all the difficulties of the things to be done ... the difficulties that derive from the discrepancy between the tempo of organisation and that of the clash ... (quoted in Scarpari 1979: 269)

Looking back in 1979, Bologna would argue that 'for the intermediary and rank-and-file cadre in Potere Operaio, the primary reference always remained the armed party rather than the composition of the class' (quoted in Galante 1981: 482). While this insight does much to explain the group's growing loss of contact with political reality, it is not the whole picture. At least until the middle of 1972, when the activity of undergound formations began to proliferate, Potere Operaio envisioned the construction of the armed party as a project embracing the 'overall movement' or the 'class left', rather than any one specific sector within it, clandestine or otherwise (Scarpari 1979: 268). Such hopes would go unrealised, however. Certainly, the early 1970s were a period of heightened class antagonism in Italy, characterised both by the open mobilisation of the forces of fascism and a growing sympathy in some government circles for an authoritarian resolution of the 'social question' (Ginsborg 1990: 335–7). Still, neither the rest of the left, nor any significant section of the working class itself, showed signs of taking up Potere Operaio's call. If the project of an armed party found a certain resonance within some of Milan's factories (Silj 1979; Alfieri et al. 1984), it fell largely on deaf ears elsewhere. True, the leadership of Lotta Continua responded to the changing political climate by replacing its programme to 'Take Over the City' with talk of an imminent 'general clash'. Then again, they intended by this less a convergence with Potere Operaio's catastrophist perspective, than an accentuation of those elements of physical force already present within the culture of the far left. In particular, the line of a 'general clash' meant the greater formalisation and centralisation of the stewards' organisations which all the groups had formed to protect their members from police and fascists (Cazzullo 1998: 183–97).

Polemicising later with a different 'armed party', Mario Dalmaviva would hold that

> the politically motivated subjective exercise of violence, if it is not to be a simple reflection of class behaviour already present in the social

confrontation, needs legitimation. Not the formal legitimation of the state, or of legislation, which is 'legitimated' by the ferocity of its adversary, but a *class* legitimation. Such a class legitimation comes about when a credible political project of 'changing the status quo' meets with, roots itself in, and is recognised by, a significant element of the class. (Dalmaviva 1981: 37)

Potere Operaio's failure to win any such sanction in 1972 was to prove the greatest blow to its goal of militarising the class struggle, sending the group into a turmoil from which it would never recover. In the ensuing debate, however, the perplexities which some within Potere Operaio had earlier admitted privately now came into the open, helping to clarify those differences concerning class and politics which all the talk of insurrection had swept under the carpet. At first the nuances were subtle, but over time two distinct positions were to evolve: the first advanced by Negri's wing of the organisation, intent upon reviewing the meaning of working-class autonomy and the insurrectional model; the other that of the 'party-builders' around Piperno and Scalzone. 1972 would see Negri (1976a: 59) begin a re-reading of Lenin and the party-form adapted to the circumstances of labour's real subsumption:

> I believe that the most important thing we need to learn from Lenin is not so much abstract models or phrases, as his way of relating to the revolutionary process and to the subjectivity of the working class. We need to ask how the working class is composed today, and what need for organisation follows from its given determinate composition, a composition that is undoubtedly different from that which Lenin described. (ibid.: 31–2)

What was now needed, wrote one member of Negri's faction in June of 1972, were 'new experiences of struggle' richer than those of the far left groups. 'Only in this sense – of working-class direction of the organisation – can the problem of the unity of revolutionary forces be posed concretely' (Potere Operaio 1972h: 3). In this respect, it was suggested, a lot could be learned from the linking of factory vanguards in Lombardy by rank-and-file committees at Alfa, Pirelli and Sit Siemens (Cantarow 1972; 1973). The response to such arguments from those in the group most committed to the Leninism of *What Is To Be Done?* was predictable, ridiculing their opponents for ignoring the necessary mediating function of the vanguard party. Left to its own devices, these workerists claimed, working-class autonomy 'lives for and in the capitalist relations of production': only a political-military organisation committed to the destruction of the state was capable of breaking such stagnation (Potere Operaio 1973a: 3). 'The practical inefficiencies of a workers' assembly' were simply not up to such a task; in any case, the form and function of the revolutionary organisation could not be dictated by the nature of struggles, but only by the task of wresting political power from the class enemy. It was thus misleading to talk of a 'working-class leadership' as the Negri wing did, since the party was a voluntary organisation whose members entered it on the basis not of social background but commitment to communism. Only those, in sum, who turned their back upon Leninism in favour of a view in which 'party, workers' struggles and mass movement are all fused into one sublime identity' could fail to see that 'the construction of the party is a party affair' (Potere Operaio 1973c: 3, 4).

With some justification, Piperno and Scalzone could claim that their position was consistent with the doctrine handed down from *Classe Operaia*, and that it was Negri who had broken with the premises upon which Potere Operaio had been founded. Such criticisms Negri accepted with aplomb, countering that the whole strategy of the extra-parliamentary groups – Potere Operaio included – had been on the wrong track since at least 1971, when

> [t]he real task – of rearticulating from within itself the compactness of the newly unified strength of the working class – was transformed into an external undertaking of guidance and abstract leadership ... In the same span of time that the working-class struggle was advancing, extending and consolidating its destruction of the factory hierarchy, launching the slogan of the guaranteed wage, and beginning the first struggles on that front, the groups were mustering their attacking capacity (which was now becoming impotent and abstract because it had no bite on the mass level) into what was claimed to be an attack 'directed against the state' ... They were to be heavily defeated; the repression would find them isolated, and was able to savage them. In addition, their detachment from the class was now total: the groups were completely absent from the contract negotiations at the end of 1972. (Negri 1973c: 57)

If the two factions were to share one thing in common, it was a continuing championing of the project of armed struggle as a necessary and imminent moment in the transition to communism. According to Negri, for example, it was not the strategy of armed struggle that should be abandoned; rather, the likes of Scalzone and Piperno were too blinkered to see that any vanguard organisation had to be 'rooted immediately within the composition of the class', since

autonomy has represented a terrain of constant innovation of political initiative, and above all it has opened up the horizon of armed struggle. (Negri 1973c: 59)

But to what exactly did such a statement refer in the Italy of the early 1970s? For Negri, two incidents sprang immediately to mind. The first had taken place in Porto Marghera where, after the failure of police attempts to break up mass pickets, a general strike had been proclaimed which saw three days of street battles before the forces of law and order finally regained control of the situation (Moriani and Ruffato 1979: 33–4). Just as Potere Operaio had dubbed Corso Traiano an 'insurrection', in Negri's hands (1973c: 57) the dramatic events of August 1970 were transformed into 'a possible model of urban guerrilla [warfare]'. Even more outlandish was his interpretation of the workers' blockade of FIAT Mirafiori in early 1973 where, following six months of struggles over the new contract, the complex had been sealed off for three days by mass pickets. The struggles of that March, in their ferocity, had brought temporary relief to those on the far left most closely bound up with the experience of Mirafiori. For one worker militant in Lotta Continua, the blockade signified 'the fulfilment of four years of struggle at FIAT'; while for *Potere Operaio*,

'[t]aking power' at FIAT, and in all of Turin, contains an explicit allusion to the seizure of political power and to the revolutionary programme of the abolition of wage labour. (Potere Operaio 1973d)

In Negri's opinion, the FIAT action represented nothing less than the 'general arming of the factory' which hailed the birth of the 'Mirafiori party', a party-form inseparable from the vanguards immersed in mass struggle (Negri 1973a). Once again, however, such triumphalism bore little semblance to reality. Indeed, soon it would be clear that the combativeness of the FIAT pickets stood more as a final gesture of open defiance by the protagonists of 1969 than the portent of a new wave of militancy in the large factories (Portelli 1985: 12).

If the more recent instances of unofficial factory committees quickly became the chief point of reference for Negri's faction, the other wing of Potere Operaio (1973a) looked increasingly to what it called the 'area of the party'. While it was not always clear just what forces the latter embraced, amongst them were included a number of those groups committed to the clandestine organisation of a proletarian military apparatus: above all the Brigate Rosse; to a much lesser extent, the Gruppi Armati Partigiani led by the publisher Feltrinelli. It is easy, with hindsight, to become emotive about Potere Operaio's interest in the former, but it must be remembered that in the spring of 1972 the Brigate Rosse's activities bore rather different connotations to those which they would assume after 1975. Led by militants once noted for their violent verbal attacks upon workerism, the core of the Brigate Rosse had participated in the Hot Autumn as part of a Milan-based Marxist-Leninist group well-grounded in local workplace committees, and in good standing with Potere Operaio (Balestrini and Moroni 1988: 222). Choosing to go underground in anticipation of a fascist coup, their earliest actions were largely symbolic and didactic, ranging from the incineration of cars owned by strike-breakers and fascists to the kidnapping and public humiliation of unpopular magistrates and factory managers (Silj 1979: 96–116). In turn such practices found, if not endorsement, then certainly indulgence within those sections of the Italian working class where the flame of the Resistance and present-day Third World struggles burned strong. Through such actions, which emphasised the armed group's orientation to the workplace, the Brigate Rosse were initially to strike both factions of Potere Operaio as an important anticipation of the tasks ahead. None the less, there was also a certain coolness towards them from many in Potere Operaio, suspicious that the Brigate held pretensions to monopolise the political-military functions which were by rights the property of the revolutionary movement as a whole. 'The working class is the only subject which interests us', declared an article in *Potere Operaio* from June 1972.

Every other form of subjectivism is only an attempt to supplant the working class ... the problem of militarisation therefore is completely subordinate to the development of mass struggle and must be directed, even in its technical aspects, by the current form of the party (the mass organisms under working-class direction) ... The military 'specific' is such only if it refers to mass struggle. To think of the militarisation of the mass movement in terms of von Clausewitz is worthy of fascists. (Potere Operaio 1972f: 3)

Deeply divided as to the significance of class behaviour and the function of political organisation, Potere Operaio collapsed in all but name by the middle of 1973. While Negri's compatriots moved off to embrace the nascent 'Area of Autonomy', their opponents attempted for a while to keep the organisation alive. Before long they too were to be drawn into Autonomia, albeit as a current with little initial sympathy for either Negri's circle or their schemas. Others still were to follow the road already taken by Tronti, Asor Rosa and Cacciari, which ultimately led to militancy within the Communist Party (Paolozzi 1980). In their own way, each of these divergent paths offered different solutions to the problems that workerism continued to ponder. In each case, however, the most valuable lesson of the 1960s – the attentive study of working-class behaviour – was to be sacrificed in a greater or lesser degree to political impatience and an increasingly rigid conceptual apparatus. As the middle of the decade approached, fewer and fewer within the political tendency which had first introduced the debate on class composition into the Italian left were to take as their starting point the vicissitudes of broad sectors of the working population itself.

7

Toni Negri and the Operaio Sociale

I don't believe that anything I am saying is less than orthodox Marxism.
It is, anyway, the truth, even were it not orthodox; orthodoxy is of very
little importance to me ... (Partridge 1981: 136)

Following the collapse of Potere Operaio, the workerist current which
would generate both the greatest political influence and theoretical
controversy within Italy's revolutionary left was that associated with the
class and state analysis developed by Antonio Negri. The hypothesis
of a new proletariat disseminated throughout society, congregating in
the spheres of both production and reproduction, a 'socialised worker'
of which the mass worker of the Fordist assembly line was at best a
poor prototype, would be Negri's most controversial contribution to the
exploration of class composition.

LAST TANGO AT MIRAFIORI

From the beginning, the development of Negri's arguments about the
'socialised worker' was to be inseparable from that of a new political
tendency: Autonomia Operaia. Making sense of Autonomia as a whole
is no simple matter. Ideologically heterogeneous, territorally dispersed,
organisationally fluid, politically marginalised: Giorgio Bocca's (1980:
87) analogy of an archipelago is an apt one. Never a single national
organisation, much less the mass wing of the armed groups, as certain
judges would later charge, the 'Area' of autonomist organisations and
collectives would begin to disintegrate almost as soon as it had attained
hegemony within the Italian far left. Autonomia had first crystallised as a
distinctive political entity in March 1973, when a few hundred militants
from around the country gathered in Bologna to take some provisional
steps towards a new national organisation of the revolutionary left
(Comitati Autonomi Operai 1976: 33). A number of those assembled
in Bologna were members of the Negri wing of Potere Operaio; the
majority, however had already abandoned the far left groups, angered by
the latter's growing involvement in the unions and institutional politics.
The words of the conference's introductory report neatly summed up

the strategic orientation that united those present. In today's situation of crisis, it argued, *'The only path possible is that of attack'* (ibid.: 40). Furthermore, such an offensive could only base itself upon those class needs that the artificial ideological divisions introduced by both the historic and new left tended to obscure. To articulate such needs, organisation was to be rooted directly in factories and neighbourhoods, in bodies capable both of promoting struggles managed directly by the class itself, and of restoring to the latter that 'awareness of proletarian power which the traditional organisations have destroyed' (ibid.: 43).

During the following 18 months Autonomia's programme was to strike a responsive chord amongst a small but growing number of Italian leftists. The decision of many Potere Operaio members to 'dissolve' into the Area was an example soon followed by a number of smaller radical groups. The most important of these would be the Gruppo Gramsci, itself a minor organisation with a certain presence in the left of Milan's union movement. Reconstituted as the Collettivi Politici Operai (Workers' Political Collectives), the group was to produce the most profound self-critique of any of the Leninist currents which entered Autonomia. In the words of the December 1973 issue of its paper *Rosso*, what was now needed was nothing short of a new form of political practice, one which broke with the 'logic' of far left groups and

> the parochial language of political 'experts', who know the ABC – and even the L and the M – of Marxism-Leninism, without being able to speak concretely about ourselves and our experiences. (Gruppo Gramsci 1973: 96)

Rather than a politics which dealt with an abstract worker, 'male, adult, normal, unburdened by feelings and emotions; rational, a democrat or revolutionary, always ready to attend meetings on the history and tendencies of capitalism' (ibid.: 92), *Rosso* sought a new perspective which examined questions of sexual and emotional domination, of the nature of the family and the marginalisation of those deemed 'abnormal', through which 'the slavery of the factory and life imposed by capital manifest themselves'. It was to be this, the most libertarian of the major tendencies within the Area, that Negri and his closest associates would join the following year, and help to build into the strongest autonomist formation in the North. Unlike *Rosso*, however, the majority of the autonomist collectives were to keep their eyes firmly upon the vicissitudes of the industrial workforce during 1973 and 1974. So too with Negri (1973b: 126) himself, whose major essay of the period centred upon the factory as *'the privileged site of both the refusal of labour and the attack upon the rate of profit*. In this respect, the most interesting aspect of the essay was to be its effort to clarify workerism's often posited relation between working-class struggle and the accumulation process. Potere Operaio had conceived the relationship between class composition and economic crisis in the blunt, mechanical terms of a zero-sum game between wages and profits. In 'Partito operaio contro il lavoro', Negri set out to detail what he had earlier termed that 'long' but 'qualitatively homogeneous' path linking disputes within the terrain of production to the problems faced by the reproduction of capital (Negri 1968: 65).

The possibility of capitalist collapse, and the place within it of working-class struggle, had first been raised in a systematic manner amongst workerists with Negri's exploration of 'Marx on Cycle and Crisis'. Although written before 1969's 'Hot Autumn' of industrial unrest, this essay presaged a number of the central themes later addressed by the tendency. In doing so, it represented *operaismo*'s first attempt to offer a political reading of that part of Marx's critique of political economy traditionally most susceptible to the charge of objectivism. The piece's most interesting aspect, however, was its discussion of the efforts by John Maynard Keynes and Joseph Schumpeter to offer a solution to the difficulties faced by capital in guaranteeing its own reproduction as a social relation. Following Tronti against Lukács, Negri did not believe that such an undertaking was impossible for capital's 'critical awareness'; indeed, both Schumpeter and Keynes were able to perceive that capitalist development was an essentially open-ended process wracked with internal contradictions (Negri 1968: 57). Negri showed particular admiration for Schumpeter, who did not shy away from the fact that the capitalist economy lacked any internal tendency towards equilibrium. Further, by grasping the moment of crisis as not only unavoidable, but 'a fundamental stimulus within the system' that was 'productive of profit', Schumpeter had glimpsed the relations of force between classes which underlay the apparently autonomous movement of economic categories (ibid.: 54).

Negri's approach to the problem of crisis was expanded in 'Partito operaio contro il lavoro', a work which emphasised the profound changes to accumulation and class struggle which stemmed from the arrival of the real subsumption of labour to capital. Drawing upon both the *Grundrisse* and Marx's 'Results of the Immediate Process of Production', Negri (1973b: 109) grappled with the central tendency in capitalist development, namely 'the abbreviation of that part of the working day necessary to the reproduction of the value of labour-power'. The division of the working day between necessary and surplus labour, he insisted, had become a struggle between two independent variables. Not only did the traditional disciplining mechanism of the industrial reserve army no longer function, with growing numbers of young people refusing factory work, but the wage increasingly assumed a rigidity indifferent to the needs of accumulation (ibid.: 123–4).

Such an argument, like so many others advanced by workerism, had little in common with conventional Marxist precepts. On the other hand, while Negri's notion of labour as an independent variable within the class relation clearly contradicted the letter of *Capital* Volume I (Marx 1976: 770), it could yet claim support from Volume III of Marx's *magnum opus* (Marx 1981: 486). More important than the verification offered by sacred texts, however, was the eloquent testimony of the Italian economy's growing problems with productivity and profitability. Later, in *Marx Beyond Marx*, Negri (1984: 100–1) would clarify the nexus in the class struggle between necessary and surplus labour, arguing that through its rigidity in the labour process, the working class could cut into capital's potential profit. In 'Partito operaio contro il lavoro', this tendency remained implicit to the depiction of the working day as a field of permanent civil war between the two major classes (Negri 1973b: 113–14). Instead of elaborating this point, however, the essay chose to build upon the analysis of Negri's 1971 work *Crisi dello Stato-piano* ('Crisis of the Planner-State'). Even as capital held to the firm as the heart of its valorisation process, it continually pressed towards a greater socialisation of labour, stretching beyond the simple extension of the immediate process of production, towards a complete redefinition of the category *productive labour*. The dimensions of this category, it concluded, could only be grasped in a historically specific sense, being *'relative to the level of the advancement of the process of subsumption* of labour to capital ... we can now say that the concept of wage labourer and the concept of productive labourer tend towards homogeneity' (Negri 1971: 127), resulting in the constitution of 'the new social figure of a unified proletariat' (ibid.: 129).

'Partito operaio contro il lavoro' was thus clearly a transitional piece in Negri's understanding of capital and class. By locating traditional workerist formulations within a discourse based upon the tendency outlined in the *Grundrisse* (Marx 1973), it already stretched a hand out towards the hypothesis of the 'socialised worker' [*operaio sociale*]. As with most transitional works, however, its author seemed not at all aware of the contradictions contained within the text itself. Negri did little, for example, to substantiate his historically dynamic definition of productive labour; what concerned him, rather, was the argument that, in the present conjuncture, the mass worker's attacks upon the rate of profit remained the rallying point of the proletariat as a whole. Factory and society, production and reproduction, were not yet identical, but continued to exist in a 'dialectical' relationship. Capital itself sought to maintain this relationship by attempting 'to isolate the fall of the rate of profit in the factory (and its agents) from the process of the socialisation of productive labour unfolding throughout society' (Negri 1971: 129). As a consequence, Negri was satisfied to conclude that the workers of the large factories, as the 'privileged subject of exploitation', remained '*absolutely hegemonic*' politically and theoretically with respect to the rest of the class (ibid.: 128).

To Negri, encouragement for such a view was to come from the mass picket and occupation of FIAT's Mirafiori plant in March 1973. At the same time, his discussion of the 'Party of Mirafiori' did offer some insight into that notion of a socially homogeneous proletariat which, discarded in the latter days of Potere Operaio, would again soon become pre-eminent within his thought. If any limit existed, he argued, for the mass vanguard formed in the years since the Hot Autumn, it lay in the reluctance to venture beyond the factory gate and join with the struggle of appropriation in the social sphere. Seeking to surpass this weakness, Negri was to posit instead a drastic form of value-reductionism that obliterated all the distinctive features of those with nothing to sell but their labour-power. Taking up Potere Operaio's theme of the crisis of the law of value as a crisis of command over labour, Negri argued that the common basis for the recomposition of the class lay in a 'unity of abstract social labour'. This in turn overrode 'the "specific" problems of the various sectors of the social sphere (young people, women, marginalised elements etc.)' and the factory (Negri 1973a: 192, 193). The terrain of value, as *Crisi dello Stato-piano* had already argued, no longer assigned meaning in any terms other than those of power. Thus the peculiarities of the sites in which such organisation sprang up, and the content of the needs whose non-fulfilment prompted their formation, could only be subsumed to a project of 'counter-power' against the state. In this manner the Gordian knot of class composition, which could only be unravelled by slowly and carefully identifying the elements common to the often divergent sectors in struggle, was to be hacked away instead with the weapon of mass armed struggle. Writing in a 1974 essay dedicated to class strategy in a global context, Negri assured the reader that armed struggle

represents the only fundamental strategic moment – i.e. the only possibility of achieving a recomposition of the proletariat and a consolidation of the struggles, and destroying, along the way, capital's weapons of provocation, of repression and containment that are designed to isolate and newly compartmentalise the various class sectors. (Negri 1974: 53)

And yet, when Negri was not collapsing the intricacies of social conflict into a one-dimensional thematic of power, he did sometimes pursue lines of enquiry that placed emphasis upon the material contents of struggle. In 'Partito operaio contro il lavoro', for example, he would argue that the liberation of individual needs must now be considered an integral part of the class struggle:

> Perhaps for the first time, outside of utopia or those formidable moments of enthusiasm which are insurrections, the objective that the class proposes today – in its intensity, in its totality – also encompasses the needs of individuals. *Liberation cannot be left until communism* ... The new needs introduced by the most recent generations of the working class are needs of liberation. *Nothing is richer or finer than being able to connect the immediate needs of individuals to the political needs of the class.* (Negri 1973b: 159)

Negri's position here is far removed from his views of 1971, when he had intoned that 'Today, the class's only real "enjoyment" lies in its relationship with class organisation and in the confrontation with the hateful apparatus of capitalist power' (Negri 1971: 138). On the other hand, Negri's new insight remained bundled in old theoretical baggage. For example, he continued to try and squeeze the whole thematic of needs into the paradigm of the wage. In his view, 'the historic structure of the wage' continued to be the privileged expression of '*the objective level of needs*' through which the struggle both within and without the factory must be filtered (Negri 1973b: 143).

'WE'LL PAY WHAT AGNELLI PAYS'

During 1974, as the West's energy crisis exacerbated domestic inflation, Italian society exploded with new struggles that pushed those 'socialised' tendencies already nascent in Negri's thought into the centre of his consciousness. The common theme of the new turmoil was the practice of 'self-reduction', through which working people organised to protect themselves against the increased service charges unleashed by the Rumor government. Beginning in Turin, where workers from FIAT's Rivalta plant refused to pay an increase in bus fares, the self-reduction of prices soon spread throughout the Northern cities and Rome, where it became particularly popular as a means to fight rises in electricity and phone charges.

As such activities quickly assumed the dimensions of a mass movement able to mobilise 180,000 families in Piedmont alone, the labour movement found itself divided over the question. Whilst many Communist union functionaries questioned the efficacy and value of this new form of struggle, others saw its advocacy as crucial to their continued legitimacy. 'In these last months, the credibility of the unions has hit a low ebb', argued the secretary of Turin's Labour Council. 'What is at stake here is our relationship with the people; what is being questioned is our ability to build an alternative' (quoted in Ramirez 1975: 190). The practice of self-reduction also proved fertile ground for the autonomous collectives. The Romans of the Comitati Autonomi Operai (Workers' Autonomous Committees) – known commonly as the 'Volsci' – had sufficient members at the state-controlled electricity commission ENEL (Ente Nazionale per L'Energia Elettrica) to restore power to those disconnected for defying the new rates. It was not difficult for them, therefore, to convince many of the local populace to pay the tariffs at the industrial rate (about one quarter of the domestic price) rather than at the 50 per cent reduction most commonly proposed by the unions. Without such a draw card, autonomist groups in the Veneto and elsewhere were none the less still prominent in the struggle, if necessarily more cautious than their Roman counterparts (Big Flame 1974: 13–14).

Nor were these the only struggles occurring outside the factory. To the threat of cuts to education spending and staff, a new movement amongst high school students responded with demonstrations and occupations. In Turin, students organised a march to Mirafiori to attend the plant's first open assembly. A new wave of housing occupations also began early in the year, starting in Rome and spreading to Turin by October. The Rome squats were dominated by members of the group Lotta Continua, but there was also room for the involvement of the Roman autonomists, one of whom became in September the first from the Area to be killed in clashes with the police. In Turin, on the other hand, the occupations became notable for the numerically large presence of factory workers involved in an activity which in the past had chiefly engaged the productively marginalised and 'poor' (Comitati Autonomi Operai 1976: 205–11, 214–19). Finally, 12 October saw one of the first organised instances of 'proletarian shopping', when demonstrators entered a supermarket in Milan and forced the manager to sell merchandise at reduced prices (*Controinformazione* 1974: 12–13).

Changes were also then occurring within the movement of Autonomia itself. In the middle of 1974, a debate concerning the guaranteed wage revealed major differences of outlook. The central rift ran between those who privileged the refusal of labour as the basis of revolutionary strategy, and the Assemblea Autonoma dell'Alfa Romeo, for whom the development of class consciousness – and human potentiality – was inseparable from the experience of labour:

> By guaranteed wage we understand the right to life conquered with the guarantee of a job. Because in a communist society, each must contribute according to their abilities and receive from society according to their needs ... The comrades of Marghera say: when all men [sic] are freed from the necessity of labour, because they no longer need to work in order to eat or clothe themselves or satisfy their desires, then we will have true freedom! To this we reply that we are not against labour, but against the capitalist organisation of labour whose end is not social progress but profit ... [in the South] the proletarian masses seek to resolve their problems with jobs. (Assemblea Autonoma dell'Alfa Romeo 1974: 14–15)

Finding themselves alone on the matter, the Alfa militants were to quit Autonomia a few months later. Differences within the Area did not, however, dissipate with their departure. Whilst sympathetic to the notion of communism as the liberation from labour, other participants in the debate were becoming increasingly concerned with the political weight within the Area of the workerists and their allies. For the Romans especially, neither the ex-members of Potere Operaio nor those of the Gruppo Gramsci had shown any signs of establishing 'a new relationship with the movement'. Instead, the Volsci claimed, these militants remained particularly vulnerable to the 'temptation' of reconstructing Autonomia along the outmoded and bureaucratic lines of the groups formed out of the student movement of the late 1960s (Comitato Politico ENEL and Collettivo Policlinico 1974: 14; Comitati Autonomi Operai 1976: 71–4).

Such fears would soon prove prophetic. By 1975 the self-defined 'organised' components of Autonomia, stretching from the group around Negri or the remnants of Oreste Scalzone's wing of Potere Operaio, to a number of Marxist-Leninist organisations and the Romans themselves, had already begun their transformation into an ensemble of political 'micro-factions' (Scalzone 1978). While their contempt for institutional politics led them to work on a different terrain to that chosen by the major groups outside the PCI (Lotta Continua, Avanguardia Operaia and the PDUP), the political style of most of the 'organised' autonomist groups increasingly acquired a similiar heavy-handedness. For this reason, many a potential sympathiser already disenchanted with the 'big three' (*triplice*) of Italy's far left chose to enter not Autonomia 'with a capital A', but rather the burgeoning number of 'diffuse' collectives that began to swell the broader autonomist movement (Soulier 1977: 92–3).

Looking back, it would be easy to sense an inevitability in this process, given the flaws inherent in that 'anti-revisionist' culture which the autonomists shared with the majority of Marxists to the left of the PCI. Of particular note was the regularity with which new insights were to be grafted on to the existing Marxist-Leninist corpus, rather than utilised to question the latter's continuing claim to revolutionary veracity. Yet it would be wrong to obscure what were, particularly in its early period, the positive elements which Autonomia contributed to the culture of the Italian far left. Perhaps the most important of these was its refusal of separate political and economic spheres of struggle, and with it the dichotomy of party and union which had been the left's organisational norm since the days of the Second International. In doing so, the Area was to go much further than any other of its major Italian rivals in challenging the practical sensibilities of traditional Communist politics. In its initial manifestation as a predominantly factory-based network, Autonomia had represented a small but significant experiment in revolutionary politics based upon the self-organisation of that generation of workplace militants thrown up by the struggles of the 1960s. That the pursuit of such a project was quickly frustrated within the Area itself attests both to the dead weight of past ideologies and the growing shift of social forces attracted to Autonomia's banner. Thus, despite the criticisms of conventional Leninist precepts voiced by quite diverse autonomist formations in their early years, none would attempt a critique as fundamental as that then emerging from within certain feminist circles, let alone that traditionally advanced by the libertarian left. Rather, in opposition to the increasingly tame politics of the *triplice*, most tendencies within Autonomia were to formulate a brand of Leninism which, if often harshly critical of the armed groups' understanding of tactics, none the less sanctified armed struggle as the pinnacle of class struggle. Faced with the Italian state's apparent determination to criminalise social protest, which in mid-1975 saw fascists and police kill six leftist demonstrators in as many weeks, such a 'Leninism under arms' seemed to hold a certain practical relevance. This was true above all for many of the young high school activists formed in the new season of self-reduction and clashes in the streets. As Autonomia began, through political disaffection or layoffs, to lose much of its base in Italy's large factories, it was to be amongst this generation that the Area would now recruit most strongly. Having earlier cut their teeth within the stewards' organisations of the *triplice* – Lotta Continua above all – many of them were impressed by the autonomists' preparedness to meet the attacks of the *carabinieri* and fascists with physical force. Later still, those amongst them who found Autonomia inadequate on the 'military' front would again move on, either joining established armed groups or founding their own (Stajano 1982).

Writing in early 1976, Negri had identified one of the fundamental contradictions facing the Area and the social forces which it sought to organise as that between those who privileged 'the movement', and the champions of 'a "Leninist" conception of organisation' (Collettivi politici di Milano 1976: 229). Unfortunately, his optimism that Autonomia was capable of overcoming this problem would soon prove misplaced. Choosing instead to 'act as a party' in the tradition of Potere Operaio and Lotta Continua, the dominant forces within Autonomia would unknowingly doom themselves to repeat the trajectory of those groups whose failures they had once so vehemently criticised (*Collegamenti* 1974: 262; 1977: 23).

FAREWELL TO THE MASS WORKER

Gasparazzo is not eternal ... (Longo 1975: 30)

It was against this background that Negri's *Proletari e Stato* was written in mid-1975. A short work, the pamphlet brimmed over with hypotheses on the changing nature of class struggle. Finally casting aside all hesitation concerning talk of a new class composition, the dominant theme was one of renewal in crisis, of a continuity in rupture for both the critique of political economy and the process of social antagonism. For Negri, capital's attempts in the wake of the Hot Autumn to divide the class through an alteration of its technical composition and the further socialisation of the wage relation had backfired badly. Like a modern sorcerer's apprentice, capital's efforts to regain control had only multiplied its difficulties, for whilst the offensive of the mass worker had been halted, new proletarian layers – indeed a new class figure – had entered the fray in its stead. If this new class figure was the child of the preceding round of struggles, its midwife was the crisis of capitalist development. Like 'Partito operaio contro il lavoro', *Proletari e Stato* sought to locate its analysis of class composition within a discussion of the tendential fall of the rate of profit. In following the arguments developed by the workerist journal *Primo Maggio*, however, Negri now called for a substantial modification of crisis theory. Certainly, he agreed, the 'Marxian tendency' had become actual, and the problems associated with the rate of profit exacerbated by working-class struggle. Precisely because of this, however, capital's traditional counter-tendencies had so far failed to take effect,

> despite the greater flexibility imposed on labour-power, despite attempts at the territorial disarticulation of production (at all levels: local, regional, national, multinational), despite capital's new mobility in the world market, despite the disconcerting effects of the inflationary process: despite all this and many other attempts, therefore, the aggregate rigidity of the proportion between surplus value and total capital – namely the rate of profit – has not been dissolved ... Profit 'stagnates' ... even in the presence of inflation and all the other antagonistic operations. (Negri 1976b: 12–13)

As a consequence, capital was forced increasingly to rely upon the peculiar properties which the money-form offered to the task of re-establishing a correct proportion between the mass and rate of profit. Given this, the critique of political economy had now to be extended so as to grasp money's new function as command. At the same time, capital's difficulties had not prevented it from reorganising its organic composition and with it the technical composition of the working class. Yet, even as restructuring had 'devastated' the mass worker, it had also entailed a greater socialisation of capital with an attendant 'further massification of abstract labour, and therefore of socially diffused labour predisposed to struggle'. Whilst *the category "working class" has gone into crisis*, Negri (ibid.: 14–15): concluded, '*it continues to produce all its own effects on the entire social terrain, as a proletariat*'.

Similar arguments were then not unknown in workerist circles. Franco Berardi (1974: 8), for example, had already written of the emergence of a new class composition in the wake of the 1973 Mirafiori occupation. The new class subject was one, he argued, within which 'intellectual and technical labour, productive intelligence (*Wissenschaft-tecknische-Intelligenz*) tends to become determinant'. And it had been Alquati (n.d.: 90–3) who had first coined the phrase 'socialised worker' in the early 1970s, understanding by this a new political subject which was overtaking the mass worker, and as such bound up with the proletarianisation and massification of intellectual labour. Negri's definition, by contrast, both encompassed this stratum and stretched far beyond it. To his mind, as he was to put it when interviewed in 1978, 'the fundamental thesis underlying the theory of workerism is precisely that of a successive abstraction of labour parallel to its socialisation' (Negri 1979a: 11). If the mass worker was the 'first massified concretisation' of this (Negri

1976b: 15), its figure was yet tied to determinate sectors of the class, in particular to those producing consumer durables. The mass worker did not therefore encompass a whole class composition, but rather only its vanguard. Or, as Alquati would then say,

[t]he mass worker, and even before it the skilled worker in relation to peasants ... have taught us that hegemony resides not in numbers, but in the quality of the relation within accumulation and within the struggle against accumulation. (Alquati 1976: 75–6)

As the logical conclusion of the line of thinking which Negri had first postulated with *Crisi dello Stato-piano*, his understanding of the socialised worker represented therefore a radical break in the genealogy of class figures classified by Italian workerism. To begin with, it had not been forged wholly within a qualitative remoulding of the immediate process of production. Even less was the *operaio sociale* tied to a particular industrial sector: rather, it was the whole proletariat, subject qua abstract labour, constituted throughout the arc of the valorisation process. This time round, Negri (1976b: 36) insisted, the socialisation of the capital relation had failed to break the continuity and generalisation of struggle. Rather than a technological defeat, restructuring had generated a new class *re*-composition.

Proletari e Stato discussed its subject in a very general, indeed generic manner; after proclaiming its profoundly social nature, the text was to say very little about the changes to the physiognomy of the mass worker which have led to the new class figure's formation. For Negri, rather, the most important questions revolved around what he saw as the socialised worker's 'massive revolutionary potential', and an unfolding process of recomposition 'extraordinary in breadth and intensity' (Negri 1976b: 36). Capital's project of restructuring had not destroyed, but rather invigorated the political composition of the proletariat, uniting the various strata it had sought to divide. There was now, *Proletari e Stato* told its readers, 'a single law of exploitation present over the entire process of planning of capitalist society', making it obligatory 'to read *in restructuring the formation of an increasingly vast unitary potential of struggles*' (ibid.: 36–7).

The pages of *Rosso* help to flesh out the constituent elements of this novel class figure somewhat better than *Proletari e Stato* itself. In 1975 a new cycle of disputes had opened for the renewal of contracts; as in 1972–73, the autonomists' emphasis was placed upon the need for workers to take the offensive over the price of labour-power. In this way, they hoped, the class struggle would aggravate what many business and political leaders continued to see as the Italian economy's chief problem: its blown-out wage bill. On the fundamental terrain of the division between necessary and surplus labour, the paper argued, the only working-class response possible was a campaign for a further reduction of the working day with no loss of pay, a demand Negri's organisation proceeded to propagate amongst Milan's carworkers (*Rosso* 1975).

Whilst large factories had remained the pinnacle of Italy's industrial pyramid, widespread territorial dispersion of many labour processes, along with the traditional importance of minor firms producing components, lent more and more weight to workers in smaller workplaces. In line with this shift, *Rosso* began to document the early efforts at self-organisation amongst young workers in the small shops of Milan and Turin. Known as 'proletarian youth circles', these precursors of today's social centres attempted to coordinate disputes in different firms, whilst also engaging in new forms of self-reduction such as the mass gatecrashing of cinemas, concerts and other cultural activities (Comitati Autonomi Operai 1976: 361–5; Balestrini 1989).

Moving beyond the workplace, the paper kept a watchful eye upon the 'organised unemployed' movement of Naples. Combining direct action and lobbying in a city synonymous with both squalid living and government by patronage, the Neapolitan movement quickly mobilised thousands of unemployed workers, becoming the region's central reference point for militant activity (Comitati Autonomi Operai 1976: 156–8). Elsewhere, the burgeoning women's movement began to move from the problem of divorce, over which it brought down the national government in 1974, to challenge all aspects of social domination. Like the unemployed, the feminists were also seen by *Rosso* as an integral component of the new social subject, and the journal now began to speak of the emergence of 'a new female proletariat' (*Rosso* 1976a; 1976b). Finally, the continuing practice of self-reduction, and in particular the increasing instances of organised looting, was seen by Negri's organisation as one of the red threads which tied these layers into a unifying process of recomposition (Comitati Autonomi Operai 1976: 246–9).

All these struggles, Negri argued, sought to fulfil the needs of their protagonists outside the logic of capitalist social relations. Since needs are by nature historically determinate, he reasoned, those of the *operaio sociale* could only be constituted within the universe of capital. Not surprisingly, here his reading again bore the mark of the *Grundrisse*. Only one use-value could possibly break the vicious circle of capital's reproduction: living labour. This, the former's very life-blood, could subvert the class relation when it became refusal of labour, creativity directed towards the reproduction of the proletariat as antagonistic subject. What was urgently required, therefore, was the substitution of the existing system of needs with a '*system of struggles*', the promotion of which remained the chief justification for a revolutionary party (Negri 1976b: 44–6). Again, like the *Grundrisse*, Negri insisted on couching this discussion in terms of the dialectic between productive forces and relations of production. At the very moment when 'the old contradiction' seemed to have subsided, and living labour subsumed to capital,

> the entire force of insubordination coagulates in that final front which is the antagonistic and general permanence of social labour. From here the productive force – the only productive force that is social living labour – opposes itself as struggle to the 'relations of production' and to the 'productive forces' incorporated in the latter. (ibid.: 44–5)

In this manner, Marx's traditional formula could now be recast as the direct antagonism between proletarians and state.

If here *Proletari e Stato* simply gave a characteristically 'Negrian' twist to Marx's schema, elsewhere the essay subverted one of the central workerist categories of old – the wage. Long the privileged moment of class recomposition, now Negri criticised the official labour movement for understanding class relations only within such terms. For a whole period, he argued, the wage in the immediate process of production and appropriation in the social sphere had marched separately but struck together. Today, however, the former tended to become the latter, as the working class sought the 'direct reappropriation of the productive forces' (Negri 1976b: 51). Indeed, for Negri, direct reappropriation was no longer 'a vague appendix to the communist programme but its essence'. Once the wage struggle had subordinated all others to its logic; now it retained meaning only as part of a society-wide attack on the state. To the struggle over division between necessary and surplus labour had been added the struggle to reduce necessary labour itself, as the proletariat strove to accelerate capital's tendency and so hasten the fall of the economy's tyrannical reign (ibid.: 47–8).

According to *Proletari e Stato*, the hypothesis of the *operaio sociale* stood or fell with its practical veracity (Negri 1976b: 9). To what extent, then, did its account of a massive process of recomposition – a qualitative leap in class unity – actually tally with the Italian experience of the time? In the pamphlet itself, Negri would offer only the briefest of discussions of the problem of 'marginal disarticulation', by which he meant the idiosyncrasies associated with new socially 'marginalised' layers. Even here, the needs of subjects such as women and the unemployed appeared to possess a political significance only to the extent that they could not be reduced to 'the demand for wage labour' (ibid.: 64). Certainly, it is not at all difficult to point to the temporal continuity of struggle linking the mass worker of the Hot Autumn to the new social subjects of the mid-1970s. It is much harder, however, to uncover traces of that concrete unification between sectors upon which Negri's whole argument rested. For the most part, instead, such potentiality was to remain sadly unfulfilled, with the front of fiercest industrial struggle – that of the small factories of the North – finding itself almost hermetically sealed from other sectors of the class. Later, in 1977, a case could be made for the role of the university as one such moment of aggregation. In 1975–76, by contrast, only the practice of self-reduction – especially that advanced by the 'proletarian youth circles' – was able to provide some linkage between the increasingly variegated layers of the Italian working class. To add insult to injury, many of the youth circles, like the swirling array of local, non-aligned 'diffuse' collectives with which they partially overlapped, continued to regard the micro-factions of 'organised' autonomists with considerable wariness (Farnetti and Moroni 1984; Moroni 1994).

The most dramatic and significant divides of the period served both to mark off the workers of the large Northern factories from the rest of the subjects grouped within Negri's class figure, and to force a widening fissure within the mass worker itself. After half a decade of struggle, the chief protagonists of the Hot Autumn now found themselves at best in the limbo world of a 'productive truce' within the factory, at worst engaged in industrial disputes both defensive in tone and subordinate to the institutional ambitions of the official labour movement. Due chiefly to their ability to guarantee the rigidity of labour-power in an increasingly centralised contractual arena, the union confederations had succeeded after 1973 in winning the support of the great majority of factory councils, bureaucratising them in the process. In practice this had meant two things. First, there was the resumption, in a new guise, of the traditional union discourse of a qualification-based pay hierarchy amongst workers which pushed hard against the egalitarian spirit of recent years. Second, there was an explicit union commitment to tailor labour's demands to the requirements of accumulation (Graziosi 1976; Regini 1980). With the centre–left of the 1960s supplanted by increasingly authoritarian governments, and conscious of the Chilean experience, the PCI leadership now committed itself to the path of a 'Historic Compromise' with the ruling Christian Democrats. Following the party's successes in the 1975 regional elections, this goal seemed to be one step closer to fruition. Even as it utilised the CGIL to rebuild a workplace presence lost in preceding years, such political ambitions only strengthened the Communist Party's traditional hostility to what it deemed 'corporatist' struggles against the necessary restructuring of the economy (Redazione romana di Rosso 1976; Hellman 1980).

On the industrial front itself, there were signs that many employers, far from being cowed by the struggles of the mass worker, had only intensified their quest to subdue the 'labour factor'. At FIAT, for example, management had begun an elaborate war of manoeuvre aimed at undermining the power over production which workers had acquired in the struggles of the Hot Autumn. Making use of the national layoff fund of the Cassa Integrazione to reorganise the whole cycle of production, management wound down output in some shops, while pushing ahead in others through extensive use of overtime. At the same time, more and more components were assigned to smaller plants within the conglomerate, including those recently established outside Italy. Such a disarticulation of the production cycle sharply eroded that capacity for disruption and communication which in previous years the more militant shops within Mirafiori had used to their advantage, while simultaneously allowing management to experiment with new production processes based upon robotics. With natural wastage and sackings for absenteeism combining to cut the total FIAT workforce by 13 per cent in the two years up to September 1975, more and more FIAT employees were forced by mounting inflation to turn to moonlighting, a practice which further blocked the transmission of militancy. As if all this was not enough, in July 1975 FIAT management was to win union agreement on its right to control mobility within the firm, a victory which provoked a spree of transfers between its various plants, and further reduced the rigidity of employees (*Collegamenti* 1978). As Marco Revelli would later indicate:

> This was a period in which FIAT was used by the employers more as a means for the enlarged reproduction of political mediation (and social consensus) rather than as a means of production of commodities, and it was clear that the union was able to survive, as a shadow, a fetishistic form of a hypostasised 'workers' power'. But it was also clear that, as the class composition which had made the material and social base of that model of the union broke up, so the moment was approaching in which the boss aimed to settle a few accounts. (Revelli 1982: 99)

Whatever other problems they faced, the core of the mass worker formed at FIAT still remained sufficiently strong in those years to retain their jobs. Manufacturing workers elsewhere, however, were not to be so secure. In Lombardy, for example, hundreds of firms now began to decentralise and rationalise their production processes. The most emblematic case – that of the British Leyland-owned Innocenti plant – also offers some insight into the divisions which then ran through the body of the industrial working class. The first round of troubles at Innocenti had opened in April 1975, with management introducing Cassa Integrazione for some workers, and speed-ups for the rest. The situation worsened at the end of August, when employees found themselves facing the prospect of redundancies for a third of their number and permanently increased worktime and production rhythms for those left behind. The most intransigent opposition to these attacks was to come from a small number of militants who, having distanced themselves from the groups of the far left, had formed a rank-and-file body possessed of a certain following in key shops within the plant. Faced with a hostile majority on the PCI-dominated factory council, increasingly outmanoeuvred as the struggle shifted from the shopfloor to the terrain of negotiations between union and company, the Coordinamento Operaio Innocenti soon found itself, in the words of one former member, 'in the eye of the cyclone'. Matters came to a head at the end of October, as PCI and CGIL stewards clashed with members of the group and their supporters. The following day six of its members were sacked, effectively destroying the Coordinamento as a force within the plant, and with it the possibility of a struggle unencumbered by the historic left's commitment to the 'management' of the nation's economic difficulties (*Primo Maggio* 1976b).

Hailed in certain circles as the new programme of Autonomia, *Proletari e Stato* would receive a stormy reception from others for its disinterest in such setbacks for the mass worker. If some of Negri's erstwhile opponents within the Area now embraced many of its precepts as their own, the pamphlet was to bring little pleasure to those of his longstanding associates who had remained apart from the 'organised' wing of Autonomia. Particularly disappointed was Sergio Bologna, who had continued to collaborate with Negri in a number of research projects. With *Proletari e Stato*, Bologna argued, Negri had grasped some of the 'objective mechanisms of political composition' present in Italian society, only to neglect completely the no-less substantial tendencies running counter to them:

> How many workers, how many factories have found themselves in the past two years faced with the problem of closure, and how many struggles have been burnt out in the alternatives between defence of the wage independent from the exchange of labour-power, and production cooperatives? Between guaranteed wage and self-management, closure of the factory or acceptance of restructuring?

In such circumstances, the revolutionary left has either not known how to offer other alternatives or, in the best cases, has limited itself to saying that the problem was wrongly posed and as such should be rejected. At its most coherent, the revolutionary left has said that the destruction of the worker as labour-power was a good thing that could only aid the recruitment and selection of the vanguard. There have been many small (or big) battles, but in their course the political composition of the class has changed substantially in the factories, and certainly not in the direction indicated by Negri. Not only that: what has taken place is the opposite of that greater unity of which he talks. Rather, a deeper division has occurred: not between factory and society, but within the factory itself, between the working-class right and left. In sum there has been a reassertion of reformist hegemony over the factories, one that is brutal and relentless in its efforts to dismember the class left and expel it from the factory. (Bologna 1976a: 27, translation based partly on Lumley 1980: 132)

Rather than come to grips with such disarray and confusion, Bologna complained, Negri had preferred to ply the traditional trade of the theorist in possession of some grand synthesis. Indeed, in choosing to invent 'a different social figure with which to impute the process of liberation from exploitation', Negri had simply washed his hands of the mass workers' recent difficulties, along with his own organisation's failure to make any headway within it. Far from being at the beginning of a new era, Bologna concluded,

[w]e are not at year one, we are not back at the reawakening of the 'new left' of the 1960s: we are not even at the redefinition of a social figure different to the mass worker. Even if it were true that the relation between *operaio sociale* and party is different, that civil society no longer exists, that the theory of consciousness has also changed, why continue to exercise the consummate craft of theoretician and ideologue? The form of political discourse is obsolete, the millenarian language is just a 'ballbreaker', and this form of theory deserves to be negated like every other 'general theory' ... let us conclude by saying that on this ground debate is no longer possible, it's boring. Better find new ground. Certainly, '*great is the disorder under the sun*, the situation is therefore excellent'. (Bologna 1976a: 28, translation based partly on Lumley 1980: 133)

Equally scathing in its critique was the Roman wing of Autonomia. After a year of participating in the production of *Rosso*, the Comitati

Autonomi Operai had finally had enough by late 1976. Agreeing with Bologna that Negri's abandonment of the sphere of direct production as the central terrain of class struggle could have only disastrous consequences, the Romans believed that such differences were underlaid by a deeper one of method. Complaining that the contribution of Negri's circle to Autonomia's analysis of class composition was characterised increasingly by assertions 'as emphatic as they are unconvincing', they acknowledged that

> [y]our interest for the 'emergent strata' (proletarian youth, feminists, homosexuals) and for new, and reconceptualised, political subjects (the *'operaio sociale'*) has always been and is still shared by us. But precisely the undeniable political importance of these phenomena demands extreme analytical rigour, great investigative caution, a strongly empirical approach (facts, data, observations and still more observations, data, facts) ... (*Rivolta di classe* 1976: 136)

Turning his back upon such counsel, Negri would henceforth devote the greater part of his energies to the development of a new 'mode of enquiry' adequate to the socialised worker.

NEGRI BEYOND MARX

In the late 1960s Negri, like other workerists of the time, had run the risk of subsuming the specificity of different working-class strata to those of the mass worker. His work in the second half of the 1970s, on the other hand, threatened to dissolve even this partially concrete understanding of class into a generic proletariat. As debate around the *operaio sociale* unfolded, the indeterminate nature of Negri's abstraction would become increasingly clear. Perhaps the gentlest critic would be Alquati (n.d.: 90–1), for whom the *operaio sociale* remained a 'suggestive' category; but even he, however, warned against the danger of constructing an ideology around a class figure which had yet to appear as a mature political subject. For Roberto Battaggia (1981: 75), writing in the pages *of Primo Maggio*, Negri's new subject was a category derived only by analogy from the mass worker, lacking as it did the latter's central characteristic: namely, a close bond between 'material conditions of exploitation' and 'political behaviours'. In reality, therefore, as a pot-pourri of different subjects 'with completely autonomous motivations', the notion of a socialised worker was of limited heuristic value. Such a line of reasoning would be pressed home by Vittorio Dini (1978: 5, 7), who considered the manner in which Negri had drained his conceptual apparatus of its content to be particularly damning. Earlier, Negri had indicated the historically determinate nature of this category; now, by deeming all moments of the circulation process as productive of value, he was to resolve workerism's longstanding tension around the factory–society relationship by theoretical sleight of hand. Similarly, the delineation of a new class figure, a project that required considerable care and time, had been accomplished simply by collapsing tendency into actuality.

Another disappointing aspect of Negri's new analysis of class composition was that part of it dealing with the PCI. Emphasising the frequently punitive nature of the Communist party's efforts to win the battle for hearts and minds within the workplace, Negri seemed unaware that this was only part of the picture. In particular, he overlooked what Lapo Berti (1976: 8) was to call the growing disjuncture between the 'behaviours of struggle and the "political" attitudes' of many workers formed in the Hot Autumn. In other words, the gulf between the continued practical critique of the organisation of labour evident in many factories, and working-class support for a party leadership which saw the existing relations of production as in the natural order of things. Insistent, instead, that the reformist project lacked any material basis in a time of capitalist crisis, Negri (1977b: 110, 117) was satisfied to paint the relationship between workers and PCI as one of pure repression, or else hint darkly at the parasitic nature of the workforce in the large factories. Closer to the truth stood one of the contributions to the June 1976 special edition of *Rosso* (1976c) devoted to the PCI. This elaborated upon the Communist intellectual Badaloni's portrayal of his party as the representation of one facet of working-class existence, that of the 'organised commodity' labour-power prepared to accept its subordinate place in society. Even here, as the Comitati Autonomi Operai were to point out, only their contributions to the same issue had advanced any practical discussion of Communist policy and its implementation, particularly in that sector where the PCI already operated as a governing party – the municipal administration of some of Italy's major cities (Rivolta di classe 1976: 137).

Thus, despite the growing intricacy of Italian working-class politics in the late 1970s, the simplification of Negri's schema was to proceed apace. While he continued to reject traditional Marxist conceptions of crisis, Negri's own framework became no less catastrophic. '*The balance of power has been reversed*', he wrote in a 1977 pamphlet which went on to become a bestseller:

[T]he working class, its sabotage, are the stronger power – above all, the only source of rationality and value. From now on it becomes impossible, even in theory, to forget this paradox produced by the struggles: the more the form of domination perfects itself, the more empty it becomes; the more the working class refusal grows, the more it is full of rationality and value ... We are here; we are uncrushable; and we are in the majority. (Negri 1977b: 118, 137)

There was much to commend in Negri's subjectivist reading of Marx. These ranged from his denunciation of the state capitalism found in the Eastern bloc and his search for a new measure of production beyond that of value, to his clear depiction of the revolutionary process as one based upon the pluralism of mass organs of proletarian self-rule. As a consequence of such triumphalism, however, these features of his work would be crippled. Devoid of the contradictory determinations of Italian reality, the promising notion – again fleshed out from Alquati (1976: 40–1) – of a working class 'self-valorising' its own needs within and against the capital relation lost all substance. None of this is to deny the suggestive aspects of Negri's work. Unfortunately, these were again and again overridden by a framework that depicted class struggle as the mortal combat of two Titans (Boismenu 1980: 192). Despite, too, Negri's acceptance of the notion of difference as a positive attribute within movements of social change, his conception of the *operaio sociale* continued to filter out all the specific and contradictory discriminants within it, leaving only their common attribute as embodiments of abstract labour. Since the latter in turn held meaning only as a form of pure command, Negri's understanding of the problem of political recomposition came to be overdetermined by a stress upon violence. This emphasis, as the practice of much of Autonomia now showed, would prove no less impoverished – if profoundly different in culture and form – than that of the Brigate Rosse (Negri 1977b: 134).

One might reasonably suppose that to an outlook so infused with triumphalism, the relative ease with which Autonomia was to be crushed by the mass arrests of 1979–80 could only come as an immense shock. Rather than restoring a note of caution to Negri's thought, however, the Area's political defeat would serve simply to exacerbate the flattening out of his conceptual framework. Breaking in 1981 with the dominant group within the Autonomia of North-Eastern Italy, Negri (1981b: 8) would accuse its exponents of holding fast to 'a Bolshevik model of organisation outside time and space'. This was linked to their embrace of a class subject – the mass worker – that was, 'if not anachronistic, at the very least partial and corporative'. In doing so, he argued, they had chosen to ignore 'a new political generation (not only children) which situates itself in the great struggles for community, for peace, for a new way of being happy. A generation *without* memory and therefore *more* revolutionary'. This line of argument had been developed more fully earlier that year in the pages of the journal *Metropoli*, where Negri had insisted that memory could only be understood as an integral moment in the logic of capitalist domination:

> [T]he class composition of the contemporary metropolitan subject *has no memory because it has no work*, because it does not want commanded labour, dialectical labour. It has no memory because only labour can construct for the proletariat a relation with past history. It has no dialectic because only memory and labour constitute the dialectic ... proletarian memory is only the memory of past estrangement ... The existing memory of 1968 and of the decade that followed it is now only that of the gravedigger ... the youths of Zurich, the Neapolitan proletarians and the workers of Gdansk have no need of memory ... Communist transition is absence of memory. (Negri 1981a: 50–1, 52, 53)

'Your memory', Negri (1981b: 8) had accused his former comrades, 'has become your prison'. In his own case, however, this embrace of an eternal present simply meant the abnegation of past responsibilities. Surveying the defeat of the workerist tendency that same year – a defeat that had left Negri and thousands of other activists falsely imprisoned as 'terrorists' – Sergio Bologna would recognise the nature of this problem clearly:

> I have a sense of both fear and repugnance when I see comrades who hate their past or, worse still, who mystify it. I'm not denying my past, for example my workerist past; on the contrary, I claim it. If we toss everything away, we live in a condition of permanent schizophrenia. (Bologna 1981: 17)

Tracing Negri's passage to this dismal point beyond both *operaismo* and Marxism is a depressing task. Behind the evident haste that has characterised much of his work (Leonetti 1979: 4), there lies what Negri himself would later concede as

> this damning pretence, that runs through all our writings; it is the language of the Marxist tradition, but it carries a residue of simulation that creates a distorted redundancy. (Quoted in Portelli 1985: 12)

Such an aberration stemmed from that peculiar mode of thinking which Negri had inherited from the father of Italian workerism, Mario

Tronti, and honed to perfection, a mode of thinking which took its starting point from real social processes only to rapidly turn in upon itself. Seeking for his part to avoid such a fate, Marx had abandoned the dazzling heights of conceptual flight displayed in the *Grundrisse* for the sombre, but historically specific, passages of *Capital*. Unconvinced by such a choice, Negri might have done worse than to heed the advice of Tronti (1971: 16) himself, who had once warned that 'A discourse which grows upon itself carries the mortal danger of verifying itself always and only through the successive passages of its own formal logic.'

8

The Historiography
of the Mass Worker

We, with our 'Americanism', with our metropolitan ideology, with the two great 'locations' set at the centre of our historical memory, of our theoretical and ideological identity: the class struggles of the American proletariat, and the gigantic and tragic German communist movement of 1918 to 1932. (Scalzone 1981: 9)

Workerism in the years before the Hot Autumn had secured only a minor foothold within Italian left historiography. The dominant school in the immediate postwar period was that associated with the Communist Party, which saw the purpose of history as tracing the development of the institutions of civil society. Gramsci himself had recognised in the *Prison Notebooks* that 'the history of a party can only be the history of a determinate social group' (quoted in Bermani 1975: 37). Despite this, the majority of his followers waged a fierce polemic in the early 1950s against those whose interest in working-class and popular culture led them beyond the institutions of the labour movement, there to explore both dissident political experiences and the daily life of workers and peasants (Bermani and Bologna 1977: 21–4). Indeed, even the best of Communist historiography, such as Paolo Spriano's chronicle of the PCI's development – a work whose sense of balance was at that time unique amongst party histories – continued to advance this focus upon the internal dynamic of the organisation's leadership. Here, as Mariuccia Salvati (1980: 8) has justly noted, 'Whatever fell outside the party, fell outside history, and vice versa.' Given the similarly narrow optic of historiography in the universities, the few intellectuals committed to the pursuit of a properly social history were forced literally to be autodidacts, particularly in economic matters (Bologna 1981: 10).

By the beginning of the 1960s, however, the introduction to Italy of the work of the foreign Communists Eric Hobsbawm and Jurgen Kuczynski did much to legitimise the notion of a history of working people. In a similar fashion, the incursion of American sociology and modernisation theory prompted a reconsideration of economic history (Pitassio 1976).

The first of the new Communist studies was that of Giuliano Procacci (1962, 1970), which examined the class composition of Italian workers at the turn of the century. Far from evoking sympathy within *operaismo*, however, this and similar studies would be dismissed by the tendency as proof of the PCI's refusal to confront the most pressing contemporary questions, beginning with the state of working-class organisation at FIAT (Alquati 1975: 310; Bermani and Bologna 1977: 32). For its part, workerism's earliest historical forays were largely schematic, their chief purpose being to set out 'new "interpretative frameworks"' capable of surpassing existing left historiography (Bologna 1964: 27).

In a series of short review essays published in late 1963 and early 1964, Sergio Bologna was to explore the significance of fascism from the working-class point of view. Despite the specific contexts within which they had arisen, the German and Italian interwar experiences both touched upon matters of current relevance. That of Nazism, for example, presented the problem of working-class passivity *in extremis*, revealing at the heart of the fascist rise to power the violent subordination of labour-power to production, along with the disposition of all available means to the pursuit of accumulation (Bologna 1963a: 19). In Germany the institutions of the old labour movement had either been destroyed or integrated into new Nazi organisations in 1933, as re-armament protected by autarchy made possible industry's full utilisation of productive capacity. During the war itself, the use of foreigners as slave labour filling the bottom rungs of the production process had destroyed the last remnants of class solidarity, the 'primary condition for the existence of the working class as a political class' (Bologna 1963b: 62). It was precisely under the regimes of Mussolini and Hitler, moreover, wherein the bonds between labour and its erstwhile representatives were violently sundered, that the reduction of working-class history to that of party and union bureaucracies appeared 'truly grotesque' (Bologna 1964: 28). Later, as Bologna (1981: 12) would acknowledge, the critical reading of official records by radical historians would help to reconstruct the many instances of resistance to the workplace regime imposed by the Nazis. In the process, their efforts would also make plain what Timothy Mason (1979) once called the fundamental divide between the political resistance of the German left, and working-class opposition in the factory and labour market.

As to the Italian case, Bologna was chiefly concerned in the early 1960s to challenge the prevalent leftist view of fascism as the product of Italy's social and political backwardness. As the liberal economist Rosario Romeo's recent work had shown *contra* Gramsci, the absence of agrarian reform had in no way impeded the advance of Italian capitalism. While Gramsci's line of argument had been tenable in his own time, Bologna (1963b: 63) believed that it had since been confuted by the impetuous development of Italy's economic 'miracle', which had encouraged a growing economic and political unity within the hostile camps of capital and labour. Thus, despite his weaknesses, Romeo had to be acknowledged as the only Italian historian currently capable of

> undertaking economic research, simply because his work possessed the undoubted merit of having returned historical discussion to the proper terrain, because it refuses the level of so-called superstructures, of perceiving history only through political institutions. (Bologna 1963b: 64; 1964: 28)

'Some hypotheses of Marxist research on contemporary history', which appeared in the third number of *Quaderni Rossi*, made explicit the alternative vantage point from which workerism chose to survey the question. The essay pushed very hard against Communist historiography, and in particular its understanding of fascism, taking instead as its starting point the recent wave of industrialisation. This, argued its authors Umberto Coldagelli and Gaspare De Caro,

> objectively poses class relations at the purest and most mature level of their antagonism ... the science of this present indicates the general direction of development itself, and explains the causes of deviations, oppositions and delays to it. In other words, [from this standpoint] history becomes a biography of the collective capitalist in its incessant struggle with the individual capitalist and in its struggle with the working class. (Coldagelli and De Caro n.d.: 104)

Like Bologna, the essay presented fascism as 'the political expression of a determinate level of development', a response to 'objectively revolutionary' conditions in which Italy found itself after the First World War (ibid.: 106, 107). Conceiving of fascism as a peculiarly modern reply to this stalemate, Coldagelli and De Caro were also harsh in their assessment of the eventual formula with which the Communist movement had chosen to meet it. To their minds, the Popular Front was a convergence of interests between those committed to defending the Soviet bureaucracy, and sections of Western capital concerned with political and economic reform. Yet, while such a critique evoked those advanced both by contemporary dissident leftists like Fortini (n.d.; 1974) and the traditional Communist heresies, it was not to be expanded at any length by Coldagelli and De Caro (n.d.: 107–8). Similarly, their analysis of fascism as a political form of capitalist domination, which was to be developed with rigour a decade later by Marco Revelli (1975), was depicted here simplistically as corresponding 'perfectly' to the needs of capital (Coldagelli and De Caro n.d.: 107).

Instead, in another brief essay devoted to the *biennio rosso*, De Caro (1964) turned his gaze to the Turin factory councils of 1920, which 'Some hypotheses' had defined as 'the only initiative responding to the necessity of a revolutionary rupture at this determinate level of capitalist development' (ibid.: 106). Polemicising with Spriano's study of the period, De Caro located the importance of the councils not in their efforts to defend the interests of labour-power within capital more capably than the unions, but in their reference to a project of political power. Thus, if Gramsci had considered the councils as organs that accepted and took root in the existing organisation of labour, they could not simply be dismissed, as Bordiga had believed, with the charge of reformism. Rather, their true significance – precisely because they anticipated a more advanced form of capitalism based upon co-management – lay in their ability to block the state's efforts to assert a greater role in economic life. That they ultimately failed in this enterprise, De Caro believed, was primarily the fault of the historic left parties, which had been unable to arm workers with an adequate form of political organisation.

TRONTI IN DEUTSCHLAND

The implications of De Caro's arguments were to be spelt out more fully three years later, in what has become the piece of workerist historiography best known to the English-speaking left. 'Class Composition and the Theory of the Party at the Origins of the Workers-Council Movement', Bologna's contribution to *operaismo*'s 1967 conference on the interwar period, is a piece wide-ranging in scope. Its domain stretched from the international cycles of class struggle of 1900–20 to encompass such questions as the nature of Fordism, the specificity of the Industrial Workers of the World (IWW) in the prewar US, and debates in the Second International concerning spontaneity and organisation. Its central aim, however, was to make sense of the class composition of the German *Rätebewegung*, the failure of which had sealed the fate both of the Bolsheviks and the postwar world revolution. In Bologna's (1972: 25) view, the distinguishing feature of the councils lay in the political weight within them of skilled workers, particularly those of the machine industry. Deemed indispensable by management, such workers exercised a considerable degree of control over the labour process. Conceived as the self-management of the existing mode of production, their practice of working-class autonomy ultimately ran aground due to the lack of any project to confront the obstacles posed by the existing state, seeking at most to democratise and renovate it in a socialist sense. In this respect, the essay was also part of the ongoing workerist polemic against contemporary arguments which grounded revolutionary politics in a productivist ethic:

> The concept of workers' self-management could not have had such a wide appeal in the German workers-council movement without the presence of a labour force inextricably linked to the technology of the working process with high professional values and naturally inclined to stress their function as 'producers'. The concept of self-management pictured the worker as an autonomous producer, and the factory's labour-power as self-sufficient ... This relation between occupational structures and determining political-ideological attitudes is well-known. It has to be emphasised both because Germany provides the most substantial illustration, and as a reminder to those who love confused and inconclusive discussions of 'class consciousness', as if the latter were a spiritual or cultural fact. (ibid.: 5–6)

Following De Caro, Bologna was careful to avoid a critique which either dwelt upon the ideological shortcomings of self-management, or else dismissed it as something tainted with the odour of the labour aristocracy. That such a conception of socialism was a dead end in the age of the assembly line did not in any way detract from its political efficacy in the Europe of the early 1920s. After all, 'the revolutionary import of a movement must be calculated on the basis of the historically determined stage of development in a specific situation' (Bologna 1972: 12). True, this particular figure of the 'worker-inventor' was already in 1919 'objectively doomed to extinction' by Fordism (ibid.: 7). Given this, the political importance of the council movement lay above all – as a consequence both of its international significance and the rigidity of German industry – in its ability 'to provoke the crisis and to freeze capitalist development' (ibid.: 26).

Amongst other things, Bologna's essay was a useful illustration of classical workerism's habit of stressing the contents of radical struggles whilst reducing the question of their organisational form to a purely secondary matter. If such a stance indicated a legitimate wariness of those who made a fetish of workers' councils, it also did nothing to challenge the argument – common to proponents and detractors of the council-form alike – which equated the working-class practice of direct democracy with productivism. When one turns to examine the events of 1918–23, however, it becomes clear that this formulation is far from adequate. As Bologna (1968: 128–9) was to point out in another essay of the period, historiography has not been kind to the German revolution, preferring – whether through myopia or bad conscience – to leave it in the shadow of Weimar and the Russian October. Indeed, so widespread had this collective dismissal become that even so astute an observer and former participant as Paul Mattick (1968: 348) could look back upon it half a century later and see nothing but the 'dreary story' of 1918. Without doubt, the general thrust of the councils was simply towards their own extinction in favour of a National Assembly, whilst their most extreme limit lay in ambiguous attempts to combine councils and parliament. Yet, even if skilled workers such as Bologna had described had been the 'most typical' representatives of the movement, the experiences of the latter could hardly be said to exhaust those of the German working class as a whole in the five years which followed Wilhelm II's abdication.

When later he was to review the work's failings, Bologna (1974) would note the 'hasty and schematic' manner in which it sought to separate the epoch of the mass worker from that of its predecessor. Following the predominant historiography's preoccupation with the events of 1919, however, the most glaring oversight of 'Class Composition and the Theory of the Party' lay in its neglect of a whole series of struggles that ran counter to – and, in their political significance, went beyond – those of the *Rätebewegung*. Indeed, the absence of any discussion of the postwar struggles of the Ruhr miners was all the more strange given the essay's designation of this sector as the 'most advanced' in the class composition of prewar Germany (Bologna 1972: 9, 11).

The emergence after 1968 of a new generation of radical historians has done much to improve our understanding of the revolution in the Ruhr, and of the miners' existence generally (Geary 1980; Brüggemeier 1981). Even so, the major study by von Oertzen, from which Bologna was to draw so much of the ammunition for his 1967 argument about skilled workers, already contained a detailed discussion of the radical nature of working-class organisation in the Ruhr after the war. The only reasonable conclusion to draw from this, therefore, is that Bologna had been in such haste to make his basic point concerning the craftworkers of the *Räten* that he failed to register another class faction. Ironically, this was one within which the determinant weight of unskilled migrants indicated obvious parallels with the Italian mass worker of the 1960s (Baluschi 1981). Finally, if Bologna was correct in concluding that the real failure of the German Revolution lay in its inability to join class autonomy to a project of armed power, it was also the case that in 1920 the Ruhr had seen a unique attempt to address this question. There thousands of miners had first abandoned the old trade unions for new organisations modelled upon the industrial unionism of the IWW, and had then gone on to form Red Armies – replete with heavy artillery – to engage the Reichswehr and the Freikorps (Jones 1987: 176–83).

Criticising the workerists in the introduction to his massive study, *Proletariato di fabbrica e capitalismo industriale*, Stefano Merli argued that 'at least in the historiographical field', the tendency had offered

> a manichean history, with a working class without internal articulations, monolithic in its revolutionary fixity, and a 'bureaucracy' which, having never exercised hegemony, having never become the ruling group, was forced to satisfy itself with the manipulation [*strumentalizzazione*] of the masses. (Merli 1972: 11)

It was a harsh judgement, yet not far from the truth. While *operaismo* had provided some new perspectives for the interpretation of labour history, its work still remained marked by that simplistic and one-dimensional view of proletarian behaviour prevalent in the philosophical reflections of Tronti. This was particularly evident in the other workerist contributions to the 'Workers and State' conference, which had been even more prone than Bologna to represent the working class as a homogeneous entity. Indeed, it was very revealing that none of the contributions to this survey of the interwar period were to devote much attention to the experiences of either fascism or Stalinism, both of which had imposed massive defeats upon the working classes of Europe. Instead, the problem of decomposition, of the destruction of the class as political subject, had remained conspicuously absent from their discourse. Significantly, the strongest historical piece in the book – Ferruccio Gambino's (1976) careful reconstruction of the history of Ford workers' struggles in Britain – was written three years after the 1967 conference, and benefited both from its author's acuity and the changed circumstances which followed the Hot Autumn.

Interestingly, the most sustained piece of classical workerist historiography was not to be produced in Italy at all. Written largely by Karl-Heinz Roth, who had been prominent during the late 1960s within the German student movement, and first published in 1974, *The 'Other' Workers' Movement* offered an interpretation of German working-class history from that nation's unification a century before. Presenting the vicissitudes of a working-class movement ignored by party and union alike, the book provoked a considerable controversy within the German left upon its appearance, which would be further fuelled by Roth's own subsequent arrest in obscure circumstances the following year (*Primo Maggio* 1976a).

Unlike Bologna, who had seen the autonomy of the unskilled emerge only after the destruction of the skilled workers' centrality to production, Roth (1976: 36) placed great emphasis upon the formation – even before the First World War – of a new working class. This class was 'crude, homogeneous even as it was divided in the workplace by a refined hierarchy, but always ready to revolt'. Present in textiles, the ports and above all the mines (where Polish migrants played a fundamental role), this sector of the working class was separated from the craft workers who dominated the official labour movement by a profound gulf of behaviours and values (ibid.: 35). With the militarisation of labour during the war, dramatic transformations had taken place within the industrial workforce, weakening the influence of skilled workers in favour of the unskilled and unorganised. After the failure of the armed insurrections of 1920–23, both strata of the class again succumbed to the discipline of capital, which now sought to introduce productive techniques inspired by Ford so as to prevent the repetition of such outbursts. Given that for much of the Weimar regime both the Social Democrats and Communists looked primarily to skilled workers as their privileged reference point, the 'other' working-class movement came again to be abandoned to its own devices (ibid.: 49–56). Driven underground but never fully extinguished by the Nazis, as the pivotal chapter by Elisabeth Behrens sought to document, its struggles would resurface sporadically after 1945. With West Germany's use of immigrant labour – first from East Germany then increasingly from the Mediterranean – the gulf between the two components of the class had become starker than ever before. Written in the immediate aftermath of a strike wave that had swept through much of German industry during 1973, Roth's conclusion was quietly optimistic. Despite the currently spasmodic outbursts of confrontation, the 'multinational worker of mass production' would be pushed by growing repression in the factory to organise a new guerrilla war able to strike out from the workplace against 'the entire social machinery' (ibid.: 241).

While Roth was to polemicise at length with the specific reading of German events presented by Bologna in 1967, it was clear that his own method of enquiry was little different. For example, in depicting the decision in 1920 of the most intransigent wing of the German Communist Party to form a new political body – the KAPD – linked to militant workplace organisations, Roth would present the coherence of a small if significant minority of activists as the property of the unskilled as a whole (Roth 1976: 63). Further, this latter stratum was portrayed as a compact force, whose documented diversity of gender, age and nationality appeared to pose no great barriers to its internal unification. Nor, apart from a passing reference to the famous chemical workers of Leuna, did Roth seek to examine the condition of workers outside the factory, or what bearing this might have upon their behaviour (ibid.: 54–5).

In a brief review which dismissed *The 'Other' Workers' Movement* as 'confused to an unacceptable degree', Paul Mattick (1978: 88) also made plain his lack of interest in the problem of class composition. Instead, he offered his longstanding 'conjunctural' analysis of working-class subjectivity as a product of capitalist crisis (Meriggi 1978c: 11). A more pertinent savaging occurred at the hands of the historian Erhard Lucas (1978: 96), whose work on the failed German revolution had been much cited in Roth's study. What particularly offended Lucas about the book, beyond what he deemed its superficial use of sources, was that it used the category of mass worker not as a hypothesis to be tested, but rather as a 'machete' with which to hack a way through conventional historiography. Yet even as he documented a number of the errors and gaps in the work, Lucas would himself fail to confront Roth's central proposition concerning the relation between class behaviour and the technical structure of labour-power (Behrens et al. 1978: 109–10). More balanced was the assessment of Massimo Cacciari (1978: 41, 42), who argued in the pages of *Rinascita* that Roth's 'strongly reductive' approach and 'continual ideologisation' of the 'other' workers' movement did not obscure the book's strengths, in particular its account of the evolution of military-style repression in German factories. The most perceptive critique of Roth's study, however, was to come from Tillman Rexroth (1978: 33). As he pointed out both its method, which depended more upon a counter-reading of existing research than original excavation of its own, and its exclusive focus upon 'the male world of the factory, a male world even when women work within it', were characteristic of classical workerist historiography. In this sense, he concluded, *The 'Other' Workers' Movement* remained 'a book that describes alternative working-class history in a non-alternative way'.

TOWARDS A MILITANT HISTORY

A greater receptivity to the complexities of working-class politics was to come in the early 1970s with the establishment of the history journal *Primo Maggio*. Grouped around Sergio Bologna (1973a: 162), its editors were committed to the development of a new, militant history 'subordinate to struggle'. While their common past in Potere Operaio and Lotta Continua bestowed a distinctly workerist bent to their enquiry, the vanguardism and political intrigues of those organisations had left the editors acutely aware of the disjuncture between working-class autonomy and past attempts to organise it from without. According to *Primo Maggio*, 'autonomy is not only a permanent contradiction of the relations of production, but also a permanent contradiction in the construction of the party'. For this reason, it refused from the beginning to succumb to that 'unreal pretence of political organisation' which had so marred the judgement of *Classe Operaia* (Bologna 1976b: 29, 39). This, together with the collaboration of a number of young historians formed in Gianni Bosio's exploration of popular culture – an experience which had left them both committed to the use of oral sources, and sensitive to the complexities of working-class life – lent to this 'rational' workerist undertaking a sobriety at odds with Negri's triumphalism. While one early reflective piece by Bologna (1974: 5) denied that there was any 'necessary relationship between class composition and organisation, in the terms of a subordination of the political programme to class composition', the opposite argument would soon emerge as one of *Primo Maggio*'s most important contributions to workerist sensibilities.

Sympathetic to much of the radical history written in the US since the late 1960s, those involved in *Primo Maggio* were none the less sharply critical of historians whose work displayed the simplistic features earlier criticised by Merli. Writing in 1975, Peppino Ortoleva examined Jeremy Brecher's study *Strike!* (1980), which had drawn exclusively upon conventional sources such as written documents to reconstruct the relation between the institutions of the labour movement and the highpoints of working-class struggle. Brecher, he argued, betrayed an 'Enlightenment view of the historian's role' as one whose task was to restore in class memory a past scrubbed clean by capital. Against this, Ortoleva wrote approvingly of the efforts of Alice and Staughton Lynd (1981), who had started instead

from a quite different presupposition, which is constantly verified in the course of [their] investigation: the hegemony of capitalist culture, and its version of American history, does not translate into a *tabula rasa* of the 'collective memory' of the American working class. A store of working-class traditions remains, but it is the patrimony not of the American proletariat as a whole, but rather – disarticulated and sectionalised – of individual groups of workers, of rank-and-file union experiences etc. (Ortoleva 1975: 52)

As the workerists of *Primo Maggio* soon began to discover, class composition – contrary to Bologna's curt dismissal of 1967 – was indeed a cultural product. Drawing upon his work with Bosio, Cesare Bermani (1975: 48) insisted upon the 'non-homogeneous nature of culture within a class society'. Both inside and outside the workplace could be found the culture of those who were 'exploited but not submitted', within which memory served to filter, order and transmit experience. Used critically, oral testimony could throw light upon the internal workings of class subjectivity; for this to happen, however, the historian must also be a political militant, who as such had won 'the complete trust of the interviewee. History of and for the workers' and peasants' movement can only be a history written by a militant for militants.'

It was no longer possible, then, to see political composition as merely the result of an immediate and exclusive relation with the labour process. The best work of classical workerism had been made possible by the recognition of material divisions existing alongside that formal unity provided by the shared condition of wage labour: in Alquati's case back in the 1960s, the identification of a generation gap at FIAT. For Bologna, writing during the social 'earthquake' of 1977, political composition had come to mean

> not only the technical composition, the structure of labour-power, but also the sum and interweaving of the forms of culture and of behaviours of both the mass worker and all the strata subsumed to capital. The mass worker's peasant past, its links (or break) with the familial clan, its past as migrant worker in contact with the most advanced technologies and with the society of the most advanced command over labour-power, its past as political or union militant or its past as a member of a patriarchal Catholic clan: these attributes are all translated into the acquisitions of struggle, into political wisdom, the sum of subcultures which catalyse on contact with the massification of labour and with its inverse process of fragmentation and territorial dispersion. Machinery, the organisation of labour, transmute and bring to light these cultural pasts; mass subjectivity appropriates them and translates them into struggle, refusal of labour, organisation. Political class composition is above all the result, the end point of a historical process. But it is also, and in a dialectical manner, the starting point of a historical movement in which the labour subsumed to capital interprets the productive, social and political organisation of exploitation and overturns it into the organisation of its own autonomy. (Bologna 1977d: 62)

Thus, if in *Primo Maggio*'s understanding the factory continued to be 'the most important site of socialisation and strength', its notion of the workplace was considerably richer and more complex than that advanced by the workerism of the 1960s. Indeed, in introducing the journal's readers to one contemporary American account of factory life, Ortoleva (1976: 42) was to criticise its author for failing to see that 'the division and stratification of workers outside the factory also acts within it'.

Primo Maggio was also increasingly critical – if not always to the satisfaction of some of its younger associates (Scarinzi 1984: 67) – of that Leninism which Potere Operaio had expoused for most of its existence. In the years when Negri (1976a: 201–23) went out of his way to defend Lenin's polemic against 'infantile leftism', *Primo Maggio* would make clear for the first time the debt which *operaismo* owed to earlier proponents of class autonomy. Reflecting upon the vicissitudes of the Comintern, whose initial aim of creating 'a multinational instrument of command over the rhythms of world revolution' he still considered praiseworthy, Bologna (1975: 94) emphasised that at the beginning of their quest the Bolsheviks had turned to the various forces of left extremism, from the ultra-left of Germany and Holland to the revolutionary unionists of Britain and the US, as the privileged interlocutors of their project. Only when these currents spurned the Russian model of organisation did Lenin begin his offensive against them, which would be won at the cost of ignoring the specificities of class composition in Europe and North America. If the bulk of the Western working class for its part refused to abandon the traditional labour movement for the militant factory organisations advocated by syndicalists, industrial unionists and left communists, it also refused to follow the Communists upon putschist manoeuvres such as the March Action of 1921. As a result, the growing stress that the Zinoviev-led Comintern placed upon the party function led it to privilege relations with other parties and their social bases through the so-called United Front. This choice was made at the expense of relations with workers themselves, a problem that became confined to the fight for hegemony within the unions. This tactic had failed in turn, according to Bologna, because the Comintern had no sense of the wage struggle as anything but a defensive measure to maintain the most minimal level of subsistence in the epoch of capitalism's decline (ibid.: 92–3, 94).

Of all the competing factions of the early Communist movement, then, the clearest conception of both the need for independent organisation within the workplace, and the long term prospects of social change could be found amongst those advocates of class autonomy dubbed 'infantile leftists' by Lenin. As Bologna indicated, however, the left extremists of the IWW and the KAPD were themselves often sharply divided in their perspectives, and ultimately ineffectual in pursuit of their goals (Bologna

1975: 92). To avoid *Primo Maggio* simply becoming 'an anthology of "'marginalised" working-class movements', as Bologna wrote to Primo Moroni (quoted in Bermani and Cartosio 1984: 7), the recovery of such experiences had to be set firmly against the current dialectic between the working class, the labour movement and the state. Examining the past through the eyes of the present was no longer enough: the journal must also engage in the direct discussion of contemporary political problems.

MARX IN DETROIT

One of the most distinctive aspects of workerist historiography in the 1970s was to be its reconsideration of revolutionary unionism. The cavalier dismissal of syndicalism during the preceding decade was now commonly replaced by an appreciation of that 'patient daily' mass work (Sereni 1974: 27) practised by the less demagogic of Italy's own revolutionary syndicalists during the early years of the twentieth century (Antonioli and Bezza 1973). So too that of the Catalonian movement before the Second World War, which offered many parallels, in the opinion of Roberto Bordiga (1976), to the modern Italian situation. In both the textile and building industries, which were then central to Barcelona's economy, unskilled migrants had possessed a determinate weight, just as they did in the industrial triangle of the 1960s. Scattered across a multiplicity of small enterprises, such workers found a reference point in the syndicalists' territorial forms of organisation, much as their Italian counterparts had made use of the *case del popolo* in the years before Mussolini's rise to power. Constantly challenging the legitimacy of class relations in the labour process, the anarcho-syndicalist-led Confederacion Nacional del Trabajo (CNT) was to be illegal for much of its existence. One of its most important lessons had been the fight to hire unemployed workers through a reduction in working hours, a goal which had been pursued not for the sake of a work ethic, but rather to preserve unity in the sphere where labour could do most damage to capital. Yet the most interesting aspect of the Spanish experience, according to Bordiga, lay in the libertarian movement's efforts at insurrection. Whatever its self-image, he argued, the relations between the CNT and the Spanish anarchist groups of the FAI (Federación Anarquista Ibérica – the Iberian Anarchist Federation) represented 'one of the few examples of a genuine "party of autonomy"' alien to both councillist ideology and Leninism (Bordiga 1976: 82, 83). On the other hand, he continued, if a political body separate from the mass movement was needed to impose a 'break' upon the pattern of class struggle, it was also clear that 'the "premature insurrections" betrayed a fundamental extremism which impeded the anarchists' passage from a function of provocation and rupture of the movement to the tasks of the political recomposition of the Spanish proletariat'. Above all, the Iberian libertarian movement had lacked a 'modern theory of power', and was thus unable to surpass the crisis of insurrectionalist politics which followed the failed uprisings of 1934 (ibid.: 86).

Despite this curiosity about both the Italian and Spanish experiences, it was to be to the Industrial Workers of the World that workerist historians returned again and again. Such interest was part of a broader fascination with the American working class already evident in the mid-1960s, and which had been stimulated further by the growing social unrest which characterised the US as the decade progressed. A riddle to many European leftists, for whom its often bloody struggles and indifference to socialist politics spelt only a provincial backwardness, it was precisely this combination which made the American working class so appealing to *operaismo*. To some degree, this line of thought had been inspired by workerism's earlier contact with associates of C.L.R. James, such as George Rawick and James Boggs. At the 1967 conference 'Workers and State', Rawick (1972a: 53; 1972b: 137) had argued that the gains won during the New Deal period – 'when the American workers, in a direct clash, conquered the highest standard of living ever known by a working class' – were second in revolutionary significance only to the Russian proletariat's seizure of power in 1917. This view was echoed by Tronti (1972: 27): 'the American class-struggles are more serious than European ones', he wrote, 'in that they obtain more results with less ideology'. Where he went further than Rawick, however, was in asserting that this factor lent a clarity to class struggle in the US which was absent in its European counterpart:

The history of the European working class is literally submerged in the ideas of Marxist intellectuals. But the history of the American working class is still naked, without anyone having thought it out. The less critique of ideology needed, the easier it is to further scientific discoveries. The smaller the contribution of leftist culture, the more the class pregnancy of a given social reality comes forward. (ibid.: 56)

Yet naked or not, little was known of American labour historiography in the Italy of the early 1970s. Indeed, for those who did not read English only a few texts, critical or otherwise, were then available. One of *Primo Maggio*'s most important functions at the time, therefore, was to help in introducing the American experience to the left of its own country. In the journal's third issue, for example, Ortoleva (1974: 37) offered a survey of a variety of interpretations of American class relations, from Rawick and Daniel Guerin to the work of G.D.H. Cole. Stressing the 'commonly neglected dialectic between class struggle and the transformation of the state', Ortoleva's gaze, like that of many of his contemporaries in the American new left, focused upon the 'Progressive Era' at the turn of the century. This was a time when federal state involvement in industrial matters had first taken a systematic form. At the centre of this period, too, stood a unique experiment on the labour front: the revolutionary union movement popularly known as the 'Wobblies'.

Already in 'Class Composition and the Theory of the Party', Bologna (1972: 9) had praised the IWW as 'a class organization anticipating present forms of struggle'. The chance to explore a political tendency whose origins and development were 'completely independent from the traditions of both the Second and the Third Internationals' was forced to wait, however, until the failure of Potere Operaio's born-again Leninism. From the very first issue of *Primo Maggio* (Buonfino 1973; Cartosio 1973), it was clear just how much importance its editors placed upon the experience of the One Big Union. Then again, the workerist interest in the IWW is not difficult to explain. The most immediate point of attraction lay in the priority that the Wobblies had given to the organisation of the unskilled components of the American working class. From its foundation in 1905, the IWW had committed itself to organising the increasingly 'uniform mass of wage slaves' called to tend the factories of the Machine Age (IWW 1905: 7). Such workers were new to the American labour movement, then dominated by the craft unions of the American Federation of Labor, and often new to the continent itself. 'Before World War One', notes David Brody (1980: 15) 'close to 60 per cent of the industrial labor force was foreign born', condemned to those jobs with the poorest pay and conditions. In the North in particular, where industrial development was then concentrated, divisions between the skilled and unskilled largely followed those which separated unionised, native-born male workers from the predominantly European immigrants. Concerned to protect their power over the labour process from the encroachments of management, and imbued with a sense of superiority over the 'Hunkies', the majority of American skilled workers perceived the new levy of machine operators as a threat. Barred even from voting due to gender or nationality, immigrant workers for their part found themselves outside the formal political sphere no less than the world of organised labour. In a similar fashion, many of the Western rural labourers were likewise excluded from civil society through their mobility and lack of a recognisable craft. For both groups, the IWW offered a form of organisation which cut across trade lines, and an approach to industrial disputation which relied upon the direct action at work of 'the workers themselves, without the treacherous aid of labor misleaders or scheming politicians' (Justus Ebert, quoted in Kornbluh 1972: 35).

The second aspect of the IWW's attraction for *operaismo* lay with its attitude to the problems that faced workers from day to day. Certainly, many Wobblies saw strikes and action on the job as 'mere incidents in the class war ... tests of strength, periodic drills in the course of which the workers train themselves for concerted action' (Andre Tridon, quoted in Kornbluh 1972: 36). All the same, few dismissed the fight to improve wages, hours and conditions as inconsequential in themselves. For the IWW, the struggle between capital and labour at the point of production was by definition a political struggle, uniting the socially marginalised even as it attacked the rate of surplus value. As 'Big Bill' Haywood put it in 1911,

industrial unionism is the broadest possible interpretation of the working-class political power, because by organizing the workers industrially you at once enfranchise the women in the shops, you at once give the black men who are disenfranchised politically a voice in the operation of the industries; and the same would extend to every worker. (Haywood 1911: 50)

There was also an earthiness about the IWW's approach to working-class aims which struck a chord with workerism's own thematic of needs. Contempt for 'pie in the sky', whether of the religious or political variety, led to a number of splits between the Wobblies and more conventionally minded leftists, and fuelled a running ideological battle with the 'Starvation Army' and other evangelists (Hill n.d.: 133; 1913: 129). Behind the IWW's frequently repeated maxim that the new society must grow within the old there lay, not only a rather mechanistic conception of change, but also a sense that the materialism which drove contemporary America held a grain of rationality lost to those motivated by socialist or Christian asceticism. It was not a sign of corruption by the capitalist Mammon to fight 'bread and butter' struggles for more money and less work. The real problem, Haywood claimed, lay with a system which placed the machine – a potential source of collective freedom from toil – at the disposal of a minority committed to nothing more than their private gain (Bock 1976: 121). The Star of Bethlehem, another Wobbly propagandist once insisted, led 'only to Heaven, which nobody knows about. These are the three I.W.W. stars of education, organization, and emancipation. They lead to porkchops which everybody wants' (quoted in Kornbluh 1972: 71).

The most important workerist discussion of the Wobblies during the 1970s was again the work of a German historian. Published in Feltrinelli's 'Marxist Materials' column, it was flanked by contributions from two editors of the North American journal *Zerowork*, both similarly concerned with *The Formation of the Mass Worker in the United States 1898–1922* (Carpignano 1976; Ramirez 1976). The centrepiece of the volume, Gisela Bock's contribution focused upon the problem of the adequacy of the project and practice of the IWW – America's own 'other' workers' movement – to its working class in the first quarter of the century. Despite its title, however, the essay cannot be dismissed simply as a transposition of Roth's work on to the US of the Progressive Era. To begin with, the narrower timeframe of Bock's essay freed the text from some of the more sweeping generalisations that had characterised her compatriot's efforts, leaving the reader with a sense of the complex nature of the divisions running through the American workforce. Certainly for Bock (1976: 65–70), like Roth, the major fracture within the class was that between those organised in craft unions and the rest. Not only did the former wield considerable power by dint of their knowledge of production, they were also often successful in exercising control over the means of entry to their professions. If the craftworkers' oft-voiced fear that immigration threatened their jobs was sincere in its conviction, the reality of the time seems to tell another story. Rather, a dual labour market then acted in America to exclude the majority of wage labourers from sharing in the relative privilege won by their skilled brethren (ibid.: 68). Yet while the position of the individual craft worker was often secure, the continued predominance of their stratum as a whole was less certain, as industrial expansion increasingly took the form of mechanised production demanding only common labour. In the decade before the US entry into the First World War, the simplification and interchangeability of factory labour took impressive strides. In such circumstances it was often tempting to assume, as the IWW itself frequently did, a commonality of collective interest amongst workers which their situation 'objectively' promoted. Such a peccadillo, however, was firmly resisted by Bock. As she was well aware, ethnic and sexual divisions interlaced and further complicated distinctions of wage and industry within the unskilled and semi-skilled layers of the workforce:

[F]ar from immediately homogenising the class, the devaluation of skills and the expropriation of knowledge and skill over the labour process often reinforced the mechanisms of competition amongst the workers themselves. Then there were the welfare and profit-sharing programmes in the manufacturing industry which, together with the new hierarchies created by scientific management, often succeeded in melding the interests of the firm with those of the American and skilled section of the workers. This was capital's reply to the political risk of a tendential homogenisation of the class and of struggles. (ibid.: 107)

Second, Bock's treatment of the relation between organisation and class was more sophisticated than that of Roth's book. At no point in her account, for example, did the Wobblies appear as the logical-historical emanation of class autonomy that Roth made of the revolutionary *Unionen* and Red Armies of 1920. If anything, the protagonists of the struggles of 1909–14 were presented as the saviours of the IWW itself, restoring to it a sense of direction and purpose which the repression and factional brawls of its early years had all but destroyed (Bock 1976: 108). Paul Buhle (1973) and Serena Tait (1973), she argued, were right to emphasise the clarity with which some American exponents of industrial unionism perceived the vanguard anti-capitalist role of unskilled machine operators. None the less, Bock (1976: 107) also made plain the often mechanical manner in which the Wobblies expressed the relation between class organisation and industrial structure, with the first commonly seen as an unambiguous response and adaptation to the second. Nor, unlike Roth, did Bock's discussion of the collapse of the organisational forms of the 'other' workers' movement hinge solely upon the ferocity of state persecution; after all, the Red Scare which followed the war had also driven the nascent Communist movement underground, without however destroying it. As Bock was to indicate, an important part of the answer for the IWW's decline lay in its inability to grapple with the changes to working-class experience ushered in with the 1920s, especially the influx of women and African-American workers on to the labour market. Instead, the sympathy within certain Wobbly circles for technicians and Taylorist principles betrayed a growing detachment from the IWW's initial rejection of the capitalist organisation of labour (ibid.: 179–87).

The true novelty of Bock's work when compared to earlier workerist efforts, noted Tillman Rexroth (1978: 36–7), was its extension of the notion of class composition beyond the bounds of the factory. Drawing upon the ideas of Lotta Femminista, Bock had placed emphasis upon the contribution of the unpaid domestic labour of women to the reproduction of labour-power. While the links established in the essay between struggles and the vagaries of the business cycle were somewhat sketchy, she had broken with the prevalent mechanistic reading of the nexus between technical and political composition. In the process, she had discovered the identity of the mass worker to be above all one of a certain relation to labour and the wage, rather than the immediate reflection of a given sociological structure. Thus, unlike Roth,

> if G. Bock avoids the theory of recomposition in the sense of a mere series of manoeuvres to divide and rule ... she also avoids the danger of teleologising the theory of recomposition in the sense of the so-called mass worker thesis. Already the fact that the book begins with the period in which the passage from skilled to mass labour had already essentially occurred – that passage whose European variant continues even today to inflame passions – indicates that G. Bock does not intend by 'recomposition' the secular constitution of the mass worker. Rather she is interested in the more subtle differentiations within the model of class composition, without which all the contours of that theory collapse; she speaks of a 'permanent' or better 'periodic' restrat-ification of the class, and not of a unitary development verifying itself by degrees up to the arrival of massified labour. (Rexroth 1978: 32)

Reviewing Bock's essay in the winter 1977–78 issue of *Primo Maggio*, Bruno Cartosio (1978: 56) indicated the pertinence of the study in the fact that in the Wobblies' time, as in the Italy of the 1970s, there existed 'a phase of very strong political recomposition of the class which did not produce the party'. In this respect, Negri (1978: 62) had been quite right to consider the success of a Comintern-style party as 'impossible' in the US. Praising Bock's piece as 'perhaps the best' of the works on the IWW to appear so far in the Italian language, Cartosio also drew attention to what he saw as its occasional ideological distortions. One of the more striking of these was its use of Tronti's 'suggestive but void' notion of passivity as a form of 'organisation without organisation' to explain the relative quietude of the American industrial front during the 1920s. Struggles did continue in that decade, despite the effective curtailment of immigration after 1924; these, however, had been confined for the most part to technologically primitive industries such as mining and textiles. Here too, he argued, lessons could be derived for the present, given the tight relation which such efforts to resist restructur-ing illustrated between political behaviours and the organic composition of capital. Still, works such as Bock's were only the beginning of the workerist appraisal of labour history, an undertaking to which Cartosio (1978: 56) looked forward with some confidence.

Barely three years later, such quiet optimism would be shaken by the reverses – both political and theoretical – that *operaismo* had come to suffer. Now, *Primo Maggio* would see its role in quite a different light, as

the conservation of a thread, however tenuous, of proletarian memory in times in which the destruction of social identity seems to have assumed devastating dimensions, and the re-elaboration of categories of theoretical reflection, however partial and provisional, in a world in which, as never before, the left appears deprived of a cultural and ideal identity. (Revelli 1981a: 9–10)

9

The Collapse of Workerism

1977 was a decisive year for the Italian far left. Coming in the wake of its disappointing showing in the previous year's general elections, the tumult of a new wave of struggles by students scornful of the 'cadavers' of 1968 was a stark indication of the mounting discontent of politically minded youth with the *triplice* and its style of politics. Having long posed as the privileged interpreters of Italy's oppositional forces, the three major organisations to the left of the PCI now found themselves contaminated or even overtaken by a new politics which emphasised needs over duty, difference over homogeneity, the localised and personal over a class-wide struggle. Always the most sensitive to the moods of the broader movement, Lotta Continua was the first to enter into crisis, dissolving as a formal organisation in late 1976 under the hammer blows of its disgruntled and divided membership (Red Notes 1978). The PDUP fared little better: torn between its established role as the critical conscience of the Communist Party, and the possibilities for broader influence outside the sphere of the PCI, it painfully split in two (Garzia 1985). Even Avanguardia Operaia, traditionally the most staid member of the *triplice*, found its congress besieged by 'Metropolitan Indians' dressed in feather bonnets and war paint, and demanding a new approach to political activity (Libera 1977: 738).

1977 was also a decisive year for *operaismo*. The various organisations of Autonomia were able – for a brief time – to fill the vacuum created by the *triplice*'s crisis. None the less, the multitude of problems which the new political mood exemplified would push workerism's conceptual apparatus, in Negri's words (1979a: 147, 148), to its 'extreme limits': 'To speak still in the old terms, after the experience of 1977, is to be dead.' As has been seen, Negri's own efforts to delineate a new approach simply repeated the tendency's old errors in a different guise; within two years, his political project would lie shattered. For the editors of *Primo Maggio*, by contrast, the so-called 'Movement of '77' would inspire their most important internal debate, throwing into question once again the significance of the categories bound up with the thematic of class composition. Together, the incursion of new elements into the FIAT workforce, and the intensification of industrial conflict within

Italy's service and transport sectors, served to revitalise aspects of the journal's reflections. In the end, however, neither of these processes could ultimately prevent the collapse of those grand themes that the rational wing of workerism had long sought to preserve and enrich. The cycle of struggles that opened in 1977 would end badly: retrenchment, addiction, imprisonment, even suicide were not uncommon. In the aftermath of its defeat came the 1980s, 'the years of cynicism, opportunism, and fear' (Balestrini and Moroni 1988: 387). Yet as Bologna would come to argue, whatever the havoc it unleashed, 1977 had posed fundamental questions about political recomposition. And while no section of the Italian far left had been able to find practical answers to them at the time, none the less these were questions that all future revolutionaries would be obliged to address:

> [T]he movement of 1977 was not only a totally different way of conceiving of the relation between life and politics, but a series of contents and values that had never been placed on the agenda of the political project. Despite having apparently left a void in its wake, despite having apparently only laid bare the crisis of political forms, including the crisis of the party-form, 1977 has to be considered one of the greatest anticipations of the forms and contents of political and social life seen in recent years. After 1977 there is no turning back, despite all the errors committed, and for which many are still paying in an atrocious manner. 1977 was a year in which the wealth and complexity of problems was such that the political form able to contain and organise them all adequately could not be found. (Bologna 1980c: 28–9)

THE PIAZZA STATUTO OF THE *OPERAIO SOCIALE*?

On 3 February, the University of Rome was occupied by thousands of students protesting against both government proposals to restrict access to tertiary education, and the wounding of two students on campus by fascists the previous day. For a fortnight the university became a 'no-go area', within which flourished a lively political culture which rejected traditional leftist sensibilities in favour of themes championed by the likes of Milan's proletarian youth circles (Lumley 1990: 295–312). Yet if most preferred *risate rosse* ('red laughter') to the Brigate Rosse, the use of force was not alien to consistent sectors of the new movement. At times this took the form of mass looting as acts of illegality assumed epidemic proportions after 1976; at others it was a preparedness – hardly new in the Italian far left – to settle political differences by physical means. When the CGIL's leader Luciano Lama came to the university, determined to chide those within, he was to inspire the derision of Metropolitan Indians chanting that '*Nessuno L'ama*' ('No one loves him'). More than this, Lama's expedition also provoked a physical confrontation which saw members of the Comitati Autonomi Operai and others remove both him and his bodyguard of union functionaries from the campus. Later that afternoon, as riot police cleared the occupiers from the university in turn, 1000 PCI members, in the words of one account, 'stood outside and clapped and cheered' (Anonymous 1980: 101).

In early March the unrest resurfaced at the University of Bologna – in the heartland of Communist-dominated Emilia-Romagna – after a militant of Lotta Continua was killed there by police. Two days of rioting followed, spreading to the national level with a massive demonstration in the centre of Rome on 12 March. In the latter's aftermath, which had seen no less than ten police and two demonstrators wounded by gunfire, tension continued to run high. A policeman was shot dead at a Roman demonstration in late April, then in mid-May a young woman was killed by police during a rally held in the capital. Two days later another policeman was gunned down at a Milan demonstration, in what many saw as a revenge killing carried out by a fringe of the autonomist movement (Del Bello 1997: 316, 326–7). These events were sufficiently disturbing for the major components of Autonomia in Milan to issue a statement suggesting that the shift from what Marx once termed 'the weapons of critique' to 'the critique of weapons' must be predicated upon an intelligent appraisal of the relations of forces rather than 'desperation'. That said, rather more of the leaflet was devoted to a condemnation of those mainstream Leninist groups accused of choosing social democracy and the state over genuine revolutionaries; such 'adventurists' were reminded

> of what was written at the Putilov works during the Bolshevik revolution: 'There is only one place for traitors, and it is a few metres long!' (Castellano 1980: 161)

According to some members of the PCI, the unrest in Rome and the North could be attributed to sinister foreign forces determined to upset the implementation of the Historic Compromise (Cowan 1978). Less prone to paranoia, other Communists sought to locate their explanation of the new movement's emergence within the logic of Italy's social relations. Writing in the pages of *L'Unità* immediately after Lama's expulsion from the University of Rome, Asor Rosa (1977: 103) depicted Italy as a country of 'two societies'. One of these was based upon the organised working class, committed to the transformation of existing institutions, the other upon the nation's marginalised and unemployed, whose behaviour was symptomatic of the disintegration of the old order. From this perspective, the restlessness of Italy's most recent generation of students revealed them as practitioners of a new form of anti-Communism. Unlike the new left of 1968, he claimed, the rebels of 1977 dismissed as revisionist and counter-revolutionary not only the leadership of the historic left, but also their followers. Those who abolished the centrality of the (factory) working class, Asor Rosa would add in September,

> and conceive of capitalist society as a disintegrated and incoherent 'structure' of equally significant social forces, fail to understand that the working class and capital (conceived here not only in their pure state, as bookish abstractions) can still find a long phase of common interest *in development*, and that in this they are opposed by both privileged and non-privileged parasitic strata, the latter not seeing beyond the hard and desperate perception of their own needs. (Asor Rosa 1977: 63)

Talk of a new class composition with its point of gravity in the university inevitably raised the problem – abandoned by most workerists after the Hot Autumn – of the nature and function of intellectual labour-power. Here, as in a number of important discussions during the 1970s, the terms of debate had already been partly set by a former collaborator of *Classe Operaia*. Writing at the beginning of the decade, Massimo Paci (1973) had sought to explain the increasing rigidity of the industrial working class by postulating the development within Italy of three labour markets, based upon mutually exclusive groups. The first involved *lavoro operaio* within the larger, unionised firms; the second those employed within the smaller-scale, marginal economy; and finally, those who, as a result of the expanding urbanisation and mass education induced by Italy's 'miracle', were engaged in intellectual labour within both private and public employ. While Paci had refused to establish a political hierarchy within his model, others would be less cautious. Inverting the significance of Asor Rosa's dichotomy, one contributor to the Bologna journal *A/traverso* held that the often state-subsidised world of large-scale industry had become the dispenser of 'a sort of social welfare for unproductive workers'. This was in marked contrast to the workers employed in Italy's burgeoning non-guaranteed, underground economy, who were characterised as 'carriers of technical-scientific knowhow' (Alliez 1980: 119).

A similar emphasis upon the peculiar productive force of the subjects organised within the new movement, if not the parasitic nature of the mass worker, can be found in the work of Franco Piperno. Recently converted, like his friend Scalzone, to the *operaio sociale* thesis, Piperno depicted this class figure as the emanation of *lavoro non operaio*. By this he understood that indirectly productive labour which, while extraneous to the physical production of commodities, embodied the 'general intellect' of the workforce. Such a stratum, he believed, was the product both of capital's growing incorporation of science, and the refusal of thousands of young people to follow their parents into the world of the assembly line. In a softer version of Negri's hypothesis, Piperno presented the new subject as one that rejected the law of value as an adequate mediation of its needs and reproduction. In this sense, at least, Asor Rosa had been right: a fundamental divide in culture and politics did indeed exist in Italy, separating that part of the working class which still accepted the logic of commodity production from a 'movement of use-value' which challenged the social legitimacy of the money-form:

> [T]he counterposition between different segments of living labour is destined, at least in Italy, to accentuate itself, fuelling a clash which, to the extent that it involves millions of men [sic], can be regarded as a form, albeit subterranean, of civil war. (Piperno 1978a: 12)

More considered and sophisticated were the reflections of Alquati (n.d.: 13, 16) upon the formation of intellectual labour-power. 1977, as a '*second* rebellion of working students', had been a 'brutal surprise' for the labour movement in Turin. Then again, despite the volumes written on the problems of university and schooling since the 1960s, almost no one in the Italian left had been disposed to examine the condition of students themselves. The starting point of his analysis, which was consistent with the whole trajectory of *operaismo*, emphasised the tendential process of proletarianisation unfolding within modern capitalist society. In Italy, however, such a course was a relatively recent development, lending confusion to many appraisals of class location: 'only now do we have many proletarians who are children of proletarians; few, however, have proletarian grandparents' (ibid.: 23).

If intellectual labour was concentrated in sectors quite distinct to those inhabited by the mass worker, Alquati insisted that the gradual 'factoryisation' of the labour process to which it was subsumed pointed to a convergence with the behaviours of more traditional sectors of the working population. Thus it was important that the specific attributes of intellectual labour not be mystified; after all, this was a form of labour which in a certain sense was '*like all others*' (Alquati n.d.: 32). At the same time, it was simplistic to conflate the category of intellectual labour with office workers. When the fragmentation of labour endured by most white-and blue-collar workers was examined carefully, Alquati argued, it was obvious that the distinction between the two was more ideological than material. For example, there was at least some element of manual labour in most forms of office work, while many jobs on the factory floor demanded some decision-making on the part of employees (ibid.: 89). Separate as a category from white-collar workers, then, was what Alquati called the 'intellectual proletariat': 'proletarians who study (a very large number of whom are white-collar workers)' (ibid.: 117). While white-collar workers as such were beginning to lose the features which distinguished them from the rest of the class, the intellectual proletariat engaged in the consumption of tertiary education was capable of becoming the vanguard within an emerging *operaio sociale* (ibid.: 118). This role, he emphasised, existed only as a possibility: at present, each of the various layers of labour-power to be found in Italy remained sharply divided from the others, enclosed within its particular corporative interests. Given this, he believed, it was misleading to explain the recent behaviour of the PCI with terms such as 'social-democratisation'. Such a notion could not be removed from its original historical context; what the current direction of the party pointed to, on the contrary, was the constitution of

> a new working-class right which seems disposable only to forms and objectives within the system. Often this has a determinate 'professional' base; sometimes instead it has a determinate political formation within the union, and recently in encounter with the party, where the ideology and ethic of labour, particularly productive labour, has left its mark. (ibid.: 128)

Perhaps the most novel aspect of Alquati's discourse, at least in terms of workerism's traditional conceptual apparatus, lay in its attempt to account for the 'middle strata' of modern Italian society. In his opinion, a complex system of social stratification, far from discrediting the centrality which Marx's *Capital* had assigned to the relation between capital and labour, had been encouraged by Italian capital 'precisely because of the exceptional acuteness of the struggle between the two strategic classes' (Alquati n.d.: 75). Thus it was quite proper for Marxists to talk of *ceti medi*, since 'the word "middle" is associated with the verb "to mediate" which, as everybody knows, is the fundamental verb of "political parlance"' (ibid.: 76). In the Italy of the late 1970s, the stabilising function of such strata had been called into question, forcing them to polarise towards either capital or labour. Here, Alquati believed, the university could be seen as a privileged site of this crisis where, as greater sections of the middle strata were driven towards the 'working-class political bloc', they would become not only the latter's allies, but even 'integrating and "propulsive forces" of its recomposition' (ibid.: 77).

A STRANGE MOVEMENT OF STRANGE STUDENTS

Primo Maggio's efforts to grasp the significance of the new movement opened with Bologna's essay on 'The Tribe of Moles', the basic premises of which had been set out in a letter penned to the *Lotta Continua* daily in early March. Unlike Asor Rosa, Bologna insisted that the behaviour exhibited by the new social protagonists did not stem from a material location extraneous to the world of production. Indeed, it was a mistake to conclude that, since the universities served as their common meeting point, those in struggle could best be understood as students comparable to those of 1968:

> [T]he best way to distort these University struggles is to pretend that they are only about the University reforms, and therefore only of interest to University workers and students. This is false – because we have seen an *entire class composition* coming together around the Universities ... (Bologna 1977c: 98–9)

Furthermore, if the participants in the new movement were marginalised, this was first and foremost a form of political marginalisation by a party system which deemed their needs and forms of struggle 'pathological aspects of late capitalism' to be cured or else expunged. For Bologna, as he went on to explain in 'The Tribe of Moles', the roots of the 'Movement of '77' were firmly set in the world of labour, albeit one radically different to that found in Mirafiori. Unlike the social protagonist of a decade before, this new class composition was not prepared to see either its collective or individual needs subordinated to the organisational structures championed by Marxism-Leninism. Whereas the average militant of 1970 had tended to view politics as the clash of contesting apparatuses, that of 1977 was conscious that the personal sphere was also political, preferring work in affinity groups based on friendship to the party branches of the *triplice* (Lerner et al. 1978). Beyond the intrusion of feminist and libertarian norms into the culture of the mainstream far left, this shift was a consequence of a profound alteration in the reproduction of classes, which had now become a problem of political legitimation rather than material intervention: a question of social and cultural identity, of acceptance or refusal to accept the norms of social behaviour required and laid down by the form of the state. Classes have tended to lose their 'objective' characteristics and become defined in terms of political subjectivity. But in this process the major force of redefinition has come from below: in the continuous reproduction and invention of systems of counter-culture and struggle in the sphere of everyday living, which has become ever more 'illegal'. (Bologna 1977b: 44)

This new subjectivity was not, however, without certain material determinants: above all, the dense undergrowth of small factories which had flourished since the early 1970s, along with the service sector, which had also seen the number of its employees rise significantly over the same period.

Interest in the workers of small firms was still something of a novelty for *operaismo* in the 1970s. While Guido Bianchini (1990) had attempted to direct *Potere Operaio*'s attention to the peculiarities of small-scale production in Emilia-Romagna, it was only from the middle of the decade that others in the tendency began to take a sustained interest in the significance of Italy's 'marginal' economy. For Massimo Paci (1973), such curiosity was prompted by the growing cycle of accumulation – and industrial disputation – outside traditional epicentres like FIAT. If the thrust of Paci's pioneering research lay in demonstrating the historical importance of marginally located small firms for Italy's economic development, the apparent halt of the mass workers' forward march lent a sense of political immediacy to the question. In what was to be an engaging debate between Italian Marxists of varied formation, a composite picture began to emerge of the intricate structure and robust vitality of the country's 'submerged' economy. In certain cases, the spread of smaller units of production could be seen as a strategy pursued by those large industrial capitals. These hoped, either by means of 'in-house decentralisation (splitting up) or inter-firm decentralisation (putting out) within the domestic economy ... [and] in conjunction with automation, to begin to dismember the large factory proletariat' (Murray 1983: 76, 93). Yet this strategy did not exhaust the phenomenon: other cases, indeed, indicated that the small firm, far from being an anomaly indicative of Italy's backwardness, stood at the centre of the nation's most dynamic accumulation process. Located in the North-East and Centre of the country, this cycle represented nothing less than a new, third pole of development comparable in importance only to the industrial triangle of the North-West and the continuing stagnation of the South (Bagnasco 1977).

Back in 1973, when the debate upon restructuring was just beginning, Bologna (1973b) had been inclined to focus his attention upon the industrial bloc associated with the production of petrochemicals. This, he had argued, was rapidly becoming the driving force of a new cycle of capital accumulation that refused the traditional Keynesian model with its goal of balanced development throughout the economy. Subsuming their employees in an almost militaristic fashion to fixed capital, the state-backed chemical conglomerates appeared to Bologna as the cutting edge of an attempt to supplant the productive centrality of those industries (and working-class vanguards) engaged in the manufacture of consumer durables. In such circumstances, he believed, the proliferation of small-scale industry, through either independent initiative or the productive decentralisation of larger firms, could only be understood as an interregnum presaging the ascent of petrochemical capital.

Criticised by some members of Lotta Continua for imposing the logic of classical workerism upon a reality more complex than that of the 1960s, Bologna's argument was to shift significantly thereafter (1973b), privileging instead the part played within restructuring by credit and the state management of the money-form. This account of 'money as capital' served to draw *Primo Maggio*'s attention to those proletarians consuming revenue outside the terrain of immediate production as an important complement to the mass worker. At the same time, the intensity of industrial conflict within many of Italy's 'marginal' firms – a sharp contrast with the stalemated war of position found in so many of the larger workplaces – had led Bologna to re-examine the problem of small factories in some detail by early 1977.

As commentators such as Paci, Brusco, Bagnasco and Messori had made plain (Graziani 1979: 235–62), the type of firms involved in Italy's 'marginal' economy were extremely diverse. These ranged from cooperatives to the satellites of large companies, from labour-intensive production for the domestic market to capital-intensive production geared towards export (Bologna 1977b: 50–1). Given the lack of a common thread derived from the nature of the labour process itself, the process of class unification within the sector stemmed from other determinants, above all age and gender. The presence of women and younger men, excluded from many of the larger enterprises by the rigidity of the mass worker, coupled with working conditions frequently exempt from regulation by the Statuto dei Lavoratori, were perhaps the most important points of commonality within this *operaio disseminato*. As a consequence, its most militant components, while taking up the torch of rebellion let fall by the mass worker, had been forced to invent new forms of organisation quite different to those of the Hot Autumn (ibid.: 47, 48). Of these, the most spectacular were the *ronde operaie* ('workers' patrols') found in Milan and Turin, which ranged from mobile pickets to genuine forms of 'diffuse' terrorism evocative of Spanish anarchism's 'pistoleros' 50 years before (ibid.: 52; *La Fabbrica Diffusa* 1977; Balestrini 1989).

Besides the small manufacturing concerns, the new movement also drew its membership from Italy's service sector (Bologna 1977b: 52). Here again, the structure and behaviour of labour-power was far from homogeneous. Instead, it stretched from the increasingly militant hospital employees subjected to quite primitive working conditions, to the relatively privileged bank employees and clerks in state employ; from jobs guaranteed through relations of patronage to those precarious, casual positions offered by subcontractors. If any 'element of homogeneity' existed within this fraction, it was the 'increasing political pressure' to which the various components of the service sector were subjected by Italy's spreading fiscal crisis. Of particular interest for Bologna within this mosaic of class fragments were the growing numbers of casual workers employed at one remove through contractors. Their status, he believed, pointed to a process in which the very structure of the firm began to dissolve 'as a means of producing commodities':

> [T]he firm remains merely as chief clerk, as mere administration of decentralised labour; in fact, the firm dissolves itself as a subject or protagonist of conflict, as an institution of the class struggle ... The chain of infinite decentralisation of production breaks the rigidity of age and sex, of geographical location, of social background, etc., all this is a weighty factor in fusing the new composition of the class.
> This chain of infinite decentralisation is one of the more 'progressive' elements of capitalism today; it is a far more powerful weapon of massification than the assembly line. (ibid.: 54)

Within this class composition, he continued, the autonomist groups had early won a hegemonic role because of their ability to anticipate political themes profoundly different to those of the late 1960s. Yet hardly had 'the echoes of the clashes in Bologna' died down 'when everyone whipped out their Lenin masks from behind their backs – in particular the Workers' Autonomy (Autonomia Operaia) tendency in the North' (Bologna 1977b: 56). The very failure of Autonomia to force the pace of struggle, however, made it clear that now, against previous vanguardist notions of class politics,

*organisation is obliged to measure itself day by day against the new
composition of the class; and must find its political programme only in the
behaviour of the class and not in some set of statutes.* (ibid.: 58)

To map a path back from the inertia which the very complexity of the
movement's structure threatened to impose, Bologna sought to locate
some 'new Mirafioris' around which a political programme could
be constituted (ibid.: 60). In time-honoured workerist fashion, this
meant looking for a segment of the class which was both dynamic in
its behaviour, and employed in a sector of strategic importance. Such
a stratum, Bologna believed, could be found in the world of transport,
and in particular amongst truck drivers whose militancy was becoming
increasingly evident:

> Less well-known [than the rail sector], but infinitely more explosive,
> is the situation in road transport. Here we are faced with a mass of
> waged workers and independent operators equal to 20 Mirafioris
> rolled into one. The 'objective' weight of this workforce is frightening,
> and it is perhaps the only section of the class today whose movement
> could paralyse the whole capitalist cycle. (ibid.: 53–4)

The arguments of 'The Tribe of Moles' would provoke controversy
amongst many members of Italy's historic left. The Communist historian
Gian Mario Bravo (1978: 128), for instance, was particularly scandalised
by Bologna's emphasis upon the subjective determinations of class
identity. According to this critic, the essay elevated individual desires
into political principles: '"Revolutionary impatience", already extolled by
the classical extremists, becomes a moment in the development of the
personality'. No less harsh was the judgement of some within *Primo
Maggio*. Writing from Bologna, where the influence of Gilles Deleuze
and Felix Guattari was strong within the local movement, Franco Gori
(1978: 115, 117, 122) criticised 'The Tribe of Moles' for attempting
to impose 'an abstract factory relation' upon the new social subjects.
Taking the 'meta-economic' categories of Marxism beyond their realm
of 'coherent applicability', he insisted, could only lead to an 'abstract
formalism' which painted the mass worker as the harbinger of the new
movement. Neither the richness of personal politics, nor the intricacies
of gender and sexuality, could be grasped within the interpretative
schema of workerism, 'this mystical way of conceiving the dynamic of
social processes'; rather, a whole new frame of reference was needed.
    Less hostile in tone was Lapo Berti (1978: 128, 139), who accepted
the basic validity of Bologna's dissection of the new movement. In his

opinion, however, the crisis of the large factory as a touchstone of class politics threw into question the continuing relevance of that nexus between technical and political composition traditionally established by *operaismo*. With the state playing an increasing role in social life, class identity was less and less a simple product of the sphere of production; more and more, the starting point of proletarian politicisation lay outside the workplace, in arenas such as the education system. Within this new articulation of the relation between factory and society, the emerging 'molecular' movement constituted itself above all by challenging the legitimation of class society.

A similar approach, if more critical of Bologna, was taken by Christian Marazzi (1978: 85, 86). In looking to small factories and the service sector as the new movement's sites of formation, he argued, 'The Tribe of Moles' continued to situate the class struggle 'within the capital–labour nexus'. In doing so, Bologna failed to realise that the state, through its strategy of bypassing the factory as privileged instrument of command in favour of the regulation of revenue, had begun to induce the formation of a new subject outside the relations of production:

> If today it is no longer fixed capital, but the territory as social place of the reproduction of antagonism, which determines class behaviours, then this means that capitalist organisation passes within the functionalisation of the political system. The system of political relations between classes must become productive, politics must act like fixed capital in its relation with living labour. The fetishisation of machinery is no longer enough; politics must also be fetishised, must appear to be 'relatively autonomous'. (ibid.: 89)

In these circumstances, a new definition of productive labour was needed, one which recognised the central part played in the reproduction of capital by that labour-power exchanged with, and under the direct command of, the political system.

Starting from a different point of view again, Giulano Buselli and Mario Zanzani (1978) would also emphasise the collapse both of the factory as an interpretative category, and of any specific productive figure as the embodiment of the overall working-class political project. Like other critics of Bologna within *Primo Maggio*, they were to criticise 'The Tribe of Moles' for not dissolving the specificity of the large factory into the tendency's longstanding, but little-developed, thematic of modern capitalism as a social factory. For two of the journal's Turin editors, by contrast, Bologna's chief failing lay in his too-ready dismissal of the potential for social antagonism still extant in the traditional strongholds of the industrial working class. By overemphasising 'subjectivity' at the expense of a materialist analysis of the relations of production, the perspective laid out in 'The Tribe of Moles' risked burying the mass worker prematurely, at a point in time when closer bonds between the old and new class compositions still remained possible. Messori and Revelli (1978: 44, 46) did not deny that a profound disjuncture presently existed between the two; rather, their chief concern was to assess the problem from the point of view of workers in the large factories. Examined in this way, the relation between technical and political composition as a determination of class behaviour remained as crucial as ever, as capital's attempts to alter it through restructuring testified.

Above all, Messori and Revelli believed, the mass worker's situation was far from stable. To begin with, the use of productive decentralisation and inflation to sidestep the mass worker's power could only be effective as short-term solutions. And if the PCI had so far stood by the core of this 'central' working class in exchange for support in the electoral sphere, such a project could not long sustain itself when capital eventually summoned the courage to dismantle the technical composition which underpinned the mass worker's power (Messori and Revelli 1978: 56–7). In this context, they insisted, the rigidity of the mass worker within the 'productive truce' of the large factories needed to be seen not merely as an indication of its subordination and passivity, but also as a measure of its strength (ibid.: 62–3).

For its part, Italian capital continued to face a dilemma. On the one hand, the reorganisation of the international division of labour following the recent energy crisis required the introduction of new technology to keep local industry competitive. On the other hand, the necessary restructuring that such a project demanded – a massive reorganisation of the productive structure – was denied it so long as major pockets of working-class rigidity stood in its path. When capital finally embarked upon the path of confrontation, and the welfare system was called upon more and more to regulate the expulsion of labour-power from the large factories, new stresses would be placed upon the already precarious bond between the state's functions of legitimation and domination. In such circumstances, the meaning of the Communist Party's reformism would be stretched to the limit, opening up possibilities for a meeting point between the proletarian generations formed before the mid-1970s and the more recent protagonists of the Movement of '77 (Messori and Revelli 1978: 69–73, 80).

It was wrong, therefore, for Bologna to downplay the strategic centrality of those workers engaged in the immediate process of production. If a crisis existed within the factory, it pertained to its traditional role of defining the universe of working-class values, when recent struggles pointed instead to 'the pre-eminence of the social terrain as the site of the individual management of "living-time" reappropriated as "use-value"' (Messori and Revelli 1978: 76). Whatever the path followed, Messori and Revelli concluded, the quest to join struggles in the workplace with those in the social sphere must start from 'a more attentive analysis of the concrete manifestations of working-class initiative' (ibid.: 81).

THE MOVEMENT LOSES DIRECTION

Summing up the debate in early 1978, Bologna (1978b: 149) would dub the arguments advanced by most of his critics within *Primo Maggio* as unreasonably optimistic. Based upon assumptions that portrayed the development of the new revolutionary movement as a univocal process, they forgot that 'The autonomy of the subject cannot elide power, its *reality*.' Qualifying the elastic reading of subjectivity in 'The Tribe of Moles', Bologna reiterated his belief that any effort to understand contemporary proletarian behaviour required 'a sector of concrete labour-power' as its focus (ibid.: 156). Preferring the perspectives advanced by Messori and Revelli, he recognised that these were, in their own way, no less partial than the views of Marazzi or Berti. On the other hand, he believed, the interpretative framework held out by the Turin editors possessed a materiality absent from explanations advancing undifferentiated notions of social control. Even more importantly, Messori and Revelli had directed attention back to workerism's original enquiry into the composition of the working class. This was all the more important given that the latter, faced with the competing models of 'radical bourgeois *operaismo*' offered by the Communist Party and Autonomia, was as much 'without allies' as it had been in the 1960s (ibid.: 157).

The terms of *Primo Maggio*'s debate over the efficacy of workerist theory would remain unresolved. In the meantime, the new movement had entered deeper and deeper into crisis as 1977 unfolded. Despite their dramatic scale, the almost weekly encounters with police and *carabinieri* soon proved to offer no programme for the movement's consolidation and extension. Matters were not helped, according to the Volsci, by those within it who chose to play up the movement's attributes as primarily a 'youth' phenomenon, and so turned their backs upon older generations within the emergent class composition (Pifano 1997: 366). Hemmed in by extensive state repression, and by a Communist Party increasingly determined to legitimise itself as a 'party of government' at the expense of 'deviant' social forces, the movement began to falter. Above all, it proved incapable of finding a productive way of harnessing its own internal tensions, and on that basis of reaching out to broader working-class circles. Instead, as Marco Melotti would later argue,

> [t]he perverse spiral of raising the stakes in the direct clash with the repressive apparatuses of the state IN PRACTICE conceded hegemony to the deliriums of the armed struggle ideology [*combattentismo*]. (Melotti 1984: 64)

In this context, the refusal of politics became 'the exclusive privileging of the "military"' dimension, while "'revolutionary radicalism" became measurable only in terms of the hardness of the clash with the adversary, whether this be the state or the "deviationist comrade"'. At the same time, in many parts of the movement,

> the unconscious/thoughtless [*inconsapevole*] introjection of the thematic of 'two societies' turned snobbish, the total exclusion of any relation with the city's working-class and proletarian fabric. (ibid.)

Little by little, these behaviours began to generate two distinct camps within the movement. At one pole stood those who emphasised the libertarian themes of autonomy and personal development only to turn inwards, refusing to confront the obstacles which limited the movement's extension. At the other stood those who glossed over both the political implications of the libertarian stream's critique of traditional Italian 'anti-revisionism' and any serious discussion of class composition in favour of debates concerning the feasibility of civil war. During the movement's Bologna conference of September 1977, the gulf between these two approaches to politics assumed a tangible form, with most components of Autonomia and a number of the more conventional political groups choosing to turn their back on other participants, instead sealing themselves off within the city's Palasporto stadium, there to battle for 'hegemony' (Balestrini and Moroni 1988: 334). Despite Negri's (1977c: 29) optimistic appraisal of the times – 'Political conditions favour us ... Italy is not Germany' – Autonomia would emerge from the conference more isolated than before. Its predicament would be made plain three months later when, snubbed by the organisers of a national metalworkers' march in Rome, its contingent of demonstrators remained trapped by police within the university campus. Having lost their reference point in the broader class composition, sections of the autonomist movement increasingly vented their frustration through the physical intimidation of those they identified as enemies (Petter 1993). In the face of such behaviours, only a few revolutionaries would argue that the role of the movement's 'political class' lay not in building 'the party', but rather in identifying and promoting an anti-capitalist programme generated from within the new class composition itself (Collettivo Politico Alitalia e Aeroporti Romani et al. 1978; *Collegamenti* 1979).

The Moro kidnapping of 1978 would throw the implications of the Brigate Rosse strategy of carrying the struggle 'to the heart of the state' into bold relief. While all the major currents within the autonomist movement would condemn the killing of the Christian Democrat leader (Castellano 1980: 179–97), their growing disorientation was plain to see. Meanwhile, the Area continued to lose activists to the armed formations, a process accelerated by the increased preparedness of fascist groups – above all in Rome – to use deadly force against members of the movement (Lombardo-Radice and Sinibaldi 1979). Their sway now declining within their own organisations, many of Autonomia's most prominent thinkers finally began to suspect that the continued influence of the *triplice* might not be the greatest threat to the movement's development. Negri (1979a: 24–5, 28), for example, remained scathing of those he called the 'party of the ghetto', who washed their hands of all questions of 'power' and 'violence' only to unwittingly glorify the omnipotence of the state, before which they stood paralysed. At the same time, he also began to distance himself from those circles within the Area that either stretched out a hand towards the Brigate Rosse, or else aspired to compete with them on the military front. The terrorists and their sympathisers, Negri argued, were so obsessed with destabilisation that they had become oblivious to the significance of the new mass subjectivity. His own response, however – an insistence upon the privileged function of the party-form within the process of recomposition – was itself anything but new. More a shield and sword than the movement's command centre, the construction of a 'party of autonomy' (*Rosso* 1978: 193–4) as the watcher on the wall of proletarian freedom remained essential, he argued, if the growing bifurcation between 'the ghetto' and 'the insurrectionalists' was to be overcome:

> The party, if I may make a jest, is a combatant religious order, not the ecclesiastical totality of the process ... [it is] the army which defends the frontiers of proletarian independence. (Negri 1977a: 62)

That the majority of autonomist groupings, by their arrogance, had recently squandered enormous opportunities was now also apparent to Scalzone. The 'micro-factions' of the Area, he noted in December 1978, had begun to reveal their fundamentally conservative nature earlier that month, when they had chosen to isolate themselves from the demonstrating metalworkers, 'not all of whom, certainly, were union functionaries'. Amongst other things, this demonstrated that the attempt to apply 'the classic model of democratic centralism' within the various segments of the 'organised' Area had only generated '*monsters*'. How then could the process of political recomposition be relaunched? Scalzone was not so sure, beyond a return to the exploration of class composition; what was certain, he held, was that Negri's project for a 'party of autonomy' could only be stillborn, since it did nothing to rethink the experience of the micro-factions (Scalzone 1978: 34, 60, 62, 63). For Piperno, a starting point for resuming the class struggle's forward advance lay in trying to understand the origins of the armed groups within the revolutionary movement and the class composition that had generated it. According to him, the deciding vote lay with the terrorist groups themselves: would they choose to place themselves at the disposal of the movement as a whole, or would they instead continue to wage their almost private feud with the state? In other words, were the armed groups capable of joining 'the frightening beauty' of the movement's 12 March 1977 rampage in Rome with 'the geometric power displayed in Moro's kidnapping'? (Piperno 1978b: 226).

Isolated from the rest of the Area, yet with much stronger roots in their local proletariat, the Comitati Autonomi Operai (1978b: 15) in Rome were by contrast harsh in their criticism of the Brigate Rosse. The Volsci had no doubt that the Moro affair represented an attempt by the armed group to force 'the vanguards and advanced sectors of the class' into the political underground, all the better to exercise its sway over them. Not that the Roman autonomists had not made their own mistakes in the face of a class composition as complex as that which emerged in 1977. With hindsight, Daniele Pifano would look with regret upon his organisation's 'often instrumental' approach to direct democracy, along with its inability to work with those currents it deemed to be on the moderate wing of the movement (Pifano 1995: 287). Above all, he later argued, Autonomia's failure 'to represent a general political force' had opened a programmatic void that the armed groups on its fringes and beyond were more than willing to exploit (Pifano 1997: 366). Even in 1978, however, the Roman group proved to be more prepared than most of its Northern counterparts to face up to some of the autonomist groups' failings. In particular, the response of the Volsci to Autonomia's crisis of late 1977 and early 1978 was to propose a 'slow, patient, intelligent entrance into the large factory' in conjunction with the hundreds of 'autonomous' workplace committees that had maintained their distance from the organised Area (Comitati Autonomi Operai 1978a: 19).

Such views would resonate with a number of *Primo Maggio*'s editors; Bologna (1978b: 153) above all. During 1979, the journal worked hard and long to bring together some of the workplace activists who refused both the policy of sacrifice and austerity promoted by the Communist union leadership (Vannicelli 1983: 508–45) and the born-again Leninism of much of Autonomia (Crespi 1984). In the process it became clear that if the industrial front was still quiet at FIAT, elsewhere things were hotting up. As the hospitals saw a groundswell of strikes outside the direction of the confederations (Arrighetti 1978), the port of Genoa offered the unique example of a delegates' council dominated by 'autonomous' militants elected ahead of the CGIL's chosen candidates (Collettivo operaio portuale 1978). Finally, within the complex network of manufacturing firms surrounding Milan, the union austerity policy inspired open opposition from growing numbers of factory delegate councils.

None of this, however, led the editors of *Primo Maggio* to assume that a class-wide wave of struggle lay just around the corner. In Bologna's opinion, the PCI had for the most part remained successful in maintaining its hegemony amongst industrial workers, despite the disappointments and confusions that its behaviour since June 1976 had evoked. In those regions where it held sway, the party was already engaged in a sophisticated experiment to establish a new state-form. Here it was '*the masses themselves who act as judge and jury*', a process Bologna (1977b: 58) held 'would be innovative were it not happening within a framework of a freezing of the class power balance, with a restoration of capitalist control at all levels'. More generally, the PCI's support found its material basis in the mass worker's desire '*to continue to function as labour-power*'. For such a demand, Communist reformism represented 'the most concrete mediation of the interests of the working class'. While the extent to which such a programme was workable largely depended upon the resolution of Italy's difficulties within the international division of labour, Bologna firmly rejected any interpretation of the PCI's role that rested upon its function of repression alone. On the contrary, he maintained, the party and the CGIL could be expected soon to reaffirm their mediating role, '*not through paralysis of the struggle but through the promotion of struggle*' (Bologna 1977c: 119, 120).

Considered absurd by many, it was a prophecy that would reveal its full meaning only three years later, in October of 1980. In the meantime, one of the most novel features of Italian working-class politics during the late 1970s began to unfold at FIAT. Having frozen its staff intake for four years, the auto giant's management once again opened its gates to new employees in 1978. Because of recent legislation favouring the hiring of women and young people seeking their first job, FIAT was to draw a disproportionate number of its 12,000 new staff from these categories (Revelli 1989: 73–4). Overnight, the terms of the earlier debate on the 'two societies' would take on new meaning, as large numbers of the protagonists of 1977 – 'the children and wives of Gasparazzo' (Deaglio and Manenti 1979: 6) – entered the terrain of the mass worker for the first time.

THE FAMILY GASPARAZZO GOES TO FIAT

Upon their arrival, the latest levy of FIAT workers discovered that the firm had changed quite markedly since the Hot Autumn. Reorganised into eleven operating sectors, the Agnelli family's holdings had become diversified, adding interests in telecommunications and energy production to the traditional preoccupation with vehicle construction (Cipriani 1981). Within the latter field, FIAT had built or acquired automobile plants elsewhere in Italy and overseas. In its Turin plants of Mirafiori and Rivalta, the creeping restructuring which characterised the 'productive truce' of the mid-1970s continued to remove labour-power from those moments of the cycle most directly involved in the production of vehicles (Mantelli and Scianna 1978: 38). As automated systems insinuated themselves into the traditional domain of the mass worker, the ability of employees to utilise the old production norms for their own ends began to melt away:

> The 1950s and 1960s were the Tayloristic phase [at FIAT]. Workers knew how much they produced. Controlling this by slowing down or stopping was their power. Now with centralized computer systems and robots, the Tayloristic phase is over. The worker produces so much more that all perspective on work is lost. Between 1973 and 1979, the work time required to produce a car was cut by 50 percent. (Marco Revelli, quoted in Barkan 1984: 240)

According to the Turin editors of *Primo Maggio*, the process by which the factory 'again becomes a universe unknown to the worker' was playing an important part in fragmenting the mass worker. Now its previous collective identity had become a myriad of 'partial and contradictory' points of view (Redazione torinese di Primo Maggio 1977: 25). Faced with such confusion, many of workerism's long-held typologies of class behaviour, if not its basic assumption of 'the hard materiality of production and the workers' relation with labour as the driving axis of the definition and structuring of social antagonism', were less than useless (ibid.: 21). In proposing a return to the tendency's old project of a workers' enquiry, Revelli and his associates were conscious that the experience of *Quaderni Rossi* could not be replicated after a space of 15 years. Once, it seemed, 'The factory produced politics. And the enquiry was struggle.' In reality, however, and despite the commitment of Panzieri's group to 'co-research', the traditional dichotomies between workers and intellectuals, and between the political project's 'theoretical elaboration and practical realisation', had often reproduced themselves in *Quaderni Rossi*'s work (ibid.: 21, 22). Now, by contrast, not only was the enquiry obliged to follow workers outside the factory; many of the workplace militants formed in recent years possessed both the confidence and ability needed to undertake the task of research themselves (ibid.: 23).

During the Moro affair of 1978, while others speculated upon the true identity of the kidnappers, Bruno Mantelli and Marco Revelli sought to gauge the reaction of FIAT workers. Presenting some of their findings to the readers of *Lotta Continua* that July, they reflected:

> When we returned to the gates of Mirafiori – not to 'speak', this time, but to listen and to try and understand – we had in mind two things. The first was the feeling that today the 'enquiry' was an obligatory point of passage, a specific form of political practice without which every other series of considerations remained fatally arid and blocked. The second was the impression that the way of living politics is today the most obscure, yet central, node within the ambit of the enquiry. (Mantelli and Revelli 1978a: 5)

Casting off the misconception 'that working-class opinion could be pre-fabricated in the laboratories of ideology', and seeking out the views of those 'others' who had never been in the forefront of struggle, Mantelli and Revelli discovered – beneath the initial impression of silence – a Tower of Babel. The opinions expressed as to Moro's fate had varied in the extreme. There were those who enthusiastically supported the unions' calls for protest stoppages. There was also the comrade who argued that 'Look, this is terrorism, the fact that I'm about to enter [the factory] and be held against my will for eight hours, this is a kidnapping' (Mantelli and Revelli 1978b: 12). At the same time, nearly all portrayed political experience, in the formal sense of that term, as an alien, hostile craft monopolised by the parties and unions. Unlike in the past, the mass worker's ability to translate its technical composition into a form of power no longer functioned, with external, socially defined considerations increasingly impinging upon the labour-power employed at FIAT. On the contrary, they argued, a void of working-class initiative had opened up. This was bounded on one side by 'a terrorism that wants to find its own legitimation in the political paralysis of that working class', on the other by a Communist Party that sought 'to establish its own autonomy as a political class on the "centrality" of a silent working class' (Mantelli and Revelli 1979: 197). Given this, Mantelli and Revelli (1978a: 12) could only conclude their survey with a series of questions, the most anguished being: 'What are the steps through which the class can once more render its own material composition politically subversive?'

Fifteen months later, the editors of *Primo Maggio* were again to ponder such problems at a conference, 'Old and New Workers at FIAT'. It was a seemingly disparate gathering which came together in October 1979, its almost two dozen speakers covering an arc which stretched from the Communist Party to Autonomia, from the local union left to the many non-aligned positions to be found in the Italian new left. Running through almost all of their contributions, however, could be found a number of shared themes. These included the arrival at FIAT of new workers with their own distinctive view of factory life, the crisis of the older generation of employees' political identity, the collapse of any glibly homogeneous notion of 'working class', and the inability of the union apparatus to address the concerns of the new arrivals. Dismissed contemptuously as 'the bottom of the barrel' by the local PCI leader Alberto Minucci (Revelli 1981b: 99–101), many of the latest recruits to FIAT had played a leading role in the contract struggles of that summer. Against this optimistic note, the wave of arrests that had struck Autonomia six months before lent a certain poignant backdrop to the conference's proceedings. To this had been added on 9 October the dismissal for 'non-consonant behaviours' of 61 FIAT employees, amongst them many prominent workplace activists of the far left (Scarponi 1979).

Examining the make-up of the FIAT workers taken on since 1978, Silvia Belforte (1980: 12) of the workerist-influenced journal *Quaderni del territorio* found 65 per cent of them to be women, usually in their mid-thirties, and married with children. As for the other new starters, many had just left school, or were still studying; most had been born in Turin itself, often of Southern parents (Barkan 1984: 188–9). Some sense of the difference in age between these new arrivals and the older hands can be gleaned from a mass survey conducted by *Rinascita* in 1979: even counting the younger workers, the average age of male respondents stood at 37–38 years (Accornero 1980: 146). Perhaps the most striking difference between the new starters and the generation formed within FIAT since the time of the Hot Autumn concerned their respective attitudes to work and the factory.

According to Pietro Marcenaro, the reasons for this lay in the very different processes of socialisation experienced by the two:

Unlike the Southern migrant who came, in the 1960s, to a hostile and foreign city which held no prospect of friendship, and for whom the factory represented practically the exclusive terrain of socialisation, the young new starters enter the factory with a life already rich in relationships. It is not the factory which shapes them according to its needs: unlike the preceding generation, which started work at 13 or 14 years of age, a significant section of young workers enter the factory at 18 or 19, their personality formed in the city and school. If in recent years things have already changed for the mass worker, with the factory no longer determining exclusively the forms of aggregation, now the process accelerates. 'The things which unite workers are not constituted by labour per se.' (Marcenaro 1980: 6)

When asked their opinion, many of the new hands were to define their time at work only in negative terms. In an anecdote of which he never tired relating, Revelli recounted the view of one of his worker-students, who had proclaimed that 'Every day when I leave, I say to myself, I've lost eight hours of my life' (quoted in Barkan 1984: 239). Such views would appear incomprehensible or even hurtful to many of FIAT's longer-serving employees, prompting comments to the effect that 'Before Fiat made us work too much, but with these kids, it's too far in the other direction' (ibid.: 219). Then again, the encounter with the 'older' workers could induce a similar disenchantment amongst the new hands – such as the discovery that, no less than outside, there were 'pigs' and sexual harassers aplenty to be found amongst the legendary workers of FIAT Turin (Deaglio and Manenti 1979: 7). And there were many apparent contradictions in behaviour, too: for example, the young, with their supposed contempt for work, seemed less prone to absenteeism and more committed to union organisation. By contrast, the same 49-year-old who complained that the new starters were workshy could also boast to an American writer in 1979:

I do my seven hours' work in three and a half or four hours. I'm responsible for 78 pieces every day. I work the way I want and decide how to do it. When I finish, I talk or do crossword puzzles, even though we're not supposed to. I walk around. There's also a room for relaxing where we play cards ... Management doesn't react to what we do because of the union. The work times are agreed upon and that's it. (Quoted in Barkan: 219)

Nino Scianna (1980: 41) of *Primo Maggio* – himself a FIAT worker – attempted to make sense of this apparent jumble for the October conference. He concluded that the divisions traditionally established by workerism upon the basis of labour-power's technical composition 'appear secondary' in a factory 'divided into a plurality of subjects, the identities of which are not defined on the terrain of production'. Contemplating a passage 'Beyond the Culture of the Mass Worker ...', Revelli (1980b: 64) now believed that nothing short of a factory-wide 'cultural revolution' was required if the rich diversity of the new class composition at FIAT was to ward off management's designs. A member of the Genoa dockworkers' collective reminded those present that 'none of us can imagine that they possess an overall strategy'. Instead, he pointed to the risks that faced the most militant sectors of the class if they turned their backs upon the 'old majority' within the proletariat (Amancio 1980: 57, 59). Meanwhile, the major sour note of the gathering was to come from one of the Volsci. Agreeing with the dockworker's warnings, Riccardo Taviani (1980: 64) accused the workerists present of engaging in *trasformismo*: 'It strikes me as an old way of doing politics, reinterpreting everything from scratch in order to survive as a political class [*ceto*].'

A year later, not only had the workerist component of the Italian far left been destroyed as a political force, but a generation of FIAT workplace activists with it (Guarcello et al. 1990). As Hilary Partridge (1996: 98) would later put it, 'Shop-floor radicalism at Fiat was not so much absorbed or defeated as torn out by the roots.' With hindsight, the path of management's strategy can be mapped clearly: the criminalisation of the 61, around which both the unions and PCI were forced to polarise; the shutting of new recruitment; the creeping retrenchments which removed 20 workers a day for absenteeism; finally, the big push for the 'temporary' layoff of 25,000 staff (Revelli 1989: 84–103). In a dramatic settling of accounts, 10,000–15,000 FIAT workers, with the local PCI apparatus in tow, were to defend the gates of Mirafiori for 35 days. In the end, they would be undermined by the defeatism of a national union apparatus shocked by FIAT's 'counter-mobilisation' of thousands of foremen and white-collar staff (and more than a sprinkling of line workers). Reading over Revelli's almost tender depiction of the 'gate people' defending the pickets, each layer carefully peeled back for examination, one is struck by the enormous distances which *Primo Maggio* had travelled since the heyday of classical workerism:

> Faced with this heterogenous yet compact human totality, we have been forced to admit the schematic nature of our analyses, which sliced up the various strata of the workforce into 'skilled workers', 'mass workers', 'social workers', 'diffuse workers' etc., without grasping the thousand subtle threads that interweave the fabric of the working

class, which communicate the experience and language of the old, skilled sections, to the raw young immigrant (transmitting a heritage of experiences that has never been entirely subdued), or which permit the young metropolitan proletariat to go 'beyond' work precisely because, in fact, the area behind the front line is well-defended by a working class strength that has been moulded and formed *in* work. (Revelli 1982: 102)

In such circumstances, however, the collapse of a theoretical framework, and its principal point of political reference, seemed rather too high a price to pay for such heightened sensitivity. Not surprisingly, the events of 1979–80 were to have a profoundly disorientating effect upon those workerists not directly implicated in the '7 April' case. To Revelli's mind (1980a: 13, 14), the 'traditional terms of the primacy of the factory and of labour' were no longer sufficient to define the behaviour of the waged. Faced with efforts 'to lobotomise' workers' memory of struggles, along with the new relation now demanded between subject and researcher, the role of the latter was increasingly akin to that of the psychoanalyst. Bologna's (1980a: 28, 29) assessment was bleaker still: even as the prosecution of the 7 April case sought to blot out all record of the past 20 years of social conflict, workerism's time-honoured indicators had gone haywire. On the one hand, 'the bosses and machines no longer unite'; on the other, it was increasingly apparent that 'mechanisms internal to the class function in opposite ways: in Turin as dynamism, in Milan as paralysis'. Trapped between the 'silence' of most workers and the 'enormous fragmentation' of the militants, he concluded, 'we have almost theorised disintegration'.

Looking back a decade later, Bruno Cartosio (1987: 13) would consider *Primo Maggio*'s reaffirmation of 'working-class centrality' in the wake of the Movement of '77 as somewhat forced. The journal would have done better, he believed, if it had given the notion of *centralità operaia* a thorough examination from top to bottom. As Asor Rosa (1987: 100) came to concede, however, Bologna had been right after all in insisting upon the political rather than social basis of the split between what the communist writer had called 'the two societies'. The events of 1977, Rossana Rossanda added, had opened for Italy 'an irreversible crisis for the union, an irreversible rupture between political society and civil society, a very grave crisis of representation' (Adornato and Lerner 1987: 92). For the rational workerists of *Primo Maggio*, the most enduring legacy of that year would remain the fragmentation of their theoretical apparatus. While conceding that a historiography 'which digs within individual and local things is important', Bologna would confess at the beginning of the 1980s to

> a very great need to reacquire a broad dimension, a respite of *'grande storia'*, a great need to reacquire … I won't say a theory, but something that doesn't force me into a relationship of abjuration and schizophrenia towards an intellectual course within which general and historical categories were not only well-defined, but functioned perfectly in helping us to understand reality and to participate within it in a militant manner. (Bologna 1981: 17)

Conclusion

In defeat, workerism would endure a savage beating from its critics. Its precepts, Giorgio Bocca admonished, were more 'an intellectual drug than a serious analysis' (quoted in Scandaletti 1979: 170); *operaismo*'s proponents, proclaimed another, were 'wicked teachers' who had led an entire generation astray (quoted in Nicotri 1980). Perhaps the lowest blow, because unexpected, was to come from one of the tendency's former adherents. In October 1981, Valerio Marchetti dismissed the efforts of *Primo Maggio* with the glib advice that henceforth those concerned with a 'dead' past should restrict themselves 'to the only trade worthy of the historian: pure and simple necrophilia':

> [W]hat can we make ... of this defeated working-class *ceto*, which seeks here to speak of its own defeat, of its own end, of its own past, of its shattered dreams? This is a political *ceto* whose own relation with the present has closed definitively. For this they call themselves – militant historians. (Quoted in Bermani and Coggiola 1986: 351, 353)

In assessing the often tortuous path of *operaismo*'s efforts to understand working-class behaviour, many of its weaknesses have come to the surface. The first of these consists in its penchant for all-embracing categories that, in seeking to explain everything, too often would clarify very little. Amongst them, that of the *social factory* always alluded to a significant rethinking of the process of class composition, yet rarely seemed to deliver on its promises. Another is *passivity*, too easily conjured forth as a means to avoid facing the problem of class decomposition, a process every bit as real as that of recomposition. Most damaging of all, however, would be *operaio sociale*, a category that, like Negri's use of the phrase *self-valorisation*,

> was a very elegant instrument for synthesising a plurality of social behaviours, but which, precisely for its excessive synthetic aspect, flattened them, negating their specificity. (Battaggia 1981: 76)

Each such category had this in common: it was an ideal construct into which certain members of the tendency attempted, with considerable obstinacy and ingenuity, to force the reality of working-class composition.

In doing so, however, they were to forget one of Marx's (1913: 9) most fundamental lessons: namely, the refusal to anticipate 'results that are still to be proven'.

In many cases, such failings within workerism had been prompted by another flaw common within the tendency: political impatience. Indeed, at each crucial stage of its development – from the break with Panzieri, or the unexpected outcome of the Hot Autumn, to the rise of the Movement of '77 – many of *operaismo*'s exponents seemed prepared to sacrifice their previous commitment to the study of the problem of class composition for a chance 'to seize the moment'. And if every such display of impetuousness was to reap no more than paltry rewards, only a minority of workerists seemed able each time to draw the appropriate conclusions.

Another of the more obvious weaknesses of Italian workerism – but one which it could hardly be said to have monopolised – would be a too-narrow focus upon what Marx termed the immediate process of production as the essential source of working-class experience and struggle. On this score, at least, the majority of workerists would show themselves after 1970 as more prepared than most Italian Marxists to examine the world beyond the factory wall. Where their focus often remained restricted, none the less, was in their choice of working-class behaviours to privilege, frequently confusing those minority practices deemed most 'advanced' for the activity of the class as a whole. Such a syndrome was to be clearly identified by Marco Gazzano at the 1979 FIAT conference: it entailed

> inferring our ideas on the actual composition of the class from enquiries concerning a single working-class stratum. That is, the stratum which interests us the most, the one closest to our culture and to external influences, such as from France for example. (Gazzano 1980: 15)

Similarly, Lapo Berti (1980: 32) would reflect that workerism had too often offered a 'symptomatic' reading of class composition. In other words, it tended to latch onto a particular stratum – the mass worker of mass production, for example – to the detriment of 'a more articulate, and even perhaps more contradictory, analysis of the class dynamic as a whole'.

Is it reasonable, then, to depict the records of Italian workerism, as Tronti (1978b: 16) has done, as one of 'Many flowers, little fruit'? A number of considerations would seem to mark such a judgement as unnecessarily harsh. To begin with, the tendency produced a whole series of studies that have contributed to an enhanced understanding of working-class politics: amongst others, these include Alquati's interviews at Olivetti and Mantelli and Revelli's at FIAT; Bock's narrative of the IWW; Bologna's topography of the 'Tribes'. Beyond this, *operaismo*, and its rational component in particular, had the merit of probing issues too long ignored by the majority of its contemporaries within the Italian left. In the process, it helped to undermine 'the use of all-inclusive categories such as *the* working class' (Ruggiero 1987: 26). Instead, it would force attention towards an exploration of the inherently contradictory experiences of workers, whether waged or otherwise, and from this to the terms upon which their struggle to turn such contradictions against the capital relation become feasible.

As to workerism's unrelenting preoccupation with the technical composition of labour-power as a key element in the explanation of behaviour, such a standpoint can be characterised more as partial than mistaken outright. Polemicising with Bologna in 1977, Berti had presented the tendency's traditional supposition as follows:

> To a determinate technical composition of labour-power, conditioned by the concrete configuration that the labour process assumes, there necessarily corresponds a system of social behaviours that, allowing for secondary socio-political factors, can be considered typical, in the sense that they tend to reproduce themselves in all the situations in which the fundamental determinants are contemporaneously given. (Berti 1978: 127–8)

As has been seen, even the homogeneity of the mass worker during the Hot Autumn could not be attributed exclusively to the question of its technical composition. By the end of the following decade, the editors of *Primo Maggio* had begun to probe those other determinants – gender, age, race, language, schooling, past struggles or defeats – which played their part in distinguishing the history of one ensemble of labour-powers from the next. Indeed, it might even be the case, as Francesco Ciafaloni (1980: 72) would argue, that in its efforts to comprehend FIAT's 'new starters', *Primo Maggio* had bent the stick too far in the opposite direction, downplaying the stamp which their encounter with the factory had left upon Gasparazzo's family.

'To know more about the workers of Turin, to know more in general about the oppressed classes, is not a small problem. It is *the* cultural and political problem of any left worthy of the name' (Ciafaloni 1980: 70). While such sentiments would hold decreasing appeal in the years after 1980 for Italy's notoriously 'mercurial intellectuals' (Sergio Bologna, quoted in Preve 1981: 53), they have lost none of their force in this new millennium. And if *operaismo*'s enquiry into the FIAT workforce of the late 1970s can be seen to have brought the tendency full circle, the questions that it posed then, as two decades before, stubbornly refuse to go away (Emery 1995). Here, as Roberto Battaggia (1981: 77) has rightly argued, 'The best way to defend workerism today is to go beyond it.' Having helped to force the lock (Bologna 1979: 36) obstructing the understanding of working-class behaviour in and against capital, only to disintegrate in the process, the workerist tradition has bequeathed to others the task of making sense of those treasures which lie within.

Postscript
Once More, With Feeling:
A Bibliographic Essay

The gathering of archival materials for this book – monographs, journals, and to a lesser extent, ephemera such as leaflets – had mostly been completed by the late 1980s, when an earlier version of the text was submitted for examination as a doctoral thesis. Indeed, much of that printed matter had been secured in the space of just two months, spent first in Britain (January) and then Italy (February) in 1982. Back then, in the immediate aftermath of Autonomia's collapse, tracking down a comprehensive selection of publications connected in some way to Italian workerism could at times prove a challenging task. As one of the most memorable passages in *The Unseen* (Balestrini 2011: 87) puts it,

> all the newspapers all the magazines all the leaflets all the documents all the posters all the publications of the movement destroyed vanished all bundled in cardboard boxes and plastic rubbish bags and burned or thrown on rubbish tips tons of printed matter the written history of the movement its memory dumped among refuse consigned to the flames through a fear of repression a fear well justified because all it took then was a leaflet found in a search to put you in prison for a year or two

Hours spent scrounging around movement bookshops (notably Calusca in Milan and Padua, Comunardi in Turin) and the Feltrinelli stores in Rome and elsewhere, plus the generosity of friends in Italy and Britain (above all, Vicky Franzinetti in Turin and Ed Emery in London – Ed in turn introduced me to Hilary Partridge, who played an absolutely crucial role opening doors for me in Padua), meant that I was ultimately able to accumulate complete or almost complete runs of many important journals (*Quaderni Rossi, Classe Operaia, Primo Maggio, Lotta Continua, Collegamenti, Potere Operaio veneto-emiliano, i volsci*).

With other magazines, though (*Rosso, Autonomia, Potere Operaio, Controinformazione*), the extent to which I could lay my hands on full sets of issues was considerably more patchy. On more than one occasion during that first visit to Italy, I met individuals who told me that they would have been happy to have given me their complete collection of –

say – *Potere Operaio*, if only the police hadn't confiscated it in one of the many raids of private residences that came in the wake of the 7 April arrests. On the book front, at least, the situation was happier, in part because a friend of a friend had visited Italy a year or two before and then kindly given me many of the books in Feltrinelli's *Materiali Marxisti* and *Opuscoli Marxisti* series. Upon my return home, library searches turned up more gems (*Contropiano, Aut Aut, il manifesto*), and a few books and journals were also ordered by mail from publishers like Dedalo.

With my thesis finally finished and consigned to a drawer, I still kept my eye out for such materials as made their way into print during the 1990s; some of these I managed to acquire during trips back to Italy across that decade. Although radical publishing in that country underwent something of a minor renaissance during those years (Dazieri 1996), such texts were more likely to chart the rise of new alternative unions and rank-and-file groupings, or the political and cultural activities in and around the country's self-managed social centres, than to reflect upon the previous cycle of struggles. By contrast, a wealth of new sources – both primary and secondary – has appeared since the first edition of *Storming Heaven* was published in 2002.

There are a number of possible routes to take when reviewing the sources that have appeared over the past 15 years, but one obvious starting point is undoubtedly the volume *Futuro Anteriore*, which like *Storming Heaven* was also published in 2002. Written by Guido Borio, Francesca Pozzi and Gigi Roggero, this book offers an extended reflection on 'the riches and limitations of Italian workerism' – a current, as they argue in a later work, that was 'neither a homogenous doctrinaire corpus, nor a unitary political subject', but rather 'multiple pathways with their roots in a common theoretical matrix' (Borio, Pozzi and Roggero 2005: 34–35). In advancing their case, Borio, Pozzi and Roggero drew upon nearly 60 interviews: conducted mostly with *operaisti*, both prominent and less well known, but also with individuals from other Marxist traditions. Utilising categories developed by Romano Alquati, the authors of *Futuro Anteriore* explored the experiences of different generations of workerists, their views on the tendency's heyday (as well as what came afterwards), and finally the challenges raised by the defeat of the 1980s. Originally included on a CD accompanying *Futuro Anteriore*, a selection of the interviews themselves were later published as a separate volume. Although *Futuro Anteriore* has yet to appear in English, a small number of the interviews have since been translated, such as Vittorio Rieser's account as one of those within *Quaderni Rossi* who chose to side with Panzieri against the nascent *operaisti*, and Alisa Del Re's recollections of her passage from the student movement to Potere Operaio, and then beyond into workerist-feminist projects. In the meantime, Roggero has also written a number of other relevant books: the latest, from 2016, addresses the relationship between subjectivity and class composition.

The various publications produced since the new millennium seem to fall into four broad (and sometimes overlapping) categories:

1. reprints of material from the 1960s and 1970s;
2. reflections recorded more recently by former participants;
3. studies of particular organisational experiences within the history of *operaismo* or the broader revolutionary left;
4. discussions of workerist theory and theorists.

Most of this material, not surprisingly, has come out in Italian, but in what follows I will also look at other publications, especially in English. Taken as a whole, these works have deepened our knowledge not only of *operaismo* as a lens through which to view the world, but also of the various practices undertaken by those influenced by workerist perspectives.

LENIN IN ENGLISH[1]

A useful place to begin is with the translations, since these are the most likely materials that readers will encounter first. In terms of primary sources, one of the largest groups of published material – particularly on the translation front – is essays and books originally penned by prominent workerist authors. Starting with Negri, 2005 saw the appearance of *Time for Revolution*, a title consisting of two essays, one of which ('The Constitution of Time', written in 1981) was an early effort to move beyond what he then saw as the limitations of workerist analysis. In the same year *Books for Burning* instead collected a series of Negri's programmatic statements from across the 1970s, most of which – 'Workers' Party Against Work', 'Proletarians and the State', and 'Toward a Critique of the Material Constitution' – had not previously appeared in English.[2] Then in 2014 came *Factory of Strategy: 33 Lessons on Lenin*, a crucial early-1970s book by Negri that in hindsight I wished I had examined in more depth in *Storming Heaven*. Penned at a time when Potere Operaio was slowly collapsing as an organisational project, *Factory of Strategy* continues to be important for its close reading of key texts by Lenin, from which Negri advanced a distinctive brand of Leninism that attempted to incorporate class composition into its

---

1 I would like to 'thank' an anonymous reviewer for suggesting this truly awful pun.
2 An earlier collection of Negri's writings, published by Ed Emery in 1983, never received the attention it deserved, and is now hard to find except online in digital form.

reckoning of the art of politics, while expunging the socialist/statist/ productivist aspects of Lenin's brand of Bolshevism. That this could sometimes be a delicate procedure is evidenced by the challenges faced in enunciating a perspective that rejects any orientation towards the parliamentary sphere or the union form, whilst simultaneously denouncing Lenin's 'leftist' opponents in the Comintern. Beyond that, a few small gems from the period have also popped up in English, chief amongst them being a 1976 introduction written by Negri for the Italian edition of former Yippie leader Jerry Rubin's third book, an essay that contains a number of interesting surprises for the attentive reader.

The novel *Vogliamo tutto* has long been one of the most striking narrations of a key event in the history of Italian workerism. Thanks to the Melbourne publishing house Telephone Company, run by Sonya Jeffery and Matt Holden, a version was finally brought out for the Anglophone market in 2014. Soon picked up and distributed in a new edition by Verso, Holden's translation captures Balestrini's vivid telling of a young male Southerner's adventures in Italy's labour market, culminating in the FIAT wildcat strikes of mid-1969. In the admiring words of *Publisher's Weekly*, 'This compelling novel works well as both historic relic and parallel to many contemporary workplace conflicts'.

Four conditions have made the appearance of these works much more likely over the past 15 years. One has been the persistence, in the aftermath of the 'alter-globalisation' movement, of a leftist culture curious about the writings of the 'post-workerists' (but considerably less curious about their earlier formation – one important exception is Nicholas Thoburn's 2003 work *Deleuze, Marx and Politics*). A second was the interest within sections of the publishing world for texts able to ride the coattails of the commercial success enjoyed by *Empire*, a work that made Negri known to a wider English-speaking audience in the first place. A third has been the reprinting of these materials in Italy itself, after many years of unavailability – most typically by smaller leftist publishing houses like DeriveApprodi and manifestolibri (which is connected with the daily newspaper *il manifesto*). The last has been the support of translators such as Arianna Bove, Ed Emery, Matt Holden, Matteo Mandarini, Timothy Murphy, Peter Thomas, Alberto Toscano and Evan Calder Williams, who are able both to work fruitfully with often difficult Italian texts, and are intimately familiar with the context and contours of Italian revolutionary politics during workerism's glory days.

Alongside their translation work, many of these writers have also made important contributions to the analysis of *operaismo* in the form of essays: for example, Toscano's 'Chronicles of Insurrection' from 2009, or Bove's examination (with Erik Empson) of 'Negri's contribution to the critique of power'. As for discussions of Negri's work as a whole, Timothy Murphy's 2012 overview continues to be the best introduction to the topic, setting out a well-written and balanced guide to the central themes that have preoccupied Negri for close to 60 years. Murphy has also co-edited for Pluto Press a two-book series of critical assessments of Negri's writings, such as Sergio Bologna's searing indictment from the mid-1970s of the pamphlet *Proletari e stato*. As things stand, a number of other translation projects are currently underway, one of the most important of which is Mandarini's rendering into English of Asor Rosa's text *Scrittori e popolo*. If, on the other hand, Tronti's *Operai e capitale* continues to be accessible to English readers only in part, there is talk of its eventual appearance, along with this mid-1970s classic *The Autonomy of the Political*. As for Negri, only one significant work from that time still awaits translation, this being his 1979 extended interview *Dall'operaio massa all'operaio sociale*.[3]

One of the best forums for the discussion and translation of workerist materials in recent years has been the online journal *Viewpoint*. Granted, its interests range far beyond *operaismo* – in the words of its editorial collective, 'Many of the best political ideas emerge when different currents find themselves forced to speak to each other' – but in the process of fostering that dialogue, *Viewpoint* has played a notable role in making materials by and about workerists available to a wider audience in the Anglophone world. Whether it be Leopoldina Fortunati's reflections on her time spent as a member of Potere Operaio, a dossier of pieces by other workerist-feminists such as Mariarosa Dalla Costa, Anna Culbertson's detailed analysis of the arc of Alisa Del Re's thought, Maya Gonzalez introducing Fortunati's classic *The Arcane of Reproduction* of 1981, Williams' presentation and translation of some early texts by Alquati, Daniel Spaulding's contextualisation of his translation of Sbardellas's 1980 critique of Tronti, or Asad Haider and Salar Mohandesi's comprehensive introduction to a special issue on workers' enquiries, the journal has been at the forefront of the circulation and discussion of *operaismo* as one tendency within the complex lineages of revolutionary Marxism. In this regard, *Viewpoint* has documented less known, but equally important moments within workerism's development, from Tronti's early critical encounter with Gramsci, to polemics amongst the workerists themselves, as when Raffaele Sbardella – a former member of *Classe Operaia* – savaged both that journal's limitations of as a political enterprise, and the subsequent political path taken by Tronti and his

---

3 Given the uncharacteristic clarity with which Negri presents his interpretation of workerism's evolution in this interview, the production of an English-language edition of this work remains a priority.

closest associates. In a passing reference in his latest autobiographical work, Negri (2015b: 517) dismisses any affinity made between Tronti's perspective and the idealism of Giovanni Gentile as 'an idiocy'. As it happens, it is precisely such an association between the author of *Operai e capitale* and the long-dead Italian philosopher that Sbardella establishes in this essay, a piece which is still relatively unknown even to an Italian audience. Upcoming translations likely to appear in *Viewpoint* include writings from *Primo Maggio*'s important working group on money, a topic about which there is now a small but growing body of research (Lucarelli 2013; Wright 2014). As for contributions to debates within the English-speaking left, Mohandesi's 2013 essay in *Science & Society*, entitled 'Class Consciousness or Class Composition?', is a clear exposition of just how different *operaismo*'s approach can be to other, better known Marxist analytical frameworks.

Generation online is another major online resource for translated workerist texts assembled by Arianna Bove, Erik Empson and others. Here too the holdings stretch well beyond *operaismo* to include works by or about C.L.R. James, Alfred Sohn-Rethel, Isaak Rubin, Louis Althusser, George Bataille, the Situationists and Michel Foucault, although workerism is clearly a constant reference point. Alongside interviews with Del Re and Rieser from the *Futuro Anteriore* volume, there are texts by Federici, Panzieri, the Wages for Housework collective, and others. There is also a host of writings from the period of 'post-*operaismo*', beginning with discussions of immaterial labour by Emiliana Armano, Maurizio Lazzarato, Paolo Virno, Christian Marazzi, Vercellone, and extending into more recent writings by Franco Berardi. Many later pieces by Negri have likewise been rendered in English; in addition, the Italian edition of his 1987 book *Fabbriche del soggetto*, which contains a number of his shorter (but still important) earlier writings, is also to be found there. While smaller in scale, Harry Cleaver's *Zerowork* website offers an excellent archive relating to that important English-language journal of the 1970s, including its connections with Italian workerism.

Historical Materialism is likewise a serial that has published interesting essays concerning Italian workerism. Along with a talk by Tronti himself (2010) on 'workerism and politics', there has been Sara Farris' analysis of Tronti's relationship with Weber, and Matteo Mandarini's 2010 intervention on Tronti and the notion of the autonomy of the political. A further issue of the journal contains Adelino Zanini's reflections on the 'philosophical foundations' of *operaismo*, while David Camfield (2007), Maria Turchetto (2003) and others have provided critical engagements with the work of Negri, albeit mostly addressing his 'post-workerist' phase.[4] As for the book series that *Historical Materialism* hosts for Brill and Haymarket, one notable volume is *Beyond Marx*, edited by Marcel van der Linden and Karl Heinz Roth, and showcasing many pertinent essays by (amongst others) Ferruccio Gambino, Devi Sacchetto, Bologna, Maria Mies, Silvia Federici, Massimiliano Tomba, Riccardo Bellofiore, George Caffentzis, and Carlo Vercellone.

Some of the most extended investigations into workerism have been conducted as research theses. One key resource in this respect is Patrick Cuninghame's doctoral dissertation on Autonomia, completed in 2002. This major study can be found online, and is recommended reading for anyone trying to unravel the shifting complexion of Italian autonomist politics. This thesis is in part a critical engagement with, and corrective to, Sydney Tarrow's 1989 analysis of protest cycles in 1960s and '70s Italy. While the latter work is important as one of a number of pioneering texts from the 1980s (also worthy of mention is David Moss' research on politically motivated violence and the Italian far left), Cuninghame rightly takes it to task, starting with its failure to pay sufficient attention to mass struggles in the latter half of the 1970s. For his part, Cuninghame provides a detailed account of Autonomia's rise and fall across that decade, utilising a rich array of printed materials and interviews with former participants. As his thesis makes clear, although certain constants remained in terms of ideology and practice, Autonomia's social roots and perspectives shifted as the movement spread from larger workplaces to find increasing resonance in communities and schools. Here the two-dozen interviews that Cuninghame conducted are key in identifying important tensions within Autonomia: around the nature and use of political violence; between approaches centred on the mass worker, and those focused on other layers within the proletariat; between different understandings of political organisation, whether Leninist or libertarian; between generations of militants, each with their own experiences and outlook. In doing so, the interviews also provide clues as to not only Autonomia's collapse, but the reasons for the wider revolutionary movement's demise. In the words of one of Cuninghame's respondents,

> (the kidnap and killing of) (...) Moro was the end (...) it was very sad, because that was the moment we all thought it had become very, very dangerous to be in politics. Most of us, like '*Boccalone*', like myself, started feeling the *riflusso*. There is this moment in which you play

---

4   On this score, one of the best critiques of the post-workerism of Negri and others can be found in Mark Gawne's 2014 PhD thesis.

your identity collectively. It seems you are touching history in being with others. And then it doesn't happen, it doesn't work any more (...) and you start feeling: 'So what am I doing?' In that period I started taking heroin, a lot of people did. There was a lot of self-destruction, either in terrorism or in drugs. (Quoted in Cuninghame 2002: 194)[5]

As for other pertinent theses in English, Phil Edwards' 2009 monograph *More work! Less pay! Rebellion and Repression in Italy, 1972–7*, which was based upon his earlier doctoral research, is similarly indispensable both for the wealth of detail it offers about radical social movements of the time, and for the corrections which it too provides to Tarrow's reading of that cycle of struggle. Equally of note is Mark Howard's 2014 dissertation, which extends Cuninghame's and Edwards' engagement of Tarrow to encompass a range of sociological treatments of the Sessantotto decade, starting with the influential work of Donatella della Porta. Particularly interesting is Howard's forceful discussion of primary source materials used in certain accounts of the period: as he notes, when seeking to interpret a decade as contentious as the Italy of the 1970s, the political (not to mention judicial) status of those providing first-hand accounts – say, a former member of an armed group or autonomist collective turned state evidence, as opposed to a former member who did not – carries enormous repercussions for the discourse that is eventually constructed.

Another informative thesis is the 2014 dissertation crafted by David Palazzo, which traces the category of the 'social factory' across the trajectory of workerist thought. Focusing in turn on the writings of Panzieri, Tronti, Negri and Dalla Costa, Palazzo provides a clear analysis of the varying nuances held over time by a concept that is both central to *operaismo*, yet too frequently taken for granted. What makes Palazzo's analysis especially engaging is the manner in which, like Cuninghame and Howard, he situates this exposition within the context of social conflict in Italy, and the efforts by workerists and others to organise political instruments adequate to that conflict. In this respect, Palazzo's discussion of the efforts, first by *La Classe* and then Potere Operaio – and partly in response, by Lotta Femminista – to influence the dynamics of class struggle, and the ways in which the notion of social factory helped to inform those efforts, are well worth reading with care, as are the insights offered in earlier chapters regarding *Classe Operaia*. Evan Calder

---

5 'Boccalone' is the narrator who recounts the 'Movement of '77' in Bologna in the eponymous novel written by Enrico Palandri. First appearing in 1979, it has been republished a number of times, the most recently being in 2011. For informative discussions, see van den Bossche (2006) and Righi (2011).

Williams' 2013 doctoral thesis, on the other hand, has a rather different focus: the place of cinema in Italy's mass upheavals of a half-century ago. In its own way, however, his work is likewise infused with the 'working-class point of view' as outlined from *Quaderni Rossi* onwards. In the process of building his argument that 'cinema is a particular mode of spatial, economic, and historical circulation that itself provides materials for social critique', Williams subjects the writings around class and power produced by Tronti, Negri and – first and foremost – Alquati to a careful examination that is both fascinating and timely.

The decision to concentrate in *Storming Heaven* on the dominant components within *operaismo* meant that some of the more interesting streams within the tendency did not receive their due. Fortunately, others have since produced works that do provide insights into a number of these experiences. In terms of workerist-feminism, an important collection of Federici's writings from the 1970s onwards appeared under the Common Notions imprint in 2012, as did a volume by Dalla Costa (2015) entitled *Family, Welfare, and the State*. Translations of texts by various groupings of the period have been published by *Viewpoint*, while Maud Ann Bracke (2013, 2014) has looked at the Italian workerist-feminists within the wider setting not only of the Italian dimension of second wave feminism, but also the international campaign for Wages for Housework. The significance of the feminist threads that arose in and against *operaismo* cannot be overestimated, both for the history of the tendency, and even more importantly for what those threads can contribute in their own right to efforts to challenge the present state of things. On this score, we still don't know enough about the evolution of Lotta Femminista and its successor organisations, although the website *Femminismo: gli anni ruggenti* for one can now be consulted for its rich array of Italian language publications, with a particular emphasis upon the activities of circles in and around Padua. And as noted earlier, some of those who took part in this experience have since shared their thoughts on the meaning of their work during those years, and its implications for the future. For example, Leopoldina Fortunati (2013) has recently argued that

> The feminist movement had the great merit of giving women an overall bargaining power at the social level. However, as we had anticipated, the problem of 'housework' or domestic labor did not disappear from the political agenda of women. Unfortunately, a reflection on the failure of this strategy has not yet been made. New generations of women need to learn from this political error and understand that

housework, in its material and immaterial aspects, must be socially recognized as productive labor.

For her part, Mariarosa Dalla Costa (2002) has stated that only in the 1980s was she able to encounter a different kind of politics, one that might move beyond the limitations imposed by an earlier way of understanding the world around her:

> The fact is that as I was trying to find the cause of my lack of joy, I had to admit that the context within which I had struggled in the 70s, in front of the factories or in the houses – basically the coupling of time-money [...] constituted a ground which had failed to move my deep currents in order to produce fluxes of energy. This is the reason why I had felt no joy [...]. What I missed was something which could positively generate emotions, a strong imaginary, which could open different scenarios. I needed to encounter other questions and new subjects, who desired and were able to effectively think a different world. Therefore for part of the '80s I continued to wander around, from room to room, in the house of reproduction. Until, at a certain point, I saw the door to the garden, I saw the issue of the earth.

A second overlooked milieu – that of theorists of space, design and capital – has attracted considerable attention in recent years amongst those attentive to the so-called Venice Group and/or the Faculty of Architecture at the University of Florence. Useful accounts of the nuances amongst thinkers as diverse as Massimo Cacciari, Claudio Greppi, Francesco Dal Co and Manfredo Tafuri can now be found in books by Gail Day (2010) and Pier Vittorio Aureli (2008), a thesis by Emre Özyetiş (2013), as well as shorter texts by Amit Wolf (2012), Alexandra Brown (2010) and James Dunbar (2016). With any luck, this research will soon be extended to a critical engagement with the journal *Contropiano*, with which many of these Italian theorists were also linked. Thinking more generally about *operaismo* and design, one researcher to watch out for in the future is Jacopo Gallimberti, whose 2012 account of the N group from Padua forms part of a wider research project which promises to be a thorough and erudite excavation of the workerist legacy on this front.

In a generous review of *Storming Heaven*, Sergio Bologna (2003: 99) rightly noted other failings in the book, such as its lack of attention to Genoa-based militants like Gianfranco Fiana, and the links established between the Italian workerists and American leftist circles, above all by

Gambino.[6] Nicola Pizzolato's exploration of 'Labor Migration, Radical Struggle, and Urban Change in Detroit and Turin' – the subtitle of his 2013 work *Challenging Global Capitalism* – looks both at the exchanges between revolutionaries in Italy and the US, and the similarities and differences between the mass upheavals in two leading auto cities of the period. In a long and sober conclusion, Pizzolato (2013: 205) spells out his views not only as to why militants in both countries could and did draw inspiration from each other, but also the limits of the broader cycle of struggle within which they were obliged to operate:

> As the successors of an earlier generation of intellectuals who had critically analyzed the expansion of the Fordist system and gauged the opportunities for resistance by considering parallel developments in the two cities, radicals of the late nineteen sixties interpreted the cogent similarities in the industrial and urban conflicts as evidence of an ongoing global revolutionary process. At the same time, this transnational circulation, though it might offer inspiration, could provide no over-arching solutions. Though international in scope, the fate of any one struggle was always inextricably linked to local circumstances and to the specific national framework.

On a related score, the late Stuart Hilwig's 2009 book is a contrarian (but all the more stimulating as a consequence) take on relations between students and workers in 1968, while Gerd-Rainer Horn's presentation of *The Spirit of '68* (2007) is a superb general history of movements across North America and Western Europe from the mid-1950s to the mid-1970s. Apart from its many strengths as a comparative study, Horn's survey draws upon an enormous range of sources in order to present a lively account of an age when mass social subversion in schools, the workplace and communities was a reality, before closing with the barbed comment that 'the sentiment that it can never happen again is somewhat bemusing to anyone with a historical memory' (Horn 2007: 238).

Back in 2003, in the journal *Strategies*, I suggested a dozen titles by Tronti, Negri, Panzieri and others that should be published in English. So far, only *The Factory of Strategy* has made that transition, thanks to Arianna Bove. Of the remainder, the most important by far is still *L'orda d'oro*, a hefty anthology about the movements of the period, compiled by Balestrini and Moroni. Configured from a clearly workerist perspective, this book is unmatched for its range of materials, and the

---

6   More details of Gambino's time spent in the US, where he met the likes of Murray Bookchin and the *Facing Reality* group, are recounted in Gambino 2001.

skilful commentary with which its editors have woven its contents together. With any luck, it will find its way into translation sooner rather than later.

TOGLIATTI IN ITALIAN[7]

Turning to relevant materials produced in Italy itself, a good place to start is with the most significant publisher of workerist-related texts: DeriveApprodi, based in Rome. This enterprise was established early last decade in the wake of a journal of the same name, one which provided a forum that brought together younger members of the Italian movement alongside veterans of days gone by. Its founders included Sergio Bianchi, whose tale of *autonomia diffusa* and subsequent prison life is captured in Nanni Balestrini's novel *The Unseen*. Having begun its series on *operaismo* with *Futuro Anteriore* in 2002, DeriveApprodi has gone on to produce volumes that encompass the full gamut of relevant works: reprints of earlier materials, recollections of former participants, history of related movements, and discussions of theorists and theory.

One of DeriveApprodi's most valuable columns contains essays about important journals of the past – not only *Classe Operaia* and *Primo Maggio*, but also *Rosso* and *A/traverso*. Typically, these have been accompanied by disks holding digitised reproductions of the original print publications: another book, yet unpublished, is touted to include all the serials associated with the organisation Potere Operaio. Amongst them, the weightiest tome produced by DeriveApprodi is a volume, nearly 900 pages in length, containing archival material and interviews relating to the years of *Quaderni Rossi* and *Classe Operaia* (Trotta and Milana 2008). It begins with a long reflective essay by Tronti – since brought out as a book in its own right (Tronti 2009), as well as being translated in part and reprinted in the pages of *New Left Review* (Tronti 2012). The bulk of *L'operaismo degli anni Sessanta* is taken up with hundreds of internal documents, transcriptions of meetings, letters, and leaflets, each carefully and thoughtfully placed in context by the editors. Rounding out the book are interviews with many of those writing for these iconic journals, as well as a detailed chronology and bibliography. It may have been this very volume that once inspired Alberto Toscano to remark that never had a political tendency been so exhaustively minuted as *operaismo* – and even more so in terms of its political-ideological debates, as opposed to its overt interventions into political struggle. If

---

7   One of Alquati's witticisms from the *Classe Operaia* period concerned how quickly Tronti's novel project for establishing 'Lenin in England' had transmuted into the tired old approach of 'Togliatti in Italy' – see Alquati (n.d.: 10).

so, such scepticism towards this kind of 'archive fever' is more than a little justified, but it also has to be said that this book, at least, does offer important access to the multiple streams and rivulets that had come together and merged in the early 1960s to launch the classical workerist experiment of rediscovering 'Lenin in England'.

Another notable output from DeriveApprodi is its three-volume (soon to be four) series called *Gli autonomi*. Opened by an excellent reflective essay from Pino Tripodi, the first of these is mostly taken up with chronicles of Autonomia in different regions of Italy during the 1970s: some are the recollections of former participants, others essays by younger researchers. Alongside the obvious cases of Milan, Rome, and the Veneto, there are portraits of the movement in places such as Florence and Genoa; most importantly, given the scarcity hitherto of such things, there are at least a couple of chapters on autonomist politics in the country's South. The book as a whole makes a fascinating read, even if the contributions by former participants vary considerably both in their level of detail and self-reflection, ranging from those that are uncritically celebratory, to those prepared to concede that Autonomia's defeat may have been at least partly of its own making.

The second volume, based in part upon an anthology edited by the Rome-based Comitati autonomi operai (CAO) back in 1976, gathers together many documents produced by a variety of autonomist collectives, as well as a chronology of events and some essays concerning autonomist politics in other countries. The fourth volume, which is in press as I write, will provide a history of Autonomia in Rome – one of the most crucial experiences in the movement as a whole, with deep roots in that city's popular quarters – which with any luck will prove to be rather more self-critical than the chapters offered by former members in the first books of the series.

Of particular interest is the third book in the set, which explores, on the front of print, radio, music and film, the society-wide cultural clash of which Autonomia was a central component. Here 'autonomist' is taken in the broadest sense of the term, stretching far beyond the groups of Autonomia organizzata to encompass, on the front of comics for example, the likes of the situationist-inspired zine *Puzz* or the cartoonist Andrea Pazienza. Then again, as the afore-mentioned Negri (2012) introduction to Jerry Rubin makes clear, the relationship between the autonomists and 'underground' or counter-cultural politics during the 1970s was as rich as it was contradictory. Recalling the period of Potere Operaio's decline, Negri speaks of a time when

Resistance became a sort of disease, a malignant isolation, a tiring interaction of theoretical formulas. In these conditions, every relationship between me and the other was, and still is as one can easily continue to observe now paternalistic. I had understood and lived through big struggles, but now in this moment of recession and defeat I was falling back into the dodgy purity of 'third-internationalism', and I had a difficult, asthmatic, relationship with the reality of class. Then, as suddenly as it had disappeared, the 'spirit reappeared again' first a pistol shot, then a burst of gunfire. The auto workers started up again at Mirafiori in 1973, the proletarians in S. Basilio in 1974, the youth in Milan in 1974 and then, gradually, more and more. I am approaching this reality of struggles with caution, I open this dialogue again with much difficulty: youth, workers, women! Strange, I can sense in these people a familiar smell yes, a thousand, a million brothers and sisters. I recognize them. Just when I was almost done with my struggle and I felt that my work was at the very end, these people brought back to the movement the energy and desire to react again from inside the defeat by sneaking through the folds of class divisions, by expressing the material conditions of new proletarian categories in revolt, by using their bodies as means of liberation. Their actions had infused new cheer and will to attack into the movement, restoring it for the years to come.[8]

Then again, not everything between these two forms of social revolt was sweetness and light, and Alessandro Bertante's book-length 2005 history of the journal *Re Nudo* does a good job in documenting the often conflicted ways in which Autonomia and 'freaks' continually crossed paths, in Milan and beyond, before both were driven from the political stage.

Two other overviews of Autonomia are worthy of note. If Emilio Quadrelli's 2008 text begins in the late 1960s and continues into the 1980s, it nonetheless revolves around the autonomist movement of the 1970s, and is distinguished amongst other things by long and fascinating interviews with anonymous militants recounting the period. Marcello Tari's *The Ice was Thin*, which first appeared in French in 2011, is the most gripping as well as the most intricate history of Autonomia produced so far, and gives a powerful sense not only of the movement's dynamism at its peak, but also the complexities of the practices and belief systems

---

8 Also important in this regard are the political writings of Elvio Fachinelli, a psychoanalyst who together with Lea Melandri brought out the important 'alternative' magazine *L'erba volgio* during this period – see Dario Borso's (2016) collection of Fachinelli's work, published by DeriveApprodi.

to be found within it. One of Tarì's most worthy attributes is that while his admiration for the project of Autonomia as a whole is unequivocal, he does not pull punches when recounting the many significant errors committed by its *ceto politico*, above all as the urge to 'conquer' the broader far left finally overtook the earlier espousal of class self-organisation.

An area in which recent publications have increased our understanding of the evolution of workerist politics involves studies focused on the regional level. *L'eresia bolognese* is a 2015 collection of documents (digitised on DVD) spanning the years from 1967 to the end of the 1980s, while Matteo Montaguti's 2013 thesis charts the fortunes of workerists in Modena. Another work, *Quelli dell'Alberone*, published in 2000, is the history of an important autonomist grouping in Rome notable in part for functioning outside the hegemony of the so-called 'Volsci' of the CAO. Having compiled a useful and detailed overview of revolutionary tendencies in and around the northern city of Bergamo, Emilio Mentasti has since written the first detailed account of the Comitato operaio active in the Magneti Marelli plant on the edges of Milan. A key firm in the automobile components sector, Magneti Marelli was also well known in the 1970s for the militancy of its workforce, prominent amongst which was a collective aligned with Oreste Scalzone's wing of Autonomia. *La Guarda rossa racconta*, which appeared in 2007, charts the rise and eventual fall of that Comitato operaio and the distinctive demands that its members developed in seeking to challenge management authority in the factory. Mentasti followed this up in 2011 with another work, this time a history of the autonomist group Comitati comunisti, with which the Marelli militants were associated. Both books draw heavily on primary source materials – the first primarily using workplace leaflets, the second also encompassing broadsheets like the newspaper *Senza Tregua* – to record these groups' actions and declarations. This is a story that has been told before, but never in such detail, even if one is still left wanting to know more about the exact circumstances in which this current finally disintegrated.

More controversial are the 2015 memoirs of Alessandro Stella, which speak of Autonomia in Vicenza before and after the period of repression. This text, published by a social centre in regional Veneto, has been sharply criticised by other veterans of the time for its 'unacceptable' interpretation of a number of events, including the explosion that killed three autonomists in the town of Thiene (Tagliapietra et al. 2015). For their part, writers associated with DeriveApprodi have used photographs, documents and the memories of participants in an effort to make sense of two other dramatic moments in the movement's history, both from 1977: a shootout at a demonstration in Milan from May that left one policeman dead and pushed the city's autonomist formations into a disarray from which they never recovered (Bianchi 2011), and another clash with firearms from earlier in the year in Rome that led to the wounding and imprisonment by police of two members of stewards' organisations linked to the Comitati Comunisti (Caminiti et al. 2012).

In a different way, Sergio Bianchi's portfolio of 'Orphans' (*Figli di nessuno. Storia di un movimento autonomo*) from 2015 mixes movement documents of the period with individual and collective reminiscences to offer a history of Autonomia in and near Varese, a key urban concentration in Lombardy. *Figli di nessuno* can be read in its own right, but it also forms a kind of backdrop and afterword to Nanni Balestrini's novel *The Unseen*, recently reprinted by Verso with an introduction by Negri. This latter book tells of Bianchi's experiences in the late 1970s and early '80s, including the difficult period of mass arrests that finally defeated Autonomia as a significant political force within Italian society. Indeed, Balestrini's technique of 'novelizing' the life stories of militants has inspired its fair share of worthy imitators. The best known of these is probably Marco Philopat's *La Banda Bellini* (2015), which charts the varying fortunes across the 1970s of the most famous group of street fighters in Milan's far left. Equally entertaining is Paolo Pozzi's *Insurrezzione* (2007): likewise set in Milan, this is a droll retelling of the rise and fall of the autonomist group gathered around the journal *Rosso*.

With the appearance of volumes such as *Vittorio Rieser. Intellettuale militante di classe* (Gaddi 2015), we have also come to know much more about the ideas and practices of individuals in and around the milieu that first generated *operaismo*. Although not formally a workerist in the sense used in *Storming Heaven*, Rieser was an important figure first in *Quaderni Rossi*, and then in the enlarged far left that emerged with 1968. Respected for his personal integrity and acumen, Rieser continued to cross paths with the workerists in various undertakings of the 1960s, of which perhaps the most notable was the Assemblea Operai Studenti, a body that played a key role in fomenting the wildcat strikes at FIAT in 1969. The same publishing house that brought out this book – a collection of Rieser's writings as well as others' appreciation of his work – also produced *1969–1977 lotte operaie a Torino. L'esperienza dei Cub, comitati unitari di base* (Allara et al. 2009), which examines the workplace collectives built by Rieser and others in the wake of the Assemblea's collapse. Useful here as well is Damiano Palano's (2015a) thoughtful review of Rieser's political path across the decades, viewed through the prism of the workers' enquiry.

Unlike Lotta Continua, there had been no book-length treatments of Potere Operaio when *Storming Heaven* was first published. Instead, at best there was Franco Berardi's *La nefasta utopia di Potere operaio* from 1998, and the brief for the 7 April trials written by the judge Giovanni Palombarini (1982), each of which devoted at least a couple of chapters to the history of the workerist group. That changed in 2003, with the appearance of Aldo Grandi's volume *La generazione degli anni perduti*. In a savage review, Negri (2003b) dismissed the journalist's book as exaggerating the militaristic culture within that organisation, as well as failing to examine in any detail the experiences of workplace organising, such as in its stronghold of Porto Marghera. Many of Negri's objections are well-founded, although the book has a number of merits all the same – not least being its extensive use of interviews with former members of the group, many of which subsequently appeared in a second volume edited by Grandi a couple of years later. While certain regions in Italy (Florence and Rome) are overrepresented in *Insurrezione Armata* (a title which again frames the organisation too simplistically), these testimonies are nonetheless important for what can be gleaned from them, involving as they do not only the leading members of Potere Operaio such as Scalzone and Alberto Magnaghi, but also the thoughts of middle-ranking cadre (the likes of Lauso Zagato), and factory militants like the Sbrogió brothers.

What about the Internet as a source of materials? If the long-term persistence of documents placed there is less certain than that on DVD or CD, at present one can find the first five numbers of the newspaper *i volsci* online, while the website of the Archivio Primo Moroni contains full sets of *Senza Tregua*, *L'Erba Voglio*, and *Sinistra Proletaria*, as well as early issues of *Autonomia* and *Metropoli* (which in 2016 was reproduced in hard copy by Pgreco Edizioni of Milan). On the other hand, materials previously on the Internet have since disappeared, recalling Jeff Rothenberg's quip that 'It is only slightly facetious to say that digital information lasts forever – or five years, whichever comes first'.[9] Amongst the history journals currently in print and accessible via the Internet, *Zapruder* is a constant source of studies and reflections concerning the period in question, with most numbers containing at least one or two articles relating to the far left of the 1960s and '70s, including various workerist groups. From its very first issue, which dealt with the theme of conflict in the streets, special issues or dossiers have

---

9 To cite just one case for illustration: the second edition of the anthology *L'Orda D'oro*, compiled by Balestrini and Moroni, contains a short section summarising a number of interviews, conducted years later, with members of the dominant autonomist group in the Veneto region during the 1970s. For a while these materials, entitled 'Liberiamo gli anni '70', could be accessed at a website associated with Radio Sherwood; today they have long since vanished.

been common: for example, no. 34, from mid 2014, deals with movement radio, with articles on Radio Alice (Bologna), Radio Sherwood (Padua), and Radio Onda Rossa (Rome), as well as other pieces concerning the political use of the airwaves across Europe. Another notable feature of *Zapruder* is the attention paid to archives, with most issues containing short but insightful profiles of repositories relevant to the study of cycles of popular culture and conflict.

More extended treatments of autonomist radio can be found in a number of university theses written in the past 15 years. Valentina Antoniol's study of Alice and Sherwood draws, amongst other sources, upon interviews with those involved in running these iconic stations during the 1970s, while Emanuela Fiorletta's 2001 history of Onda Rossa is even more extensive in its treatment and its pool of sources. In all, there is now a considerable body of research available that, whilst often not addressing *operaismo* at length, still helps to frame the contours within which it developed.

Other dissertations worth mentioning on this front include Giulia Vergottini's 2012 dissection of the impact of feminism within the major New Left groups of the 1970s, especially as represented within their press; Alberto Pantaloni's history of Lotta Continua's organisational collapse in Turin, a process which fed both the autonomists and the armed groups (indeed, which fed those sections of Autonomia that spawned their own armed groups aiming to rival the Brigate Rosse); Daniele Franco's 2009 exploration of the influence of French 'sociology of work', including the publications of *Socialisme ou barbarie*, on the method and practice of enquiry within Italy; and Marilisa Malizia's discussion of the 'unsolved relationships' between the women's movement and politically-motivated acts of violence. Meanwhile, focusing on the petrochemical plants of the Venice lagoon, Omar Salani Favaro's 2013 doctorate provides an intricate narrative of workplace struggles that both echoes and complements Cesco Chinello's (1996) magisterial, two-volume history of 'Union, PCI, movements in the 1960s: Porto Marghera-Venezia 1955–1970'.

In terms of other works that help us better grasp the place of *operaismo* within Italian traditions of radical theory, again a number of important books have appeared over the past decade and a half. In terms of general background, Cristina Corradi's *Storia dei marxismi in Italia* (2011) supplies both a keen dissection of the dominant threads of local 'Marxisms' from Labriola onwards, and a provocative but well-informed discussion of workerism in particular – and if the book itself has yet to appear in translation, at least Peter Thomas' thoughtful introduction has managed to grace the pages of *New Left Review*. A matching volume, edited by Riccardo Bellofiore (2007) and also published by manifestolibri, brings together essays inspired by Corradi's history. Mariamargherita Scotti's comprehensive *Da sinistra* (2011) is narrower in focus, skillfully delineating the rise of dissident Marxists within the PSI of the 1950s, foremost of whom was of course Raniero Panzieri. A volume commemorating Panzieri, published just over 40 years after his death (Ferrero 2005), is also worth a look, above all for the personal reminiscences that it brings together from those in and around *Quaderni Rossi*. The *Enciclopedia del '68*, edited by writers from the newspaper *il manifesto*, is a rich reference text that looks at events, ideologies, organisations, and the kinds of resources brought to bear during the mass mobilisations of the period, while Salvatore Ricciardi's *Maelstrom* (2011) weaves together his personal narrative of life as a militant with a collective portrait of the Hot Autumn, the rise of Autonomia, and the years in which the Brigate Rosse came to prominence. Also relevant in this regard is Diego Giachetti's (2008) analysis of the ways in which class, gender and generation intersected and redounded in and around the social movements that took the stage from the late 1960s.

Other militants in the orbit of *Quaderni Rossi* have likewise been the object of excellent studies published in Italian. The Centro Documentazione Pistoia has brought out short studies of Panzieri (Pianciola 2014) and Giovanni Pirelli (Bermani 2011) as part of its *Quaderni dell'Italia Antimoderata* series, while Danilo Balicco's 2006 book *Non parlo a tutti* ('I don't speak to everyone') still remains the best guide to Franco Fortini's writings. If Danilo Montaldi's impact upon the early workerists was not comparable to that of Panzieri, nonetheless his views on working-class politics were a constant touchstone for many in the tendency, especially Alquati. Papers about Montaldi presented at a conference in Cremona have since been published in a volume edited by Gianfranco Fiameni (2003), while a special issue of the journal *Parolechiave* from 2007 is likewise devoted to Montaldi's efforts on the artistic as well as political front, with Sergio Bologna's contribution to the Faimeni collection reprinted in a 2007 anthology of his essays that contains three other pieces relating to the history of *operaismo*.

A respectable number of books by or about individual workerists have also appeared during the new millennium. Negri, not surprisingly, is the most common subject here, and Mimmo Sersante's relentlessly sympathetic treatment of Negri's political journey from the 1950s to the late 1970s is an effective overview, as is the recent sequel co-authored with Willer Montefusco. For his part, Bologna provides a lengthy introduction to *Dal fordismo alla globalizzazione*, a posthumous gathering together of Luciano Ferrari Bravo's most influential essays, while Negri's moving

2003 biography of his friend continues to be one of the best texts that he has written to date. From a different angle, the recent re-issue of Asor Rosa's essays from the 1960s contains a 'historical preface' that offers his take on, amongst other things, the project of classical workerism. The posthumous work by Primo Moroni, *La luna sotto casa* (2007), offers incisive portraits of social conflict in Milan during and after 1968, and is a worthy complement to an earlier anthology of his writing from 2001 (since reprinted in 2012). There have also been some studies of historians who, together with Moroni, helped edit the journal *Primo Maggio* – from Damiano Palano's (2015b) review of Sergio Bologna's approach to historiography, to a collection of papers dedicated to the oral history of Cesare Bermani (Bellamio et al. 2012).

Considerations in print of Tronti's significance as a political theorist are a low-intensity but nonetheless regular feature in Italy. The volume *Politica e Destino*, which came out in 2006, brings together a dozen essays first drafted when Tronti retired from teaching back at the beginning of the millennium. Most of the authors are the usual suspects, chiefly collaborators from the *Classe Operaia* days. Tronti's (2006: 28) own introduction to the book contains the following aphorism, demonstrating yet again that when it comes to the composition of memorable lines, if not always their execution, he remains second to none:

> It is right to rebel: but one needs to do it well, to know how to do it well, to learn how to know how to do it well – and this is the task of a lifetime.

As for essays on Tronti's work, Michele Filippini has written a number of important reflections in both Italian and French (one of these, centred upon the *Classe Operaia* period and co-authored with Emilio Macchia, has now come out in book form in English). The most detailed introduction to Tronti's trajectory continues to be Franco Milanesi's 2014 tome, *Nel Novecento: Storia, teoria, politica nel pensiero di Mario Tronti*. Here the author, who has also produced an excellent book on the function of militants as a driving force within radical movements, develops a lucid guide to the path taken by Tronti, from his early dissent within the PCI of the 1950s, through to the formulation of classical *operaismo* as a doctrine, and then the shifts and turns of his perspective once he had thrown his lot in again with the Community party and its successors.

Not long before his passing in 2016, Italo Sbrogiò (2016) was able to see the publication of his personal history of struggle alongside other petrochemical workers employed in Porto Marghera, an account that is interwoven with primary sources from the period. Seven years earlier, manifestolibri had issued *Quando il potere è operaio*, a work co-edited by Devi Sacchetto and Sbrogiò's brother Gianni. Some of the contributions to that book – those of Massimo Cacciari, Toni Negri, and Karl Heinz Roth – were originally presented at a 2007 conference about 'Settanta. Gli anni sospesi', and the latter two have since been translated into English and can be found at www.libcom.org. These offer privileged views into particular aspects of the Marghera experience of workers' self-organisation, first in the Comitato Operaio, and later the Assemblea Autonoma. They are framed in turn by two longer and very detailed accounts of the period, each penned by one of the book's editors, and complemented by a documentary film on an accompanying DVD – also entitled *Gli anni sospesi* – along with one of the Marghera Comitato Operaio's most famous texts, 'Il rifiuto del lavoro'. Of these longer pieces, Gianni Sbrogiò's is a blow-by-blow account of the formation and development of workers' power in the factory and community. Devi Sacchetto's closing essay instead draws upon more than 20 interviews to paint an intricate picture of the political subjectivity of those who shaped the Marghera story. His interviewees are mostly worker militants who had taken part in these organisations, but there are 'external militants' here too, as well as those who remained within the unions.

We also hear some of the few female voices in what, as Sacchetto notes, is 'a terribly masculine history'. It is a rich, complex chorus that emerges here – 'a mosaic' – that reverberates in the film directed by Manuela Pellarin, where excerpts from the interviews are blended with original footage of the times. Without nostalgia, but rather a quiet passion and some humour, these men and women tell us how they came to challenge the circumstances of their daily lives. As Bellofiore and Tomba note in the afterword to this new edition of *Storming Heaven*, much of what happened in the tumultuous realm of chemical plants sitting across the bay from Venice is testament to how 'the *operaismo* of male and female workers were more advanced than the reflections of the current's theoreticians'. Although *Quando il potere è operaio* and the film *Gli anni sospesi* have not yet appeared in English, an earlier documentary about Marghera by the same director can be found on another DVD issued by the German group Wildcat (2004) – indeed, this latter film, *Gli ultimi fuochi*, can at the time of writing be viewed (with English subtitles) on YouTube.

In terms of visual materials, more and more of such documents can be found online these days. One cycle of recorded seminars (available on Vimeo) contains contributions not only by a younger generation of politically engaged scholars, but also central figures of *operaismo* such as

Negri, Bologna, Del Re and Marazzi, discussing class composition, the state, and workers' enquiries; another related series of talks features the likes of Mario Dalmaviva reflecting on the meaning of political militancy in the 1960s and '70s.[10] In terms of striking still camera work, there are now a number of books with photographs by Tano D'Amico (see for example, D'Amico 2008), who snapped many of the iconic images of that epoch for the pages of journals such as *Lotta Continua* and *I volsci*. Another work to mention here – once again from the DeriveApprodi stable – is William Gambetta's survey of political posters as a means of communication, *I muri del lungo '68* (2014). Finally, social media was the trigger for one of the most intriguing books about the movement in Bologna, *I ragazzi del '77* (2011), a kind of family photo album with commentary by dozens of participants that first began to accumulate within, of all things, Facebook.

As Sergio Bologna has long pointed out, the discourse of 'militarising the movement' in the early 1970s was one of the more evident signs of Potere Operaio's growing crisis in the face of a class composition that proved richer, more complex and more resistant to being 'nudged along' than anticipated.[11] In this respect, Antonio Lenzi's 2016 book-length treatment of Lotta Continua and the Manifesto group during the early 1970s is instructive here, since Potere Operaio frequently crossed the path of both these far-left groups, as it attempted to find its bearings after 1969. A number of studies, of which one of the most impressive is Marco Grispigni's *Quella sera a Milano era caldo* (2016), have deepened our appreciation of the circumstances within which 'the critique of arms' came to preoccupy more and more sections of the Italian movement in the wake of the Hot Autumn. Grispigni's book is important not only because it discusses the broader context wherein certain forms of violence became normalised within the Italian revolutionary politics of the time, but because it sets this within the subsequent historiographical debate, as well as within a comparative framework gauged against the French far left of the period. Other notable works on the same question include Guido Panvini's *Ordine nero, guerriglia rossa* (2009), which lays out a very detailed account of events and debates in the early 1970s as it seeks to argue that clashes with neo-fascists came to overdetermine many revolutionaries' understandings and practice of political violence; Aldo Gianulli's vivid account of insurgent actions and repression in

---

10 The Vimeo-based talks have now been transcribed and published as *Genealogie del futuro* (Roggero & Zanini 2013).

11 'What interested us was endowing workers' struggles with a specific offensive capacity, an extra "oomph" that they would not otherwise have had' – Massimo Casa, former member of Potere Operaio, in Grandi 2005: 98.

Bombe a inchiostro (2008); a 2010 volume of essays edited by Angelo Ventrone; another anthology of papers from 2012 compiled by Simone Neri Serneri and featuring excellent historical work, and even Gabriele Licciardi's rather sensationalist and mistitled *Macchie rosse: L'operaismo italiano tra politica e lotta armata* (2014).

If the practice of militant anti-fascism could be read from the early 1970s as one response to the maneuvering of both sections of the state and the fascist camp to terrorise and disorient mass unrest in the workplace and the community, the rationale for politically-motivated force was nonetheless somewhat different within Potere Operaio. The development of the workerist group's discourse on violence is treated in an exhaustive way in Gabriele Donato 2014 book *La lotta è armata*, which also examines the polemics in and around Lotta Continua and the nascent Brigate Rosse. Donato's careful reconstruction of the debates and programmatic positions assumed by each of these groups at the time is a key text for anyone who wants to make sense of what later befell them, as well as the inadequacy of, in the author's words, any collective undertaking unable to 'elaborate a political project that does not exhaust itself in the pure and simple will to mete out punishment [*farsi giustizia*]' (Donato 2014: 369).

Talk of political violence inevitably raises the links between *operaismo*, Autonomia, and the armed groups of the 1970s – and thus the 7 April case and the wider state repression within which that case was central. The weakest of the literature on this front is undoubtedly the various texts produced by some of the trial judges and their closest associates, starting with Pietro Calogero, whose famed 'theorem' refused to differentiate between the autonomists and the Brigate Rosse. Emblematic here is the 2010 collection of essays *Terrore rosso: dall'autonomia al partito armato*, of whose authors it can be said, like the Bourbons, that they have forgotten nothing and learned nothing. In contrast, Giovanni Palombarini's 2014 title *Il processo 7 aprile nei ricordi del giudice istruttore* is well worth a look, even if it continues to be overshadowed by his 1982 work *7 aprile: il processo e la storia*, which was the first serious attempt by an outsider to write a considered intellectual and political history of Potere Operaio and those sections of Autonomia descended from it.

Over the years, anniversaries of 1968 in Italy have been marked by spates of memoirs by former participants, in a manner that recalls (not always favorably) an earlier generation's recollections of the Resistance years. All the same, some of this material is worth more than a cursory glance. Before his return to Italy from France in 1997, Negri had already written one rather stylised book-length account of his personal history (published in English in 2015 as *Pipeline*), as well as a further book concerning his 1983 flight from Italy (Negri 2010). Nearly 20 years later, 2015's *Storia di un comunista* is the most detailed by far of Negri's memorialist endeavours, spanning the first half of his life, up until his arrest on 7 April 1979. What Negri deems to be his central experiences are recounted in considerable detail and with great enthusiasm, even exuberance – and if some readers will sometimes be left wondering how consistently his version of events squares with what else is known of the period, still the book is unavoidable for anyone trying to make sense of the impact of *operaista* politics upon those who lived through it. Of note too is the considerable attention paid in this book not only to organisational matters and industrial campaigns, but to the content and function of various workerist publications as weapons of struggle.

We can conclude our survey of material published since the turn of the millennium by noting that 2017 is the 40th anniversary of 1977, a truly tumultuous year for Italian society as a whole, as well as for those circles aiming to subvert it. A modest outpouring of publications on the topic has already begun, one of the first being Oreste Scalzone's (2017) recollections of Autonomia in conversation with Pino Cassamassima (who had earlier recorded Franco Piperno's 2008 account of Sessantotto). While less has appeared in print over the past 15 years specifically about 1977 compared to studies concerning 1968 and its aftermath, what has been written is nonetheless instructive, and sometimes even informative. A disproportionate number of such works appeared in 2007 – Italian publishing houses have long been big on commemorations – of which some of the better journalistic accounts were then written by Annunziata and Cappelini (Vecchio's account is more dubious). Better still is Danilo Mariscalco's 2014 look at the so-called 'creatives', a well-argued and researched treatise that avoids earlier commonplaces about hard and fast political and cultural divides within this new wave of mass unrest, such as that between 'peaceful' versus 'violent' elements.

Amongst the best reporting of 'the movement' at the time came from the journalist and political militant Carlo Rivolta, and two volumes about his life, each with selections of his writings, have also latterly come out (Monti 2010; Favale & De Lorenzis 2012). As a study of events that year in Bologna, and how these have been remembered by those who took part, *Omicidio Francesco Lorusso* (2015) by Franca Menneas is similarly an excellent resource. The finest and most thematically comprehensive work to date on 1977, however, would only appear in bookstores in late 2015, in the form of Luca Falciola's *Il movimento del 1977 in Italia*. Addressing the question through thematic chapters such as 'The crisis of the work society', 'The crisis of faith in politics', 'Violence', 'Repression', Falciola displays a masterly command of primary and secondary sources to weave together a complex but coherent and plausible portrait of a very different mass movement to that which had emerged in the late 1960s. One does not have to accept all of Falciola's conclusions to recognise that this book, with its careful attention to the myriad nuances at work within and around 'the movement of '77', is likely to remain an obligatory touchstone in debates over radical Italian politics for some years to come.

With 2018 being the 50th anniversary of 1968, we can expect even more published matter relating to mass social unrest in the 1960s and '70s, and some of these works no doubt will concern *operaismo* and the *operaisti*. As with the centenary of 1917, one of the hardest tasks we face is trying not to read such events simply as formulaic lessons able to provide a model (or worse, a 'recipe') for how to change the world. What precisely will be uncovered in future research about what Arrighi, Hopkins & Wallerstein (1989) once called 'the great rehearsal' of the 1960s and 1970s remains to be seen. Whatever that entails, I think there is much to learn in the views of Kristin Ross (2016), who has recently provided us with a fresh and exciting take on the Paris Commune:

> I don't think it is wise to consider historical events from an omniscient perspective, nor from the vantage point provided by our present, fat and complacent with all the wisdom of the 'back-seat driver,' correcting the errors of the past ... By focusing on the words and agency of concrete individuals acting in common to dismantle, little by little and step by step, the social hierarchies that make up a state's bureaucracy, I've tried to think the Commune historically – as belonging to the past, as dead and gone – and, at the same time, as the figuration of a possible future. I tried to stage it as very much a part of its historical era, yet in a way that exceeds its own history and suggests to us, perhaps, the deepest and most durable demands for worldwide democracy and revolution. The book is my way of reopening, in other words, from the midst of our current struggles, the possibility of a different historiography, one that allows us to think and do politics differently.

Afterword*

Riccardo Bellofiore
and Massimiliano Tomba

The new millennium has seen the revival of a growing interest in *operaismo*, as testified by the republication not only of histories, but also of some classic texts. These latter have until recently been impossible to find, either because their print run was long exhausted, or else had been sent to be pulped at the end of the 1970s. The international success of Michael Hardt and Toni Negri's book *Empire*, which has been translated into many languages, has contributed to this revival of interest. *Empire* came out in 2000, not long after the mass challenge to the WTO in Seattle, in November 1999, followed in turn by the blockades of the WEF summit in Melbourne, September 2000, of the World Bank in Prague the same month, and then the G8 counter-summit in Genoa in 2001. Throughout the 1990s, too, there had been uprisings linked to price hikes for food and against the overwhelming power of the IMF.

These are only some of the events that have come to assume symbolic power. None was a simple repetition of what preceded it, and each experimented with forms of political innovation. A new generation was forced to come to terms with the dynamics of capitalist globalisation, with the casualisation of work, with the metamorphoses of the old as well as the new economy. It was prodded, therefore, to seek new forms of both political analysis and intervention. Moved by this need, some young militants discovered *operaismo*. And it is from this perspective, too, that Steve Wright's history of Italian *operaismo* needs to be read. A book written by a scholar living on the other side of the world to the province of Europe, and perhaps for this reason, the best on a topic that is no antiquarian matter.

Sergio Bologna is right when he says that *operaismo*, linked to the 'Fordist' historical context of the 1960s, in Italy, would never have been rediscovered without the theoretical work of a generation that provided a bridge between the intellectuals of that time and younger generations: without the work of transmission and contamination of those experiences undertaken by comrades like Primo Moroni, without the attempt to read

---

* First published in the Italian edition, translated by Steve Wright.

the dynamics of so-called 'post-Fordism'. Indeed, what is probably most fascinating about *operaismo* is its refusal of any air of defeat, its ability to read social dynamics from the point of view of political subjectivities and class insurgencies. This is an authentic 'attitude' that seeks, today as in the past, to produce a series of reversals in perspective, able to open new possibilities of political analysis and action.

When Mario Tronti, in 'Lenin in England', read workers' passivity, non-collaboration with unions, standoffishness and refusal, as 'organised passivity', 'planned non-collaboration', 'polemical standoffishness' and 'political refusal', he was on the one hand preparing new lenses with which to read new working-class behaviours, and seeking on the other new modalities of reading marked by a strongly performative value. Tronti did not intend to produce an objective reading of reality, but rather effects on that reality. The illusions of an objective historiography were demolished by Marx in what is perhaps his most brilliant text, *The Eighteenth Brumaire* – an example of historiography from the workers' point of view, aimed not at photographing reality, but at producing a new reality.

Many of *operaismo*'s historiographical works deserve to be republished and reread with care. In a section significantly entitled 'Tronti in Deutschland', Steve Wright mentions important works such as Sergio Bologna's essay on the German council movement, Ferruccio Gambino's reconstruction of workers' struggles in Britain, as well as Karl Heinz Roth's book *The Other Workers' Movement* and Gisela Bock's writing on the IWW. Wright's book is one of the few that grasp the importance of this historiographical innovation, an innovation that would continue into the 1970s with the journal *Primo Maggio*, which sought to develop a new militant history, subordinate to struggles. Placing the relationship between history and memory at the centre, *Primo Maggio* anticipated the battle against historiographical revisionism in the following years, while placing the accent upon proletarian memory, against the refusal of memory celebrated by Negri in his writings of the early 1980s.

In the 1960s Tronti founded what became, in its grandeur but also its limits, the workerist 'gesture' of overturning: the necessity of a partisan reading – simultaneously a partisan intervention – in the processes underway and in the given situation. During the same period, Romano Alquati refined the methodology of 'co-research', and articulated the discourse on class composition: that is, on the forms of behaviour that arise when particular figures of labour-power are inserted in specific processes of production. This element would become particularly significant, and while not all *operaisti* would attribute primary importance to class composition, Steve Wright makes it the red thread of his history of workerism. The analysis of class composition and co-research were amongst the fundamental ingredients of a workerist mode of conducting 'enquiry', intended to establish collaboration between intellectuals and workers. And it was sometimes capable of keeping its promise, as demonstrated with the Comitati operai of Porto Marghera, an experience recently debated at a conference held in Mestre together with the old protagonists.

But the history of Italian workerism was not quite a monolithic bloc that developed in a linear fashion, even if the 'ideological' *operaismo* of the 1960s and '70s (the decades upon which Steve Wright's narration concentrates) can appear so. Workerism's development is worth following for one very simple reason. For a certain generation, *operaismo* was an inevitable reference point – more than that, a genuine, inescapable legacy – whatever the disagreements concerning specific aspects. At the same time, the branches that followed, that gave life to the various 'post-*operaista*' lineages of the last 30 years, cannot easily be separated from their origins, and their successive limits are rooted precisely in the contradictions of the workerism from which they originated.

If we examine the classic figures of the operaista *pantheon* – Mario Tronti and Toni Negri (but also, at least in part, Raniero Panzieri, whom Wright also examines, while not addressing the history of *Quaderni Rossi* after the split with *Classe Operaia*) – it is not difficult to identify some of workerism's undoubted strong points. In the first place, the break with the 'stagnationism' that constituted an ulcer within the traditional Italian left, in particular the Italian Communist Party (PCI) (some important internal dissidences excluded), leaving it incapable of grasping the country's lively capitalist growth, including the 'economic miracle' itself. Along with an attentiveness to the non 'backward' nature of economic (but also social) reality, there was a rich theoretical innovation: the theorisation by Tronti of the labour-power/working-class duality, rediscovered through a reading of Marx. As a consequence, *operaismo* broke with a good part of the received tradition of the Second and Third Internationals, with its economistic and passified vision of workers. More than this, Tronti also opened the way to a new theory of crisis (in certain ways, if you like, a theory of collapse): a 'social' crisis, premised immediately on the capital–labour relation, light years away from the various and competing mechanistic visions of crisis (from disproportionality to underconsumption, to the tendential fall in the rate of profit).

Tronti was, in many senses, the central (if not the only) figure of the *operaismo* of the 1960s, who needs to be located, as Steve Wright does, in a relationship of continuity/rupture between Panzieri and Negri. As for Panzieri, here it is sufficient to underscore three aspects of his reflections within the experience of *Quaderni Rossi*. Before anything else, the strong emphasis on the non-neutrality of the productive forces and machinery: an intuition that was not only original, but liberating. Secondly, the invention of the category of 'capital's plan': the idea, namely, that 'total capital' was able to plan both the economy and society as a whole. However problematic this category, with it Panzieri rightly dealt a death blow to the traditional left vision of socialism, understood reductively as the summation of state ownership of the means of production and planning. Finally, the method of 'enquiry': knowledge of workers' reality demanded a cognitive method (that was also political intervention and struggle) independently of the analysis of capital.

The limit of capital, for Panzieri, was not 'objectivist', but lay if anywhere in labour. Not, however, as an integrated part of capital, but in the measure to which it has the capacity to produce political contents in struggles. Here, broadly, is the point of departure for Tronti who, in starting from Panzieri, then breaks with him (we are thinking above all of *Operai e capitale*). There are two Marxisms, argued Tronti: Marxism as science of capital, and Marxism as revolution. Marxism as science views workers as 'labour power'. It is a theory of economic development, in which labour is seen from the point of view of capital, and is fully integrated within the latter. Against this, Marxism as revolution views workers as 'working class', as labour that actively, and therefore also politically, refuses to be incorporated by capital.

Here we can locate the distant origin of a forcing of this thesis later typical of Negri. Reading Marx's theory of value politically, in the spirit of overturning that distinguishes *operaismo*, Tronti wanted to pose labour power first, capital second. From this it followed that capital was not only conditioned by labour power, but that the latter constituted the measure of value even before production. This occurred in the wage relation, where capital faced not the individual worker, but the working class, and therefore class conflict, that preceded, provoked and produced the capitalist relation. If in Tronti this leads to a sort of political measure of value, its definitive liquidation will be given thereafter, in the assertion that every human activity (and non-activity) is productive of value. Labour will be hypostasised in its presumed independent ontological reality, 'naturally' antagonistic, implicitly and intrinsically productive of value before its inclusion in capital. And capital will be reduced to a merely reactive reality that lives increasingly by autosuggestion. Here not only the political composition of the class comes before, and determines, its technical composition, but the very power of capital is increasingly stripped down to nothing more than pure 'command'. In the process it loses every feature of 'objectivity' (Marx's 'fetish character'), to the point where the capitalist reply to antagonism simply unifies and homogenises labour (materially and politically), at the time simplified in the figure of the 'mass worker' (later on in '*operaio sociale*', cyborg, multitude, etc.). The performative act still remains, but now increasingly akin to the postmodern way of constructing discourses upon discourses, of forced discourses upon forced discourses, with the illusion that capital, in the end, works for communism.

Before returning to the author of *Empire*, however, at least one other significant point of Tronti's framework needs to be remembered, one that will profoundly mark both *operaismo* and post-workerism. According to the author of *Operai e capitale*, antagonism, through which the workers rise out of the dimension of labour power and enter the dimension of working class, is concretised in 'struggles over the wage', when these demand increases that outstrip productivity, and in the 'refusal of labour' within immediate production. In the absence of these two dimensions of struggle, labour is reduced to mere variable capital. Steve Wright's book is valuable in identifying the couplings through which this 'wage-ist' version of class conflict – typical of *operaismo* – unravels over time. Clearly, the *operaismo* under discussion here – no less than Negri himself, up until the mid-1970s – recognises workers as subjects in struggle, irreducible to the dimension of labour power, always exclusively in so far as their antagonism is immediately subversive. Capital's reply to struggles over the wage or to antagonism in the workplace is no less than capitalist development itself. This simply generalises the capitalist condition from the factory to society, strengthening the working class and radicalising the revolutionary face-off between the two classes. Struggles within this crisis are overturned into development, which is translated in turn into capital's incessant antagonistic overcoming.

Tronti quickly drew back from reducing class struggle to a struggle over wages that would transcend the mediation of the party and politics. The journal *Contropiano* began publication in 1967, and Tronti returned to the ranks of PCI, while keeping the accent almost exclusively on wage struggles. The sequence typical of 'ideological' *operaismo* – antagonism within and against capital / leaps in capitalist development / 'recomposition' – was reproblematised, however, since the passage from workers' struggles to capitalist development was no longer automatically given. Between the workers and capital opened the space of politics: better, of the Political. Producing capitalist development in the wake of workers' struggles required intervention from above: it was not spontaneous, it had to be imposed on capital by the 'workers' party. This is the time of tactics and the party. If the 'autonomy of the political' can be glimpsed on the horizon, at the end of the 1960s the wage as 'independent variable' was conceived in ways not so different from Napoleoni's reflections in *Rivista Trimestrale*. In both cases, the conflict over distribution opens to, and becomes the instrument of, an arbitrary and groundless intervention in the sphere of politics and the state: a sphere that is parasitic of struggles, from which it must inevitably separate itself, demanding their subordination.

Moving from the same trunk, but along a different path, is Toni Negri, who proposes an original development of Marx's theory of crisis that is brilliant, in its own way. Disproportionality and overproduction both depend upon changes in the conditions of valorisation that necessarily determine continuous upheavals within those exchange ratios that make equilibrium possible, exploding sooner or later as crisis: this is the Marx of the nineteenth century. The twentieth century opens with the October revolution, which translates into reality the risk that the struggle in the factory will transmute – once again, and immediately – into the struggle for power, spreading everywhere like wildfire. This process breaks up the class composition of the craft worker, giving life to the 'mass worker', through the production of that stage-sequence Taylorism-Fordism which Negri (like nearly all of workerism) reads in a non-problematic way. In this way class decomposition is once again negated, because crisis and restructuring come to be indistinguishable from the development of capital – and the reunification of the antagonistic subject, which is the other side of the coin. The massification of workers in itself recomposes them as working class. Keynesianism is nothing more than the bourgeois attempt to translate the now inevitable autonomy of the class within capital into a stimulus for demand, fighting off the tendency towards stagnation connected to organisational and technological innovations. In the process, Keynesianism seeks to subordinate the independence of the wage to the goal of productivity, and so guarantee balanced and proportional development.

Here, in Negri's work, we see the return of the theoretical-political centrality of the wage, seen as an 'independent variable' when it has been uncoupled from productivity. This occurs within the context of the transition from absolute to relative surplus value, seen (contentiously) as mutually exclusive. 'Necessary' labour, if understood in the traditional sense as production for subsistence, now tends towards zero. At the same time, the wage as an 'independent variable' instead maximises 'necessary' labour, here understood as the reappropriation of income separated from labour. Distribution is reduced to a mere relation of force. Wage struggles make the social relations of production explode, squeezing surplus labour. During the same period, some young followers of Sraffa, positively quoted by Negri himself, likewise called for a 'standing fast' on the wages front, imposing on capital the road of innovation in response to the profit squeeze. Certainly, though, the language, intentions and categories were far from similar. The passage matures from planner state to crisis-state, when public spending becomes wage spending of the factory-state. Exploitation and perception of the wage reflect each other: the demand for wages, and then for income, are for Negri simply an attack upon capital and the state. The capitalist response, which combines inflation with outsourcing, in reality sets the whole society to work. According to this way of seeing things, typical of Negri in the middle of the 1970s, no substantial modification of the reality of the labour process is possible, only a deepening of the structure of command.

Having reached this point, it's clear that Negri – building directly upon foundations provided by Tronti himself – has given life, with undoubted visionary powers, to a workerism with strongly irrational characteristics, as Steve Wright himself indicates on a number of occasions. This is an *operaismo* that develops in a self-referential manner, almost without further relationship to the social reality it seeks to draw upon and express. Development, crisis, revolution are now the same thing. It is pointless to seek mediations, or to claim verifications of reality, in an idealist and subversive apparatus that is self-reproducing, and where reference to the concrete has no other function than to validate a purpose-built philosophy of history.

To be honest, these flaws can be detected from the beginnings of *operaismo*. *Classe Operaia* judged as paltry the results of the struggles of 1962–63, when in actuality these bestowed some empirical validity upon the category of the wage as an 'independent variable' in distribution that led in turn to a violent reaction on the part of the system. Potere Operaio forced the Hot Autumn and its aftermath into the straightjacket of a wage-centred vision, failing to see that the struggles of 1968–69 directly attacked the intensity of labour that the 'restructuring without investments' of the mid-1960s had already stretched to breaking point – at the same time also posing constraints to the full exploitation of the potential increase in the productive power of labour. It is not surprising, then, that a few years later Potere Operaio failed to recognise the 'deconstruction' of labour through which capital responded to class struggle within the sphere of production.

It's true that the 'mass worker' assumed an increasing significance within Italy's postwar development. But it does not follow from this, as part of Potere Operaio hypothesised, that this figure could dominate and subsume other strata of the class composition. Increasingly from the 1970s onwards, however, the schema for reading capitalist and antagonistic dynamics was ossified and projected forward. The 'mass worker' ceded its place to the 'socialised worker', to the 'cyborg', to the so-called 'cognitariat' or even, coining a category lacking all meaning, to the 'immaterial worker'. The method was, and is, the same: always and come what may, identifying some 'tendency', focused at its most advanced point upon a sector which assumes strategic significance, and upon which a new political 'wager' is staked. The whole theoretical system is thus politically geared towards new figures, declared hegemonic in the process. These figures are said to express new forms of conflictuality on which to place a new bet.

Toni Negri recalls that without the reading of the *Grundrisse*, many workerist texts would not have been possible. The *Grundrisse*, translated into Italian in 1968–70, became a sort of bible of the movement of the 1970s. Workerism was, in many ways, a Marxism of the *Grundrisse*. Certainly, this is a text that can in many senses be unavoidable and liberating, but only if read whilst conscious of all its limits and backwards, via Marx's Capital. Instead, *operaismo* read the *Grundrisse* against *Capital*. And if Panzieri, against numerous passages in *Capital* and the *Critique of the Gotha Program*, discerned in the *Grundrisse* a model for passing directly from capitalism to communism, Tronti judged the *Rough Notebooks* to be more politically advanced than either the first volume of *Capital* or *A Contribution to the Critique of Political Economy*. But if Tronti attributed these political outbursts to a formal reason, to a more rough Marxian exposition, not yet constrained into a rigid logical disposition of arguments, the Negri of *Marx Beyond Marx* discovered in the *Grundrisse* the action of a revolutionary subjectivity not yet trapped in *Capital's* objectified categories. The *Grundrisse* became not only the most advanced text, but also the text that contained a surfeit of subjectivity to deploy against the reified state of *Capital's* categories. For many epigones, such as the enthusiasts of cognitive labour, only the *Grundrisse* exists – and of this, perhaps only a few pages, those of the 'Fragment on Machines'.

Having transformed the *Grundrisse* into the book of the 'tendency', Negri could now outline certain equations: convinced that the multitude is to the metropoles as the working class was to the factory, he could deduce the passage from the hegemony of the factory working class to the hegemony of the multitudes in the metropoles. Everything that destroyed the Fordist wage society – productive subjectification, the globalisation of markets, worldwide financial integration and automation, the affirmation of the knowledge economy – places a new social figure at the centre, in a universe where the nexus between wages and productivity would now be impossible to establish. For this Negri, now beyond workerism, all forms of labour are socially productive. If the industrial labour of the nineteenth and twentieth centuries has lost its hegemony, in the final decades of the twentieth century 'immaterial labour' assumed the key place. The General Intellect becomes hegemonic in capitalist production, cognitive immaterial labour becomes immediately productive. The 'cognitariat' is the fundamental productive force that makes the system function. The result of this approach is almost Eurocentric: hi-tech capitalist forms of production in the West become dominant and represent the tendency for the rest of the world, which is constituted by residual and backwards forms.

Even before developing any critical considerations of these stances, it is clear how such positions contribute to and nourish, within the young generations of the 1990s as well as well as those from older generations, like ourselves, an indifference towards working-class labour: transforming hatred against work into an indifference, when it is not an aversion, towards a working class deemed residual and reactionary in its attachment to jobs. At the same time, these positions impede the perception of new forms of labour productive of value, because they cancel concrete reality by substituting a stereotype in its place, dissolving the quite material forms that today characterise the fragmentation of labour employed by capital into an indistinct and indeterminate category. The immediate production of value as place both of conflict and antagonism, and of capitalist hegemony and cooperation, are never truly addressed, as if they never existed. The capitalist labour process as 'contested' terrain is missing, which means that workers when they work are missing as well: if they are not insubordinate, they are labour-power; if they are working class, they are against labour. 'Ideological' *operaismo* only sees them when they demand wages, or when they negate the performance of labour: the rest of the time, they are the same thing as machines. In the absence of labour as such, attention to the real characteristics of capitalist restructuring, to the effective and efficacious modes of political intervention against the class of workers, is missing as well. What remains is a total blindness to what is authentically new in contemporary capitalism.

In this workerism, antagonism is transformed into the movements of a hegemonic, mercurial subject, while the forms of conflictuality of subjects no longer considered hegemonic from the point of view of the tendency become residues, memories in a Fellini film. A rather different discourse, clearly, can be seen in the work of other authors who have played an important role in *operaismo*, such as Vittorio Rieser, Romano Alquati, Ferruccio Gambino, Sergio Bologna, Marco Revelli and others still. Theirs is a workerism that could be called 'materialist', one that succeeds in escaping the meanderings of 'ideological' workerism. And yet it has been the latter that has succeeded in imposing itself in the imaginary as workerism *tout court*, generating various post-*operaista* threads that have cancelled the memory of others. Rather than following the hegemonic subjects of a presumed tendency, it would be more useful today to start from the bodies and minds incorporated in the monstrous and deadly mechanism of a self-valorisation that renders simultaneous the tempos of exploitation. A process that, without the historicist image of stages, encompasses both relative and absolute surplus value, increasingly combining various forms of surplus labour and labour extraction into the same productive weave, from hi-tech to new forms of slavery spreading within a world globalised today by capital. Here the leaps in the productive force of labour are inseparable from the accelerated intensity of labour, from the push to lengthen the social working day.

If Steve Wright's book brings to light the irrational drifts of one part of *operaismo*, it also demonstrates the richness of experiences that the memories of post-workerist literature too often overshadow, when they do not simply forget them. What seems precious to us about Wright's book is its capacity to trace the *operaismo* of those women and men who have conducted struggles – within labour as it is, and against the initiative of a spiritualised capital. Exemplary, from this point of view, are the pages concerning the struggles against harmful, deadly working conditions, or the struggles at FIAT, that demonstrate how the *operaismo* of male and female workers were more advanced than the reflections of the current's theoreticians. Notable too in the book is the capacity to draw out the subterranean experience of that 'rational' *operaismo* that entails not only *Primo Maggio*, but also continues into the 1990s with *Altreragioni*.

Continuing today to press the tendency of the capitalist mode of production whilst awaiting liberation from development means increasingly accelerating the path towards a scenario of self-destruction, that which Marx himself dreads in the gloomiest pages of *Capital*. Today the liberation 'of' labour and liberation 'from' labour are again, tragically separated: the first is sucked into the horizon of the job to be defended, the second seems shipwrecked upon ecological concerns. This rendering becomes an open opposition when the job in question is work in a polluting factory, as has happened recently at the Petrolchimico plant in Porto Marghera, or as was seen in the tragedy of Thyssen Krupp, neither of which can be reduced to exceptional situations symptomatic of backwardness. Taking dangerous working conditions as a starting point, as the Marghera group of Potere Operaio did 40 years ago, means putting up for discussion the deadly nature of the capitalist mode of production. This means, as Sergio Bologna has reminded us, addressing not only the toxicity of chemical production, but also the new forms of harmful, deadly working conditions, such as the lack of social life, the endless cigarettes, the psychic disturbances and the haemorrhoids of our ultra-modern knowledge workers.

The developmentalist schema that, according to some post-*operaisti*, has now led, after formal and real subsumption, to 'total' subsumption, presupposed then and now the liquidation of the notion of value and the extension of the notion of productive labour to the entire sphere of human activity (and also non-activity). This is a theoretical framework that has literally fallen from the sky, and that has yet to furnish an analytic. Rather, as Wright argues, with the figure of the 'socialised worker' Negri simply washed his hands of the difficulties facing the 'mass worker'. But that schema presupposed, then and now, a stage-ist representation of capitalism, where to each form of subsumption there seems to correspond new types of revolutionary subjectivity: in this way the 'mass' worker steps aside for the 'socialised' worker, which leaves the stage in turn for the 'immaterial' worker.

This is a schema that, as anticipated, bears the stigma of a purpose-built philosophy of history – one that, not by chance, beyond its resounding antagonistic rhetoric, seeks to twist to its own advantage the analyses of the French 'regulation' school, in the process flattening this into a social-liberal reformism. When the 'regulation' school abandons Marxism, becoming little more than an updated, bastardised version of Keynesianism, the response of this post-workerism is little short of enthusiastic. It translates basic income, now put forward by some regulationists like Aglietta, into a mere subsidy for casualised workers, paving the way for a lowering of living standards, to the reproduction of that Speenhamland system, about which it would be worth rereading not only Marx, but also Polanyi. In the process, this *operaismo* unwittingly favours capital's current process of permanent restructuring.

The assumption of a paradigm of stages, that today as in the past characterises various tendencies of the workerist tradition, impedes an understanding of the reciprocity and synchronic combination of different forms of exploitation, and mistakenly locates the centre of theoretical and practical critique outside labour. Within a conception of history that identifies a hegemonic subject able to drive the tendency onwards, one finds Tronti's recent decadent-Spenglerian vision of history, which defines the working class as the Pauline *katechon* that has constrained the devastating, levelling and depoliticising aspects of modernity. Here there is no sight of the motor of history, the class struggle that forced capital to respond continually through development: all that remains is the arrow of history with a 'minus' sign at the front. This is, at bottom, the trajectory of those seeking refuge in the wake of defeat. Against this, Negri seeks to position himself on the terrain of the tendency by assuming the point of view of the hegemonic figure of labour, confining the rest to a secondary position, the upshot of which is a triumphalist vision that moves from victory to victory. All of which raises a question worthy of further discussion: is it possible that Tronti and Negri share the same philosophy of history, albeit in inverted form? For Tronti, the dusk of the working-class subject loses the engine of history; for Negri, it is continually searching for new hegemonic figures capable of determining the tendency.

What is required is to return to the beginning: to the reconstruction of the conditions that make possible antagonism within and against capital, in a world that has not overcome the present order of things, but is rather the scene of the gigantic, planet-wide re-formation of the 'working class'.

Bibliography

Accornero, A. (1965) 'Operaismo sterile', *Rinascita* 42, 23 October.

Accornero, A. (1980) 'Le idee dell'operaio Fiat su lavoro, sindacato, politica', now in L. Barca et al., *I mestieri del sindacato: Il dibattito di 'Rinascita' attorno al caso Fiat* (Rome: Rinascita, 1982).

Adagio, C. et al. (eds) (1999) *Il lungo decennio. L'Italia prima del 68* (Verona: Cierre edizioni).

Adornato, F. and G. Lerner (1987) 'Quell'urlo lungo un anno', *L'Espresso*, 18 January.

Agazzi, E. (1977) 'Prefazione', in M. Alcaro, *Dellavolpismo e nuova sinistra* (Bari: Dedalo).

Agosti, A. (1971) *Rodolfo Morandi* (Bari: Laterza).

Ajello, N. (1979) *Intellettuali e PCI 1944–1958* (Bari: Laterza).

Alasia, F. and D. Montaldi (1960) *Milano, Corea: Inchiesta sugli immigrati* (Milan: Feltrinelli).

Alcaro, M. (1977) *Dellavolpismo e nuova sinistra* (Bari: Dedalo).

Alfieri, V. et al. (1984) *Frammenti ... di lotta armata e utopia rivoluzionaria* (Milan: Controinformazione).

Allara, C. et al. (2009) *1969–1977 lotte operaie a Torino. L'esperienza dei Cub, comitati unitari di base* (Milan: Edizioni Punto Rosso).

Alliez, E. (1980) 'Hegel and the Wobblies', *Semiotext(e)* III(3).

Alquati, R. (1975) *Sulla FIAT e altri scritti* (Milan: Feltrinelli).

Alquati, R. (1976) 'Università, formazione della forza lavoro intellettuale, terziarizzazione', in R. Tomassini (ed.) *Studenti e composizione di classe* (Milan: Edizioni aut aut, 1977).

Alquati, R. (1980) 'Cani e morti, cani morti, cani sciolti; intellettuali e terrorismo rossi, nel Bel Paese', in R. Alquati et al., *Terrorismo verso la seconda repubblica?* (Turin: Stampatori).

Alquati, R. (1994) 'Su Montaldi (Panzieri, io) e la conricerca', in *Camminando per realizzare un sogno comune* (Turin: Velleità Alternative).

Alquati, R. (n.d.) 'Sul secondo operaismo politico'. Manuscript, available on the CD accompanying Borio, G. F. Pozzi & G. Roggero (2002) *Futuro Anteriore. Dai «Quaderni Rossi» ai movimenti globali: ricchezze e limiti dell'operaismo italiano* (Rome: DeriveApprodi).

Alquati, R. (n.d.) 'Ulteriori note sull'università e il territorio', in R. Alquati et al., *Università di ceto medio e proletariato intellettuale* (Turin: Stampatori).

Amancio (1980) 'Non vogliamo rappresentare avamposti di frontiera, ma capire la maggioranza di classe', *Inchiesta* 44, March–April.

Amendola, G. (1966) *Classe operaia e programmazione democratica* (Rome: Riuniti).

Amyot, G. (1981) *The Italian Communist Party: The Crisis of the Popular Front Strategy* (New York: St Martin's Press).

Annunziata, L. (2007) *1977. L'ultima foto di famiglia* (Turin: Einaudi).

Anonymous (1980) 'Lama Sabachthani', *Semiotext(e)* III(3).

Antoniol, V. (2010) *1977: Alice e Sherwood: tra rivoluzione dei linguaggi e linguaggio della rivoluzione*. Tesi di laurea, Facoltà di Lettere e Filosofia, Università degli Studi di Padova.

Antonioli, M. and B. Bezza (1973) 'Alcune linee interpretative per una storia dell'Unione Sindacale Italiana: un inedito di Armando Borghi', *Primo Maggio* 1, June–September.

Apergi, F. (1978) 'Sulle origini di una sociologia marxista in Italia: Il caso dei "Quaderni Rossi"', *Critica Marxista* 16(1), January–February.

Arrighetti, L. (1978) 'Firenze: ospedali in lotta', *Primo Maggio* 12, Winter.

Arrighi, G. T. Hopkins & I. Wallerstein (1989) *Antisystemic Movements* (London: Verso).

Artioli, G. (1967) 'Un salto politico da preparare', *Classe Operaia* III(3), March.

Asor Rosa, A. (1962) 'Il punto di vista operaio e la cultura socialista', *Quaderni Rossi* 2.

Asor Rosa, A. (1965) 'Quattro note di "politica culturale"', *Classe Operaia* II(3).

Asor Rosa, A. (1966) 'Le ambiguità si chiariscono', *Classe Operaia* III(1).

Asor Rosa, A. (1967) 'Su "Operai e capitale" di Mario Tronti', *Giovane Critica* 15–16, Spring–Summer.

Asor Rosa, A. (1968) 'A Separate Branch of the Working Class', *International Socialist Journal* 26–7, July.

Asor Rosa, A. (1975) 'La cultura', in *Storia d'Italia: dall'unità a oggi* (Turin: Einaudi).

Asor Rosa, A. (1977) *Le due società: Ipotesi sulla crisi italiana* (Turin: Einaudi).

Asor Rosa, A. (1987) 'Le due sordità', *L'Espresso*, 18 January.

Assemblea Autonoma dell'Alfa Romeo (1974) 'Rivoluzione e lavoro', *Rosso* 11, June.

Assemblea operaia di Torino (1969) 'Appello dell'Assemblea operaia di Torino a tutta la classe operaia italiana', now in L. Castellano (ed.) *Aut. Op. La storia e i documenti: da Potere operaio all'Autonomia organizzata* (Rome: Savelli, 1980).

Aureli, P. (2008) *The Project of Autonomy. Politics and Architecture within and against Capitalism* (New York: Princeton Architectural Press).

Bagnasco, A. (1977) *Tre Italie: La problematica territoriale dello sviluppo italiano* (Bologna: Il Mulino).

Balestrini, N. (1971) *Vogliamo tutto* (Milan: Feltrinelli).

Balestrini, N. (1989) *The Unseen* (London: Verso).

Balestrini, N. (2011) *The Unseen*. Translated by Liz Heron (London: Verso).

Balestrini, N. (2014) *Vogliamo tutto*. Translated by Matt Holden (Melbourne: Telephone Publishing).

Balestrini, N. and P. Moroni (1988) *L'orda d'oro* (Milan: SugarCo).

Balestrini, N. and P. Moroni (1997) *L'orda d'oro 1968–1977. La grande ondata rivoluzionaria e creative, politica e esistenziale*. Nuova edizione a cura di Sergio Bianchi (Milan: Feltrinelli).

Balicco, D. (2006) *Non parlo a tutti. Franco Fortini intelletuale politico* (Rome: manifestolibri).

Baluschi, M. (1981) 'Il movimento dei consigli e la formazione della ideologia consiliare', *Collegamenti Quaderno 3*.

Baranelli, L. and G. Cherci (eds) (1977) *Quaderni Piacentini Antologia 1962–1968* (Milan: Gulliver).

Baranelli, L. and G. Cherci (eds) (1978) *Quaderni Piacentini Antologia 1968–1972* (Milan: Gulliver).

Barkan, J. (1984) *Visions of Emancipation* (New York: Praeger).

Barnes, S. (1967) *Party Democracy: Politics in an Italian Socialist Federation* (New Haven, CT: Yale University Press).

Bascetta, M., S. Bonsignori, M. Grispigni and S. Petrucciani (2008) *Enciclopedia del '68* (Rome: Manifestolibri).

Basilico, V. (1976) 'Pirelli. Un decennio di lotte viste da un protagonista', *Classe* 12, June.

Battaggia, R. (1981) 'Operaio massa e operaio sociale: alcune considerazione sulla "nuova composizione di classe"', *Primo Maggio* 14, Winter.

Bedeschi, G. (1983) *La parabola del marxismo in Italia 1945–1983* (Bari: Laterza).

Behrens, E. et al. (1978) 'Alla fiera delle presunzioni. Contro Erhard Lucas', now in M. Meriggi (ed.) *Il caso Karl-Heinz Roth: Discussione sull'"altro" movimento operaio* (Milan: Edizioni aut aut).

Belforte, S. (1980) 'I nuovi assunti alla Fiat', *Inchiesta* 44.

Bellamio, D. et al. (2012) *La libera ricrca di Cesare Bermani* (Rome: DeriveApprodi).

Bellofiore, R. (ed.) (2007) *Da Marx a Marx. Un bilancio dei marxismi italiani del Novecento* (Rome: Manifestolibri).

Benzoni, A. (1980) *Il partito socialista dalla resistenza a oggi* (Venice: Marsilio).

Berardi, F. (1974) 'Mirafiori è rossa', in *Scrittura e Movimento* (Venice: Marsilio).

Berardi, F. (1998) *La nefasta utopia di Potere operaio* (Rome: Castelvecchi).

Bermani, C. (1975) 'Dieci anni di lavoro con le fonti orali', *Primo Maggio* 5, Spring.

Bermani, C. (ed.) (2010) *La rivista «Primo Maggio» (1973–1989)* (Rome: DeriveApprodi).

Bermani, C. (2011) *Giovanni Pirelli* (Pistoia: Centro di Documentazione Editrice Pistoia).

Bermani, C. and S. Bologna (1977) 'Soggettività e storia del movimento operaio', *Il Nuovo Canzoniere Italiano* III(4–5), March.

Bermani, C. and B. Cartosio (1984) 'Dieci anni di "Primo Maggio"', *Primo Maggio* 19–20, Winter.

Bermani, C. and F. Coggiola (eds) (1986) *Memoria operaia e nuova composizione di classe* (Milan: Magioli).

Bermani, C. and A. Cuzzaniti (1977) 'Biografia di un militante: Gianni Bosio', *Il Nuovo Canzoniere Italiano* III(4–5).

Bertante, A. (2005) *Re Nudo. Underground e rivoluzione nelle pagine di una rivista* (Rimini: NDA).

Berti, L. (1976) 'Tra crisi e compromesso storico', *Primo Maggio* 7.

Berti, L. (1978) 'Astrattizzazione del lavoro', in S. Bologna (ed.) *La tribù delle talpe* (Milan: Feltrinelli).

Berti, L. (1980) 'Appunti per un dibattito possibile', *Collegamenti* 8, June.

Bianchi, S. (ed.) (2011) *Storia di una foto. Milano, via De Amicis, 14 maggio 1977. La costruzione dell'immagine-icona degli :anni di piombo".* Contesti e retroscena (Rome: DeriveApprodi).

Bianchi, S. (2015) *Figli di nessuno. Storia di un movimento autonomo* (Milan: Milieu edizioni).

Bianchi, S. and L. Caminiti (eds) (2007a) *Gli autonomi. Le storie, le lotte, le teorie.* Volume 1 (Rome: DeriveApprodi).

Bianchi, S. and L. Caminiti (eds) (2007b) *Gli autonomi. Le storie, le lotte, le teorie.* Volume 2 (Rome: DeriveApprodi).

Bianchi, S. and L. Caminiti (eds) (2008) *Gli autonomi. Le storie, le lotte, le teorie.* Volume 3 (Rome: DeriveApprodi).

Bianchini, G. (1990) *Sul sindacato e altri scritti* (Padua: Edizioni Quaderni del Progetto).

Bianchini, G. and M. Pergola (1980) 'Prefazione', *Potere Operaio 1967–1969* (Padua: Edizioni cooperativa libreria calusca).

Big Flame (1974) *Class Struggle in Italy: October '74* (London: Big Flame).

Binstock, A. (1971) 'Socialisme ou Barbarie: Examination of a Revolutionary Project'. MA thesis, University of Wisconsin.

Boato, M. (1978) *Il '68 è morto: viva il '68* (Verona: Bertani).

Bobbio, L. (1979) *Lotta continua: Storia di una organizzazione rivoluzionaria* (Rome: Savelli).

Bobbio, L. and G. Viale (1968) 'Student Political Organisation', *International Socialist Journal* 26–7, July.

Bocca, G. (1973) *Palmiro Togliatti* (Bari: Laterza).

Bocca, G. (1980) *Il caso 7 aprile* (Milan: Feltrinelli).

Bock, G. (1976) L'"altro" movimento operaio negli Stati Uniti: l'operaio massa e gli Industrial Workers of the World, 1905–1922', in G. Bock et al., *La formazione dell'operaio massa negli USA 1898/1922* (Milan: Feltrinelli).

Bock, G. et al. (1976) *La formazione dell'operaio massa negli USA 1898/1922* (Milan: Feltrinelli).

Boggs, J. (1963) *The American Revolution* (New York: Monthly Review Press).

Boismenu, G. (1980) 'Review of A. Negri, *La classe ouvriere contre l'Etat. Paris: Galilee', Canadian Journal of Political Science* 13(1), March.

Bologna, S. (1963a) 'La storiografia sul nazismo', *Quaderni Piacentini* 9–10, May–June.

Bologna, S. (1963b) 'Fascismo e capitale', *Quaderni Piacentini* 11, July–August, now in L. Baranelli and G. Cherci (eds) *Quaderni Piacentini Antologia 1962–1968* (Milan: Gulliver, 1977).

Bologna, S. (1964) 'Storici e storia contemporanea', *Quaderni Piacentini* 14, January–February.

Bologna, S. (1965) 'Il discorso sui tecnici', *Classe Operaia* II(4–5), October.

Bologna, S. (1968) 'Problemi di storia della classe operaia: Germania 1917–1920', *Quaderni Piacentini* 33, February.

Bologna, S. (1972) 'Class Composition and the Theory of the Party at the Origins of the Workers-Council Movement', *Telos* 13, Fall.

Bologna, S. (1973a) 'Una storia di classe del proletariato italiano', *Quaderni Piacentini* 50, July.

Bologna, S. (1973b) 'Questioni di metodo per l'analisi del piano chimico', *Quaderni Piacentini* 48–9, January.

Bologna, S. (1974) 'Rapporto società-fabbrica come categoria storica', *Primo Maggio* 2.

Bologna, S. (1975) 'Per la storia dell'Internazionale comunista', *Primo Maggio* 5, Spring.

Bologna, S. (1976a) '"Proletari e Stato" di Antonio Negri: una recensione', *Primo Maggio* 7.

Bologna, S. (1976b) 'Il dibattito sull'"altro" movimento operaio in Germania', now in M. Meriggi (ed.) *Il caso Karl-Heinz Roth: Discussione sull'"altro" movimento operaio* (Milan: Edizioni aut aut, 1978).

Bologna, S. (1977a) 'Il PCI e la classe operaia a Milano', *Lotta Continua*, 12 September.

Bologna, S. (1977b) 'The Tribe of Moles', *Semiotext(e)* III(3).

Bologna, S. (1977c) 'What is "The Movement"?', now in Red Notes (ed.) *Italy 1977–8: 'Living with an Earthquake'* (2nd edn) (London: Red Notes, 1978).

Bologna, S. (1977d) 'Otto tesi per la storia militante', *Primo Maggio* 11.

Bologna, S. (ed.) (1978a) *La tribù delle talpe* (Milan: Feltrinelli).

Bologna, S. (1978b) 'Amo il rosso e il nero, odio il rosa e il viola', in S. Bologna (ed.) *La tribù delle talpe* (Milan: Feltrinelli).

Bologna, S. (1979) 'Usa il grimaldello per scoprire dei tesori', *L'Espresso*, 27 May.

Bologna, S. (1980a) 'Dibattito fra gruppi di ricerca dell'Italia Settentrionale – 19 aprile 1980 Milano', *Comunicazione di massa e di classe* 2.

Bologna, S. (1980b) 'Workerist Publications and Bios', *Semiotext(e)* III(3).

Bologna, S. (1980c) 'Composizione di classe e sistema politico', in R. Lauricella, R. et al. (1981) *Crisi delle politiche e politiche nella crisi* (Naples: Libreria L'Ateneo di G. Pronti).

Bologna, S. (1981) 'Per una "società degli storici militanti"', in S. Bologna et al., *Dieci interventi sulla storia sociale* (Turin: Rosenberg & Sellier).

Bologna, S. (1988) 'Memorie di un operaista', *Novembre 1968*, supplement to *Il manifesto*, 30 November.

Bologna, S. (2003) 'A Review of *Storming Heaven: Class Composition and Struggle in Italian Autonomist Marxism* by Steve Wright', *Strategies. Journal of Theory, Culture & Politics*, 16(2), November, https://libcom.org/library/review-storming-heaven-sergio-bologna.

Bologna, S. (2007) *Ceti medi senza futuro? Scritti, appunti sul lavoro e altro* (Rome: DeriveApprodi).

Bologna, S. and F. Ciafaloni (1969) 'I tecnici come produttori e come prodotto', *Quaderni Piacentini* 39, March, now in L. Baranelli and G. Cherci (eds) *Quaderni Piacentini Antologia 1968–1972* (Milan: Gulliver, 1978).

Bologna, S. and G. Daghini (1968) 'Maggio '68 in Francia', *Quaderni Piacentini* 35, July, now in L. Baranelli and G. Cherci (eds) *Quaderni Piacentini Antologia 1968–1972* (Milan: Gulliver, 1978).

Bologna, S. et al. (1972) *Operai e Stato: Lotte operaie e riforma dello stato capitalistico tra rivoluzione d'Ottobre e New Deal* (Milan: Feltrinelli).

Bologna, S. et al. (1974) *Crisi e organizzazione operaia* (Milan: Feltrinelli).

Bologna, S. et al. (1981) *Dieci interventi sulla storia sociale* (Turin: Rosenberg & Sellier).

Bolzani, P. (1978) 'Le lotte di fabbrica dal "luglio '60" al centro sinistra', *Classe* 16, December.

Bonini, L. (1978) 'Vittorio Foa protagonista e inteprete della "svolta" del 1955', *Classe* 16, December.

Bordiga, R. (1976) 'Per la storia degli anarchici spagnoli', *Primo Maggio* 6, Winter.

Borio, G. F. Pozzi and G. Roggero (2002) *Futuro Anteriore. Dai «Quaderni Rossi» ai movimenti globali: ricchezze e limiti dell'operaismo italiano* (Rome: DeriveApprodi).

Borio, G. F. Pozzi and G. Roggero (2005) *Gli operaisti* (Rome: DeriveApprodi).

Borso, D. (ed.) (2016) *Elvio Fachinelli. Al cuore delle cose. Scritti politici (1967–1989)* (Rome: DeriveApprodi).

Bosio, G. (1975) *L'intellettuale rovesciato* (Milan: Edizioni Bella Ciao).

Bossi, G. (1975) 'Classe e composizione di classe – Per una riconiderazione delle ipotesi della nuova sinistra', *Aut Aut* 149–50, September–October.

Botta, F. (1975) 'Nota introduttiva', in L. Barca et al., *I comunisti e l'economia italiana 1944–1974* (Bari: De Donato).

Bottomore, T. and M. Rubel (eds) (1965) *Karl Marx: Selected Writings in Sociology and Social Philosophy* (Harmondsworth: Penguin).

Bracke, M. (2013) 'Between the Transnational and the Local: mapping the trajectories and contexts of the Wages for Housework campaign in 1970s Italian feminism', *Women's History Review*, 22(4).

Bracke, M. (2014) *Women and the Reinvention of the Political: feminism in Italy, 1968–1983* (New York: Routledge).

Bravo, G.M. (1978) *L'estremismo in Italia* (Rome: Riuniti).

Brecher, J. (1980) *Strike!* (Boston, MA: South End Press).

Brody, D. (1980) *Workers in Industrial America: Essays on the 20th Century Struggle* (New York: Oxford University Press).

Brown, A. (2010) 'Operaismo, Architecture and Design in Ambasz's New Domestic Landscape', 27th Annual Sahanz Conference, Newcastle.

Brüggemeier, F.-J. (1981) 'Ruhr Miners and their Historians', in R. Samuel (ed.) *People's History and Socialist Theory* (London: RKP).

Brunetti, P. (ed.) (2015) *L'eresia bolognese. Documenti di una generazione ribelle (1967–1990)* (Rome: Beniamini).

Buhle, P. (1973) 'Debsian Socialism and the "New Immigrant Worker"', in W. O'Neill (ed.) *Insights and Parallels: Problems and Issues of American Social History* (Minneapolis: Burgess).

Buonfino, G. (1973) 'Il muschio non cresce sui sassi che rotolano: grafica e propaganda IWW', *Primo Maggio* 1.

Buselli, G. and M. Zanzani (1978) 'Sistema politico-società', in S. Bologna (ed.) *La tribù delle talpe* (Milan: Feltrinelli).

Cacciari, M. (1968) 'Sviluppo capitalistico e ciclo delle lotte. La Montecatini-Edison di Porto Marghera', *Contropiano* 3.

Cacciari, M. (1969) 'Teoria e Organizzazione in Francia, dopo il maggio', *Contropiano* 2.

Cacciari, M. (1975) 'Note intorno a "sull'uso capitalistico delle macchine" di Raniero Panzieri', *Aut Aut* 149–50.

Cacciari, M. (1978) 'Problemi teorici e politici dell'operaismo nei nuovi gruppi dal 1960 ad oggi', in F. D'Agostini (ed.) *Operaismo e centralità operaia* (Rome: Riuniti).

Calogero, P., C. Fumian and M. Sartori (2010) *Terrore rosso: dall'autonomia al partito armato* (Rome: Laterza).

Camboni, G. and D. Samsa (1975) *PCI e movimento degli studenti 1968–1973: ceti medi e stategie delle riforme* (Bari: De Donato).

Caminiti, L. et al. (2012) *Daddo e Paolo. L'inizio della grande rivolta. Roma, piazza Indipendenza, 2 febbraio 1977* (Rome: DeriveApprodi).

Cantarow, E. (1972) 'Women's Liberation and Workers' Autonomy in Turin and Milan I', *Liberation*, October.

Cantarow, E. (1973) 'Women's Liberation and Workers' Autonomy in Turin and Milan II', *Liberation*, June.

Cappellini, S. (2007) *Rose e pistole* (Milan: Sperling & Kupfer).

Cardan, P. (1969) *The Meaning of Socialism* (London: Solidarity).

Carli, G. (1977) 'Guido Carli with Eugenio Scalfari', in F. Colombo (ed.) *In Italy: Postwar Political Life* (New York: Karz, 1981).

Carpignano, P. (1976) 'Immigrazione e degradazione: mercato del lavoro e ideologie della classe operaia americana durante la "Progressive Era"', in G. Bock et al., *La formazione dell'operaio massa negli USA 1898/1922* (Milan: Feltrinelli).

Cartosio, B. (1973) 'Note e documenti sugli Industrial Workers of the World', *Primo Maggio* 1.

Cartosio, B. (1976) 'Introduzione' to M. Glaberman, *Classe operaia imperialismo e rivoluzione negli USA* (Turin: Musolini).

Cartosio, B. (1978) 'Storie e storici di operai americani', *Primo Maggio* 11, Winter.

Cartosio, B. (1987) 'Il peso dell'emergenza: il sistema dei partiti e il '77', *Primo Maggio* 26, Winter.

Casamassima, P. (ed.) (2008) *Franco Piperno: '68 – L'anno che ritorna* (Milan: Rizzoli).

Castellano, L. (ed.) (1980) *Aut. Op. La storia e i documenti: da Potere operaio all'Autonomia organizzata* (Rome: Savelli).

Castellina, L. (1969) 'Rapporto sulla FIAT', *Il manifesto* 2–3, July–August.

Cazzaniga, G. (1967) 'I giovani hegeliani del capitale collettivo', *Giovane Critica* 17, Autumn.

Cazzaniga, G. et al. (1968) 'Tesi di Sapienza', in *Università: l'ipotesi rivoluzionaria* (Padua: Marsilio).

Cazzullo, A. (1998) *I ragazzi che volevano fare la rivoluzione. 1968–1978: storia di Lotta continua* (Milan: Mondadori).

Cerrato, R. (1999) 'Dal concilio al 68. Il mondo cattolico italiano negli anni sessanta', in C. Adagio et al. (eds) *Il lungo decennio. L'Italia prima del 68* (Verona: Cierre edizioni).

Chinello, C. (1996) *Sindacato, Pci movimenti negli anni sessanta. Porto Marghera-Venezia 1955–1970* (Milan: FrancoAngeli).

Ciafaloni, F. (ed.) (1968) 'Riposte di operai FIAT al referendum', *Quaderni Piacentini* 35, July.

Ciafaloni, F. (1970) 'Sul Manifesto ed altro', *Quaderni Piacentini* 42, November.

Ciafaloni, F. (1980) 'Produrre automobili a Torino', *Inchiesta* 44.

Ciafaloni, F. and C. Donolo (1969) 'Contro la falsa coscienza nel movimento studentesco', *Quaderni Piacentini* 38, July, now in L. Baranelli and G. Cherci (eds) *Quaderni Piacentini Antologia 1968–1972* (Milan: Gulliver, 1978).

Cipriani, L. (1981) 'La lunga vicenda Fiat', *Quotidiano del lavoratori*, 20, 27 March; 3, 10, 17 April.

Ciuffreda, G. and B. Frabotta (1975) 'Introduzione' to B. Frabotta (ed.) *Femminismo e lotta di classe in Italia (1970–1973)* (Rome: Savelli).

Classe e Partito (1966) 'Vietnam e classe operaia' *Classe e Partito* 0, November.

Classe Operaia (1964a) 'Che fare del sindacato?', *Classe Operaia* 1.

Classe Operaia (1964b) '"Si" al centro-sinistra: No al riformismo', *Classe Operaia* 1.

Classe Operaia (1964c) 'Verso la nuova programmazione', *Classe Operaia* 1, January.

Classe Operaia (1964d) 'Il sindacato', *Classe Operaia* 4–5, May.

Classe Operaia (1964e) 'Intervento politico nelle lotte', *Classe Operaia* 6, June.

Classe Operaia (1964f) 'Il partito come istituzione', *Classe Operaia* 10–12, December.

Classe Operaia (1964g) 'Ricordo di Raniero Panzieri', *Classe Operaia* 10–12.

Classe Operaia (1964h) 'Venti anni di vita democratica', *Classe Operaia* 10–12.

Classe Operaia (1965a) 'La riposta operaia c'è', *Classe Operaia* II(1).

Classe Operaia (1965b) 'Rapporto tra sindacato e partito nel 1964', *Classe Operaia* II(3), May.

Classe Operaia (1965c) 'Milano – un'unica lotta di classe e di partito', *Classe Operaia* II(4–5), October.

Classe Operaia (1966) 'L'alternativa alla socialdemocrazia: unificazione a sinistra', *Classe Operaia* III(2), October.

Cleaver, H. (2000) *Reading 'Capital' Politically* (Leeds: Antitheses).

Clough, S. (1964) *The Economic History of Modern Italy* (New York: Columbia University Press).

Coldagelli, U. and G. De Caro (n.d.) 'Alcune ipotesi di ricerca marxista sulla storia contemporanea', *Quaderni Rossi* 3.

Collegamenti (1974) 'Organismi autonomi e "area dell'autonomia"', *Collegamenti* 6, December, now in G. Martignoni and S. Morandini (eds) *Il diritto all'odio: dentro/fuori/ai bordi dell'area dell'autonomia* (Verona: Bertani, 1977).

Collegamenti (1977) 'Appunti sul movimento', *Collegamenti* 2, August.

Collegamenti (1978) 'Lotte operaie a Torino 1974–1978: Ipotesi sugli sviluppi della ristrutturazione alla FIAT', *Collegamenti* 5, November.

Collegamenti (1979) 'Editoriale', *Collegamenti* 6–7, May.

Colletti, L. (1974) *From Rousseau to Lenin: Studies in Ideology and Society* (New York: Monthly Review Press).

Colletti, L. (1978) 'A Political and Philosophical Interview', in New Left Review (ed.) *Western Marxism: A Critical Reader* (London: Verso).

Collettivi politici di Milano (1976) 'Documento Politico della Segretaria dei Collettivi politici di Milano', *Rosso* 7, 13 March, now in G. Martignoni and S. Morandini (eds) *Il diritto all'odio: dentro/fuori/ai bordi dell'area dell'autonomia* (Verona: Bertani, 1977).

Collettivo operaio portuale (1978) 'I portuali di Genova', *Primo Maggio* 9–10, Winter.

Collettivo Politico Alitalia e Aeroporti Romani et al. (1978) 'La rivoluzione sta dietro una porta? Cerchiamo di aprire quella giusta!', now in *Vis-à-vis* 5, Winter 1997.

Comitati Autonomi Operai (1978a) 'Un pò di massa, un pò violento, un pò illegale ed anche un poco armato', *I Volsci* 1, February.

Comitati Autonomi Operai (1978b) 'Br e lotta armata', *I Volsci* 3, April.

Comitati Autonomi Operai (eds) (1976) *Autonomia Operaia* (Rome: Savelli).

Comitato di Quartiere Alberone (2000) *Quelli dell'Alberone* (Rome: Massari editore).

Comitato Politico ENEL and Collettivo Policlinico (1974) 'Centralizzazione e responsabilità delle avanguardie', *Rosso* 11.

Contini, G. (1978) 'Le lotte operaie contro il taglio dei tempi e la svolta nella politica rivendicativa della Fiom (1955–1956)', *Classe* 16.

Controinformazione (1974) 'Milano: la spesa politica', *Controinformazione* 5–6.

Corradi, C. (2011) *Storia dei marxismi in Italia* (Rome: manifestolibri).

Cowan, S. (1978) 'The Unhappy Adventures of "Alice" in Blunderland: Counter-culture, Revolt and Repression in the Heart of Italy's "Red Belt"', *Radical America* 11(6)–12(1), February.

Craveri, P. (1977) *Sindacato e istituzioni nel dopoguerra* (Bologna: Il Mulino).

Crespi, G. (1984) '"Primo Maggio" e i trasporti', *Primo Maggio* 19–20.

CUB (Comitato Unitario di Base) (1969) 'Lotta alla Pirelli', *Quindici* 16.

CUB et al. (1970) 'Le lotte alla Pirelli. Documenti', *Classe* 2.

Cuninghame, P. (2002) *Autonomia: a movement of refusal: social movements and social conflict in Italy in the 1970's*. PhD thesis, Middlesex University, http://eprints.mdx.ac.uk/6688/1/Cunninghame.phd.pdf

D'Agostini, F. (ed.) (1974) *La condizione operaia e i consigli di fabbrica* (Rome: Riuniti).

D'Agostini, F. (ed.) (1978) *Operaismo e centralità operaia* (Rome: Riuniti).

D'Amico, T. (2008) *Volevamo solo cambiare il mondo. Romanzo fotografico degli anni '70* (Naples: Edizioni Intra Moena).

Daghini, G. (1971) 'Towards a Reconsideration of Lukács' Theory of the Offensive', *Telos* 10, Winter.

Dalla Costa, M. (2002) 'The door to the garden', www.generation-online.org/p/fpdallacosta1.htm

Dalla Costa, M. (2015) *Family, Welfare, and the State* (Brooklyn: Common Notions).

Dalmaviva, M. (1981) 'Hunger Strike by Political Detainee', now in Red Notes (ed.) *Italy 1980–81: The Attempted Destruction of a Communist Movement* (London: Red Notes).

Day, G. (2010) *Dialectical Passions: Negation and Postwar Art Theory* (New York: Columbia University Press).

Dazieri, S. (ed.) (1996) *Italia overground. Mappe e reti della cultura alternativa* (Rome: Castelvecchi).

De Caro, G. (1964) 'L'esperienza torinese dei consigli operai', *Classe Operaia* 1.

De Cecco, M. (1972) 'Economic Policy in the Reconstruction Period, 1945–51', in S. Woolf (ed.) *The Rebirth of Italy 1943–1950* (London: Longman).

De Martinis, A. and A. Piazzi (1980) 'Alle origini dell'autonomia del politico', in A. De Martinis and A. Piazzi (eds) *Soggetti crisi potere/Mario Tronti: antologia di scritti e interventi* (Bologna: Cappelli).

De Meo, G. (1966) 'Productivity and the Distribution of Income to Factors in Italy (1951–63)', *Banco Nazionale del Lavoro Quarterly Review* 76, March.

Deaglio, E. and C. Manenti (1979) 'Fiat: è arrivato un bastimento carico di …', *Lotta Continua*, 4–5 February.

Del Bello, C. (ed.) (1997) *Una sparatoria tranquilla. Per una storia orale del '77* (Rome: Odradek).

Del Carria, R. (1979) *Proletari senza rivoluzione*, Volume 5 (Rome: Savelli).

Della Mea, L. (1967) 'Panzieri tra "Mondo Operaio" e "Quaderni Rossi"', *Giovane Critica* 15–16, Spring–Summer.

Della Mea, L. (1972) *Proletari senza comunismo* (Verona: Bertani).

Della Volpe, G. (1980) *Logic as a Positive Science* (London: New Left Books).

Di Leo, R. (1964) 'Operai e braccianti', *Classe Operaia* 3, March.

Dina, A. (1969) 'Un'esperienza di movimento politico di massa: le lotte interne alla Fiat (fine 1968–giugno 1969)', *Classe* 2.

Dina, A. (1972) 'La sindacalizzazione dei tecnici', *Ulisse* 73–4, December.

Dini, V. (1978) 'A proposito di Toni Negri: note sull'operaio sociale', *Ombre Rosse* 24, March.

Dolci, D. (1960) *To Feed the Hungry: Enquiry in Palermo* (London: MacGibbon & Kee).

Donaggio, F. (1977) *In fabbrica ogni giorno tutti i giorni* (Verona: Bertani).

Donato, G. (2014) *La lotta è armata. Sinistra rivoluzionaria e violenza politica in Italia (1969–1972)* (Rome: DeriveApprodi).

Donolo, C. (1968) 'La politica redefinita', *Quaderni Piacentini* 35, now in L. Baranelli and G. Cherci (eds) *Quaderni Piacentini Antologia 1968–1972* (Milan: Gulliver, 1978).

Dunayevskaya, R. (1958) *Marxism and Freedom* (New York: Bookman Associates).

Dunbar, J. (2016) *The Making of Italian Radical Architecture*. MA Architectural History Report, The Bartlett School of Architecture, University College London.

Dyer-Witheford, N. (1999) *Cyber-Marx* (Champaign: University of Illinois Press).

Echeverria, R. (1978) 'Critique of Marx's *1857 Introduction*', *Economy and Society* 7(4), November.

Edwards, P. (2009) *More work! Less pay! Rebellion and Repression in Italy, 1972–7* (Manchester: Manchester University Press).

Ellwood, D. (1985) *Italy 1943–1945* (Leicester: Leicester University Press).

Emery, E. (1995) 'No Politics Without Inquiry!', <http:// www.emery.archive. mcmail.com/public_html/diary/inquiry.html> Engels, F. (1959) 'On Authority', in L. Feuer (ed.) *Karl Marx and Frederick Engels: Basic Writings on Politics and Philosophy* (New York: Anchor).

Farnetti, P. and P. Moroni (1984) 'Collettivo Autonomo Barona: appunti per una storia impossibile', *Primo Maggio* 21, Spring.

Favale, M. and T. De Lorenzis (2012) *L'aspra stagione* (Turin: Einaudi).

Favaro, O. (2013) *La chimica nord-orientale: L'impresa, il lavoro e la politica.* PhD thesis, Scuola Dottorale di Ateneo. Università Ca'Foscari Venezia.

Federici, S. (2012) *Revolution at Point Zero* (Brooklyn: Common Notions).

Ferrajoli, L. (1981) 'The Prosecution's House of Cards Collapses', now in Red Notes (ed.) *Italy 1980–81: The Attempted Destruction of a Communist Movement* (London: Red Notes).

Ferrari Bravo, L. (1969) 'Bologna: la costituente del Great Labour Party', *Quindici* 16, March.

Ferrari Bravo, L. (1972) 'Il New Deal e il nuovo assetto delle istituzioni capitalistiche', in S. Bologna et al., *Operai e Stato: Lotte operaie e riforma dello stato capitalistico tra rivoluzione d'Ottobre e New Deal* (Milan: Feltrinelli).

Ferrari Bravo, L. (2001) *Dal fordismo alla globalizzazione. Cristalli di tempo politico* (Rome: manifestolibri).

Ferrari Bravo, L. and A. Serafini (1972) *Stato e sottosviluppo: Il caso del Mezzogiorno* (Milan: Feltrinelli).

Ferraris, P. (1998) 'Delegati operai e democrazia diretta in FIAT nel '69. Un inedito del luglio del 1969', *Vis-à-vis* 6.

Ferrero, P. (2005) *Raniero Panzieri: Un uomo di frontiera* (Milan: Edizioni Punto Rosso).

Fiameni, G. (ed.) (2003) *Danilo Montaldi (1929–1975): azione politica e ricerca sociale* (Cremona: Biblioteca statale di Cremona).

Filippini, M. and E. Macchia (2012) *Leaping forward: Mario Tronti and the history of political workerism* (Maastricht: Jan van Eyck Academie).

Finzi, B. (1971) 'Porto Marghera: primo comitato politico', *Il manifesto*, January–February.

Fiorletta, E. (2001) *Radio Onda Rossa. Storia di una radio libera (1977–1987).* Tesi di laurea, Facoltà di Scienze Politiche, Università di Roma 'La Sapienza'.

Foa, V. (1980) *Per una storia del movimento operaio* (Turin: Einaudi).

Fofi, G. (1962) *L'immigrazione meridionale a Torino* (Milan: Feltrinelli).

Forgàcs, D. (1984) 'Franco Fortini', in M. Caesar and P. Hainsworth (eds) *Writers and Society in Contemporary Italy* (New York: Berg).

Form, W. (1976) *Blue Collar Stratification: Autoworkers in Four Countries* (Princeton, NJ: Princeton University Press).

Fortini, F. (1965) *Verifica dei poteri* (Milan: Il Saggiatore).

Fortini, F. (1972) *Dieci inverni* (2nd edn) (Milan: Feltrinelli).

Fortini, F. (1974) 'The Writers' Mandate and the End of Anti-Fascism', *Screen* 15(1), Spring.

Fortini, F. (1977) 'Da "Politecnico" a "Ragionamenti" 1954–1957', in S. Cheriotti (ed.) *Gli intelletuali in trincea* (Padua: CLEUP).

Fortini, F. (n.d.) 'Per un discorso inattuale', *Quaderni Rossi* 3.

Fortunati, L. (2013) 'Learning to Struggle: My Story Between Workerism and Feminism', http://viewpointmag.com/2013/09/15/learning-to-struggle-my-story-between-workerism-and-feminism/.

Franchi, P. (1977) *Nuove generazioni democrazia socialismo* (Rome: Riuniti).

Franco, D. (2009) *Dalla Francia all'Italia: impegno politico, inchiesta e transfers culturali alle origini della sociologia del lavoro in Italia*. PhD thesis, Alma Mater Studiorum Università di Bologna. http://amsdottorato.unibo.it/1470/.

Fraser, R. (1988) *1968: A Student Generation in Revolt* (London: Chatto & Windus).

Fugazza, M. (1975) 'Dellavolpismo e nuova sinistra. Sul rapporto tra I "Quaderni Rossi" e il marxismo teorico', *Aut Aut* 149–50.

Gaddi, M. (2015) *Vittorio Rieser. Intellettuale militante di classe* (Milan: Edizioni Puto Rosso).

Galante, S. (1981) 'Alle origini del partito armato', *Il mulino* 275, May–June.

Gallimberti, J. (2012) 'The N Group and the *Operaisti*: Art and Class Struggle in the Italian Economic Boom', *Grey Room* 49, Fall.

Gambetta, W. (2014) *I muri del lungo '68* (Rome: DeriveApprodi).

Gambino, F. (1968) 'Cancelli stretti per la sociologia americana', *Contropiano* 1.

Gambino, F. (1969) 'Le lotte a livello internazionale', *Quindici* 17, May.

Gambino, F. (1976) *Workers' Struggles and the Development of Ford in Britain* (London: Red Notes).

Gambino, F. (1986) 'Only Connect', in P. Buhle (ed.) *C.L.R. James: His Life and Work* (London: Allison & Busby).

Gambino, F. (2001) 'Intervista a Ferruccio Gambino', now in the CD-ROM accompanying Guido Borio, Francesca Pozzi and Gigi Roggero 2002, *Futuro anteriore. Dai "Quaderni Rossi" ai movimenti globali: ricchezze e limiti . dell'operaismo italiano* (Rome: DeriveApprodi).

Garzia, A. (1985) *Da Natta a Natta. Storia del Manifesto e del PDUP* (Bari: Dedalo).

Gatto Selvaggio (1963) 'Nel sabotaggio continua la lotta e si organizza l'unità', *Gatto Selvaggio* 0.

Gawne, M. (2014) *Ontology, Composition & Affect: The political limits of postworkerist thought*. PhD thesis, Department of Sociology and Social Policy, School of Social and Political Sciences, University of Sydney.

Gazzano, M. (1980) 'Quale ricomposizione operaia?', *Inchiesta* 44.

Geary, D. (1980) 'The Ruhr: From Social Peace to Social Revolution', *European Studies Review* 10.

Georgakas, D. and M. Surkin (1998) *Detroit: I Do Mind Dying* (revised edn) (Boston, MA: South End Press).

Giachetti, D. (1997) *Il giorno più lungo. La rivolta di Corso Triaino. Torino 3 Luglio 1969* (Pisa: BPS).

Giachetti, D. (2008) *Un Sessantotto e tre conflitti. Generazione, genere, classe* (Pisa: BFS Edizioni).

Gianulli, A. (2008) *Bombe di inchiostro* (Milan: BUR).

Ginsborg, P. (1990) *A History of Contemporary Italy* (London: Penguin).

Giugni, G. (1987) 'Una soluzione ci sarebbe ...', *L'Espresso*, 6 December.

Glaberman, M. (1976) *Classe operaia imperialismo e rivoluzione negli USA* (Turin: Musolini).

Gobbi, R. (1973) *Operai e Resistenza* (Turin: Musolini).

Gori, F. (1978) 'Chi scava che cosa', in S. Bologna (ed.) *La tribù delle talpe* (Milan: Feltrinelli).

Gorz, A. (1967) *Strategy for Labor: A Radical Proposal* (Boston, MA: Beacon Press).

Grandi, A. (2003) *La generazione degli anni perduti. Storie di Potere Operaio* (Turin: Einaudi).

Grandi, A. (2005) *Insurrezione armata* (Milan: BUR).

Graziani, A. (ed.) (1979) *L'economia italiana dal 1945 a oggi* (2nd edn) (Bologna: Il Mulino).

Graziosi, A. (1976) *La ristrutturazione nelle grande fabbriche 1973–1976* (Milan: Feltrinelli).

Grisoni, D. and H. Portelli (1977) *Le lotte operaie in Italia dal 1960 al 1976* (Milan: Mazzotta).

Gruppo Gramsci (1973) 'Una proposta per un diverso modo di fare politica', *Rosso* 7, December, now in L. Castellano (ed.) *Aut. Op. La storia e i documenti: da Potere operaio all'Autonomia organizzata* (Rome: Savelli, 1980).

Guarcello, E. et al. (1990) *L'altra faccia della FIAT. I protagonisti raccontano* (Rome: Erre emme).

Guastini, R. and R. Levrero (1970) 'Garantismo e programmazione democratica. A proposito di Della Volpe e del dellavolpismo', *Classe* 3.

Hardt, M. and A. Negri (1994) *Labor of Dionysus: A Critique of the State-Form* (Minneapolis: University of Minnesota Press).

Harman, C. (1982) *The Lost Revolution* (London: Bookmarks).

Haywood, W. (1911) 'The General Strike', now in J. Kornbluh (ed.) *Rebel Voices: An I.W.W. Anthology* (Ann Arbor: University of Michigan Press, 1972).

Hellman, S. (1976) 'The "New Left" in Italy', in M. Kolinsky and W. Paterson (eds) *Social and Political Movements in Western Europe* (London: Croom Helm).

Hellman, S. (1980) 'Il Pci e l'ambigua eredità dell'autunno caldo', *Il mulino* 268, March–April.

Hill, J. (1913) 'Constitutional Guarantee: – Life? Liberty? And the Pursuit of – a Job!', now in J. Kornbluh (ed.) *Rebel Voices: An I.W.W. Anthology* (Ann Arbor: University of Michigan Press, 1972).

Hill, J. (n.d.) 'The Preacher and the Slave', now in J. Kornbluh (ed.) *Rebel Voices: An I.W.W. Anthology* (Ann Arbor: University of Michigan Press, 1972).

Hilwig, S. (2009) *Italy and 1968: Youthful Unrest and Democratic Culture* (London: Macmillan).

Hoare, Q. (ed.) (1977) *Antonio Gramsci: Selections from Political Writings 1910–1920* (London: Lawrence & Wishart).

Horn, G-R. (2007) *The Spirit of '68. Rebellion in Wesern Europe and North America, 1956–1976* (Oxford: Oxford University Press).

Howard, D. (1974) 'In Memory of Serge Mallet', *Telos* 20, Summer.

Howard, M. (2014) *Italian radical social movements 1968–1978: A critical study of sociological accounts of the politics of radical social movements in Italy*. PhD thesis, School of English, Communications and Performance Studies, Faculty of Arts, Monash University.

Introduction', in K. Marx and F. Engels, *Collected Works*, Volume 31 (London: Lawrence & Wishart).

Isnenghi, M. (1980) 'Fra partito e prepartito. Il "Progresso Veneto" (1961–1963)', *Classe* 17, June.

IWW (Industrial Workers of the World) (1905) 'Manifesto', now in J. Kornbluh (ed.) *Rebel Voices: An I.W.W. Anthology* (Ann Arbor: University of Michigan Press, 1972).

Jones, N. (1987) *Hitler's Heralds: The Story of the Freikorps 1918–1923* (London: John Murray).

Joubert, J.-P. (1977) *Revolutionnaires de la sfio* (Paris: Fondation nationale des sciences politiques).

King, R. (1985) *The Industrial Geography of Italy* (London: Croom Helm).

Kornbluh, J. (ed.) (1972) *Rebel Voices: An I.W.W. Anthology* (Ann Arbor: University of Michigan Press).

Kunzle, M. (ed.) (1980) *Dear Comrades – Readers' Letters to 'Lotta Continua'* (London: Pluto Press).

La Classe (1969a) 'Corso Traiano: 1969', now in Red Notes (ed.) *Working Class Autonomy and the Crisis* (London: Red Notes/CSE Books, 1979).

La Classe (1969b) 'Unificiamo le lotte, costriuamo l'organizzazione', now in L. Castellano (ed.) *Aut. Op. La storia e i documenti: da Potere operaio all'Autonomia organizzata* (Rome: Savelli, 1980).

La Fabbrica Diffusa (1977) 'Le ronde operaie a Milano', *La Fabbrica Diffusa* 2.

Lange, P. et al. (1982) *Unions, Change and Crisis: French and Italian Union Strategy and the Political Economy, 1945–1980* (London: Allen & Unwin).

Lanzardo, D. (1965) 'Intervento socialista nella lotta operaia: l'inchiesta operaia di Marx', *Quaderni Rossi* 5.

Lanzardo, D. (1975) 'Introduzione', in R. Panzieri, *La ripresa del marxismoleninismo in Italia* (2nd edn) (Milan: Sapere).

Lanzardo, D. (1979) *La rivolta di Piazza Statuto. Torino, luglio 1962* (Milan: Feltrinelli).

Lanzardo, D. and G. Pirelli (1973) 'Nota dei curatori', in R. Panzieri, *La crisi del movimento operaio: Scritti interventi lettere, 1956–60* (Milan: Lampugnani Nigri).

Lauricella et al., *Crisi delle politiche e politiche nella crisi* (Naples: Libreria L'Ateneo di G. Pronti, 1981).

Lefort, C. (1978) 'L'esperienza proletaria', *Collegamenti* 3–4, May.

Lelli, M. (1971) *Tecnici e lotta di classe* (Bari: De Donato).

Lenin, V. (1977) *The Development of Capitalism in Russia* (Moscow: Progress Publishers).

Lenin, V. (1978a) *Imperialism, the Highest Stage of Capitalism* (Moscow: Progress Publishers).

Lenin, V. (1978b) *What Is To Be Done?* (Moscow: Progress Publishers).

Lenzi, Antonio (2016) *Gli opposti estremismi. Organizzazione e linea politica in Lotta continua e ne il Manifesto-Pdup (1969–1976)* (Reggo Calabria: Città del Sole).

Leonetti, F. (1979) 'Habermas, O'Connor, Negri: non legittimare più', *Alfabeta* 2, June.

Lerner, G. (1980) 'Avanti popolo', *L'Espresso*, 29 June.

Lerner, G. et al. (1978) *Uno strano movimento di strani studenti* (Milan: Feltrinelli).

Libera, A. (1977) 'Avanguardia Operaia's Long-Shot Bet', *Intercontinental Press*, 27 June.

Libertini, L. (1957) 'Post-War Evolution of the Italian Movement', *New International*, Winter.

Licciardi, G. (2014) *Macchie rosse: L'operaismo italiano tra politica e lotta armata* (Rimini: NDA).

Lichtner, M. (ed.) (1975) *L'organizzazione del lavoro in Italia* (Rome: Riuniti).

Lieberman, S. (1977) *The Growth of European Mixed Economies 1945–1970* (New York: John Wiley).

Lolli, G. (1962) 'Rivendicazioni ed elemento politico nello sciopero della Lancia', *Quaderni Rossi* 2.

Lombardo-Radice, M. and M. Sinibaldi (1979) '"C'è un clima di guerra" … Intervista sul terrorismo diffuso', in L. Manconi (ed.) *La violenza e la politica* (Rome: Savelli).

Longo, B. (1975) 'Meno salario, più reddito: la Cassa integrazione', *Primo Maggio* 5.

Lotta Continua (1974) 'Qui sommes-nous?', *Les Tempes Modernes* 335.

Lotta Femminista (1972) 'Alla Redazione del Manifesto', in *L'Offensiva* (Turin: Musolini).

Low-Beer, J. (1978) *Protest and Participation: The New Working Class in Italy* (Cambridge: Cambridge University Press).

Löwy, M. (1979) *Georg Lukács – From Romanticism to Bolshevism* (London: New Left Books).

Lucarelli, S. (2013) 'The 1973–1978 workgroup on money of the journal *Primo Maggio*: an example of a pluralist critique of political economy', *International Journal of Pluralism and Economics Education* 4(1), February.

Lucas, E. (1978) 'Osservazioni su un nuovo approccio di ricerca alla storia del movimento operaio', in M. Meriggi (ed.) *Il caso Karl-Heinz Roth: Discussione sull'"altro" movimento operaio* (Milan: Edizioni aut aut).

Lukács, G. (1971) *History and Class Consciousness* (London: Merlin).

Lumley, R. (1980) 'Review Article: Working Class Autonomy and the Crisis', *Capital & Class* 12, Winter.

Lumley, R. (1990) *States of Emergency: Cultures of Revolt in Italy from 1968 to 1978* (London: Verso).

Luperini, R. (1969) *Il PCI e il movimento studentesco* (Milan: Jaca Book).

Lynd, A. and S. Lynd (eds) (1981) *Rank and File. Personal Histories by Working Class Organizers* (2nd edn) (Princeton, NJ: Princeton University Press).

Magna, N. (1978) 'Per una storia dell'operaismo in Italia. Il trentennio postbellico', in F. D'Agostini (ed.) *Operaismo e centralità operaia* (Rome: Riuniti).

Magni, G. (1970) 'La sinistra italiana e la programmazione democratica', *Classe* 3.

Malizia, M. (2009) *Stories of unsolved relationships. The Italian feminist movement and political violence in Italy during the Seventies.* Masters Thesis, Faculty of Arts – Women's Studies, Utrecht University.

Malos, E. (ed.) (1980) *The Politics of Housework* (London: Allison & Busby).

Mancini, S. (1975) 'Due puntualizzazioni sull'interpretazione di Panzieri', *Aut Aut* 149–50.

Mancini, S. (1977) *Socialismo e democrazia diretta: Introduzione a Raniero Panzieri* (Bari: Dedalo).

Mangano, A. (1978) 'Fortini da "Politecnico" a "Dieci inverni"', *Classe* 16.

Mangano, A. (1979) *Origini della nuova sinistra* (Florence: G. D'Anna Messina).

Mangano, A. (1999) 'Capelloni e cinesi. I giovani negli anni sessanta', in C. Adagio et al. (eds) *Il lungo decennio. L'Italia prima del 68* (Verona: Cierre edizioni).

Mantelli, B. and M. Revelli (1978a) 'Operai senza politica', *Lotta Continua*, 19 July.

Mantelli, B. and M. Revelli (1978b) '10 aprile 1978, ore 13', *Lotta Continua*, 19 July.

Mantelli, B. and M. Revelli (1979) *Operai senza politica: Il caso Moro e il 'qualunquismo operaio'* (Rome: Savelli).

Mantelli, B. and N. Scianna (1978) 'Tregua produttiva e rivoluzione dall'alto alla Fiat', *Primo Maggio* 12.

Marazzi, C. (1978) 'La crisi del "doppio mulinello"', in S. Bologna (ed.) *La tribù delle talpe* (Milan: Feltrinelli).

Marcenaro, P. (1980) 'Vecchi e nuovi operai nella fabbrica che cambia', *Inchiesta* 44.

Mariscalo, D. (2014) *Dai laboratori alle masse. Pratiche artistiche e comunicazione nel movimento del '77* (Verona: Ombre Corte).

Marramao, G. (1975) 'Theory of the Crisis and the Problem of Constitution', *Telos* 26, Winter.

Martignoni, G. and S. Morandini (eds) (1977) *Il diritto all'odio: dentro/fuori/ai bordi dell'area dell'autonomia* (Verona: Bertani).

Martin, J. and P. Moroni (2007) *La luna sotta casa* (Milan: Shake).

Marx, K. (1913) *A Contribution to the Critique of Political Economy* (Chicago, IL: Charles Kerr).

Marx, K. (1973) *Grundrisse* (Harmondsworth: Penguin).

Marx, K. (1975a) 'Contribution to the Critique of Hegel's Philosophy of Law. Introduction', in K. Marx and F. Engels, *Collected Works*, Volume 31 (London: Lawrence & Wishart).

Marx, K. (1975b) 'On Friedrich List's Book *Das Nationale System der Politischen Oekonomie*', in K. Marx and F. Engels, *Collected Works*, Volume 4 (London: Lawrence & Wishart).

Marx, K. (1976) *Capital*, Volume I (Harmondsworth: Penguin).

Marx, K. (1981) *Capital*, Volume III (Harmondsworth: Penguin).

Marx, K. and F. Engels (1965) *Selected Correspondence* (Moscow: Progress Publishers).

Marx, K. and F. Engels (1972) *Manifesto of the Communist Party* (Peking: Foreign Languages Press).

Marx, K. and F. Engels (1975) *Collected Works*, Volume 3 (London: Lawrence & Wishart).

Masi, E. (1968) 'La "nuova sinistra" e il problema dell'organizzazione', *Quaderni Piacentini* 35, now in L. Baranelli and G. Cherci (eds) *Quaderni Piacentini Antologia 1968–1972* (Milan: Gulliver, 1978).

Mason, T. (1979) 'The Workers' Opposition in Germany', *History Workshop Journal* 9.

Massironi, G. (1975) '"Americanate"', in L. Balbo et al., *L'Inferma scienza. Tre saggi sull'istituzionalizzazione della sociologia in Italia* (Bologna: Il Mulino).

Mattick, P. (1968) 'Review of A. Ryder (1968) *The German Revolution of 1918*, *Science & Society* 32.

Mattick, P. (1978) 'Recensione a "L'altro" movimento operaio', in M. Meriggi (ed.) *Il caso Karl-Heinz Roth: Discussione sull'"altro" movimento operaio* (Milan: Edizioni aut aut).

McNeish, J. (1965) *Fire Under the Ashes: The Life of Danilo Dolci* (London: Hodder & Stoughton).

Melotti, M. (1984) 'Dibattito su "Dieci anni di 'Primo Maggio'"', *Primo Maggio* 21.

Menneas, F. (2015) *Omicidio Francesco Lorusso. Una storia di giustizia negata* (Bologna: Pendragon).

Mentasti, E. (2003) *Bergamo 1967–1980. Lotte, movimenti, organizzazioni* (Milan: Edizioni Colibrì).

Mentasti, E. (2007) *La Guarda rossa racconta. Storia del Comitato operaio della Magneti Marelli* (Milan: Edizioni Colibrì).

Mentasti, E. (2011) *Senza Tregua. Storia dei Comitati Comunisti per il potere operaio (1975–76)* (Milan: Edizioni Colibrì).

Meriggi, M. (1978a) *Composizione di classe e teoria del partito* (Bari: Dedalo).

Meriggi, M. (ed.) (1978b) *Il caso Karl-Heinz Roth: Discussione sull'"altro" movimento operaio* (Milan: Edizioni aut aut).

Meriggi, M. (1978c) 'Roth e il metodo di ricerca per una storia di classe', in M. Meriggi (ed.) *Il caso Karl-Heinz Roth: Discussione sull'"altro" movimento operaio* (Milan: Edizioni aut aut).

Merli, S. (1972) *Proletariato di fabbrica e capitalismo industriale: Il caso italiano 1880–1900* (Florence: La Nuova Italia).

Merli, S. (1977) *L'altra storia: Bosio, Montaldi e le origini della nuova sinistra* (Milan: Feltrinelli).

Merli, S. (1979) 'Appunti sulla formazione di R. Panzieri', *Quaderni Piacentini* 72–3, October.

Messori, M. and M. Revelli (1978) 'Centralità operaia', in S. Bologna (ed.) *La tribù delle talpe* (Milan: Feltrinelli).

Metropolis (1978) 'Quattro inediti di Mario Tronti', *Metropolis* 2, June.

Midnight Notes (ed.) (1990) *Midnight Oil* (New York: Autonomedia).

Milanesi, F. (2010) *Militanti* (Milan: Edizioni Punto Rosso).

Milanesi, F. (2014) *Nel novecento. Storia, teoria, politica nel pensiero di Mario Tronti* (Milan: Mimesis).

Minucci, A. (1964) 'Chi li paga?', *Classe Operaia* 4–5, May.

Mohandesi, S. (2013) 'Class Consciousness or Class Composition?', *Science & Society* 77(1), January.

Momigliano, F. (1962) 'Possibilità e limiti dell'azione sindacale', *Quaderni Rossi* 2.

Montaguti, M. (2013) *Lenin a Modena. L'intervento di Potere Operaio nelle lotte di fabbrica a Modena tra anni Sessanta e Settanta.* Tesi di laurea, Scuola di Lettere e bene culturali, Università di Bologna.

Montaldi, D. (1971) *Militanti politici di base* (Turin: Einaudi).

Montaldi, D. (1976) *Saggio sulla politica comunista in Italia (1919–1970)* (Piacenza: Quaderni Piacentini).

Montaldi, D. (1994) *Bisogna sognare. Scritti 1952–1975* (Milan: Cooperativa Co libri).

Montano, M. (1971) 'On the Methodology of Determinate Abstraction: Essay on Galvano Della Volpe', *Telos* 7.

Montefusco, W. and M. Sersante (2016) *Dall'operaio sociale alla moltitudine. La prospettiva ontological di Antonio Negri (1980–2015)* (Rome: DeriveApprodi).

Monti, A. (ed.) (2010) *Travolto dal riflusso. L'Italia nella vita e negli articoli del giornalista Carlo Rivolta* (Pisa: Edizioni ETS).

Moriani, G. and M. Ruffato (1979) 'Il lavoro d'appalto a Porto Marghera', *Primo Maggio* 13, Autumn.

Moroni, P. (1983) 'Da "Don Lisander" alla "Calusca": l'Autobiografia di Primo Moroni', *Primo Maggio* 18, Autumn–Winter.

Moroni, P. (1994) 'Origine dei centri sociali autogestiti a Milano: Appunti per una storia possibile', in F. Adinolfi et al., *Comunità virtuali: I centri sociali in Italia* (Rome: Manifestolibri).

Moroni, P. (2012) *Ca' lusca: Scritti e interventi di Primo Moroni* (Milan: Archivio Primo Moroni & Calusca City Lights).

Mosca, M. et al. (1988) 'I CUB alla Bicocca', *Marzo 1968*, supplement to *Il manifesto*, 30 March.

Moss, D. (1989) *The politics of left-wing violence in Italy, 1969–85* (Basingstoke: Macmillan).

Moulier, Y. (1989) 'Introduction', in A. Negri, *The Politics of Subversion* (Cambridge: Polity Press).

Murphy, T. (2012) *Antonio Negri: Modernity & the Multitude* (Cambridge: Polity).

Murray, F. (1983) 'The Decentralisation of Production – the Decline of the Mass-Collective Worker?', *Capital & Class* 19, Spring.

Negarville, C. (1959) 'Fallimento di Comunità', in P. Alatri (ed.) *Rinascita 1944–1962* (Florence: Luciano Ladri, 1966–67).

Negri, A. (1964a) 'I comitati di classe di Porto Marghera', *Classe Operaia* 1, February.

Negri, A. (1964b) 'Operai senza alleati', *Classe Operaia* 3, March.

Negri, A. (1967) 'Keynes and the Capitalist Theory of the State', now in M. Hardt and A. Negri, *Labor of Dionysus: A Critique of the State-Form* (Minneapolis: University of Minnesota Press, 1994).

Negri, A. (1968) 'Marx on Cycle and Crisis', now in A. Negri, *Revolution Retrieved* (London: Red Notes, 1988).

Negri, A. (1971) 'Crisis of the Planner-State: Communism and Revolutionary Organisation', now in A. Negri, *Revolution Retrieved* (London: Red Notes, 1988).

Negri, A. (1973a) 'Articolazioni organizzative e organizzazione complessiva: il partito di Mirafiori', in S. Bologna et al., *Crisi e organizzazione operaia* (Milan: Feltrinelli, 1974).

Negri, A. (1973b) 'Partito operaio contro il lavoro', in S. Bologna et al., *Crisi e organizzazione operaia* (Milan: Feltrinelli, 1974).

Negri, A. (1973c) 'One Step Forward, Two Steps Back', now in Red Notes (ed.) *Working Class Autonomy and the Crisis* (London: Red Notes/CSE Books, 1979).

Negri, A. (1974) 'Theses on the Crisis', now in Red Notes (ed.) *Working Class Autonomy and the Crisis* (London: Red Notes/CSE Books, 1979).

Negri, A. (1975) 'Ambiguità di Panzieri?', *Aut Aut* 149–50.

Negri, A. (1976a) *La fabbrica della strategia* (Padua: CLEUP).

Negri, A. (1976b) *Proletari e Stato: Per una discussione su autonomia operaia e compromesso storico* (2nd edn) (Milan: Feltrinelli).

Negri, A. (1977a) *Il dominio e il sabotaggio. Sul metodo marxista della trasformazione sociale* (Milan Feltrinelli).

Negri, A. (1977b) 'Working Class Sabotage and Capitalist Domination', now in Red Notes (ed.) *Working Class Autonomy and the Crisis* (London: Red Notes/CSE Books, 1979).

Negri, A. (1977c) 'Il teorico è sicuro che …', *L'Espresso*, 24 July.

Negri, A. (1978) 'La soggettività di classe nel metodo di Roth', in M. Meriggi (ed.) *Il caso Karl-Heinz Roth: Discussione sull'"altro" movimento operaio* (Milan: Edizioni aut aut).

Negri, A. (1979a) *Dall'operaio massa all'operaio sociale: Intervista sull'operaismo* (Milan: Multhipla edizioni).

Negri, A. (1979b) 'Nota introduttiva' to the reprint of *Classe Operaia* (Milan: Machina libri).

Negri, A. (1981a) 'Erkenntnistheorie: elogio dell'assenza di memoria', *Metropoli* 5, June.

Negri, A. (1981b) 'Cari compagni di Autonomia', *Autonomia* 26, November.

Negri, A. (1983) *Pipe-line: Lettere da Rebibbia* (Turin: Einaudi).

Negri, A. (1983) *Revolution Retrieved* (London: Red Notes).

Negri, A. (1984) *Marx Beyond Marx* (South Hadley: Bergin & Harvey).

Negri, A. (1988) *Revolution Retrieved* (London: Red Notes).

Negri, A. (2003a) *Luciano Ferrari Bravo: Ritratto di un cattivo maestro* (Rome: manifestolibri).

Negri, A. (2003b) 'Recensioni. Gli anni conquistati', *Posse*, November.

Negri, A. (2005a) *Time for Revolution*. Translated by Matteo Mandarini (London: Continuum).

Negri, A. (2005b) *Books for Burning*. Translated by Arianna Bove, Ed Emery, and Francesca Novello (London: Verso).

Negri, A. (2010) *Diary of an Escape*. Translated by Ed Emery (Oxford: Polity).

Negri, A. (2012) 'Little Brother Breaks the Fifth Commandment: Antonio Negri's Introduction to Jerry Rubin's Growing (Up) at Thirty-Seven', *Cultural Studies* 20(12).

Negri, A. (2014) *Factory of Strategy: 33 Lessons on Lenin*. Translated by Arianna Bove (New York: Columbia University Press).

Negri, A. (2015a) *Pipeline*. Translated by Ed Emery (Oxford: Polity).

Negri, A. (2015b) *Storia di un comunista* (Milan: Salani).

Negri, A. and L. Ferrari Bravo (1981) 'Reflections on a Phantom', in Red Notes (ed.) *Italy 1980–81: The Attempted Destruction of a Communist Movement* (London: Red Notes).

Nicotri, G. (1980) 'Quei cattivi maestri', *L'Espresso*, 2 November.

Ortoleva, P. (1974) 'Classe operaia e potere politico in USA (1860–1920)', *Primo Maggio* 3–4, September.

Ortoleva, P. (1975) 'Testimonianze proletarie e storia negli USA', *Primo Maggio* 5.

Ortoleva, P. (1976) 'Un operaio dell'auto racconta', *Primo Maggio* 6, Winter.

Ortoleva, P. (1987) 'La sfinge '68', in L. Bobbio et al., *Cinque lezioni sul '68* (Turin: Rossoscuola).

Ortoleva, P. (1988) *Saggio sui movimenti del 1968 in Europa e in America* (Rome: Riuniti).

Özyetiş, E. (2013) *Re-visiting the Political Context of Manfredo Tafuri's 'Toward a Critique of Architectural Ideology': 'Having Corpses in our Mouths'*. PhD thesis, School of Architecture and Design, RMIT University, Melbourne.

Paci, M. (1962) 'Aspetti della socializzazione del lavoro nell'edilizia', *Quaderni Rossi* 2.

Paci, M. (1973) *Mercato del lavoro e classi sociali in Italia* (Bologna: Il Mulino).

Palandri, E. (2011) *Boccalone. Storia vera piena di bugie* (Milan: Bompiani).

Palano, D. (2015a) 'L'inchiesta prima di tutto: Vittorio Rieser', *tysm*, 24 May, http://tysm.org/linchiesta-prima-di-tutto-vittorio-rieser/

Palano, D. (2015b) 'Nel cervello della crisi: La "storia militante" di Sergio Bologna tra passato e presente', in Alessandro Simoncini (ed.), *Pensare la politica, pensare il capitalismo. Filosofie e concetti del pensiero critico per il tempo presente* (Milan: Mimesis).

Palazzo, D. (2014) *The "Social Factory" in Postwar Radical Italian Thought from Operaismo to Autonomia*. PhD thesis, Graduate Faculty in Political Science, The City University of New York.

Palombarini, G. (1982) *7 aprile: il processo e la storia* (Venice: Arsenale Cooperativa Editrice).

Palombarini, G. (2014) *Il processo 7 aprile nei ricordi del giudice istruttore* (Padua: Poligrafo).

Pantaloni, A. (2011) *La dissoluzione di Lotta Continua nella Torino della seconda metà degli anni '70: Il tramonto di un'epoca fra movimenti e violenza*. Dipartimento di Studi Storici e Geografici, Facoltà di Lettere e Filosofia, Università degli Studi di Firenze.

Panzieri, R. (1973) *La crisi del movimento operaio: Scritti interventi lettere, 1956–60* (Milan: Lampugnani Nigri).

Panzieri, R. (1975) *La ripresa del marxismo-leninismo in Italia* (2nd edn) (Milan: Sapere).

Panzieri, R. (1976) 'Surplus value and planning: notes on the reading of "Capital"', in R. Panzieri et al., *The Labour Process & Class Strategies* (London: Stage 1 for the Conference of Socialist Economists).

Panzieri, R. (1980) 'The Capitalist Use of Machinery: Marx Versus the Objectivists', in P. Slater (ed.) *Outlines of a Critique of Technology* (London: Inks Links).

Panzieri, R. (1987) *Lettere 1940–1964* (Venice: Marsilio).

Panzieri, R. and M. Tronti (1975) 'Tesi Panzieri-Tronti', *Aut Aut* 149–50.

Paolozzi, L. (1980) 'Quando militavo in Potere Operaio', *L'Unità*, 8 February.

Partridge, H. (1980) 'Italy's FIAT in Turin in the 1950s', in T. Nichols (ed.) *Capital and Labour: A Marxist Primer* (London: Fontana).

Partridge, H. (1981) 'Interview with Toni Negri. November 1980', *Capital & Class* 13, Spring.

Partridge, H. (1996) 'Labour's Challenge to Capital at Fiat: The Influence of Southern Immigrants in a Changing Industrial Culture', *Labour History Review* 61(1), Spring.

Pasetto, E. and G. Pupillo (1970) 'Il gruppo "Potere Operaio" nelle lotte di Porto Marghera (primavera '66–primavera '70)', *Classe* 3.

Pastore, L. (2013) *La vetrina infranta. A violenza politica a Bologna negli anni del terrorismo rosso, 1974–1979* (Bologna: Pendragon).

Patrono, M. (ed.) (1980) 'Tradizioni, mutamento culturale e rivolta nel Veneto', *Schema* 5.

Peragalli, A. (1980) 'Le dissidenze comuniste tra Lenin e Mao. "Azione Comunista" (1956–1965)', *Classe* 17, June.

Perna, C. (1980) *Classe sindacato operaismo al Petrolchimico di Porto Marghera* (Rome: Editrice Sindacale Italiana).

Pescarolo, A. (1979) 'Storia della classe operaia e "operaismo" in Italia. Alcuni problemi interpretativi', *Movimento Operaio e Socialista* 2(1).

Petter, G. (1993) *I giorni dell'ombra* (Milan: Garzanti).

Philopat, M. (2015) *La banda Bellini* (Milan: Agenziax).

Pianciola, C. (2014) *Raniero Panzieri* (Pistoia: Centro di Documentazione Editrice Pistoia).

Piccone Stella, S. (1993) *La prima generazione. Ragazze e ragazzi nel miracolo economico italiano* (Milan: FrancoAngeli).

Pietropaolo, E. (1970) 'Pirelli '68: contro l'organizzazione capitalistico del lavoro e per la demo(c)razia diretta', *Classe* 2.

Pifano, D. (1995) 'Alcune riflessioni sugli anni '70', *Vis-à-vis* 3.

Pifano, D. (1997) 'L'Autonomia operaia romana', in Derive Approdi (ed.) *Settantasette* (Rome: Castelvecchi).

Pinto, D. (1980) 'La sociologie dans l'Italie de l'après-guerre, 1950–1980', *Revue française de sociologie* XXI.

Piperno, F. (1969) 'Classe e Partito', *Quindici* 16.

Piperno, F. (1978a) 'Sul lavoro non operaio', *Preprint* 1, December.

Piperno, F. (1978b) 'From Terrorism to Guerrilla Warfare', now in *Semiotext(e)* III(3).

Piperno, F. and O. Scalzone (1978) 'Piperno-Scalzone: nel bene e nel male', *L'Espresso*, 5 February.

Piperno, F. et al. (1969) 'Esperienze e prospettive di lotta nei centri di ricerca', *Quaderni Piacentini* 39, November.

Pitassio, A. (1976) 'La storiografia marxista in Italia e l'autonomia operaia', *Quaderni Piacentini* 60–1, October.

Pizzolato, N. (2013) *Challenging Global Capitalism: Labor Migration, Radical Struggle, and Urban Change in Detroit and Turin* (New York: Palgrave Macmillan).

Portelli, A. (1985) 'Oral Testimony, the Law and the Making of History: the "April 7" Murder Trials', *History Workshop Journal* 20, Autumn.

Potere Operaio (1969a) 'Operai proletari nel sud', *Potere Operaio* 1, 18 September, reprinted in *Potere Operaio del lunedi* 56, 11 June 1973.

Potere Operaio (1969b) 'Unificazione delle lotte sugli obiettivi operai', *Potere Operaio* 5, 16 October, now in C. Perna, *Classe sindacato operaismo al Petrolchimico di Porto Marghera* (Rome: Editrice Sindacale Italiana, 1980).

Potere Operaio (1969c) 'La linea di condotta', *Potere Operaio* 10, 27 November.

Potere Operaio (1971a) 'La scadenza è il partito', supplement to *Potere Operaio* 38–9, 1 May.

Potere Operaio (1971b) 'Rivoluzione femminile e lotta proletaria', *Potere Operaio* 43, 25 September–25 October.

Potere Operaio (1971c) 'Salario politico contro il fabbrichismo', *Potere Operaio* 43.

Potere Operaio (1971d) 'Il congresso il partito le scadenze', *Potere Operaio* 44.

Potere Operaio (1971e) 'La nostra proposta politica', *Potere Operaio* 44, November.

Potere Operaio (1971f) 'Riposta al Manifesto: Perchè siamo potere operaio', *Potere Operaio* 44.

Potere Operaio (1971g) 'Che cos'è potere operaio', *Potere Operaio* 45, December.

Potere Operaio (1971h) 'Il tecnico in rivolta nel comando del capitale', *Potere Operaio* 45.

Potere Operaio (1972a) 'Dobbiamo riprendere il lavoro teorico per l'organizzazione', *Potere Operaio* 46, February.

Potere Operaio (1972b) 'A proposito di un discussione di lotta continua: Approfondiamo insieme la discussione', *Potere Operaio* 47–8.

Potere Operaio (1972c) 'Lotta di classe lotta per il potere', *Potere Operaio* 47–8.

Potere Operaio (1972d) 'Note sul Manifesto', *Potere Operaio*, 47–8, May–June.

Potere Operaio (1972e) 'Proletari, è guerra di classe', *Potere Operaio* 47–8.

Potere Operaio (1972f) 'Preparare l'insurrezione', *Potere Operaio* 49, June.

Potere Operaio (1972g) 'I nostri mandati', *Potere Operaio del lunedi* 6, 2 April.

Potere Operaio (1972h) 'Il convegno di Potere Operaio', *Potere Operaio del lunedi* 14, 18 June.

Potere Operaio (1973a) 'La costruzione del partito è un affare di partito', *Potere Operaio del lunedi* 55, 4 June.

Potere Operaio (1973b) 'Operai proletari nel sud', *Potere Operaio del lunedi 56*, 11 June.

Potere Operaio (1973c) 'Potere Operaio: Lo scioglimento', in G. Martignoni and S. Morandini (eds) *Il diritto all'odio: dentro/fuori/ai bordi dell'area dell'autonomia* (Verona: Bertani, 1977).

Potere Operaio (1973d) 'Italy 1973: Workers' Struggles in the Capitalist Crisis', now in Red Notes (ed.) *Working Class Autonomy and the Crisis* (London: Red Notes/CSE Books, 1979).

Potere Operaio (n.d.) *Potere Operaio: A Selection (September 1969–April 1970)* (Milan: Potere Operaio).

POv-e (Potere Operaio veneto-emiliano) (1967a) 'È ora di muoversi nel partito', *Potere Operaio* 1.

POv-e (1967b) 'Contro il piano', *Potere Operaio* 1.

POv-e (1967c) 'La lotta dei vietcong ci insegna che la rivoluzione è possibile', *Potere Operaio* 1.

POv-e (1967d) 'Sirma', *Potere Operaio* 1, 1 May.

POv-e (1967e) 'La classe operaia contro il piano dei padroni', *Potere Operaio* 3.

POv-e (1967f) 'Per gli operai ENI lotta su due fronti', *Potere Operaio* 3, 1 July.

POv-e (1967g) 'Dalla Edison', *Potere Operaio* 4, 29 October.

POv-e (1967h) 'Classe Operaia e Piano in Emilia', *Potere Operaio* 5.

POv-e (1967i) 'Corni', *Potere Operaio* 5.

POv-e (1967j) 'Un'unica lotta contro i riformisti nel partito contro il padrone nella fabbrica', *Potere Operaio* 5, 15 November.

POv-e (1968a) *Porto Marghera/Montedison/Estate '68* (Florence: Centro G. Francovich).

POv-e (1968b) 'Cosa chiede al partito la classe operaia in lotta', *Potere Operaio* 8, 25 February.

POv-e (1968c) 'Fiat Edison Marzotto Università – una sola lotta contro un solo padrone', *Potere Operaio* 9, 10 May.

POv-e (1968d) 'Intervento di massa contro il padrone contro il suo stato contro il riformismo', *Potere Operaio* 9.

POv-e (1968e) 'Operai e elezioni', *Potere Operaio* 9.

POv-e (1968f) 'Dalla INDIGAS di Modena: una lezione esemplare', *Potere Operaio* 10.

POv-e (1968g) 'Con l'automazione il padrone attacca ...', *Potere Operaio* 11, 11 November.

POv-e (1968h) 'Montedison ieri e oggi', *Potere Operaio* 11.

POv-e (1968i) 'Operazione Francia controllata', *Potere Operaio* 11.

POv-e (1968j) 'Ferrara: Operai degli zuccherifici e studenti uniti con gli operai della Montedison in lotta', *Potere Operaio* 12, 1 January.

Pozzi, P. (2007) *Insurrezzione* (Rome: DeriveApprodi).

Preve, C. (1981) 'Ontologia dell'essere sociale e composizione di classe', *Primo Maggio* 16, Autumn–Winter.

Preve, C. (1984) *La teoria in pezzi. La dissoluzione del paradigma operaista in Italia (1976–1983)* (Bari: Dedalo).

Primo Maggio (1976a) 'Per Karl Heinz Roth e altri', *Primo Maggio* 6.

Primo Maggio (1976b) 'Lotta all'Innocenti', *Primo Maggio* 7.

Procacci, G. (1962) 'La classe operaia italiana agli inizi del secolo XX', *Studi storici* III(1).

Procacci, G. (1970) *Lotta di classe in Italia agli inizi del secolo XX* (Rome: Riuniti).

Quaderni Piacentini (1963) 'Ultime sul processo per sabotaggio alla FIAT', *Quaderni Piacentini* 13, November–December, now in L. Baranelli and G. Cherci (eds) *Quaderni Piacentini Antologia 1962–1968* (Milan: Gulliver, 1977).

Quaderni Piacentini (1964) 'I vertici e la base', *Quaderni Piacentini* 15, March–April.

Quadrelli, E. (2008) *Autonomia operaia* (Rimini: NDA).

Ramirez, B. (1975) 'Self-reduction of prices in Italy', now in Midnight Notes (ed.) *Midnight Oil* (New York: Autonomedia, 1990).

Ramirez, B. (1976) 'Lotte operaie e strategia del capitale: 1898–1905', in G. Bock et al., *La formazione dell'operaio massa negli USA 1898/1922* (Milan: Feltrinelli).

Rawick, G. (1972a) 'Anni Venti: lotte operaie USA', in S. Bologna et al., *Operai e Stato: Lotte operaie e riforma dello stato capitalistico tra rivoluzione d'Ottobre e New Deal* (Milan: Feltrinelli).

Rawick, G. (1972b) 'Anni Trenta: lotte operaie USA', in S. Bologna et al., *Operai e Stato: Lotte operaie e riforma dello stato capitalistico tra rivoluzione d'Ottobre e New Deal* (Milan: Feltrinelli).

Red Notes (ed.) (1978) *Italy 1977–8: 'Living with an Earthquake'* (2nd edn) (London: Red Notes).

Red Notes (ed.) (1979) *Working Class Autonomy and the Crisis* (London: Red Notes/CSE Books).

Red Notes (ed.) (1981a) *Italy 1980–81: The Attempted Destruction of a Communist Movement* (London: Red Notes).

Red Notes (1981b) 'Who is Gianni Sbrogio?', in Red Notes (ed.) *Italy 1980–81: The Attempted Destruction of a Communist Movement* (London: Red Notes).

Redazione romana di Rosso (ed.) (1976) *Compromesso senza operai* (Milan: Librirossi).

Redazione torinese di Primo Maggio (1977) 'Inchiesta operaia', *Primo Maggio* 9–10.

Regalia, I. et al. (1978) 'Labour Conflicts and Industrial Relations in Italy', in C. Crouch and A. Pizzorno (eds) *The Resurgence of Class Conflict in Western Europe Since 1968. Volume 1: National Case Studies* (London: Macmillan).

Regini, M. (1980) 'Labour Unions, Industrial Action and Politics', in P. Lange and S. Tarrow (eds) *Italy in Transition: Conflict and Consensus* (London: Frank Cass).

Regini, M. and E. Reyneri (1971) *Lotte operaie e organizzazione del lavoro* (Padua: Marsilio).

Revelli, M. (1975) 'Fascismo come "rivoluzione dall'alto" (1920–1925)', *Primo Maggio* 5.

Revelli, M. (1980a) 'Dibattito fra gruppi di ricerca dell'Italia Settentrionale – 19 aprile 1980 Milano', *Comunicazione di massa e di classe* 2.

Revelli, M. (1980b) 'Oltre la cultura dell'operaio massa …', *Inchiesta* 44.

Revelli, M. (1981a) 'Crisi di sistema e partito del capitale', *Primo Maggio* 15, Spring–Summer.

Revelli, M. (1981b) 'L'ultima Fiat. Appunti su un tempo perduto', *Quaderni Piacentini* 1, New Series.

Revelli, M. (1982) 'Defeat at Fiat', *Capital & Class* 16, Spring.

Revelli, M. (1989) *Lavorare in FIAT* (Milan: Garzanti).

Rexroth, T. (1978) 'L'altro movimento operaio negli USA', *Collegamenti Quaderno* 1.

Reyneri, E. (1978) 'Il "Maggio strisciante": l'inizio della mobilitazione', in A. Pizzorno et al., *Lotte operaie e sindacato: il ciclo 1968–1972* (Bologna: Il Mulino).

Ricciardi, S. (2011) *Maelstrom. Scene di rivolta e autorganizzazione di classe in Italia (1960–1980)* (Rome: DeriveApprodi).

Rieser, V. (1982) 'L'alternativa di Raniero Panzieri', *Primo Maggio* 18, Autumn–Winter, 1982–83.

Rieser, V. (2001) 'Interview with Vittorio Rieser', www.generation-online.org/t/vittorio.htm

Righi, A. (2011) 'The Personal is (Bio)Political! Italian Marxist Neo-feminism and its Historical Trajectory', in *Biopolitics and Social Change in Italy: From Gramsci to Pasolini to Negri* (New York: Palgrave Macmillan).

Rivolta di classe (1976) 'Letter aperta alla redazione milanese di "Rosso"', now in L. Castellano (ed.) *Aut. Op. La storia e i documenti: da Potere operaio all'Autonomia organizzata* (Rome: Savelli, 1980).

Roggero, G. (2016) *Elogio della militanza. Note su soggetività e composizione di classe* (Rome: DeriveApprodi).

Roggero, G. and A. Zanini (2013) *Genealogie del futuro* (Verona: Ombre corte).

Romagnoli, G. (1975) *Consigli di fabbrica e democrazia sindacale* (Milan: Mazzotta).

Romano, P. (1972) *The American Worker* (2nd edn) (Detroit, MI: Berwick).

Rosdolsky, R. (1977) *The Making of Marx's 'Capital'* (London: Pluto Press).

Ross, K. (2016) 'The Survival of the Commune', *Roar* 1, Spring.

Rossanda, R. (1968) *L'anno degli studenti* (Bari: De Donato).

Rossini, S. (1980) 'Le Tront populaire', *L'Espresso*, 17 December.

Rosso (1975) 'Alfa Romeo 35 X 40' *Rosso* III(1), 9 October.

Rosso (1976a) 'Note del sesto anno', *Rosso* III(8), 24 April.

Rosso (1976b) 'Un diverso 8 marzo', *Rosso* III(8).

Rosso (1976c) "Il partito della merce organizzata per una nuova etica del lavoro', *Rosso* III(10–11), June.

Rosso (1978) 'L'autonomia organizzata di fronte al "dopo Moro"', now in L. Castellano (ed.) *Aut. Op. La storia e i documenti: da Potere operaio all'Autonomia organizzata* (Rome: Savelli, 1980).

Rostagno, M. (1968) 'Anatomy of the Revolt', *International Socialist Journal* 26–7, July.

Roth, K.-H. (1976) *L'"altro" movimento operaio. Storia della repressione capitalistica in Germania dal 1880 a oggi* (Milan: Feltrinelli).

Ruggiero, V. (1987) 'Turin Today: Premodern Society or Postindustrial Bazaar?', *Capital & Class* 31, Spring.

Rühle, O. (1974) *From the Bourgeois to the Proletarian Revolution* (Glasgow: Socialist Reproduction).

Sacchetto, D. and G. Sbrogiò (eds) (2009) *Quando il potere è operaio* (Rome: manifestolibri).

Salvati, B. (1972) 'The Rebirth of Italian Trade Unionism, 1943–1954', in S. Woolf (ed.) *The Rebirth of Italy 1943–1950* (London: Longman).

Salvati, M. (1980) 'Cultura operaia e disciplina industriale: Ipotesi per un confronto tra correnti storiografiche', *Movimento operaio e socialista* III(1), January–March.

Salvati, M. et al. (2007) 'Danilo Montaldi', *Parolechiave* 38, December.

Sbardella, R. (1980) 'La NEP di "Classe Operaia"', *Classe* 17 June.

Sbardella, R. (2016) 'The NEP of Classe Operaia', *Viewpoint*, www.viewpointmag. com/2016/01/28/the-nep-of-classe-operaia/

Sbrogiò, I. (2016) *La fiaba di una città industriale 1953–1993. 40 anni di lotte* (Venice: Casa editrice el squero).

Scalzone, O. (1968) 'Condizione studentesca e logica rivoluzionaria', *Quindici* 10, 15 April.

Scalzone, O. (1969) 'Università: riforma e repressione', *Quindici* 16.

Scalzone, O. (1978) 'la congiuntura del movimento e i malanni della soggettività', *Preprint* 1, December.

Scalzone, O. (1980) 'Beyond Terrorism', *Semiotext(e)* III(3).

Scalzone, O. (1981) 'Compagna Cjang Cjing', *Metropoli* 3, February.

Scalzone, O. (1988) *Biennio rosso* (Milan: SugarCo).

Scandaletti, P. (1979) *La fine del compromesso* (Venice: Marsilio).

Scarinzi, C. (1984) 'Dibattito su "Dieci anni di 'Primo Maggio'"', *Primo Maggio* 21.

Scarpari, G. (1979) 'Processo a mezzo stampa: il "7 aprile"', *QUALEgiustizia* 51, May–June.

Scarponi, S. (1979) 'Licenziamenti Fiat: la vicenda dei 61', *QUALEgiustizia* 51.

Schenone, F. (1980) 'Fare l'inchiesta: I "Quaderni Rossi"', *Classe* 17.

Scianna, N. (1980) 'La fabbrica, i giovani operai … A ciascuno il suo tempo', *Inchiesta* 44.

Scotti, M. (2011) *Da sinistra. Intellettuali, Partito socialista italiano e organizzazione della cultura (1953–1960)* (Rome: Ediesse).

Scuro, E. (2011) *I ragazzi del '77. Una storia condivisa su Facebook* (Bologna: Baskerville).

Sechi, S. (1974) *Movimento operaio e storiografia marxista* (Bari: De Donato).

Sereni, U. (1974) 'Sindacalismo rivoluzionaria a Parma', *Primo Maggio* 3–4.

Serneri, S. (ed.) (2012) *Verso la lotta armata. La politica della violenza nella sinistra radical degli anni Settanta* (Bologna: Il Mulino).

Sersante, M. (2012) *Il ritmo delle lotte. La pratica teorica di Antonio Negri (1958–1979)* (Verona: Ombre corte).

Silj, A. (1979) *Never Again Without a Rifle: The Origins of Italian Terrorism* (New York: Karz).

Soulier, G. (1977) 'Autonomie–Autonomies', *Recherches* 30, November.

Spini, V. (1982) *I socialisti e la politica di piano (1945–1964)* (Florence: Sansoni).

Stajano, C. (1982) *L'Italia nichilista. Il caso di Marco Donat Cattin, la rivolta, il potere* (Turin: Mondadori).

Stella, A. (2015) *Anni di sogni e di piombo* (Schio: Edizioni Arcadia Libri).

Studer, S. (1977) 'Per un'alternativa al leninismo. Sul rifiuto operaio della "coscienza esterna"', *Metropolis* 1, October.

Tagliapietra, D. et al. (2015) 'Lettera ai compagni per una riflessione sulla pubblicazione del libro "Anni di sogni e di piombo" di A. Stella – Edizioni Arcadia Libri', *Infoaut* 8 June, www.infoaut.org/index.php/blog/notes/item/14827-lettera-ai-compagni-per-una-riflessione-sulla-pubblicazione-del-libro-anni-di-sogni-e-di-piombo-di-a-stella-edizioni-arcadia-libri.

Tait, S. (1973) 'Alle origini del movimento comunista negli Stati Uniti: Louis Fraina teorico della azione di massa', *Primo Maggio* 1.

Tarì, M. (2012) *Il ghiaccio era sottile. Per una storia dell'Autonomia* (Rome: DeriveApprodi).

Tarrow, S. (1989) *Democracy and Disorder: Protest and Politics in Italy 1965–1975* (Oxford: Clarendon Press).

Taviani, R. (1980) 'Uscire dal pantano', *Inchiesta* 44.

Thoburn, N. (2003) *Deleuze, Marx and Politics* (London: Routledge).

Thomas, P. (2009) 'The Moor's Italian Journeys', *New Left Review* 58, July–August.

Togliatti, P. (1979) *On Gramsci and Other Writings* (London: Lawrence & Wishart).

Tolin, F. (1965) 'Come si è fatta fallire la battaglia della SIRMA', *Classe Operaia* II(3), May.

Tracce (1983) 'Conversazione con Oreste Scalzone', *Tracce* 6, Winter.

Tronti, M. (1964) 'Lenin in England', now in Red Notes (ed.) *Working Class Autonomy and the Crisis* (London: Red Notes/CSE Books, 1979).

Tronti, M. (1966) 'Fronte unico contro la socialdemocrazia', *Classe Operaia* III(1), May.

Tronti, M. (1967a) 'Classepartitoclasse', *Classe Operaia* III(3), March.

Tronti, M. (1967b) 'La nuova sintesi: dentro e contro', *Giovane Critica* 17, Autumn.

Tronti, M. (1968) 'Estremismo e riformismo', *Contropiano* 1.

Tronti, M. (1969) 'Internazionalismo vecchio e nuovo', *Contropiano* 3.

Tronti, M. (1971) *Operai e capitale* (2nd edn) (Turin: Einaudi).

Tronti, M. (1972) 'Workers and Capital', *Telos* 14, Winter.

Tronti, M. (1973) 'Social Capital', *Telos* 17, Fall.

Tronti, M. (1978a) 'Quattro inediti di Mario Tronti', *Metropolis* 2, June.

Tronti, M. (1978b) 'Operaismo e centralità operaia', in F. D'Agostini (ed.) *Operaismo e centralità operaia* (Rome: Riuniti).

Tronti, M. (2009) *Noi operaisti* (Rome: DeriveApprodi).

Tronti, M. (2012) 'Our Operaismo', *New Left Review* 73, January–February.

Trotta, G. and F. Milana (eds) (2008) *L'operaismo degli anni Sessanta. Da «Quaderni Rossi» a «classe operaia»* (Rome: DeriveApprodi).

Vallauri, C. (1978) 'L'interpretazione del '56 e la "via italiana": Le posizioni dei socialisti', *Classe* 16, December.

van den Bossche, Bart (2006) 'Voci dal Settantasette : Orality and historical experience in Enrico Palandri's Boccalone and Pier Vittorio Tondelli's Altri libertini', *Italianistica Ultraiectina*, volume 1, https://dspace.library.uu.nl/handle/1874/29235

van der Linden, M. and K. H. Roth (eds) (2014) *Beyond Marx: Theorising the Global Labour Relations of the Twenty-First Century* (Chicago: Haymarket Books).

Vannicelli, M. (1983) 'A Labor Movement in Search of a Role: The Evolution of the Strategy of the Italian Unions since 1943'. Unpublished PhD thesis, Harvard University.

Vecchio, C. ((2007) *Ali di piombo* (Milan: BUR).

Ventrone, A. (ed.) (2010) *I dannati della rivoluzione. Violenza politica e storia d'italia negli anni Sessanta e Settanta* (Macerate: EUM).

Vergottini, G. (2012) *Women, comrades, and feminists: how the discourse about gender developed in the press of the Italian revolutionary Left, 1974–1976*. Masters Thesis, Department of History, University of Uppsala, Sweden.

Vettori, G. (ed.) (1973) *La sinistra extraparlamentare in Italia: Storia, documenti, analisi politiche* (2nd edn) (Rome: Newton Compton).

Viale, G. (1973) *S'avanza uno strano soldato* (Rome: Edizioni di Lotta Continua).

Viale, G. (1978) *Il sessantotto: tra rivoluzione e restaurazione* (Milan: Mazzotta).

Violi, P. (1977) *I giornali dell'estrema sinistra* (Milan: Garzanti).

Virno, P. (1989) '1969. La riscossa dell'ex crumiro', *Il bimestrale* 6, supplement to *Il manifesto*, 12 December.

Virno, P. and M. Hardt (eds) (1996) *Radical Thought in Italy: A Potential Politics* (Minneapolis: University of Minnesota Press).

Weir, S. (1981) 'The Informal Work Group', in A. Lynd and S. Lynd (eds) *Rank and File. Personal Histories by Working Class Organizers* (2nd edn) (Princeton, NJ: Princeton University Press).

Williams, E. (2013a) 'Invisible Organization: Reading Romano Alquati', *Viewpoint* 3, https://viewpointmag.com/2013/09/26/invisible-organization-reading-romano-alquati/

Williams, E. (2013b) *The Fog of Class War: Cinema, Circulation, and Refusal in Italy's Creeping '70s*. PhD thesis, Literature Department, University of California, Santa Cruz.

Wolf, A. (2012) '*Discorsi per Immagini*: Of Political and Architectural Experimentation', *California Italian Studies* 3(2).

Wright, S. (2003) '*Operaismo, Autonomia, Settantasette* in Translation: Then, Now, the Future', *Strategies* 16(2), November.

Wright, S. (2014) 'Revolution from Above? Money and Class-Composition in Italian *Operaismo*', in M. van der Linden and K. H. Roth (eds) *Beyond Marx: Theorising the Global Labour Relations of the Twenty-First Century* (Chicago: Haymarket Books).

Zandegiacomi, N. (1974) *Autonomia operaia: esperienze di giornalismo operaio* (Verona: Bertani).

WEBSITES

Archivio Primo Moroni – www.inventati.org/apm/index.php?step=primo
Commonware – https://vimeo.com/user10153968
Femminismo: gli anni ruggenti – www.femminismoruggente.it/
Giorni che valgono anni – https://movimento77.wixsite.com/roma
Libcom – www.libcom.org (excellent collection of translated materials)
I ragazzi del '77 – www.facebook.com/search/top/?q=i%20ragazzi%20del%20
%2777
Rosso vivo (includes some issues of *i volsci*) – https://rossovivo.noblogs.org/
archivio/i-volsci/
The Last Firebrands (Manuela Pellerin's 2004 documentary on Porto Marghera
workplace militants) – www.youtube.com/watch?v=CiplVIxrgdc
Viewpoint – http://viewpointmag.com/
Zapruder – http://storieinmovimento.org/
Zerowork – zerowork.org

Index

A/traverso 186
Accornero, A. 75, 203
Adorno, T. 19
AFL (American Federation of Labor) 177
Agazzi, E. 27
Agnelli family 201
Alfa Romeo, Assemblea Autonoma dell'Alfa 147
Alliez, E. 186
Alquati, R. 18, 22, 28, 29, 61, 70–1, 108, 160, 213, 220, 223n7, 230, 238, 245
    class composition and 45, 72–4, 187–9, 238–9
    Classe Operaia and 61
    FIAT study 42–9, 70, 173
    on intellectual labour 187–9
    on mass worker 130, 151
    Olivetti study 49–53
    on socialised worker 150, 158
    on unions 51
Amendola, G. 62, 68, 69, 85
anarchism 1, 175–6, 192
anarcho-syndicalism 32
Archivio Primo Moroni website 228
Artioli, G. 69
Asor Rosa, A. 10, 26, 61, 66–7, 69–70, 79, 84, 139, 185–7, 206, 216, 231
Assemblea Autonoma dell'Alfa Romeo 147
Assemblea operai e studenti 111
Aut Aut 133, 213
autonomia diffusa 223
Autonomia Operaia 1, 192
    Cuninghame on 218–19
    early debates 156–62
    Negri's theories 140–5, 149–58
    new struggles 145–9
    origins 140–1, 147–8
autonomist Marxism 1–2

autonomy 3, 16–18, 26, 55, 67–8, 70–1, 103, 107–9, 114, 133, 137, 167, 172
Avanguardia Operaia 115, 116, 119, 147, 183
Avanti 59

Badaloni, N. 159
Bagnasco, A. 191
Balestrini, N. 111, 184, 212, 215, 222–3, 227, 228n9
Barcelona 175
Basso, L. 17, 29
Battaggia, R. 158, 208, 211
Bedeschi, G. 24
Behrens, E. 170
Belforte, S. 203
Bellofiore, R. 232
Berardi, F. 4, 132, 133, 150, 217, 228
Bermani, C. 21, 22, 173, 231
Bertante, A. 225
Berti, L. 159, 193, 196, 209, 210
Bianchi, S. 223
Black Power 121–2
Bobbio, L. 85–6, 116
Bocca, G. 140, 208
Bock, G. 179–81, 210, 238
Boggs, J. 78, 121, 176
Bologna 140–1
Bologna, S. 4, 53, 108, 163, 170, 210, 211, 221–2, 230, 233, 245
    on co-research 22
    on fascism 164–6
    on German councils movement 166–8
    on memory 161
    on 'movement of '77' 184, 189–96
    on Negri 156–7, 216
    on new harmful working conditions 246–7

on PCI 200
on petrochemical sector 191
Potere Operaio and 132, 134, 233
Primo Maggio and 171–82, 189–90,
    191, 193, 194, 196, 200, 206–7
on self-management 106
on student movement 83, 92–3
on technicians 93, 94, 95–7
on wages 112, 113
on workerism 4, 75, 237–8
Bolshevism *see* Leninism
Bordiga, A. 64
Bordiga, R. 166, 175
Borio, G. 213
Bosio, G. 14, 25, 172
Bossi, G. 74
Botta, F. 7
Bracke, M. 220
Brandirali, A. 115
Bravo, G. 193
Brecher, J. 172
Brigate Rosse (Red Brigades) 130,
    138, 198–9, 234
Britain 33, 55, 169, 174
Brody, D. 177
Brusco, S. 191
Budapest 10 *see also* Hungary
Buhle, P. 180
Buselli, G. 194

Cacciari, M. 39, 74, 105, 139, 171,
    221, 232
Cahiers Rouges 29
Calogero, Pietro 234
CAO (Comitati autonomi operai)
    224
capital 1, 31, 128, 141–2, 180, 186,
    194, 240, 243
    composition of 33–4, 40, 72, 87,
        114, 150, 181
    Della Volpe on 23
    domination of labour and 6, 23,
        50–1, 53, 61–2, 69, 71–2,
        99–100, 101, 104, 112, 127,
        144–5, 173, 195

domination through money form
    149–50, 191
historical nature of 3, 23
labour's power over 6, 33–4, 39,
    100–1, 159–60, 201–2
Panzieri on 38–42
as social relation of power 33–7,
    77–80, 128, 142, 144, 188, 194
socialisation of 87
surplus value and 33, 51
technology and 37–42, 38, 43,
    47–8, 50, 94–5, 170
Tronti on 3, 34–6, 61, 65–6, 76–80
see also restructuring of workplaces
Cardan, P. *see* Castoriadis
Carli, G. 60, 61
Cartosio, B. 181, 206
Cassa Integrazione 155, 156
Castoriadis, C. 21
Cazzaniga, G. 86–7, 88
CGIL (Confederazione Generale
    Italiana del Lavoro) 9, 18, 54, 62,
    94, 100, 108, 118, 154, 156, 185,
    200
Classe Operaia on 63, 71
FIAT and 43, 44, 48
POv-e and 90–1, 101, 102–3, 104
struggles of late 1950s 30–1, 32, 38
Chile 154
China 84
Christian Democrats 12, 13, 59, 154
Ciafaloni, F. 95–7, 110, 113, 115, 116,
    210
CISL (Confederazione Italiana
    Sindacati Lavoratori) 108, 118
class composition
    in *Classe Operaia* 70–5, 79
    co-research and 238–9
    decomposition 47, 61, 169, 208,
        242
    definition 45
    at FIAT 42–9, 200–7
    in historiography 166, 167–9,
        177–8, 180–1
    'movement of '77' and 183–90

Movimento Studentesco and 82–3, 88
in Negri's *Proletari e Stato* 156–8
new composition 192–207
political organisation and 194–201
in Potere Operaio 70–5, 79
recomposition 34, 39, 47, 52–3, 65, 71, 74, 90, 117, 119, 126–8, 132, 144–5, 150–3, 160, 181, 184, 189, 198–9, 241
workerism and 3–4, 209
see also mass worker, skilled workers, socialised worker
Classe e Partito 61, 65
Classe Operaia 29, 58–81, 87, 102
on class composition 70–5, 79
decline of 80–1, 89
modern essays on/reproductions of 223
on political organisation 64–70
on politics and policy 59–63
theory and 75–80
Cleaver, H. 3, 217
CNEN (Comitato Nazionale Energia Nucleare) 94–5
CNT (Confederación Nacional del Trabajo) 175
co-research 19–23, 42–53, 238–9
Cohn-Bendit, D. 92
Coldagelli, U. 165–6
Cole, G.D.H. 177
Colletti, L. 24, 25
Collettivi Politici Operai 141
Cominform 12
Comintern 8, 12, 68, 174, 181, 215
Comitati Autonomi Operai (CAO) 140, 146, 159, 185, 199, 224
Comitati di Liberazione Nazionale 12
Comitato Nazionale Energia Nucleare (CNEN) 94–5
Comitato Operaio 109, 226, 232
Comitato Unitario di Base (CUB) 108–9, 119
Commissione Interna 9, 53, 101, 103
Common Market 9
communism 1, 128, 136, 147, 244

Confederación Nacional del Trabajo (CNT) 175
Confederazione Generale Italiana del Lavoro *see* CGIL
Confederazione Italiana Sindacati Lavoratori (CISL) 108, 118
Corradi, C. 229
Correspondence 21, 48
Corso Traiano 114, 137
councils movement 166–71
Cremona 18, 230
Croce, B. 13
Cronache Operaie 55
CUB (Comitato Unitario di Base) 108–9, 119
Cuninghame, P. 218–19

Daghini, G. 92, 97, 106, 112, 133
Dalla Costa, M. 2, 123, 216, 219, 221
Dalmaviva, M. 134–5, 233
De Caro, G. 165–7
De Gasperi, A. 8–9
De Gaulle, C. 108
De Martino, E. 14
De Meo, G. 6
Deleuze, G. 2, 193
Della Mea, L. 18
Della Volpe, G. 14, 23–8
DeriveApprodi 223–4, 225n8, 226–7, 233
Detroit 121–2, 222
Di Leo, R. 58
Dimitrov, G. 68
Dina, A. 110
Dini, V. 158
Dolci, D. 18, 20
Donaggio, F. 99
Donato, G. 234
Donolo, C. 85, 116
Dunayevskaya, R. 21, 77
Dyer-Witheford, N. 1

Ebert, J. 178
Echeverria, R. 27
Edwards, Phil 219
Einaudi firm 18

Einaudi, L. 8
Emery, E. 212, 214n2, 215
Emilia-Romagna 99, 103, 185, 190
ENEL (Ente Nazionale per
    L'Energia Elettrica) 146
Engels, F. 24, 27, 35, 78, 98–9
enquiries 42–53, 202–3, 239, 240
extra-parliamentary left 92, 116, 122,
    131, 136

factory Communists 72, 108
factoryism 126–7, 129
FAI (Federación Anarquista Ibérica)
    175
fascism, fascists 6, 7, 31–3, 125, 134,
    138, 148–9, 164–6, 169, 184,
    198, 233–4
Federici, S. 220
feminism 2, 122–3, 148, 152, 216,
    220–1, 229
Ferrari Bravo, L. 106, 130–1, 230–1
Ferrarotti, F. 49
FIAT firm
    Alquati's study of 42–9, 173
    strikes and blockades at 70, 137,
        144, 190, 227
    students at 83
    women workers at 122, 200–1, 203
    1950s 'new forces' 9, 30–1
    1960s struggles 53–4, 55, 70,
        109–15, 116–17
    1969 and Hot Autumn 109–11,
        114, 116–17
    1970s 'new starters' 183–4, 200–6,
        210
    1970s restructuring 122, 155–6,
        201
Filippini, M. 231
Finzi, A. 131
FIOM (Federazione Impiegati
    Operai Metallurgici) 31, 48, 90,
    100
Florence, University of 221
Foa, V. 14, 30, 54
Ford, H. 50, 170

Fordism 140, 166 167, 222, 237–8,
    242, 244
Fortini, F. 48, 165, 230
Fortunati, Leopoldina 220–1
France 21, 55, 82, 92
    French general strike 104–9
Friedmann, G. 20
Futuro Anteriore 213

Galileo 23
Gallimberti, J. 221
Gambino, F. 75, 122, 169, 218, 222,
    238, 245
Gasparazzo 120–1, 149, 201, 210
Gatto Selvaggio 55
Gazzano, M. 209
Gdansk 161
generalised/guaranteed wages 88, 90,
    113, 127, 146–47
Generation online 217
Genoa 5, 31, 58, 200, 205, 224, 237
Germany 40, 82, 120, 133, 163, 164,
    166–71
Ginsborg, P. 4, 134
Giovane Critica 66
Gli autonomi 224
Glucksmann, A. 105
Gobbi, R. 55
Gori, F. 193
Gorz, A. 93–4
Gramsci, A. 16, 25, 63, 163, 164–5,
    166, 216
Grandi, A. 228
Grillo, E. 127
Grispigni, M. 233
Grundrisse 244
Gruppi Armati Partigiani 138
Gruppo Gramsci 141, 147
Guattari, F. 2, 193
Guerin, D. 177
Guiducci, R. 20

Hardt, M. 2, 237
Haywood, W. 178–9
Hegel, G.W.F. 76–7
Hilwig, S. 222

Historic Compromise 154–5, 185
historical materialism 3 *see also* theory
Historical Materialism serial 217–18
Hobsbawm, E. 163
Holland 174
Horn, G-R. 222
Hot Autumn 82, 92–3, 97, 121, 125,
    131, 138, 149, 154, 155, 159,
    169, 186, 201, 209, 210, 233, 243
housework 2, 123–4, 220–1
Howard, M. 219
Hungary, invasion of 5, 10, 13, 17, 53

Il manifesto 115, 130, 215
Il Potere Operaio (Tuscany) 86–7,
    111
Ingrao, P. 10, 68
Innocenti firm 156
Ivrea 49–50, 52
IWW (Industrial Workers of the
    World) 166, 174, 177–81

James, C.L.R. 21, 176
Japan 82

KAPD (Kommunistiche Arbeiter
    Partei Deutschlands) 120, 170,
    174
Kennedy, J.F. 59
Keynes, J.M. 98, 113, 142
Keynesianism 191, 242, 247
Khrushchev, N. 10

La Classe 109, 111–14, 219
labour
    domination of by capital 6, 23,
        50–1, 53, 61–2, 69, 71–2,
        99–100, 101, 104, 112, 127,
        144–5, 173, 195
    immaterial 245, 247
    intensification of 99, 108, 109–10,
        243
    productive 37, 74, 88, 113, 143–4,
        187, 188, 194, 247

refusal of 53, 56, 92, 106, 111, 112,
    117, 143, 147, 148, 152–3, 160,
    173, 238, 241
    reserve army of 100, 143
    see also class composition; working
        class
Lama, L. 185
Lanzardo, L. 22–3
law of value 9, 77–8, 87, 125, 144, 187
League of Revolutionary Black
    Workers 121–2
Lefort, C. 21, 22
Lenin, V. 26, 36, 40–1, 45, 63–4, 66,
    80, 126, 132, 135, 174
Leninism/Marxism-Leninism 13, 21,
    45, 46, 60–1, 91, 105, 115, 126,
    132, 135–6, 148–9, 174, 177,
    189, 200, 214–50
Leonardi, S. 38–9
Leuna 171
Libertini, L. 16–17, 18
Lolli, G. 32
Lombardi, R, 60
Longo, L. 68, 149
L'orda d'oro 222–3
Lotta Continua 84, 86, 115, 116, 118,
    119, 120–1, 128– 128, 129, 130,
    131, 133, 134, 137, 146, 149,
    183, 185, 191, 202, 223, 224, 229
Lotta Femminista 123–4, 219
Lucas, E. 171
Lukács, G. 16, 34, 35, 133
Lumley, R. 4
L'Unità 69, 185–6
Luxemburg, R. 11, 16
Lynd, A. 172
Lynd, S. 172

Magneti Marelli, firm 226
Magri, L. 130
Mallet, S. 93–4, 96
Manacorda, G. 12
Mancini, S. 17, 40
Manenti, C. 201
Manifesto 116, 126, 131, 233
Mantelli, B. 202, 203 210

Maoism 64 *see also* Marxism-
 Leninism
Marazzi, C. 194
Marcenaro, P. 203–4
March Action 174
Marchetti, V. 208
Mariscalco, D. 235
Marx, K. 14, 16, 22, 23–4, 25–6, 28,
 33, 35, 37–8, 40–1, 45, 58, 76–7,
 78, 79, 127–8, 142, 153, 160,
 162, 185, 188, 209, 238, 242, 246
Marxism 1, 2–3, 4, 5, 14–15, 19, 20,
 22, 23–8, 29, 33, 36, 41, 66, 76,
 161, 188, 193, 240, 247
Marxism-Leninism 13, 21, 45, 46,
 60–1, 91, 105, 115, 126, 132,
 135–6, 148–9, 174, 177, 189,
 200, 214–50
Masi, E. 106
Mason, T. 164
mass worker
 decline of 149–58, 195, 201–7, 247
 in Germany 166–71
 in Italy 71, 74–5, 83, 93, 96, 97,
  98–101, 111, 114, 119, 120–1,
  125–6, 129, 130, 140, 143–4,
  160, 190, 191, 193, 195, 200,
  210, 218, 241, 242, 243–4, 247
 Potere Operaio on 120–1, 126–9
 in US 175–82
 in workerist historiography 166–82
Mattick, P. 168, 171
Melotti, M. 197
Mentasti, E. 226
Meriggi, M. 21
Merli, S. 169, 172
Messina 25
Messori, M. 191, 195, 196
Metropoli 161, 228
Metropolis 81
Metropolitan Indians 183, 185
Milan 5, 8, 18, 58, 84, 93, 108, 109,
 115, 116, 121, 129, 130, 133–4,
 138, 141, 146, 152, 184, 185,
 192, 200, 206, 225, 226–7, 231
Minucci, A. 203

Mirafiori *see* FIAT
Momigliano, F. 54
Mondo Operaio 15–16, 18
Montaldi, D. 14, 18, 20–1, 45, 46, 230
Montano, M. 27
Montedison firm 91–2, 101, 108
Morandi, R. 11–12, 13, 14, 15, 17, 41
Moro, A. 198, 199, 202, 218–19,
 228n9
Moroni, P. 175, 222–3, 231
Mothe, D. 21
Mouvement du 22 Mars 106
'movement of '77'
 class composition debated 183–4,
  186–90
 legacy of 184
 loses direction 196–9
 recent publications on 235–6
Movimento Sociale Italiano 31
Movimento Studentesco (MS) 82–93,
 106, 108, 109, 110–11, 114,
 115–16, 122
Murphy, T. 216
Mussolini, B. 164

Naples 152
Napoleon 66
Natella, A. 111–12
Nazism 6, 164, 170
Negri, A. 2, 5, 37–8, 48, 52, 67, 74, 76,
 89, 98, 174, 183, 239, 242–5, 248
 on class recomposition 127–8, 198
 on crisis and class struggle 71,
  80–1, 142–3, 149–50
 Empire 215, 237
 on memory and class composition
  161
 on PCI 159
 on Potere Operaio 130–1, 132, 134,
  135–7, 224–5
 recent works by/on 214–16, 217,
  224–5, 227, 228, 230–1, 234–5
 on socialised worker 140–5,
  149–58
Nenni, P. 11, 13, 16, 17–18
New Deal 98, 176

Olivetti, A. 49, 51
Olivetti firm 42, 49–53
Onofri, F. 49
operaio massa *see* mass worker
operaio sociale *see* socialised worker
operaismo *see* workerism
Ordine Nuovo 16
organic intellectuals 13, 15
Ortoleva, P. 172, 174, 176–7

Paci, M. 99, 186, 190, 191
Padua 98, 220, 221
Palazzo, D. 219
Palombarini, G. 234
Panvini, G. 233
Panzieri, R. 33, 36–7, 79, 130
   background and early activities
     14–19
   capitalist technology, critique of
     38–42
   on *Classe Operaia* 58
   on *Grundrisse* 244
   Quaderni Rossi and 19, 23, 26–31,
     32, 48, 239–40
   unions and 54, 55–6
Paris Commune 236
Parti Communiste Française (PCF)
   105–6
Parti Socialiste Unifié (PSU) 94
Partito Comunista Italiano *see* PCI
Partito di Unità Proletaria (PDUP)
   84, 147, 183
Partito Social Democratico Italiano
   (PSDI) 69
Partito Socialista Italiano (PSI)
   10–11, 32–3, 41, 48, 49, 51,
   59–60, 62, 230
Partito Socialista Italiano di Unità
   Proletaria (PSIUP) 62, 67, 69,
   84–5, 110, 118
Partridge, H. 140, 205
Pasolini, P. 60
PCF (Parti Communiste Française)
   105–6
PCI (Partito Comunista Italiano) 1,
   102, 103–4, 106–7, 125, 126,

139, 154–5, 156, 195, 196, 200,
   205, 239
   Bologna on 200
   Classe Operaia on 63, 65–70
   historiography and 163–4
   'movement of '77' and 185, 196
   Negri on 159
   postwar 7–13, 24–5, 32–3, 68
   student movement and 84, 85, 91,
     185
PDUP (Partito di Unità Proletaria)
   84, 147, 183
Petrolchimico *see* Montedison
Piazza Statuto 53–7
Pifano, D. 199
Pinto, D. 19
Piperno, F. 61, 89, 107, 114, 135–7,
   187, 199, 235
Pirelli firm 108–9, 135
Pisa 85, 86, 89, 91
Pivert, M. 29, 30
Pizzolato, N. 222
Pizzorno, A. 20
Poland 13, 53
Popular Front 11, 68, 165
Porto Marghera 52, 91–2, 99, 101–4,
   109, 116, 137, 227–8, 239, 246
Potere Operaio (Potop) 97, 106, 111,
   112, 115, 116–17, 118–19,
   120–39, 142, 174, 234, 243
   class composition, crisis of and
     120–30, 144, 233, 243–4
   decline of 120, 129, 138–9, 224–5
   founding of 53
   on the mass worker 120–1, 126–9
   militarisation, debates over 130–9
   Southern Italian proletariat,
     influence of 124–5, 129
   US Black struggles, influence of
     121–2
   women's struggles, influence of
     122–4
Potere Operaio veneto-emiliano
   (POv-e) 109, 121
   on PCI 104–5, 106, 107
   Porto Marghera and 101–4
   students and 89–93

Poznan 10, 13
Pozzi, F. 213
Preve, C. 128
Primo Maggio
    on FIAT 210
    IWW, discussion of 176–82
    Marchetti on 208
    militant history project 171–5
    modern essays on/reproductions of 217, 223
    'movement of '77' debates 183–4, 189–90, 191, 193, 194, 196, 200, 206–7
    syndicalism and 175
Procacci, G. 164
productive labour 37, 74, 88, 113, 143–4, 187, 188, 194, 247
productivity and wages 7, 9, 10, 39, 60, 62, 102, 112, 127, 242
proletarian youth circles 152, 154, 184
PSDI (Partito Social Democratico Italiano) 69
PSI (Partito Socialista Italiano) 10–11, 32–3, 41, 48, 49, 51, 59–60, 62, 230
PSU (Parti Socialiste Unifié) 94
Pugno, E. 30

Quaderni del territorio 203
Quaderni Piacentini 55, 69, 110
Quaderni Rossi 29–57, 58, 70, 72, 75–6, 79, 83, 87, 94, 111, 165, 202, 220, 227
    capital, critique of 32–42, 77–8
    on class composition 42–53
    Della Volpe and 25–8
    divisions following Piazza Statuto 53–7
    modern sources on 223–4, 230, 240
    sociology and 19–23
    unions and 29–32, 52–7
Quadrelli, E. 225

Rätebewegung *see* German councils movement
Rawick, G. 176, 177

recomposition of class 34, 39, 47, 52–3, 65, 71, 74, 90, 117, 119, 126–8, 132, 144–5, 150–3, 160, 181, 184, 189, 198–9, 241
refusal of labour 53, 56, 92, 106, 111, 112, 117, 143, 147, 148, 152–3, 160, 173, 238, 241
Regalia, I. 109
Reggio Calabria 125
Reggio Emilia 85
Renault firm 106
Resistance 6, 8, 12, 32, 84, 138
restructuring of workplaces 72, 87, 151
    1940s and 50s 5–9
    1960s 99–101, 108–11, 243
    1970s 190–1, 195, 201
    at FIAT 122, 155–6, 201
Revelli, M. 155, 166, 182, 195–6, 201–6, 245
Rexroth, T. 171, 180, 181
Reyneri, E. 111
Ricardo, D. 27, 38–9, 77
Rieser, V. 18, 213, 227, 245
Rinascita 25, 32, 75, 171, 203
Roggero, G. 213
Rome 18, 45, 58, 86, 90, 94–5, 106, 116, 133, 145–6, 184, 185, 197, 198, 199, 223, 224, 226, 227, 228
Romeo, R. 164–5
Roosevelt, F.D. 98
Ross, K. 236
Rossanda, R. 86, 206
Rosso 141–2, 151–2, 157–8, 159, 198, 223, 227
Rostagno, M. 88
Roth, K.-H. 169–71, 180, 232
Ruggiero, V. 210
Rühle, O. 73
Ruhr 168–9

sabotage 52–3, 55–6, 159–60
Salvati, M. 163
Saragat, G. 11, 13
Sartre, J.-P. 92
Sbardella, R. 63, 216–17

Scalzone, O. 86, 89, 106–7, 120, 131, 133, 135–7, 147, 163, 187, 198–9, 226, 228, 235
Schumpeter, J. 142
Scianna, N. 204–5
Second International 40, 94, 106–7, 148, 166, 239
self-management 36, 40, 44, 46–7, 50, 51, 70–1, 94, 96, 105–6, 166–7
self-reduction 145–6, 148, 152, 154
servizio d'ordine see stewards' organisation
7 April case 5, 130, 206, 213, 234
Sicily 14, 25
Sit Siemens firm 135
skilled workers 9, 43–4, 87, 101, 170, 177, 179–80 see also technicians
small firms 190
Smith, A. 27
social factory 33–7, 41, 62–3, 73–4, 85–6, 88, 125, 194, 208, 219
socialised worker 140–5, 149–58, 244, 247
Socialisme ou Barbarie 21, 47, 48
sociology 19–23, 49, 56, 163
Sofri, A. 128–9
Spriano, P. 17, 54, 163, 166
Stalin, J. 10, 12
Stalinism 5, 10, 13, 14, 16, 20, 27, 68–9, 169
state 1, 60, 61, 194, 195, 243
antagonism with 153
capitalist 35, 87, 125, 132
replacement of/anti-statism 1, 60
Statuto dei Lavoratori 119, 191–2
Stella, A. 226
stewards' organisation 134, 227
strikes 31, 53–4, 70–1, 92, 101–2, 104–5, 106, 108, 109, 110, 114, 116–17, 137–8, 170, 178, 200, 215, 227
student movement/Movimento Studentesco (MS) 82–93, 106, 108, 109, 110–11, 114, 115–16, 122, 184–9
Studer, S. 71–2

syndicalism 175

Tait, S. 180
Tambroni, F. 31, 33
Tarì, M. 225–6
Tarrow, S. 218, 219
Taviani, R. 205
Taylor, F.W. 50
Taylorism 39, 95, 180, 201, 242
technicians 43–4, 52, 53, 55, 82, 93–7
technology 37–42, 38, 43, 47–8, 50, 94–5, 170
tendency category 127
theory
in PCI 11–13, 15–19, 23–8
of student movement 86–8
in workerism 3–4, 32–42, 47–9, 58–62, 71–80, 75–80, 95–7, 121–8, 150–1, 157–62, 186–9
theory of the offensive 132–3
Thoburn, N. 215
Togliatti, P. 6–8, 10, 13, 68
Tomba, M. 232
Toscano, A. 223
Touraine, A. 20
Trentin, B. 71, 100
Trento 83, 85, 90
Tridon, A. 178
Tronti, M. 3, 25–6, 29, 94, 98, 113, 132, 139, 162, 237, 238, 239, 240–2, 244, 247–8
on capital as social relation 77–80
on capitalist development and social factory 33–7
on class composition 70–5
Classe Operaia and 58–81
modern works by or on 216–17, 219, 220, 222–3, 231
on political organisation 64–7
in Quaderni Rossi 33–7, 42, 49, 56, 57, 58
on unions 63–4
on workerism 58–9, 60–1, 132, 169, 176, 181, 209
Trotsky, L. 65
Trotskyism 64, 66

Turin 5, 18, 30–1, 42, 44, 48, 49, 53–4, 55, 58, 71, 72–3, 74, 85–6, 92, 109, 110–11, 114, 115, 116, 124, 137, 145, 146, 152, 166, 187, 192, 201, 203, 204, 206, 210–11, 229

UIL (Unione Italiana del Lavoro) 53–4, 108
unemployment and the unemployed 9, 126–7, 128–9, 152, 156, 186
Unione dei Comunisti Italiani 115
Unione Socialisti Independenti 18
unions 51, 154, 205
    division among 9, 53–4
    limitations of 44–5, 48, 53–4, 63–4, 70–1, 104, 106, 110, 146, 153
    on pay differentials 100
    renovation of labour movement and 30–1, 117, 120
    students and 90–1
    see also CGIL, CNT, IWW, UIL, CISL, AFL
United Front 133, 174
United States 2, 98, 121–2, 127, 172, 174, 175–82
USSR 5, 7, 10, 11, 13–14, 41, 53, 84
    invasion of Hungary 5, 10, 13, 17, 53

Vatican 9, 59
Veneto 37, 52, 58, 75, 89, 91, 99, 103–4, 116, 123, 133, 146, 224
    see also Porto Marghera
Venice Group 221
Viale, G. 85–6, 90, 113
Vietnam, peasants in 61
Vietnam War 121
Viewpoint online journal 216–17
Virno, P. 2
Volsci see Comitati Autonomi Operai
von Clausewitz, K. 138
von Oertzen, P. 168

wages
    differentials in 95, 97, 99–100, 110, 122–3, 154

at FIAT 43, 110–11
    generalised/guaranteed 88, 90, 113, 127, 146–47
    needs and 145
    piecework rates 52–3, 110, 112, 118
    productivity and 7, 9, 10, 39, 60, 62, 102, 112, 127, 242
    struggles 58, 153, 241, 242–3
    of women 122–3
Wages for Housework 2, 123–4, 220–1
Weber, M. 23
Weir, S. 73
Williams, E. 219–20
women workers 99, 122–4
workerism
    classical 1–2, 29, 58, 61, 72, 74, 76, 81, 94, 121, 167, 169, 171, 173, 191, 205–6, 224, 231, 243
    decline of 4, 205–10
    definition 2–4, 58–9
    Grundrisse and 244
    impact of 1–2
    legacy of 239
    mass workers and 98–101
    modern sources on 213–36; in English 213–23; in Italian 223–36
    origins 45, 53–7
    on PCI 106–7
    post-workerism 244–8
    on self-management 105–6
    student movement and 82–3, 86–93
    US, interest in 176–82
workers' enquiry 42–53, 202–3, 239, 240
workers, skilled 9, 43–4, 87, 101, 170, 177, 179–80 see also technicians
working class
    autonomy and 3, 16–18, 26, 55, 67–8, 70–1, 103, 107–9, 114, 133, 137, 167, 172
    as capital 35–6
    co-research/studies of 19–23, 42–53, 238–9

deskilling of 43–9, 94–5, 99
memory 72, 161, 173, 206
migration and 5–6, 75, 100, 123, 124–5, 177
needs of 111–14, 127, 145, 152–3
passivity 49, 71–2, 79, 164, 181, 208, 238
PCI and 7–10, 106–7
power of 6, 33–4, 39, 100–1, 159–60, 201–2
social factory and 33–7
spontaneity of 45, 52, 64

struggle 31–2, 47, 51, 55, 60, 64–7, 70–2, 79, 97, 103–4, 105, 110–11, 143–7, 151–2, 178
students, alliance with 82–93, 106, 108, 109, 110–11, 114, 115–16

Zanzani, M. 194
Zapruder journal 228–9
Zengakuren 54–5
Zerowork website 2, 179, 217
Zhdanov, A. 13, 24
Zinoviev, G. 174